Swooning Beauty

JOANNA FRUEH

Swooning Beauty

a memoir of pleasure

UNIVERSITY OF NEVADA PRESS   RENO & LAS VEGAS

University of Nevada Press, Reno, Nevada 89557 USA
Copyright © 2006 by University of Nevada Press
All rights reserved
Manufactured in the United States of America
Design by Carrie House / HOUSEdesign LLC
Library of Congress Cataloging-in-Publication Data
Frueh, Joanna.
Swooning beauty : a memoir of pleasure / Joanna Frueh.
p. cm.
Includes bibliographical references.
ISBN 0-87417-659-x (hardcover : alk. paper) —
ISBN 0-87417-672-7 (pbk. : alk. paper)
1. Frueh, Joanna. 2. Middle aged women — Biography.
3. Divorced women — Biography. 4. Pleasure. 5. Sex
(Psychology) 6. Chocolate — Psychological aspects.
7. Parents — Death — Psychological aspects. I. Title.
HQ1059.4.U6 F78   2006
306.89'3092 — dc22   2005029668
The paper used in this book meets the requirements
of American National Standard for Information
Sciences — Permanence of Paper for Printed Library
Materials, ANSI Z.48-1984. Binding materials were
selected for strength and durability.

The events described in this memoir are real; however, some
characters have been given fictitious names and identifying
characteristics to protect their anonymity.

FIRST PRINTING
15 14 13 12 11 10 09 08 07 06
5 4 3 2 1

To my sister Renee Wood, and
to my parents Erne René Frueh and Florence Pass Frueh in memoriam

CONTENTS

This book is about pleasure, death, rebirth, and revelation. Letting go looms large, because I write about my parents and their dying and about my husband and our divorce. Mourning and celebrating those processes and events, I see them in light of my history with chocolate—my lifetime engagement in erotic and aesthetic pleasures. Letting go is the outcome of learning, and it also precipitates learning. *Swooning Beauty* describes, interprets, and analyzes a process of knowing much more about love than I did before writing.

Cookbooks give repeated directions for the treatment of chocolate desserts. The verbs are imperatives for pleasure. Beat, cream, blend, stir, scrape, spread, divide, mix, bake, garnish, loosen, boil, grease, heat, sprinkle, spoon, cool, frost, remove, refrigerate, freeze, shape, pour, dip, drizzle, cover, press, fill, dissolve, split, swirl, serve: I do them all in *Swooning Beauty*, thus letting chocolate be both salve and sanctum.

Enjoyment of chocolate colors, foods, and perfumes arouses my memory of objects, places, acts, and people that I celebrate and mourn. As nurturing and erotic love and as aesthetic nutriment, chocolate is a reliable companion that one can savor with those she loves or keep to herself as a beautiful obsession, to be shared, sometimes, in need or under the duress of heartbreak.

Butter, sugar, eggs, chocolate. That combination of ingredients causes me to salivate; and it has figured in my life as a salvation. The spoken rhythm of rich and sweet ingredients creates an expectation and a melody. I anticipate a rhapsody on my tongue and throughout my mind and flesh. I'm in love with soothing luxuries. How beautiful is Queen of Sheba, a torte with brandy and ground, blanched almonds, whose glaze the chef can marble into an exquisite gestural abstraction of white and dark chocolate. How sensuously sticky are pudding, candy bars, and brownies, clinging to my lips and fingers. The brownie that I'm eating — picking up and putting down — as I write is scenting my left hand with chocolate. The brownie stirs my longing for Mom's version, whose cake-like texture I try to reproduce whenever I bake brownies, always using her recipe. How I miss my Dad's cocoa, whose infinite sweetness I am aching for on this cold autumn evening.

I have a faith in the written word that escapes or mystifies many people I talk to in both my personal and professional lives. *Words lie* is a cliché, and my faith in words may cause some people to snicker at what they consider to be my naiveté; because they believe that people are so good at misinterpreting one another through words. I stick to my faith in words — words processed through tears and over coffees, words mistily remembered from literature that has left me breathless, words that assure me I am loved. I believe that words loosen the unconscious and bring its contents to the light, and unless that happens — or we aid its happening — more than a little, we sink toward a stasis or a psychic and bodily entropy that atrophies our ability to love ourselves.

ACKNOWLEDGMENTS

My acknowledgments take three courses of gratitude as I mull over the period of conceiving and writing *Swooning Beauty* (spring 2000 through November 2003), release the ignorance and blockages that I brought to its pages, and grow wiser from having looked at my life so closely.

Thank you, friends and healers, for your love. Larry Barnum, Stephen Barr, Nancy Blakely, Rob Borges, Peggy Doogan, Pam Henning, Amber Martin, Claire Prussian, Ariana Page Russell, Renee Wood, and the fairy lover, with you I saw the light. I saw *myself*.

Larry: we turned my woe to radiance
Stephen: you loosed me on the fearless path
Nancy: the harmonies of your laughter, words, and hands both held and lifted me
Rob: we wondered at the poetry of lunches and ideas
Peggy: we explored the mysteries with your patient generosity
Pam: your eloquent plain-spokenness awakened my intuition
Amber: you trained me in strength and supple spirit
Claire: you taught me where the ground was
Ariana: when you asked me to have coffee, an angel came my way
Ren: we sang our songs in registers of love
fairy lover: we realigned my erotic being

Thank you, sites of learning, which supported the growth of my pleasure and self-knowledge. In autumn 2002 I began to regularly attend classes at Yoga Loka, where Kim Orenstein is the director. Yoga Loka's brochure reads, "Loka translates as a location or a place with an inner sense of community." Kim and Denise Barclay, the instructors whose classes I most often attended, provided a community of peace, a place in which to open my heart. The University of Nevada, Reno, granted me a sabbatical for the academic year 2003–4. Retreat mode, for writing, reading, yoga, bodybuilding, and all kinds of loving opened nodes and channels.

Thank you, students of mine, for amazements beyond measure. Especially those of you in my spring 2003 classes — B.F.A. Seminar, Performance Art, and Contemporary Art. Your love increased the fluency of mine.

I follow a fourth course of gratitude in thanking everyone associated with the University of Nevada Press for their enthusiasm and cheer. I especially thank the people with whom I had the most contact and the designer:

Joanne O'Hare — a lover, like me, of the Sonoran Desert and Tucson, one of its jewels — your sense of fun and adventure and your down-to-earth humanity made everything easy.

Gerry Anders, your perfectly precise copyediting, your knowledge and your humor were a writer's joy.

Vicki Davies, your playful intelligence and creativity awakened and delighted me.

Michelle Filippini, your kind and quick responsiveness invited me to relax and I accepted.

Kathleen Szawiola, your acuity of eye and mind roused my spirit.

Carrie House, your simultaneously bold and subtle design engages the intentions of *Swooning Beauty.*

My fifth and final course of gratitude is to the journals that published material that appears in *Swooning Beauty:*

"The Aesthetics of Orgasm" (*Sexualities*, 6.3/4 [August/November 2003]: 459–78) was presented at the 15th annual Women's Studies Network (UK) conference "Beyond Sex and Gender: The Future of Women's Studies?," hosted by Queen's University, Belfast (September 19–21, 2002), for a special section, "Exceeding Sex and Gender?" "The Aesthetics of Orgasm" is an early version of chapter 9 in *Swooning Beauty*; Moya Lloyd and Marysia Zalewski, how happy I was that you selected the text for my performance.

Sections of "Bloodred Beauty: A Meditation on Mel Gibson's Midlife Allure" (*Art Journal*, 60.3 [fall 2001]: 24–33) and "Tarts, Stars, Jewels, and Fairies" (*Art Journal*, 58.4 [winter 1999]: 88–89) appear in various chapters of *Swooning Beauty*. John Alan Farmer, senior editor of *Art Journal* during those years, how wonderful it was to work with you, who are so fairy bright and bloodred beautiful.

"Daughter of the Sunshine Fairies" (*n.paradoxa: international feminist art journal*, vol. 16 [2005]: 81–89) is a small section of chapter 3 in this book, and I thank *n.paradoxa: international feminist art journal* for permission to use it. I also thank editor Katy Deepwell for her willingness to publish an unorthodox piece of criticism and theory, "The Pink of Revolution" (*n.paradoxa: international feminist art journal*, vol. 10 [2002]: 27–35), in which I am in conversation with three scholars who are delightful and enlightening to talk and work with—Tanya Augsburg, Maria Elena Buszek, and Jill O'Bryan—though in *Swooning Beauty* I use only my own words from our collaboration and I've scattered them here and there in *Swooning Beauty*.

Parts of "Passion Pink and Heroes" (*Rhizomes*, issue 7 [2003], http://www.rhizomes.net) appear throughout *Swooning Beauty*. Thank you to Ellen Berry and Carol Siegel, editors of *Rhizomes*, who support my work with their love and enthusiasm.

"Vaginal Aesthetics" (*Hypatia: A Journal of Feminist Philosophy*, 18.4 [fall/winter, 2003]: 137–58) is an early version of chapter 7 in *Swooning Beauty*. Peg Brand and Mary Devereaux, editors of a special issue on women, art, and aesthetics, I so appreciate your solicitation of a contribution from me.

Acknowledgments take this writer deep into her recent history: conversations, discoveries, meals, performances, travels, intimacies, errors turned to awakenings—relationships. Thank you all for a magnitude of learning.

1 —

Truly Human

I ate a lot. Chocolate loomed large in my diet. Like a sweet soothsayer, it healed me and let me know that pleasure always would be available. I needed to know that, during the years when I was fearing and then enduring my parents' deaths—1997 into 2000. I needed to know that pleasure could be my companion. I ate much more than I normally do, and I ate many foods composed of grains and sugar. By the summer after Mom died, I felt my heaviness. Which meant that I could start to let it go. I read and read, that summer of 2000, on the chaise lounge in the living room, and one day, resting from reading, having placed the book on the end table next to the chaise, I noticed, as I interlaced my hands on my belly, that it felt like a large cushion. Neither my husband nor my friends remarked about my weight gain; and after I began to return to my usual leaner self, when I spoke to him and them about the heaviness, they said that it had been no big deal. They were right. The cushion was not as large in appearance as it had felt under my fingers, palms, and wrists. Yet, I wanted lightness—of both body and spirit. The archaic meaning of sooth is truth, reality. After my parents' deaths, I recognized myself as my own soothsayer. I became more truly human than I had ever been.

At the age of fifty-two I realized I was a man. This discovery followed the deaths of both my parents within eight months of each other. Dad died July 7, 1999, and Mom died March 3, 2000. I was left with a sister, Renee, eleven months older than I, and a husband, Russell, thirteen years younger. I loved them, as I loved my friends, my work, and Russell's and my home and its flourishing garden. Nonetheless, I was bereft. I told friends and acquaintances for several months after Mom died that I deeply appreciated their comforting me, but that I was inconsolable. Perhaps my manhood permitted me a bravery, self-confidence, and independence that Western civilization claims for men. I needed those qualities in order slowly to console myself.

Erne René Frueh. Florence Pass Frueh. Frueh had been Früh in Switzerland, the original homeland of Dad's father's family. Pass had been Pasovic, the native surname of my Russian Jewish grandfather, whom, my parents believed, had fled the pogroms of the Russian Revolution. Erne was masculine, an intellectual, an artist, a gourmet cook, like his father, and he was a gardener. When Ren and I were kids, Dad told us that his father had been the chef at one of Chicago's best hotels. Anything Dad cooked, he cooked well, and his veal stews were exceptionally delicious. Mom was feminine, an intellectual, a pianist, a great cook, like her mother, and she was a beauty. I miss her cherry pies. I can't bake a decent one, even having watched Mom do so many times and having asked her for tips about pastry in particular.

In the middle of the summer after Mom died, I dug out almost all the plants in a part of the front yard garden that is closest to the street. I wanted a lighter look, with brighter colors. Russian sage was overrunning the ground cover sedum, the lavender and santolina. The sage felt unnecessarily massive for its location, and the yarrow, as usual, had grown unattractively dense, sprouting and spreading too much for my taste. I spent hours finding, then yanking and chopping out the sage's root system. The yarrow, whose roots were closer to the surface and, unlike the sage's, neither thick nor woody, required only pulling, not a pickaxe.

A slender hibiscus full of small pink flowers took the sage's place, along with startlingly orange daisies and chocolate coreopsis, whose dark and delicate, tiny blooms contrasted incisively with the daisies in both color and form. I transplanted large, flowering sedums and wasn't worried about whether they would survive. When I was a less experienced gardener, I feared the mortality of transplants, but by this time I'd weathered a number of such deaths. They no longer bothered me, because nearby plants soon enough filled in empty spots or, if I wanted immediate difference and satisfaction, I enjoyed choosing a new plant at the nursery to replace any dead ones.

I changed the garden in order to change myself. The probity of the long day's sensuous labor refreshed and tired me, the daisies' brilliance amazed me into October, the coreopsis struggled, then flourished, and nothing died. I changed the garden in order to console myself. The effect was no better or worse than baking then eating a chocolate cake.

My heartbreak was so large after my parents died that now and then my heart itself seemed to fill my entire chest and to swell up—into my neck and the back of my throat—while simultaneously swelling downward, pushing into the top of my diaphragm. It seemed to take over my lungs and tongue, as if wanting to shoot out the front of my chest. By writing this book, I have acted to alleviate that congestion and explosiveness: I opened up my body that is my brain. I was afraid that otherwise my heart would fester, become so damaged that it might kill me. Sometimes my broken heart told me, Sleep, and you'll recover from exhaustion. My heart was wise, but I was a bad listener. For a few years following my parents' deaths, I slept unsoundly, occasionally too much. One remedy for insomnia and grief was to inflame my heart in such a way that soreness turned to brightness. To help my heart rest, I luxuriated in swooning beauty, which was my memory, reality, and invention of manly, girlish, and midlife pleasures. Pain mixed with the pleasure, perhaps increased it—though I've never felt comfortable with the belief that you don't know joy unless you've known shit. I'd rather create a new faith, one that relieves us of having to atone for feeling good and of having to suffer for our delights. Once you know that pleasure is the point of living, you will not let pain retard your progress in pleasure. I am not a hedonist, and I use *know* to mean a visceral rather than an intellectual understanding. Pleasure in eating, in drinking coffee with cream, in talking with one's friends, in hours of lovemaking, in quick, exuberant fucking, in weeding a garden, in gazing at its colors and assimilating its scents, in getting into bed and relaxing into the textures of cotton sheets in soft colors that comfort the spirit—pleasure in the everyday events and circumstances of bodily and psychic maintenance: these were the pleasures that kept me alive and that revived me from the melancholic energy that sapped my love of life after my parents died. You might think that my pleasures constituted avoidance of pain. I cannot deny the factuality of that thought, yet by itself, unmodified or unelaborated, it is facile.

I was adding warmth to the garden in the spring and summer after Mom died. I bought peach pink double hollyhocks, and when they bloomed I felt like I was in love. I stared at them through a glinting spider web, against the front porch's yellow railing. I planted roses, Queen Nefertiti, tight and spicy, and Singin' in the Rain, copper orange petals living up to their name. (It rains little in Reno, but the roses' simple lyric—brightness—sung into me, making my spirit, if only momentarily, so unlike the ballad that it usually was.) The subtle, varied scents of roses are like the fragrances of cunts.

When I lost my mother, I created Mel. He was my fantasy figure whose beauty of being recurred in one Mel Gibson film after another. Mel was not Mel Gibson. Gibson is a real person whose work in film, primarily as an action hero, has made him one of the most famous men in the world. Mel was an intimate and epic individual, a fetish and fixation that served mechanisms of displacement, projection, and transference. His beauties and functions did not differ from those of other movie stars, except that Mel provided me with a psychic, emotional, and intellectual sustenance that no other fantasy figure derived from popular culture ever did.

As the art historian Griselda Pollock asserts, "The subject is always massively unknown to itself," and little did I know that, in my bereft state, I needed both to love a hero and to be one.

At home I viewed almost all of Gibson's more than thirty films over the summer following Mom's death, and after it I went to movie theaters to see his more recent films, *The Patriot, What Women Want, We Were Soldiers,* and *Signs. Braveheart* and *Payback,* respectively released in 1995 and 1999, remain my favorite Gibson films. They compel me aesthetically, whereas his other films do not, and I continue to be more drawn to William Wallace, *Braveheart*'s medieval warrior, and to Porter, *Payback*'s professional robber protagonist, than I am to other Gibson characters.

Braveheart is Gibson's tour de force. He won an Academy Award for directing the film, which also took the award for best picture, and he stars as Scotland's patriot leader, William Wallace, Braveheart himself. I watched *Braveheart* for the first time in May 2000, two months after Mom's death. In June, Russell and I separated. He moved out of our house. We divorced in July 2001.

Gibson's midlife projects, more than his earlier films, allowed me, a midlife woman who realized that she was also a man, an acutely satisfying identification with Mel. Gibson made *Payback* when he was forty-two. Before I learned that he was thirty-eight when he acted in *Braveheart,* I thought he was in his mid-forties, if not close to fifty, in the film. (Wallace died at age thirty-five.) Gibson and I looked more or less the same age, even though in 2000 I was fifty-two and Gibson was forty-four. Aspects of Gibson's personal, midlife allure contributed to Mel's: the strong, round muscles of his built body, which resembled mine, and the wide face, dark hair—in some photos and television interviews it looked like it was silvering—and intense, inviting eyes—features that we shared. Mel lushly inhabited his body, and Mel and I inhabited each other. An unparadoxical weight and lightness—dense muscle, ease of movement—characterized Mel's rich corporeality, which I call "in-the-bodyness." I fell in love with Gibson's ability in film to feel both dense and light, which chocolate is, and despite the inelegance of the term *in-the-bodyness*, it describes a chocolate grace, of soul-and-mind-inseparable-from-body. Gibson's in-the-bodyness recruited me into Mel's charisma, which I came to realize was my own. *Recruit*, from the French *recrute*, new growth, and the Latin *re-*, again + *crescere*, to grow, increase. Gibson's in-the-bodyness exceeds gender designs, making him, in film, as much a poem as he is the many persons played by a grandly attractive man. That poem is the cognitive body, which persuaded me to fall in love with Mel cum Wallace and Porter; and as I fell in love with midlife Mel, I was continually falling in love with myself.

In the acts of enjoying and thinking about Mel, the charisma that had withered after my parents' deaths grew again; he stirred my blood, my heart increased, he nurtured a new life. Dense and light, like a fleshily embodied fairy.

I heard a lot of fairy songs in the spring and summer of 2000, when I didn't throw away old underwear—loose elastic, tiny holes—that I'd bought in Highland Park, Illinois, where my parents lived for fifty-three years and where I grew up. I heard the fairies when I leaned against the sides of thresholds in my house as if I didn't have the will or energy to stand up straight or to move from one room to another. I was listening when I was afraid that summer would never be summer again: how could hot, sunny weather warm my soul-and-mind-insepa-rable-from-body and charm me onto the deck for green tea and buttered toast spread with raspberry preserves or into the garden to watch the many greens grow to their full height? Fairies sang a lot from March, after Mom's last days on earth, into July, when my ten-year marriage became a disintegration whose profundity I could bear to know only unconsciously. From March into July I didn't want to open the front curtains in the living room, but I forced myself to do it each day. During that time, I left the curtains closed in my study. The fairy songs focused my attention on places in my body turned wooden, hardened in the woulds and would-nots of stagnant emotions. The fairy songs gave me hot flushes, headaches, constipation, a pain in my right eye, and tight, high, and rounded shoulders. The fairy songs hurt, poignantly, and healed me. Because of the fairy songs, I could hardly sit at my desk all summer. I completed professional and financial chores there, but I wrote notes for this book reclining on the living room chaise. All summer, as the fairies sang, I was more of a hermit than usual, spending hours reading, as I had when I was a child and teenager; watching Mel Gibson's movies; taking long walks in a nearby park where early in the morning, marmots permitted me to say hello to them from as close as five feet; bodybuilding in the gym by myself; and hanging out, in my mind, with Mel.

In my hermitude, I broodingly enjoyed the loneliness of being without my parents and without Russell in the house, and the fairy singing entertained my melancholy. Sometimes I worried about being too alone, as I indulged in fairy song.

Shimmer shimmer savage stars
Me and Mel and planet Mars
Full of plenty full of red
Full of life and full of dead
Ready for my grief to shed

Color scares people. In the art critic David Batchelor's *Chromophobia* we learn that color disorients and intoxicates, and it spurs desire. Color, often associated in the West with the primitive and the savage, is a kind of overkill, a delirium, joy, and sensuality that threaten reason and order. Wallace refers to himself as "a savage." Porter is "a real Cro-Magnon-lookin' bastard" to a petty drug dealer who wants to convey Porter's crude and frightening fierceness. Excelling in the virility tests—the ritual bloodletting of war and murder, the *kosmetikos* of red—Wallace and Porter are literally colorful characters, stunning in their displays of overkill.

Mel walked in blood, like women do.

Mel, I loved your savage sunshine. Your bloodred beauty kept singin' in the rain, despite the deaths of your parents, wives, and children. Mel, my one-man militia of the soul.

Maybe red scares us more than other colors because it is the hottest one. We yearn for its erotic brilliance yet we run from it. *I burned in empathy with you, my uncommonly masculine Mel, the man's man who was a ladies' man, which means that you were the perfect lady, though no more a proper woman than I was a proper man. You could not have burned red hot for me if your maximum masculinity had not required maximum femininity.*

Wallace rides on horseback into the market where his newlywed wife has just had her throat slashed by an English garrison chief. In slow motion, Wallace grows gradually larger onscreen as he comes closer to committing revenge. Arms raised, hands behind his head in the classic gesture that says, I am not a threat, he also resembles a marine Venus—emerging from the sea, wringing her hair—and he is ravishing. Gray blue sky appears between the strands of hair that frame his heartbroken, pink-cheeked face, which is darkened by stubble. My eyes as fingers roamed over his deltoids and solid neck, his biceps and triceps, and stroked his forearms, from elbow to wrist and wrist to elbow, tarrying where the backlight emphasizes the soft hairiness near the tenderest skin of the inner arm.

One November night the autumn after Mom died, when the fairies and I were on our own in my house and Russell and I saw a lot of each other even though we were living separately, I said to him, "Our sex is of stirring depth and expanse." He agreed. Because I was achingly full of our emotion, I couldn't bear to have sex together that night. He understood so well that no discussion was necessary. It would have dissipated our excruciating poignancy, and we wanted it intact in order to build up even fiercer sexual passion. Or it's likely that we were simply emotionally exhausted. Enough was enough.

In a different autumn, I was forty-one, Mom was seventy-seven, Russell was twenty-seven, and he and I had fallen in love a few months earlier. Recalling a recent walk, on which she admired the physical beauty of a young man who was running, Mom said she could understand my attraction to young men. I wish that I'd felt comfortable continuing our conversational admiration of men's beauty, but in front of my mother I was shy about my sexuality, even in midlife and even though I knew that its intensity was no mystery to her. Also, decades earlier, she had told me that she'd been "a passionate young woman." That autumn afternoon when we talked—too little—about why young men attracted me, Mom asked me why I loved younger men, and my answer focused on the desire in my teens and into my twenties for a brother much younger than I.

Mel was not much younger than I. But in my fantasies we shared the brotherly love that I experienced with younger lovers, including both of my ex-husbands. (Tom, my first husband, is eight years younger than I.)

The warrior exists in an altered state. Red quickens the pulse, warms the body, speeds adrenaline to the heart. Warriors, as well as societies that are engaged in combat, attain an altered state, according to Barbara Ehrenreich in *Blood Rites: Origins and History of the Passions of War.* They undergo or enforce upon themselves a psychological transformation in order to promote and endure war. Bloodred beauty uncensors the spirit. A warrior's altered state enables action. *Mel, in that altered state, you moved from regular citizen, ordinary human being, and common masculinity into bloodred beauty. You became truly human.* Batchelor asserts that color connotes escape—from words, self, sanity, and concepts. I add gender. He explains, too, that color represents loss of focus and identity. Colorful Wallace's Venus loses the conventional action hero's common masculinity. In the Venus scene, Wallace as fe-mel(le), fe-Mel, and fe-Mel(le), offers in-the-bodyness to a many-gendered or—join me in a truly altered state of mind—to a beyond-gendered gaze. Either way, color queers stability, and as the gay filmmaker Derek Jarman understood, "colour seems to have a Queer bent." How exquisite fe-Mel looked in the rope of garnet beads my mother gave me in my twenties for a birthday present. (Gibson and I, both born in January, share the same birthstone.)

Mel and I sat across from each other for sips of mocha java and for anything but dainty pieces of an unembellished chocolate cake—devil's food with lots of buttercream on the top and sides and between the layers. (That perfect stimulus of cocoa and caffeine promoted conversation with my parents, friends, lovers, and husbands.) Mel and I sat side by side on a couch in front of a coffee table on which a plate of hazelnut truffles and Pinot Noir satisfied desires of taste, scent, and touch, and opened our unique expanse of mutually lustful gazing. That led to caresses which left the boundaries and the burdens of gender in oblivion. For us, gender was like color, simultaneously formless yet exquisitely clear. No need to draw the lines that contain spillages of sexual pleasure.

— In July, four months after Mom died, I threw out my crummy underwear. I'd never again buy anything at Bette's, the lingerie store in Highland Park where I'd purchased most of my socks and underpants over the three years that Mom and Dad lived two blocks from it. In September 1997 they sold their house one neighbor away from Lake Michigan and moved into a condominium a half block from downtown Highland Park. Before Mom's strokes that gradually led Dad, in consultation with Ren and me, to incarcerate Mom in Red Oaks, a residence in Highland Park for older people recovering from surgery and for the ready-to-die and the wanting-to-die, Bette's was Mom's favorite place to shop for robes and underwear. Often Dad and I laughed when he called the Red Oaks residents "inmates," but just as often we didn't laugh, being too gloomy about Mom's imprisonment not only in Red Oaks but also within her own body.

Around the time that I threw out the underwear, I also opened the curtains in my study, amazed to realize that they'd been closed for months. Occasionally, crying dispelled my headaches, and in my sadness I told myself that the pressure in my head—and in my heart and shoulders and other places that I knew held pain but without my consciousness of them—was the pressure of being alive when my parents were not, the pressure of love unmitigated by death. Sometimes when I ate raspberries and bananas, my headaches disappeared and my energy increased, though never to what it was before my parents grew weaker and sicker over the previous few years. With two loves of my life gone from this planet, my emotions grew at such a rate that they depleted me. Having given birth to the infancy of a new adulthood, perhaps I was overly concerned about its well-being; maybe I didn't know how to feed it correctly, with sufficient ease. At any rate, staying home a lot felt nourishing, because if home is where the heart is and a large part of my home had died—for my senses could no longer visit my parents and my husband of ten years was living elsewhere—then I needed to thoroughly inhabit house and garden in mind and body in order to ground my senses in a soothing reality.

Fourth of July weekend 2000, when Russell and I met Ren and her partner in Chicago to scatter Mom's ashes in Lake Michigan, where we scattered Dad's almost exactly a year earlier, hot flushes stronger than those I experienced at Dad's bedside the day of his death and each of the five days before it, made clear to me my continuing anguish. Up until Dad's dying, I enjoyed my menopausal flushes, which over several years came occasionally, each time awakening me to the sensuousness of aging. In late June 1999, before going to Highland Park for what I knew would be my last visits with Dad, I began taking an herbal remedy for the flushes. It started to diminish them while I sat near the foot of his bed, witnessing the changes that took him from mental clarity, anxiety, and eating bits of food, to occasional hallucinations, dozing with one eye open, and sipping juice, to asking for water and saying little else, to letting his head turn toward the window and, with sunlight bright on all of him, dying.

His death in the gentle radiance of Midwest sunlight was anything but brutal; and yet I experienced a savage sunshine—because he died.

Mel's savage sunshine often manifested in a spectacle of reds. Madders, lakes, and alizarins—bluish reds; cadmiums and vermilions—warm toward orange; light, bright crimsons; deep, bright scarlets; reddish-purple carmines: Mel's body was a celebration of color, for red is a loosening of eros as it is an uncensoring of the spirit.

A gush of uterine blood ran down my leg and spotted the wood floor in varying circular sizes. I sat on the toilet as more blood left me, and it stank. Autumn 2000 in New York, at my friend Serena's apartment on the Upper West Side. I'd left a business meeting, feeling nauseous and flushing, chilling, and sweating intensely. Before that, Serena and I had eaten breakfast at the Empire Diner with my friend Peggy, and they talked with me, so kindly and wisely, about my seeing a therapist. Decaying, rotting—those words filled my mind as I sat on the toilet, smelling . . . the end of my periods? the end of my marriage? the end of the uterine infection that I wasn't tending to? I pushed toilet paper into my vagina in order to gather more blood when it stopped dripping, and I smelled the toilet paper. Smelling my menstrual blood and tasting it were familiar to me, as I started performing those sensuous acts in my teens.

The end of anyone else taking care of me. That's when the warrior emerged, again and anew, the way that enlightenment takes place—not once and for all in The Awakening, but time after time, in flashes that illuminated parts of the massively unknown self, those parts of the universe that we've kept in hiding from our consciousness.

Mel, you were my warrior, my scarlet lady, my flagrant spice and flower—pimento, poppy, pepper, and paprika. You embodied blood and lust, a bloodlust more vital than the one enforced on battlefields.

One of the bloodiest pictures of Gibson occurs in The Patriot, released around the Fourth of July of 2000. I saw the movie by myself soon after scattering Mom's ashes. Gibson plays the fictional Revolutionary War militia hero Benjamin Martin. The scene occurs after Ben has axed to death a British soldier. Ben and his two young sons have just been on a mission to save the oldest son, a teenager, from the British troops. Because the two other boys are not yet adolescents, our hero's savagery seems especially severe. He stands, for seconds, in a bloody glory, the V-neck of his white shirt spread wide, open to his sternum, exposing much of his collarbones. We see him from the waist up, and he is truly blood-soaked. The asymmetrical spread of his shirt dramatically eroticizes his skin, the shirt is more red than white, and blood covers his face, neck, throat, and chest. This image is one of the most dazzling within the whole of Gibson's work.

Mel, you were my scarlet rose, my melon-colored honeysuckle. Within our narrative of love we fertilized and watered our emotions, which unfolded like flower petals, with that delicacy and inevitability. Films thick with brutalities, such as director Terrence Malick's The Thin Red Line, in theaters the year before The Patriot, can provide such an experience. Mars, presiding over the red planet—fields of corpses and still living, but slashed or battered bodies—can play the heartstrings with Venus's passionately capricious tenderness. *Mel, my blood-covered hero, you offered catharsis differently.* Blood-covered heroes purgatively nursed my in-the-bodyness by reminding me where I came from: the interior bloodiness of my mother's body, her blood that flowed with me through her vagina—the safety of her bloodred beauty. I have heard that birth traumatizes the newborn. If that is true, the shock site had yet to reveal itself to me, and, for a while, the rich red palette of an exquisitely lurid Mel—blood-bathed birth phantasm—healed my wound, my being bloodied in soul-and-mind-inseparable-from-body by my parents' deaths. *Thank you, Mel, for healing me into the truly human.*

For about a year after Mom died, I was still bleeding from my vagina, curious about the irregular periods that heralded my menopause. *Maybe, in my imminently permanent cessation of natural bleeding, your extravagances of blood entranced me, Mel. You bled from just about anywhere. Because you didn't have my sex's gift, you did the best you could. I did my best to forgive you for savagery.*

I took the herbal hot flush remedy for many months, but it stopped working a week or so before scattering Mom's ashes. I kept taking it nonetheless and only stopped after we scattered her ashes, having decided that if indeed the curative had become ineffective, then I'd live with the flushes for a while. I never timed their appearance, but I think it sometimes may have been every thirty minutes: heat in my face, neck, and shoulders, moistness on my arms, belly, back, buttocks, and legs, especially at night along with cold sweating and removing bed linens so that air could cool my naked body, encumbered by fabric as much as by heat.

I flushed and chilled all through the summer of 2000 and into the beginning of fall semester. I never sweated much in my life, and I was sweating a lot, so much that I smelled my cunt when I was conducting a discussion in my fall 2000 Feminist Art Criticism class. The smells, sweat, and unchanged frequency of the flushes persuaded me to return to the original remedy, whose restorative qualities I believed were working again and contributing not only to the calming of my body but also to the elevation of my spirit.

As for the constipation, tight shoulders and slumped posture, and pain in my right eye, an August sojourn at Canyon Ranch, a Tucson health resort, relieved them all and guided me into practices, once I returned home, that had become haphazard during my parents' years of dying and that refreshed my soul-and-mind-inseparable-from-body. The litany of disciplines is a contemporary cliché: drink at least eight glasses of water a day, eat primarily fresh fruits and vegetables and whole grain breads and pastas, and practice yoga most days of the week. The yoga classes that I attended at the spa were especially revelatory. In our early twenties my boyfriend Jason taught me yoga, which I continued more or less regularly over thirty years, learning new asanas and ideas from books; but I never took a class. My last day at the spa, I benefitted so much from one yoga class in the morning and a longer one after lunch, that I felt extraordinarily grounded and light as I traveled home late in the afternoon. Massages, a moonlit swim in an outdoor pool—I was amazed to be the only person in the water or its vicinity—javelinas, roadrunners, and rabbits within feet of where I sat on outdoor benches, and a meeting with Diana, a practitioner of traditional Chinese medicine, all quieted me. I thought about almost nothing during my spa vacation. I didn't read the books that I brought with me. Nor did my usual sexual fantasies about Mel run rampant, even though I had swiped the July issue of *George* from a spa lounge hours after my arrival—Gibson, costumed for *The Patriot*, lured me from the cover—took the magazine to my room, and laid it on the nightstand.

Diana ordered Chinese herbal formulas for me. They arrived at my door a couple of days after I returned home from Canyon Ranch, and I began a weekly yoga class in September. I was certain that the herbs built my well-being and tranquility, enlivened my complexion, hair, and eyes, and augmented my "luminous sexuality," a phrase used by a student critic in the University of Nevada, Reno's student newspaper to describe my presence in a performance art piece that I presented in 2000. Yoga taught me, as did bodybuilding, to stand at my full length, shoulders back and down, soul-and-mind-inseparable-from-body filled with as much grace as I imagined.

— Spring came early to Reno in the year 2000, which meant that the tall bearded irises bloomed profusely in April. *Iris, messenger of the gods, messenger from beyond our planet, from fairyland, deliver me a fairy song,* I asked that spring, *so that I can see my life more clearly through these infant eyes, too innocent of grief before the process of my parents dying and the weight on me of their deaths.* Irises were my mother's favorite flowers, and they're one of my favorites, too. I hoped that she would live to see the irises from my garden, which I would have brought her in the residence—of lesser incarceration than Red Oaks—to which Ren and I moved her in Reno after Dad died. Red oaks don't grow in Reno. Aesthetic pleasure and sharp sorrow thrilled though me at the lemony white, eggplant purple, mauve to pink sorbet, and chocolate-red irises that filled the beds closest to the front of the house. If I'd opened the study curtains in April, I would have seen that mass of both highly saturated, highly reflective colors while sitting at my desk. The chocolate-red petals harbored a dark, transparent eros, as do the consequences of being human, which are engagement and engorgement with bravery, fear, and laughter.

The goddess Aphrodite is wild about flowers. She helps them grow. *Aphrodite, I asked, like I asked Iris, help me flower, like the irises, unpretentiously.*

According to the yoga master B. K. S. Iyengar, "The mind when it contemplates an object is transformed into the shape of that object." During the years of my parents' dying and of my disintegrating marriage, I was taut with overstimulations that grieved my every cell. I observed the irises unfolding, and in their presence, inches from the centers of their scents, I studied their shapely color, smell, and form. The chocolate-red flowers especially captivated me. Their tonal subtlety mystified me every year. Collecting myself in their shape, which was the shape of Aphrodite, I managed to start redeeming those cells.

I rarely fall in love with movies or characters in them, but with the same intensity that I fell in love with Mel, I fell in love with director Todd Haynes's

Velvet Goldmine, released in November 1998, the last autumn that Florence and Erne lived with each other. *Velvet Goldmine* is a fabulous fairyland, a luminous extravaganza, a cathedral of queer, all of which I explain in chapter 6. Just as Mel recalled me to myself, daring me into luxuriant self-invention, so did *Velvet Goldmine's* male characters: rock stars Brian Slade and Curt Wild, teenage fan Arthur Stuart, who later in life becomes a journalist, and Jack Fairy, living legend and apocryphal descendant of Oscar Wilde. That crew of beautiful men who love and fuck one another and sometimes women, those beautiful fairy men: I was their twin in lust and gender, their camp splendor and tenderness. All of us silly and deliriously gorgeous, celebrating ourselves, being truly human.

In *Velvet Goldmine* an infant Wilde arrives on earth wearing a green brooch. The jewelry moves into Fairy's possession, then Slade's, Wild's, and Stuart's. The fairies helped me find that heirloom, a talisman of strange masculinity. I found it because they sang to me.

In May of 2000 nature worked against my happiness and any complete redemption of my cells. A late frost killed almost all the irises. I looked elsewhere to save myself.

We look elsewhere continually, in order to save ourselves. What we want becomes what we know; so learning to want new experiences, new terms of understanding, inspires change. Without change, we know very little and stagnate in our redundant desires. *New* may be subtle, and certainly unknown to anyone but oneself. What we want and know needn't be a spectacle. Clarities and solutions continually shift when, like an action hero, one is working and playing to be fearless. Clarities and solutions shift even though one knows that she is always the center of any kind and quantity of looking elsewhere.

— "You come into the world alone," goes the aphorism. We take that aphorism's meaning as a given, but to me it feels forced on us as truth. I came into the world with my mother, her body and being ever-present in the process. I could not have accomplished birth by myself. And although *alone* connotes a spiritual state, one that continues throughout life if we're wise and staunch enough to comprehend the aphorism, a different wisdom demands our acknowledgment that every human being comes into the world with a woman. All of those women are not equally present spiritually when they're giving birth, and all women do not or cannot give birth equally. For many newborns, the process of being birthed may not be a gift. Even so, the aphorism denies the absolutely primary togetherness—at least physically—of a woman and a fetus-into-infant, a new human being. In much psychoanalytical literature, the child must separate from the mother in order to establish her or his individuality. According to such theories, that break is painful, but inevitable and necessary. This idea of separation from the mother runs culturally deep, so deep that, even while giving birth—an iconic and revered act, an event made, through language, into a gift—the woman and her body are misunderstood as a wasteland. Fairy wisdom tells us otherwise. A fairy aphorism says, "In ever-presence, the mother's body and being are fairyland."

— One summer morning in 2000, I replaced rank water sitting in a clear glass vase with fresh water from the kitchen sink. I clipped off dried-up leaves and flowers and a bit from the bottom of each stalk of the bouquet to freshen it, too. I returned the vase to my black enameled McCobb desk. Paperweights from Mom's collection sat to the side of the vase: one's design is three trumpet-shaped white flowers; another's is a butterfly suspended over a daisylike blossom whose red, yellow, green, and white petals overarch a circle of transparent bubbles and, below them, a swirl of the same colors interspersed with blue; and the third, a Tiffany piece, is iridescent like the irises. Together, the paperweights and flowers created a glittery garden on my desk.

After Mom died, several people sent me flowers. The only ones that I remember came from Peggy—irises. In Greek mythology, Iris is goddess of the rainbow. A book on Victorian painting reproduces John Atkinson Grimshaw's *Iris*, dated 1886, in the "Fairy Painting" chapter. Aglow, her fleshy curves appealed to me. In the photo their light becomes a halo emphasizing her profiled face and the top of her long, dark, streaming hair. Iris's iridescent wings, of chocolate-red and a green resembling the magically masculine brooch, give her the power to hover above a pond. Her wings almost equal the length of her legs. *Iris, steamy vision: my hero, my fairy, my desire, my twin. In my mind, you sat at the peak of a rainbow's arc, wings spread for perfect balance, arms folded over your upper abdomen, legs crossed, feet happy in sleekly high-heeled, shimmering pumps. Despite the rainbow's existence, people below continued to feel the rain that preceded it. In fact, rain inundated the earth.*

Here on earth the summer of my mother's death, the summer that was my rainy season, I thought about the smell of flowers that is simultaneously lovely and pungent, like something that is about to die but does not yet know it, so keeps living as intensely as it can.

July 9, 1999, my sister, her partner, my husband, my father's lawyer, and I scattered Dad's ashes in Lake Michigan, onto the surface of fairyland. (That, Iris told me, was where my parents went.) A year later my sister, her partner, my husband, and I scattered Mom's ashes in the same spot, so that they would meet Dad's in fairyland. Like everyone, Mom and Dad ended up missing in action. Death makes everyone into a hero.

Love, the infinite emotion, can slow time's ordinary flow. Moments are sustained and events suspended, and both feel as infinite as love itself. For those who are living, the dead body and the dying in one's presence of a loved one suspend time; death holds the living in suspense. I witnessed both of my parents' deaths. After the too clearly defined details of that suspension, the survivor may avenge the perceived assault on life. Thus the action hero's revenge. I once called this book my revenge.

Where does deep affection come from? What is its history in the body after body of human beings through the millennia of our existence? Not the *ideas* that a scholar gives us of love in literature, like Denis de Rougemont in his *Love in the Western World*. There, love is rotten — but exciting — because the romantic love between men and women that the book elaborates is an illness: love is always a lost cause; love is only lovesickness. Ideas do ground and generate reality: lovesickness embeds itself in soul-and-mind-inseparable-from-body. Yet the bond between mother and child or between mates or hunting companions or warrior brothers and sisters drives my imagination and intellectual and corporeal longing more than does rotten romance.

We will never know the growth of love in the way I wish to know it, because it is not a story that malcontents, such as many scholars are, can tell. History tells events and relations that are important enough to record. Love is more important than history is, yet love, like the actual voices of the Delphic oracles, is lost to us.

At the same time, love lives; not because history (or literary criticism or psychoanalytic theory) has narrated some of its systems, and not because history as biography has recounted the "excesses" of "great" or extreme lovers, such as Casanova, Byron, Edna St. Vincent Millay, or Frida Kahlo. History — events that matter—itself is irretrievable, but when historians take on the task of try-ing to retrieve bodies and emotions, their stories set me yearning for the love within my reach—right now—for the loving bodies available to me—right now. When historians take on the task of trying to retrieve the truly human, their work propels me into curiosity about erotic philosophers who preceded me, most of whom wrote nothing, because their wisdom existed being-to-being and body-to-body.

We know the origins and growth of deep affection, not as facts in a scholar's book, but rather as the way we feel when our own being and body constitute a love song, for whoever it is we are singing. Better that I made up Mel and asked him to sing with me—our tones were mellow, dulcet, utterly requited—than that I searched for solace, let alone warmth, in the unheated library of history.

Those who don't learn from the past are destined to repeat it: we are assured that our knowledge of history—which to a great measure is our belief in the ver-ity of history—will release us from error. Human history, family history, as writ huge in the history of art or the history of Assyrian Empire and as writ smaller and perhaps more quirkily in the history of lipstick and the history of a latest love affair: I love all of these histories, but they lead me into speculations and ques-tions about reality. If I'd let them, they could all cause me insomnia, all lure my unconscious to create the dark circles under my eyes that, over the last few years of my parents' lives, I attributed to my trauma over their imminent deaths. Like the historical origins of deep attachment, the origins of those undereye circles eluded me—when I looked for their truth (or the truth of their formation) in my own recent history. Love, not history, is truth, and we feel and see love in our bodies. Losing love, or anticipating its loss, I was losing sleep. And losing, if only temporarily, a part of my deep affection for myself. One could say that someone's history is written all over her body; and the metaphor works. But the body is simply *there* in a way that history never is.

Mom and Dad, my lost loves, came to me in dreams and in times of tremen-dous stress, as Wallace's father and Murron, his wife, come to Wallace after they have died.

In October 2001, three months after Russ and I divorced, I unexpectedly and quickly became intimate with a man. I called him my fairy lover. Together, we were romantic, passionate, profoundly taken with each other and surprised by our own intensity. He was living with another woman, which created hiatuses in our relationship and deeply disturbed his equilibrium. At breakfast a week after a distressed conversation about our deepening feelings for each other, I told him about the only dream I remembered from the previous seven days with a subject other than him and me. I related, "Mom, Russ, and I are in a store, and she collapses in my arms. I know that her death is near, and I say to Russell, 'We'll have to take her home,' which I know is a permanent adjustment. I know that she'll never recover. I wake up crying and saying, 'I want my Mommy.'"

My mom had recurring nightmares about her mom and dad after they died. She never talked with me about the dreams, even though I asked. She knew terror, I knew sadness. Permanent adjustment, permanent loss.

Be different from your stricken mother, brain lamed by stroke. Be different from your depressed father, full of every worry his own ancient history summoned.

Because Mom and Dad died and Russ moved out, I felt, from spring through autumn 2000, that I had to do everything myself, to take care of everything myself, and I didn't want to do a fucking thing. I wished that I could just be a fucking thing, assuaging my grief with many male bodies.

Autumn 2000 was full of glowing days whose golden light and warmth caressed me out of my sensual, yet sad, insularity. I felt like I was emitting light, like Aphrodite, called *golden* by the Greeks. A writer from the student newspaper felt my radiance, because he called attention to my "luminous sexuality." One gorgeous Saturday afternoon all I wanted to do was fuck, and I thought about a young male student who was paying me long visits in my office. (This is one of the only ways a student can begin to court a professor, for a grade, for a drink or coffee, for sex, for love of any kind. E-mail is another way, but for me, the physical is essential in courtship.) He had asked me to watch a film of his. "Delighted," I said. He brought the video to me: "It's only six minutes long." I assured him of my interest: "I'd watch it if it were thirty minutes." One day as we were sitting on a bench in my office, where I sit with all student visitors, he could hardly look at me. I turned toward him, and he was gazing at the wall. His film showed intelligence and passion, but when I told him so, he didn't even start the conversation that my honest compliment initiated. He made no sign that he wished to hear either my appreciation or the critique that was part of it. Intellectual clichés clouded the lovely imagery, oversentimentalizing the entire film so that I couldn't take it seriously enough. Unlike many scholars, I use and defend sentimentality in my own work. Sentimentality invigorates

Swooning Beauty because sentimentality probes soul-and-mind-inseparable-from-body. Usually, sentimentality keeps to the surface, and that was the student's problem.

We talked a little about Mel Gibson, a safe topic centered silently on the beauty of a man. My students knew that I found Gibson beautiful, and the student told me that *he* was beautiful, in a veiled but unmistakable way. (The unconscious was at the forefront of my mind. Early in the semester I read in an assignment for one of my classes — not the one in which the student was enrolled — Pollock's statement that "the subject is always massively unknown to itself." Week after week that idea resurfaced from my massively unknown depth as I contemplated or laughed at myself, my students, Russell, and others who entered my life either intimately or ever so slightly.) The student asserted that he was "prettier" than his friend with whom he collaborated on the film and who appears in it. My student's strangely bold declaration of his desirability took me aback, but I don't think that my reaction was too readable.

A couple of days before my sexually luminous performance he unexpectedly showed up in my office doorway, and I asked if he had a few minutes to help me move a pedestal that I planned to use for the piece. Of course he did. (Was he wanting an "A"? Being a good boy? Was he wanting the literal touch of my luminous sexuality? Being a bad boy?) We went to a storeroom, I couldn't get the key to fit into the lock, and I asked for his assistance. Rather than allowing me to hand the key to him the way one normally does, without any meeting of flesh, his fingers danced over mine. I wished that I'd let the electricity flow, but I wasn't ready. Nor, once when I was sitting with my legs crossed at the knees and he was standing close, did I heatedly catch his eye right after he stared at my bare, pearly inner calf. I wanted to fuck him, and a month or so later I told Peggy, miles away from me in Tucson but closer to me than just about anyone, that I asked him to have coffee with me — "That sounds like fun," he said — and that I felt trashy and exhausted and in love with Russell. And I was tired of being a saint.

I wanted sex with someone besides my estranged husband. I also wanted to be protected and taken care of, I wanted life to be safe and sane. To a great extent Mom and Dad helped me to make it that way for myself. They taught me moderation, which can keep one's life relatively clean. Or had I learned that alone?

We are all afraid, sometimes, that our parents have poisoned us, and I could suppose that in the murky places of my past, which conscious memory cannot fetch, unredeemable dirt has been collecting all my life. But I feel pretty clean—unashamed, guilt-free, unregretful—because my parents loved me and I've never doubted that. It may be the clearest knowledge I possess.

In the melancholy of parental deaths and marital separation, I could have believed that I was desperately alone, even though in general I was moderately, calmly, and resiliently negotiating my terror of being alive. I had a dream in the summer of 2000, from which I remembered a house, a grinder, a mansion, a loss, and a flagrant need for something. The something permanently slipped my mind as soon as I woke up.

In daydreams I directed the student's and my sexual acts. How breathtakingly erotic they became in their slowness: pivots of my pleasure, sharp as chilies flaming in my mouth and opening my sinuses with burning sweetness. My pleasure, raging in me like the excessive appetites attributed to teenagers, 3-D as any worthwhile fantasy is.

In fantasy I wondered which M·A·C color of mine the student imagined coating my lips when his cock enjoyed my tongue, teeth, and throat. In reality I noticed him staring at my mouth. Which color did he want to see on his skin? Did one of my matte reds excite him the most? Pivot, a scarlet, or Chili, my favorite at the time, whose brightness a cumin tone subdues. Maybe he liked colors of cunt wet with the anticipation of fucking him. Those would be two shimmering lipsticks, a maroon named Rage and a very light warm pink called 3-D.

The student and I left campus in my car for lunch. We were hungry and our date was at noon. He suggested that we go to a restaurant that has excellent sandwiches. I'd never been there and asked him if it served chocolate malts. "They're very hard to come by these days," I said. Then I told him about my memory of chocolate malts on family vacations when I was a girl. On long car trips I loved stopping for lunch and getting my standby: a cheeseburger, fries, and a chocolate malt. I kept the account of my lifetime passion for chocolate malts brief because its intimacy embarrassed me. If he sensed too much of my passion for chocolate malts, he'd sense my desire to fuck him.

Here's what it's like when both your parents died within eight months of each other: the very real, very fresh irises on the coffee table feel like a memory. Here's what it's like when your husband moves out of the home you've shared for ten years: your passion for fucking, whether him or another man, can drive you into believing that the beauty you see in a man's body and in his taste for yours means that he sees your heart as clearly as you feel his cock in actuality and in fantasy. Because what you want is his ability to open you and him to the beauty of soul-and-mind-inseparable-from-body. Here's what it's like in both cases: you end up wanting.

I needed something to sink my teeth into, something as substantive and delicious as new love. A 1994 Hershey's ad selling thick chocolate chunks reminds us that "we all deserve something we can sink our teeth into." *Vogue* food critic Jeffrey Steingarten asserts in the October 1996 issue that food is "life's most reliable pleasure," and my agreement with him takes a more particular turn: chocolate is life's most reliable pleasure, because its aesthetic intensity so often exceeds that of other foods. Chocolate desserts look more beautiful than other foods, and to many people they taste more beautiful as well. In Marcel Desaulniers's *Death by Chocolate: The Last Word on a Consuming Passion*, Lucy's Chocolate Diamonds is a typically luscious composition of umbers—little diamond-shaped cakes covered with glossy ganache and topped with a peaked swirl of glistening buttercream. The photograph features a five-pointed gold star: chocolate is the golden food of fairies, the glamorous star of any kitchen.

Chocolate desserts are foods of substance because they offer us the ability to satisfy a craving—to sink our teeth into what both they and we are: rich, deep, and sweet. The heart is a perfect shape for chocolate. The chocolate heart is meant to persuade us of its giver's love. *Sweet* and *persuade* share the Indo-European root *swad*. So the chocolate giver is playing with the beauty of a bitter substance—unsweetened in its original Mayan and Aztec home—that people have coddled into both the dearest form, a heart, and into an elegance that pleases eyes, nose, tongue, and fingers. Chocolate desserts, like love, should never be so sweet that sugariness overwhelms depth and richness. The best chocolate desserts argue for infinite sweetness, which, like beauty, never cloys.

We put our fingers on infinity. Our tongues and eyes and noses courted beauty. O Mel, my suitor, I accepted your suite of chocolate pleasures. Mel, mon beau.

At least one of Mom's obituaries reported that she "knew how to make things beautiful." That was Ren's response when asked by the *Chicago Sun-Times* or the *Chicago Tribune* what Mom's legacy was. (Neither Ren nor I recall which newspaper, and neither of us has the obituaries.) A dream that I do not want to forget, from the midsummer after her death, renewed for me her legacy of personal beauty.

The dream. I can't find my way home, home being Highland Park. Mom appears, and I do mean appears, like a miracle or an angel. She could be anywhere between thirty and seventy. She's stunningly pretty — her ivory complexion, her black hair. The style of her bright white shirt or sweater perfectly complements her red jacket, tailored and feminine like the Rodier suits she bought in Paris. She's smiling so happily and she makes me smile, she makes me happy. And she gives me directions.

I would have liked her to come to me that night of the dream, maybe each night for a week, and give me directions again, so that they would stick. I wasn't stupid, but I was still lost.

Visiting Wallace in a dream, Murron tells him that he has to wake up. He says that he doesn't want to. He's as lost as I was, even though he battles on for Scotland. Almost no one around us action heroes suspects how lost we can be.

In another summer dream after Mom's death, another dream that I do not want to forget, Dad is driving and I'm a child by his side. We're going down Marion Avenue, which, for Highland Park, is hilly and winding. The dream's season is simultaneous spring and summer, the seasons I connect with my parents' deaths, even though Mom died before March 21. Daffodils, which grew every year in my father's gardens, are blooming, and the grass is gleamingly green. The street changes into a beach with an ocean or lake on the left. I called Lake Michigan the ocean once when I was a little girl. Gaily painted metal lawn chairs sit beside the daffodils, decorating the beach houses. In the dream, Marion and Mariolatry become connected. Merry-olatry. I am venerating gaiety because its absence is pressing. Now I'm driving and I realize that Dad is, in reality, dead. But simultaneously I realize that Mom, too, is dead and Dad is looking for a place to live. Then I realize that they both are dead and I'm alive. And I cried, in the dream and as I was waking up.

The real and dream tears dampened my whole body, like a sweat. I supposed that I woke up in a menopausal flush, but nonetheless, I think that my unconscious corporeally delivered my lonely sadness to the surface. The only way to learn anything is to do it yourself: so sweating tears manifested the integrity of my grief, the fact that the psyche is never a human being's sole site of suffering. Wallace surely sweats tears. We just don't see them onscreen, we're not privy to that intimate a marker of Braveheart.

The late postclassic Maya and the Aztec symbolically associated human blood and chocolate, possibly because both the somewhat similarly shaped heart and cacao pod produced precious substances. The Aztec army ate chocolate as war rations; chocolate was a metaphor of sensuality and luxuriousness for the Aztec; and they and the Maya added the dried and ground powder of chili peppers to their chocolate drinks, creating chilcacahuatl, which, unlike our cocoa, was cool. The Aztec spiced their chocolate with various powdered flower petals. In The True History of Chocolate, by Sophie D. Coe and Michael D. Coe, we learn that the Aztec poet-king of Texcoco, Nezahualcoatl, called chocolate "flower of the cacao tree" in one of his songs. Seeds from the tree called achiote or annatto probably colored chocolate drinks reddish, and according to Gonzalo Fernández de Oviedo, reporting during the Spanish conquest of Nicaragua, natives' mouths, lips, and whiskers turned red, as if they'd been drinking blood, after they had drunk chocolate containing achiote.

One of the first cakes I baked, when I was around eight, was a heart. I cut a round cake in half, turned a square so it faced me as a diamond, then placed the straight edge of each half-round along the diamond's two upper edges. Frosting visually joined the discrete forms into a valentine for Mom, Dad, and Ren.

The daughter unconsciously developed a dark heart after her mother died: in a purgative bloodlust, I symbolically committed a Sadean crime, by hacking apart a large orchid that I gave Mom a week or two before her death. Called chocolate cymbidium, it flourished in her room. It was gorgeous. So I brought it home after her death and did my best to keep it alive, but it gradually gave up the ghost. I let it linger, thinking for a month or so during its extremely piqued condition that I could revive it and bring it back to flowering. I had also failed to keep Mom alive. I didn't feel guilty about that; I felt miserable. Trying to revive the obviously dying, whether human or plant, is a foolish but understandable position to take. Our wish is that the practical tending strategized by the darkening heart and secured through hope and love will work and that the happy outcome will not even be a miracle but rather what simply ensues from pragmatic care.

You nursed me, Mel, and let my blood and other lusts be as fluid as the tears your brave heart sometimes hid.

Bloodlust can lead to blood flow. Color, like blood let from the body, is fluid, as Plotinus (quoted in Batchelor) wrote, "devoid of parts." Nurture and nurse are cognates that share the Latin root nutrire, which is related to the Greek naein, to flow. Blood flowed around you, Mel, and from you. Blood paints the skin and clothes of Gibson's characters; splatters, stains, and smudges the men with the heat of madders, scarlets, lakes, and crimsons, as if the heroes were abstract expressionist canvases. I wondered if Gibson knew this when he offered the following description in an online interview, which I read in July 2000, about *The Patriot*: "beautiful, the whole atmosphere of it, like a painting." I learned in a July 2002 *Parade* cover story about Gibson that his mother was an artist. Like Gibson as the director of *Braveheart*. Like my father.

Like you, Mel, my artist of love.

I hacked to death the orchid and placed its remains on the compost pile that I started the day after I came back to Reno following Dad's dying. In the Highland Park condo, Ren and I hosted our celebration of him, our honoring his life and death. I called the event a party, a word that, considering the occasion, some of the celebrants found unusual, if not offensive. Axing the orchid returned me to the dream from my late twenties in which I axed off my mother's head. The dark heart sometimes demands to be in the plainest view. In those moments or hours, it's wise to take a good look. When I conscientiously regarded my own dark heart, which, like my bright heart too, was as rich as chocolate, I was relieved to disinter one agony or another. I was relieved to examine a defense, a drama, a desire — maybe even a heroic quirk — that could stay buried in the eternal oblivion or the graveyard that the unconscious can be.

— Ren, her partner, Russ, and I scattered Mom's ashes after iris season ended in Chicago. Later in the summer, Ren's partner sent me snapshots of Russell, Ren, and me at the beach below 90 Riparian Road, at the far north end of Highland Park where, above us, buyers had rebuilt our high modern house into a postmodern monstrosity — clean lines gone, arches and cupolas here and there, design enlarged beyond its original elegance into a bloated monument of trendy, run-of-the-mill architecture created by a lot of money and not enough good sense.

Both Ren's partner and Russell had taken pictures at the beach. Mom's ash-scattering morning began gray and stayed very humid.

In one picture I saw me and Ren sitting, backs to the camera, Russell standing, hands in jeans pockets, several feet to our left, giving us breathing space, crying space. Lake Michigan looks placid but not the least glassy. A vertical photo shows the three of us, all with pants rolled to just below our knees, at the shoreline, gathering ashes from the plastic bag, provided by the crematorium, that I'm holding. (I say *gathering; grabbing* or *grasping* is harsh, and a body's cremated remains slip through one's fingers.) Ren and I seem to be watching the disappearance of ashes in the water.

Ren's partner came within a few feet of my sister and me to take another picture. When I first saw the snapshots, that proximity angered me. I judged it to be invasive. But looking again a year later, I was glad for the closeness. It allowed me to see Ren's fingers playing her penny whistle and the sad intentness in her eyes. I liked looking at her thick upper arms, one of many physical features we share, and when I lingered over the pictures, my feet recalled the coarse sand as I slid them slowly over and into it. Ren is wearing socks, and between us sits a big, transparent plastic carton of caramel corn, with its top off and much of the contents eaten. Mom loved caramel corn. Dark green foliage twenty feet behind us covers the bluff that rises to the street level of Riparian Road. By the time Ren's partner took the caramel corn picture, the sun had come out a bit, but the air was still thick. Thick air and thick arms, thick trees and thick beads of sand. Sweet high piercing music thick with our mother's death, thick thighs of the Frueh sisters, sweating slightly in the torrid midwestern summer.

Two ducks about forty feet out appear as little horizontal blobs in the next photo. The ducks would be unrecognizable as such to anyone but the four of us. Ren and her partner took them as an omen that Mom and Dad were together again. Are beloved souls ever far apart, in either life or death? In fairyland?

I looked at a picture of me alone, walking, staring down, and happily noticed that the contour of my face, cheek to chin, was the same as Mom's.

Ren's partner sent three series of pictures: the beach, Ravinia Park — at the southern end of Highland Park — and Chicago near our hotel on Michigan Avenue across from Grant Park. Parks and more parks. Parks ease the heart. Flowers and more flowers — patches of reds, lavenders, sages, and yellows — compose the main subject of the Ravinia photos. We drove there after the beach for several reasons. Mom and Dad often attended the famous classical music concerts held outdoors at Ravinia in the summers. Ren and I sometimes went with Mom and Dad, and Ren, in her late teens and early twenties, before moving to the Missouri Ozarks with her husband, Ken, with whom she no longer lives, enjoyed both day and evening events at Ravinia. In a small indoor theater she listened to afternoon recitals and performances. She also sneaked in during the day to hear the

Chicago Symphony Orchestra rehearse. Ren's and my high school graduations took place in the Ravinia concert shell. Rows of flowers, masses of colors fill the snapshots. Mom and Dad would have known all the flowers' names.

In another photo, Russell poses, framed by greenery, on a walkway, and I recognize hosta behind the daylilies. Hosta blooms profusely all over Highland Park, and I came to know hosta well during my long walks through the town when I visited Mom and Dad over the several years before they died. Hosta, or plantain lily, doesn't grow in the Great Basin, where Reno is located.

The photos show different groupings of the four of us: Ren's partner and I face each other in conversation, and my red Mary Jane flats catch my eye; Ren, her partner, and I stroll together, reacting to something that I don't remember, and I like that our hairstyles differ — Ren's hugs her head to her nape, her partner's bob is the same length as Ren's, my low ponytail hangs a third of the way down my back; Ren and her partner stand close together, the latter broad, big, and tall, the former short and robust, forearms impressing me with their muscularity; me hugging Russ like I'm a little girl, with my head on his shoulder like a daughter loving her daddy; Russ and me from behind, in the midst of tall trees and formal plantings, ponytails down our backs, the similarities of our bodies and strides striking to me, as always — straight, broad shoulders, small waists, high, round buttocks, short, strong legs, proud gaits and posture.

The only city picture that stayed in my mind after I looked at it is Russ strutting toward the camera at the front of a crowd, mist veiling the top half of two skyscrapers. Six red awnings, their overall presence larger than any person or building, loom to the left and proceed to the rear in one-point perspective. Like the ducks in the Lake Michigan picture, Russell can only be spotted by those who know his form; and like the ducks, he can seem frighteningly small in the vast activity and huge expanse that appear with him in the camera's eye. Only the fairies can save the ducks and the man from death — does the lake need those ducks for it to stay alive? Does the city need that man?

Russell's pictures at Mom's ash-scattering show only the water. They are abstract expressions of fairyland's surface, and that makes them more philosophical than the rest of the photos.

Late in the summer of 2002, more than two years after my sister's partner and Russell took the photos and I first pored over them, I opened the folder in which I kept them. I hadn't touched the folder since I placed the photo packet in it after contemplating the pictures the first and only time. The impossibility of simply *looking* at the beach, Ravinia, and Chicago pictures saddened me in itself and slowed me down, to the slowness of the summer after Mom died and I was still married but living alone. Self-indulgent, sensual, almost unbearable, and necessary; I don't know which word or combination of words best describes, in retrospect, my state in the summer of 2000, but I felt it as I sat in my study writing about the pictures, and it scared me. Where was the energy for the next volley of sentences? For the semester that would begin in several weeks? For something as easy as calling my closest friends on the phone? Or getting up to make tea for breakfast?

A question to Russ, deep in that slow 2000 summer of post-death and imminent divorce, comes back: "When your parents die and you don't deal with it, do you go crazy, don't know it, and never recover?" In other words, if your parents' deaths tipped you off-balance, which is pretty likely, and you don't find a new balance, which takes both effort and the simplest being in your grieving cells, are you courting a low-grade craziness? One that bleeds your heart, so that the rest of your life is the gradual drying up that is so prevalent in people from midlife on?

In the year 2000, when more people likely believed in angels than in their own capacity for balance, which is a contented self-maintenance, I knew that I had learned, reasonably well, maintenance and moderation in my parents' house. (Do people ask their angels for help with balance?) Some of those skills they taught me, like eating a dinner that included meat or fish, a salad, and a fresh, cooked vegetable, and some of them I probably learned in self-defense, whose techniques children particularize in order to ameliorate their own upsets and discomforts in the midst of familial oddities or horrors. Lucky me — in terms of mental and physical health — my strategies didn't and haven't included extremity on a lifetime basis.

However, by the autumn of 2000 I'd been in *extremis* long enough, at least for my standard of balance, and I was having trouble normalizing. Naming my new gender, or stabilizing within that name, helped me to let go of outworn maintenance mechanisms. While being a man as a fifty-two-year-old woman may not seem normal, my manhood promised to release some traumas from my soul-and-mind-inseparable-from-body. It promised a restorative integration of love's past, poetic passages. In my new gender identification, which was a transformation in progress and will never be complete — neither has my previous one, or several, been complete — normalcy didn't mean conforming, it didn't mean being an average guy. (Despite its dictates for feminine females and masculine males, gender is a freewheeling psychic and aesthetic form.) My new gender identification did mean finding a daily rhythm, which had unraveled gradually over my parents' slow demise.

Let go. I continually relearned this.

Mel, delectable as chocolate, bloodrich as the heart from which it came, I could not determine the extent of your ravel of reds. It did disorient me from the sidewalks that I followed every day, but I was ready for more revelry. Tempt me more, flowering chocolate Mel. Test my lipstick—Chili is its name—by leaving its imprint from your lips where my mother's garnets touch my skin. Mix us chilcacahuatl, burning, bitter; but sugar me with tweaks and teasings of our gender. Inspire us to be as darkly pretty as the maroon petals of chocolate coreopsis and cymbidium, and as fierce as the reds of births and deaths and mothers often are. Sit beside me while we suck truffles until they melt, while we mourn the short-lived beauty of the chocolate-red tall bearded iris unfolding in the vase on the same table that holds the candy box, remembering that iris was my mother's favorite flower.

In summer 2002 when I reexamined the beach, Ravinia, and Chicago pictures taken the day that Mom's ashes dissolved into the fairyland of Lake Michigan, I found mixed in with them another set of photos, still lifes of the coffee table as altar in Russell's and my home, still lifes of a ritual that took place for a week or two in March 2000, right after Mom died: a vase of yellow daisies, burning candles, the box that held Mom's ashes, and her death certificate. No ritual event or still life was as real, as mystifying, as beautiful, or as overwhelming as the days and nights of my parents' deaths, but letting go . . . it opened many ways in which to resolve the loss that at first felt like a huge and compound break — a smash and a split, an injurious breach in life's little and big decorums. Creating a still life, a *vanitas* that for several days included my mother's hairbrush, holding strands of her hair, and the pajama top that she wore when she died, I was trying to balance myself by allowing the still-life items to draw out my grief. It was volcanic, squalling, foggy, seething. It was uncontrollable, like the surprises that nature bestows on human beings. My psyche labored to present a smooth surface, especially at work; but I started crying just about as soon as I walked in the door of one of my classes within the week after Mom died.

Breaches closed, but that did not produce resolution. I wished desperately for resolution, but *resolution* seemed final, and finality was false. The point of letting go was clarity, not resolution. Clarities shift and overlap, and I was glad that Mom and Dad were dead, because an end to my time and effort in behalf of their physical and mental welfare was a relief. Simultaneously I suffered after they died, because I could never touch, see, or smell them again. *Mel, so amenable as my hero, my alter ego, my lover and companion, you were necessary, but now you're not. Nonetheless, I forever thank you, which is thanking me for a self-maintaining love.*

In unconscious desperation, the subject that is always massively unknown to itself generally clings to its ancient, tightly and protectively constructed narratives, despite the fact that the psyche's poetry is always in motion. *Mel, I was in a motion that I hadn't known before.* I clung to memories that I created at eight, sixteen, or thirty-seven. I've clung to memories formed as recently as 2002. *You moved me, Mel, in one of the dreams my motion gave to me.*

Mel came to me in dreams a number of times in the summer of 2000, and the tone of my intensely voluptuous emotions in the Mel dreams startled me. From girlhood on, I've been voluptuously inclined, so maybe my surprise indicated a depth of concomitant despair and healing: I needed to be loved and moved, and Mel was doing both. My resonant emotions about Mel, when I was awake, suspended me in a starstruck empyrean, where, pining for my future that I was feeling as my past, I took up residence in his soul-and-mind-inseparable-from-body and he in mine. That state was a kind of lovemaking, which was a wish for my healing.

In a long dream or a series of dreams, my wish repeated itself. Mel and I were making love—fucking? Having sex? I didn't know which language was appropriate. For decades I felt more comfortable with *fuck* than with *making love*, but I found myself needing variation. Otherwise, I couldn't adequately articulate, to myself, the dreams' varying but always profound sensuality. While fucking as fairy intercourse heals the wounds of having been fucked over—and being fucked over happens to all action heroes—making love covers all the territory where bodies touch in gracious union.

Hyperreal details are what I most remembered when I awoke from the dream series starring Mel. He and I were . . . making love? Eventually fucking? Perhaps the precise language of love eluded me because of my freshly named gender configuration. Yet fucking is part of every gender's skills and talents. In the first of the dreams, one of Mel's forearms intrigued me. My face was an inch away from his skin — too close in real life to see clearly but perfect, in the dream, for precise erotic observation — and I was taken by his dark and fairly thick hair. (Gibson *does* have hairy forearms.) Men's hairy arms have never been my taste, but in my dream Mel's forearms were far from being gross. *Mel, my animal, so glamorously hairy. Mel, my animal, but never my pet, you were my mignon, the meat of life.*

I paid acute attention to Gibson's forearms in *What Women Want*, the fall 2000 film in which he plays Nick Marshall, a macho advertising executive who, by a literal accident, learns what women want from men. The movie was Gibson's second big-screen release after Mom's death. I wanted to find out if his hairy forearms — which resembled my Mel's hairy forearms — disturbed me aesthetically or sexually. In the film, as in the dream, they excited me. Sitting in the theater, I effortlessly, without thinking, sensed the quality of their touch, of the lovely unity of their soft skin and muscularity, and I sensed, too, how they would feel to my cheek or fingers and how warm and giving their embrace would be.

In *What Women Want* Gibson wears a watch, as he often does in his films. The watch frequently grabbed my attention, as it had in some of his films that I saw over the summer of 2000. I don't wear a watch, but the major men in my life have worn one: Gramps (Mom's father), Dad, Russell, and Tom. I don't respond to watches erotically, but in my dream the watch belonged to the warmth and eros of embrace. Because the watch was the eros of eternity: it was telling time for all time, and therefore I was safe with Mel, who, animal as he was — and consequently mortal — was also love, the timeless and the infinite emotion.

In the series's second dream, Mel and I were very close to each other, faces inches apart, as if ready to kiss. We found the situation delightfully humorous and psychically acknowledged our enjoyment of the sexual attraction between us. Dreams can be soothing sex lies as well as a sensual nutrition that heals through erotic heat.

Mel, you turned my grief to chocolate before I became bitter. Milk chocolate is my favorite chocolate flavor. I've never much liked bittersweet. You brought to me and you knew how to be my milk chocolate. You were my Mommy, full of milk that nurtured every cell.

Mel did not always make things easy in my dreams. He came to me in two dreams during a night of restlessness from which I woke up thinking that I barely slept at all. At first I told myself that the man in the first dream must have been Gibson, not Mel. Or it was Mel gone bad. I did not want the dream figure to be Mel, but, of course, it was. My anxiety and emotional obstruction in the dream did not correspond to the comfortableness that I felt, when awake, with Mel. Anyway, in the dream Mel was nuts. He had agreed to an interview with me, and I was caught unprepared for it. I had no questions, not even topics. The unpreparedness was the same as in dreams I had where I was a teacher, an art historian like I am in actuality, who not only walked into class with no lecture or no slides, but who also had no knowledge of the material that she was supposed to be teaching. (I'm not the only teacher to dream about professional insecurity through images of incompetence or irresponsibility.) In my dream, Mel was driving a brown beater from the '60s, very long and sort of cozy. I thought it was strange, a star driving a vehicle like that. I thought, Oh, he wants to be ordinary, working class. I met him at a nursery—for plants. He owned it, and I'd been told that I'd find him there.

Awake, I thought, Ah, Mel's a gardener, like my father and like me, a man of the soil, like Wallace and like Russell Crowe's Maximus Decimus Meridius, the hero in director Ridley Scott's *Gladiator.* That film, a hit in the summer of 2000 when it opened, held some healing powers for me; though not nearly as many as did *Braveheart, Payback,* or many of Gibson's earlier films—like *The Road Warrior* or *The Year of Living Dangerously.* Maximus endures the deaths of his wife and son, who are brutally done in by Roman soldiers. Dad, Wallace, Maximus, and me: all of us men have been soiled by the death of loved ones, we've all been tired of everything and have just wanted to die.

In my dream, Mel didn't say that he was paranoid about the interview, but I could tell that he was worried: maybe I'd reveal something weird about him or simply too much. He wasn't worried that I'd find out too much, but rather that I'd expose more than he'd like. I had no idea what too much would be. The dream was brown upon brown, and Mel looked more exhausted than Gibson does in his movies; and he was frenetic. My feeling was, Well, here I am, I guess I'll try to calm him down.

I was the brown beater, worn and also roomy, with cushioning for my squalls, fogs, and eruptions. I was the nursery, giving birth to a fairy-light Joanna with the help of Mel. I was nuts, unprepared for revelation of myself to me, revelations about gender, money, and marriage.

Was the brown-beater-and-nursery dream the Mel dream from which I awoke with the words in my head, "I will trouble your dreams as you've troubled my sleep"? But for me to trouble Mel's dreams was to trouble my own, since Mel was my concoction.

The summer of Mel dreams, I kept to myself a lot, even though Russ and I were in close touch, which more often than not was sexual, and I was becoming friends with Pam, a student in her late thirties of radiant spirit, leaping imagination, and striking intuition and physical beauty. Despite those intimacies — one old, intact, and lovely though exhausting, the other new and energizing — my hermitude protected me from revealing too much of myself to anyone. In the dream, Mel represented me, the exhausted hero nursing her wounds by spending a lot of time in her garden, calming herself with soil and flowers. My dreams were psychic inflammations that healed the most sensitive festerings of my sadness by offering me images that I could tolerate interpreting and analyzing.

Words can be dreams and they can be fairy songs. They can make a wish come true.

Words can be commitments. Wallace commits himself in words with passionate questions and assertions, even though we know that for the most part he keeps his cards close to his chest. Me and Wallace, we can be calm and bothersome, quiet yet impertinent. Here I feel my words flowing like hot fudge over vanilla ice cream. They flow with the sensuous sureness of Wallace, betrayed by Robert the Bruce, fallen flat on his ass, bewildered and disbelieving. Gibson looks approachably and kissably gorgeous in those frames, "dribble lines" part of his bloodstained and -splattered face.

Wallace's cosmetic excess, akin to Mel's ultrafemininity, lured me as much as did his bloodred masculinity from the overkill of bloodlust as war. Besides painting their faces with menstrual blood, women have cut themselves around their mouths and tattooed lines from lower lip to chin tip to signal menstruation. Judy Grahn, in Blood, Bread, and Roses: How Menstruation Created the World, discusses women's painting and tattooing themselves with blood as "signs of warning and instruction" and says that sometimes the chin tattoos were called "dribble lines." The betrayed Wallace warns and instructs the viewer about the wages of morality, and of being, as the Bruce's father says of Braveheart, with the skeptical and ironic wisdom of a patriot-whore, one of those "uncompromising men" who are "easy to admire." The patriot-whore's politics compromise him, weakening his already weak heart. I admired Wallace's heartbreaking beauty as both predator and prey.

Payback is based on Donald E. Westlake's novel *The Hunter*, which features the predatory hero Parker. But *Payback*'s Porter, besides being a hunter, also lets himself become prey. He bleeds from his toes, which have been hammered by the sadist minion of his enemy, Bronson. *Mignon*, which means "darling" or "favorite" in French, became *minion*, the untasty henchman who carries out the orders of evil masters. (The Bruce is King Edward's minion when he betrays Wallace.) The Marquis de Sade's libertines make their victims into meat, and Bronson notes to Porter during the toe-hammering episode that the flesh, which the camera does not show, is starting to "look like roast beef." Porter is choice meat/male. Indeed, Porter equals porterhouse.

Mel, you were prime, period. Mignon, you were like the mythic vagina dentata, which injures its prey; and you were like a predator animal that appears to bleed from its mouth, sometimes with human's blood. Mignon, you were my feminine hero, my heroic femininity. O my fe-Mel(le), you were my familiar other, a bloodied side of me that you repaired through love, the bloodied side which was my chocolate heart, profoundly glittering and dark as garnets.

In the laws of sympathetic magic, garnets, whose rich dark red resembles venous blood, relate to bleeding and wounds, blood bonds and disorders, and blood itself; people have used red stones to treat blood diseases. Venous, Venus: Mel's and my bleeding hearts, bonded through bloodred beauty, suffered from lovesickness, a disorder that Venus both creates and cures. *In the rope of garnet beads, my Mel, you were the resonating red of love's circulation.*

I imagined those beads on Porter when he's showering, sad and weary from both his wife's treachery—she shot him in the back near the beginning of the film—and his attempt, before the shower scene, to end her heroin habit, an effort that he probably knew was futile. *Mel, we tried to save our loved ones from death, knowing that we'd fail. Payback*'s color is stylishly faded, often only bluish, with reds snapping out as surprises. The garnet necklace, dark though it is, would catch our eye that way. In the shower, Porter leans, with both arms in front of him, against the wall that holds the fixtures. The camera gives us his lower back and right side, and for some seconds his head as well, before offering a close-up that features his gunshot scars. We also see most of a tattoo of the letters USMC — United States Marine Corps — on his biceps. Full of the self-consciousness associated with postmodernism, *Payback* borrows from film noir and 1970s detective movies, and its time period is ambiguous. Details and atmosphere refer to any decade between the 1930s and now. This ambiguity permitted me to think that Porter is a Vietnam vet whose bloodred beauty was born in jungles and monsoons. I saw the beads at his nape as he luxuriates with slight sinuosity in the heat and rain of the shower. If only he let us hear him moan. I loved that scene as much as I loved Wallace, as Venus, on his horse.

Me and Mel stood face to face, palms up, fingertips touching, the fairy men's green brooch glittering where our flesh met; me and Mel stood skin to skin, naked except for garnets, one necklace apiece, each bead an allusion to our broken hearts. We lingered in the erotic caress that was the energy of soul-and-mind-inseparable-from-body. We lingered, being truly human.

— I wondered where Wallace's body is tight when he feels grotesquely abandoned, as he feels when betrayed by the Bruce. Does he inadvertently hold his breath? Easy breathing promotes thinking and feeling. Thoughts and emotions flow, for better or worse, with the calm or restlessness that the air moving through us releases. Me? For at least three years preceding Mom's and Dad's deaths, my forehead and vagina were tight, tighter than my shoulders from my writing posture. One sign of that distress was a prominent vein in the right side of my forehead. I noticed it in the morning when I was getting ready to go to school. Forehead and vagina, thinking and fucking. Two things I loved to do.

Sometimes I did them with speed and power. Sometimes I did them more tenderly, less fiercely. Speed and power are qualities that the student I would have loved to fuck said that men like about cars. Then he said that men simply like speed and power.

Wallace is a master of speed and power — the way he runs, kills, and rides a horse; his skill as a military strategist; his commitments in words. Even Mel, graceful though he was in speed and power, in both fierce and tender actions, asked me to help him with his tightness. He leaned on me.

Gibson has been in danger of being an ornamental male. Mel, too, was beautiful. (Mel's physical features were identical to Gibson's.) Part of the ornamental male's allure can be "the lean," a term coined by the philosopher Susan Bordo to describe a posture assumed by beautiful male bodies in contemporary advertising. In Stiffed: The Betrayal of the American Male, "ornamental male" is the journalist Susan Faludi's phrase for the late-twentieth-century cosmetic manhood in which the solely bodily attractiveness of a man's glamorous masculine pose performs the feminine vanity for which both feminists and misogynists have criticized women. Pronounced furrows across Gibson's forehead, major crow's-feet, and deep nasal-labial folds—features disallowed for female film stars—have not detracted from his ability to sell himself in today's ornamental and celebrity culture. However, if Gibson's midlife characters were only the ornamental male, then he would be simply prime beefcake and Mel could not have existed.

Mel's ornamentality was full of heart, like the gay rock star Curt Wild's in Velvet Goldmine and like Peter O'Toole's as the real-life action hero T. E. Lawrence—who was a homosexual—in David Lean's 1962 film Lawrence of Arabia. Wallace, and even the mostly hard-boiled Porter, are bleeding hearts, poignantly so in scenes that display them at their most alluring, like jewels gleaming their secrets—like garnets.

The lean skews gender norms, for the male offers, invites, receives, and responds as he props or rests himself against something, or reclines—all, as Bordo says, "in the fashion typical of women's bodies." Porter leans in the shower, asking our eyes and bodies to take him. He also leans against Rosie, his lover, and they let his gentle yet ample weight as well as her insistence ease them onto a sofa. Some time after Murron's death, Wallace meets the Princess of Wales in a hut. She has warned him twice of her father-in-law Edward's plans against him, and the narrative has already established the attraction between princess and warrior. He steps near her, raises one arm so that his hand rests against a ceiling beam, and leans closer yet. Their kiss is seconds away. Wallace's and Porter's anthem could be AC/DC's song "You Want Blood," and it could also be "Lean on Me."

Mel, you leaned toward then on and into the full length and breadth of my in-the-body-ness, closer than most people think that close can ever be.

I leaned on my girlfriends. My grief, my change brought out their best, which was the speed and power of their hearts, and they were superb compatriots in easier times as well. In my bereavement, my girlfriends gave me their love with unstinting sweetness. Hamish and Stephen treat Wallace that way. They are not as sweet as sugar to their cherished companion, and neither were my girlfriends that to me. Best friends are sweet like bars and cakes of chocolate. The best chocolate bars, cakes, and brownies are, of course, rich with butter or eggs as well as being infinitely but not saccharinely sweet. Chocolate in its tropical American home was unsweetened, and chocolate in its natural state is bitter. Milk chocolate, my favorite, is lighter to the taste than is its bittersweet ally in pleasure.

My sorrow after Mom died brought me bittersweet dreams with no Mel. The fairy beauty in one of those dreams without Mel thrilled me with exuberance and dread. I was observing a panorama that resembled the German Renaissance painter Altdorfer's *The Battle of Issus*. This means that the scene was just about beyond comprehension. Altdorfer presents the characteristic Northern Renaissance viewpoint that the world is not ours to own, that human beings accomplish their tiny daily tasks in the cosmos, not only in the material world that Italian Renaissance painters represent in one-point perspective. That system makes earthly existence mentally graspable by placing the human figure in the limelight. In the North, however, higher powers oversee and minimize human events, history-making ones included. Almost the whole upper half of the Altdorfer depicts turbulent blue heavens. A crescent moon hangs in their upper left, and the sun blazes at the horizon in the lower right. We have night and day operating as menace and inspiration, as death and life, and beneath the celestial metaphors, in the excruciating detail of swarming patterns composed of mote-like men, Alexander the Great battles Darius, the Persian king. Banners, pennants, soldiers, horses, mountains, encampment, city, water, boats, and dizzyingly distant land untouched by battle exist in equal unimportance.

As I witnessed in my dream an *Issus*-like drama of unparalleled aesthetic and spiritual accord that also was uncompromisingly confusing, I was giving a lecture, trying to define the terms or the measure of what I was looking at, trying to explain the whole picture. I couldn't find concepts, let alone words. Then aliens entered the dream, and they took it over. They augmented my fear-ridden speechlessness, and they stayed with me as I woke up from the dream. They were presences, not visions, and in the dream's aftermath I was so scared that I lay frozen, wanting to speak to someone—although I was alone in bed—and only able to imagine speaking. I awakened growling or making some incoherent sound, and I heard it as if it were not my own, or as if my vocal and aural mechanisms functioned feet apart from each other. I swear that a light flickered in the hallway, right outside the bedroom. I wondered who or what was present with me in the house. Mother, father, fairy, killer, ghost? In confusion coupled with loss, I wanted to discern that the world I inhabited had not become pernicious.

The dream's beauty was its hugeness. With my parents' deaths, and to a lesser degree, with my additional aloneness because of Russell's and my separation, the world had become enormous. Everything was available. Anything could happen. But I was too scared, that night of the dream and that summer, to move wholeheartedly into the huge, new world. Darius and Alexander and their armies are so small in the Altdorfer, and I felt that small or smaller—amoeba little, miniature in my energy or power; and the world in my dream was an enormity of energy. I see now that the enormity of energy was me—stirred up, dreamy, turbulent—but contained by the losses that exhausted me.

Altdorfer's mastery arouses a viewer's awe of the world's spine-tingling serendipities, but it is a painting, not the world; it is a painting, not my dream; it is a painting whose rectangular format frames, and so restrains, the world. Just as my exhaustion framed my energy.

I looked down the hallway one day not long after Mom's death, into the bedroom at the gray leather club chair, whose cushiony sturdiness relaxed me even when I gave the chair only a glance. Stability and softness: they rested me at that moment, yet I thought, Who gives a fuck where you put your ass or lean your back?

— Some people might say that because neither Ren nor I have children, I am writing to save our family. They may be correct in a psychoanalytically clichéd way. But their easy surmising is wrong about this action hero and fairy man who has thought deeply about the erotic for decades and for whom the erotic is a lifesaver again and again.

I am writing to eroticize death, to believe or make believe that I am not ruined for joy. I stand in different thresholds from the ones I needed to lean against the summer after Mom died. The erotic is fluid connection, freedom of movement, whether emotional, physical, spiritual, or energetic. Standing in a threshold, one is in transit. You can't stay there forever, or even for very long, though I tried to keep from moving—or rather, my fatigue demanded that I be very still the summer of 2000. My unconscious ruled my fatigue, because my unconscious had embattled itself. The Altdorfer dream may have included a battle, one where action heroes, like Darius and Alexander and their troops, fought for life. People say to the grieving that they must continue after the death of a loved one, carry on by going back to normal. I could not continue my former life, so I was battling to create a new life. Wallace literally goes to battle after Murron's death. That's when his fellow Scotsmen know him to be a warrior, and when we, the viewers, can call him an action hero. In my summer stillness, I named myself an action hero.

Dislocation impelled me to lean in the thresholds of my home, and I didn't feel inviting in that position, not at all like Wallace with the princess. I was not the supremely erotic action hero performing the lean, but rather the hero in a slump. Surely I was in psychic transit, so my erotic energy had not entirely disappeared. Figuratively, to stand in a threshold is to site one's body and self erotically. I was getting ready to move; but I do not remember when I actually moved away from the support provided by any of the thresholds in my house. I remember standing still.

Because of that stillness, I was very aware of passing through the same thresholds the following summer, 2001. I was freshly locating myself, or locating myself anew, if only for instants, like the hummingbird whose beak in nectar locates the bird's entire body.

2 ~

An Aftermath of Animals with Wings

Everyone knew that I loved chocolate. Russell knew it more than anyone else. Most of the years that we lived together, I baked chocolate chip cookies in the evening once a week, and sometimes we ate at least a third of the batter. I often baked chocolate cake for my own birthdays: Devil's Food Cake Cockaigne, on chocolate-smudged page 676 of my Joy of Cooking. I frosted the cake with Chocolate Butter Cream from my New York Times Cook Book. The frosting, mixed in a blender, is mostly butter, egg yolks, and chocolate chips. (I skipped the two tablespoons of rum that the recipe calls for.) I loved to eat the frosting from the blender as I swirled it between the layers of the cake and onto its sides and top. The buttercream felt and tasted the way that I thought fudge should, rich and smooth as it could be, but not too sweet. Cockaigne is a fantasy land of idle and luxurious living, and Chocolate Cake Cockaigne is indeed a fairy cake. "The best chocolate cake we know," declare Joy of Cooking authors Irma S. Rombauer and Marion Rombauer Becker. "Whether made with 2 or 4 oz. chocolate, it's wonderfully light, but rich and moist." Over the years, I cut down on the sugar, but never the full four ounces of baker's chocolate. Since Mom's death I've hardly made the cake at all. Whether it's because I unconsciously associate the cake with my former life, before my parents' deaths and Russell's and my divorce, or because a spa transformed my at-home cooking and eating habits, I'm not sure. In graduate school a girlfriend of mine introduced me to the cake, and she and I baked it together. From then on, I baked it for many people I loved, including my parents; Tom; Peggy, in Tucson, and her daughter Moira; and students who came to my home for a party. Knowing my love for chocolate, students often gave me chocolate bars, which we enjoyed more than occasionally in seminars where either I or a student treated the small group to variety — organic, Belgian, dark, milk, white, sometimes plain, sometimes with hazelnuts or almonds. One male student gave me chocolate lips three inches wide. I've missed baking Chocolate Cake Cockaigne and spreading it with Chocolate Buttercream. I've thought of making the dessert for Pam's birthday.

Stillness is waiting, as I did in the thresholds of my home; and stillness is death, which found my parents; and stillness is a being that is peaceful. Stillness as being is often appropriate and beautiful action, with amazing outcomes; and with outcome after outcome that, like interlacings, appear as patterns rather than as sequences in linear time. The action hero understands and intuits such interlacings. He operates as does the sage commander to whom The Art of War is addressed. Attributed to Sun Tzu, The Art of War is a fourth-century BCE Chinese text that counsels the sage commander to take whole, to achieve victory without battle. O Mel, you helped me to pacify my embattled heart, to call it beloved.

The sage commander stands his ground and also moves beautifully within shih's eddying and flowing unpredictability. Shih is interlacings, patterns of circumstances and influences, and it is dependent on intuitive and strategic arrangements of those patterns. The sage commander is an action hero, but often without the action, because his ultimate aim is to be victorious without killing anyone. O Mom and Dad, your deaths were killing me. In actual warfare, victory without killing may be impossible, but Sun Tzu's philosophy, whose discipline "sage commanders" in all walks of life may practice, directs its audience, who read in the position of the sage commander, to resolve conflict through methods of being rather than doing. Mel, you helped me to quell my uncertainties, my impetus to master the future. I was so full of qualms and questions.

Sometimes we simply are the sage commander, although we may know nothing of Sun Tzu or Chinese philosophy or contemplative practices. We simply know how to be, so our words and actions make a sense that resolves conflict, both within ourselves and within the circumstances that surround, inform, and implicate us. You helped me to be still, so that I knew myself as interlacing, so that I knew from my perineum and the base of my spine up through my heart and chest and into my throat, knew so clearly and completely that my breath and my body's knowledge made me sing without my even thinking of a starting point or note.

In August 2001 Pam and I walked from her house to a nearby occult bookstore one hot and balmy afternoon. At her suggestion, we were looking for

Medicine Cards, which is both a book and a deck. Each card is devoted to a partic-ular animal's healing power within American Indian traditions and features an illustration of the animal in the center of a medicine shield. The book relates the animal's medicine in plain and graceful stories, facts, and observations. Pam's response to what I discerned from her description as the cards' fairy beauty intrigued me, and the hummingbirds that had visited my garden in the morn-ings intrigued me, too, because of their beauty, the regularity of their visits, and the joy that the birds were giving me.

For weeks, my garden's hummingbirds kept calling on the muted red blooms of a yucca that's a few feet away from the living room window. When I looked out the window, or watered or weeded, or stood quietly at the open front door, I saw the hummingbirds between 8:30 and 9:30 in the morning. I mentioned the birds to Pam, and she remembered that an American Indian friend had sent her a postcard wishing her the blessings represented by the hummingbird. "Hummingbird is joy and beauty," she told me, and I was struck by the repeti-tion of those attributes in *Medicine Cards*, because I was experiencing the attri-butes' reality.

Pam and I were each in the market for healing, so we were delighted when we found two sets of *Medicine Cards*, the only ones in the shop.

That night I took out Hummingbird from the deck and placed it in front of me on the pink, flowered Persian rug that filled the oak floor between the foot of my bed and the window that looked out on the back yard garden. Many Persian rugs beautified my parents' 90 Riparian Road home, and the pink one in my bedroom, which enhanced their own bedroom's oak floor and its pal-est cool pink walls, was my favorite of all the rugs at 90 Riparian Road. Sitting with Hummingbird on the gentle background of the pink rug, I read about the animal's powers.

The previous summer at the same time of year, late August, dragonflies appeared in my life. Pam had been visiting me, I was accompanying her to her car, and I spotted a small, metallic bronze dragonfly above some pink cosmos and lavender. The insect amazed me. I'd never seen a golden dragonfly before. Within the week, I noticed a large one, of colors I'm familiar with, lying on the paved walkway about three feet from the entrance to the building that I teach in. I stepped close to the dragonfly, peered at it, amazed again, this time by a dragonfly's size and stillness. At first I assumed it was alive, but I touched it and it didn't move. The stillness of death had found the dragonfly, as it had found my parents.

I wondered how long the dragonfly could have been so near the entrance of a well-trafficked building without anyone crushing it underfoot or picking it up. Part of me wanted to leave the insect where it was, undisturbed. But the part that moved me to action wanted to protect its intact beauty, so I took the dragonfly to my office and set it on my desk. Students and colleagues remarked on its perfection and size, and I enjoyed telling them the story of my finding it, even though I felt a twinge of sadness each time: why had this animal magically offered itself to me? and why was it dead? After a month or so, I brought it home, then eventually laid it in one of the backyard flowerbeds.

Dragonfly's entry into one's life is a reminder that what we believe to be true is often not. We live in a physical reality that is an illusion, but sometimes we let mystic facts, like a mythical dragon, breathe their fiery revelations into us. We surrender to circumstances that shove us beyond our material world, we scoot and glide behind illusion. If Dragonfly has flown into your life, it means that you should pay attention to these facts: the subject is always massively unknown to itself and the world is always massively unknown to the subject. Dragonfly's iridescence, its fairy appearance—shifting, energized—beckons you to break habits, to change.

I sought inspiration from *Medicine Cards*, so I believed that my morning hummingbirds signaled change; and that began my development of a faith that I had not known that I did not have. "Hummer sings a vibration of pure joy," claim Jamie Sams and David Carson, authors of *Medicine Cards*. While illusions died with my parents' deaths, I can't say that pure joy arrived quickly. I lived as though my parents would always take care of me, even when Dad, in physical therapy, could barely walk, even when Mom, whom I visited almost every day in Washoe Village—the residence in Reno where Ren, Russ, and I moved her a couple of months after Dad died—hadn't been able to talk coherently for four years. After they died, I started getting used to taking care of myself differently from how I had in the past.

The hero waited as she healed, sometimes fondling the illusion of joy's arrival. But she knew that the hero creates joy, that the hero *is* joy, and that the hero doesn't wait in a depression for joy to arrive, because maybe it will and maybe it won't.

Hummingbird medicine brings ecstatic joy, makes life worth living by renewing one's ability to experience life's magic. One reason is that, according to Sams and Carson, "Hummingbird conjures love as no other medicine does" and "embraces the highest aesthetics." Hummingbird must have visited Wallace the night his father died. In Wallace's dream that night, maybe Hummingbird brought the message spoken by the boy's father: "Yer heart is free. Have the courage to follow 'er." Hummingbird medicine is fragile, as are love and beauty if unmaintained, and Dragonfly's medicine—that magic is available to us if we're available to it—is delicate too, like the fairy wings with which Hummingbird and Dragonfly have flown for thousands of years.

Mel, my chocolate hummingbird, you flew to my nectar, for I'd been left, alone, awry, and oh so ready to go astray with you. We wandered far from beaten paths, and sometimes we traveled simply hand in hand, wearing nothing but our garnet beads. Mel, you came into my nectar, for my sweetness had not left me. We were each other's honey as you guided me on the pilgrimage from the homeland that was my parents. You were my Huitzilopochtili, also called Hummingbird on the Left, who, in Aztec mythology, guided the Mexicas from Aztlan, their land of origin. He was also a god of war, armed, like you, in readiness for bloodred feats and victories.

We do not commonly consider dragonflies or hummingbirds to be heroic animals. We bestow that characteristic on Jaguar, Eagle, Buffalo, Mountain Lion, Hawk, Black Panther, Wolf, Whale, Elk, and Horse. Our idea of heroism revolves around conventions of speed and power. Wallace rides horses. He doesn't peer at dead dragonflies or admire hummingbirds that hover nearby his material heaviness. Like all of us, Wallace is heavy because he's human, despite his in-the-bodyness. But both his dreams and that of an enemy's in which he appears are prescient, and when he is light of spirit, he is charming, spellbinding, armored in the extraordinary power of fairy beauty. Beauty makes the speediest of entries into soul-and-mind-inseparable-from-body. Beauty is so fast, so accurate, that no one can stop it. Beauty is The Patriot's hero Benjamin Martin killing the British in answer to his prayer, "Oh, Lord, let me be fast and accurate." Beauty is Wallace literally and figuratively at his enemies' throats, like Hummingbird in nectar.

Nectar derives from Greek roots meaning death-overcoming. Together, Dragonfly and Hummingbird, which look like creatures that inhabit fairy tales, shake loose the illusion that nectar belongs only to gods and flowers. Together,

I and my heroes Dragonfly and Hummingbird overcame the bitter ending of my old life.

Near an exceptionally high rainbow, Hummingbird spun around Iris's head, entertaining her with his beauty, as she entertained him with hers. They watched and they waited. In laughing stillness, they watched over me.

One morning I opened the front door and one hummingbird, only three feet from me, didn't fly away.

— A lightning bolt appears on the back of each medicine card. "Hummingbird conjures love as no other medicine does." Great balls of fire! When we pay attention, every detail of life is as cozily, intricately, and clearly yet perplexingly interrelated as in a dream. I've watched people like a hawk. I've scrutinized them like the devil. I've paced myself like a squirrel gathering nuts. I've observed the flirtation between snow and sun. I've witnessed the drama of silvering hair. I've completed tasks in the most human of ways—with a tiny understanding of mortality. Who can bear the limits of all terms? "Hummingbird conjures love as no other medicine does." I began to know that infinity exists within the embrace of love. Being both the massively unknown subject and the conscious intelligence, I began to know that love, which I earlier called the infinite emotion, was assuming new forms in my life. My own shape changed, because I was able to love it more than I had for the past several years—or ever before; and in my new form of soul-and-mind-inseparable-from-body, I attracted the gaze and lust of men so obviously that even I could not ignore or deny their desire.

Denial long had been my means to disable the joy that I could have felt when being desired by men. My lovers, friends, and husbands saw men's desire for me, but I did not. After a cross-country trip with my lover Erik when I was thirty-five, he said out of the blue, "Men just want to fuck you." Erik was twenty-two years old. His assertion thrilled me, yet I disbelieved it. I so wanted to experience and live its truth, but I was neither secure nor self-loving enough to know that Erik told me facts. He was not apprising me of his perceptions or fears or of a sexual fantasy that we share our sex with a male third party. Had a dumb and simple vanity been mine, I probably would have thought—or even said to Erik—"Yeah, and ain't it great?" But I asked him how he knew that they just wanted to fuck me, and he said that he saw it. Their desire was very plain to him. More recently, in my late forties, I was sitting in a bar one night with a writer in her twenties and a scholar who was a little younger than I, both of whom I'd just met at the conference we were all attending. I was eating a burger and enjoying our conversation. The scholar, Carol, and I shared an interest in extremely direct talking about sex, and we became friendly. In an e-mail that I received perhaps as long as a year after the conference, she wrote that every man whom the three of us women had passed as we left the bar looked at me with lust. I trusted Carol's vision and her perception, as I had Erik's, but I did not trust my own glamour. And, as earlier in my life, I literally had not seen the men's response to me.

My blindness to desire was coupled with a blindness to love. Except in select situations, like Russell's and my first time socializing by ourselves, in my favorite Tucson restaurant on a spring night. The conversation twisted and turned, sparked and sizzled — my head swam with the conversation's erotic density. And when my head swims because I'm immersed in conversation, then my heart is intoxicated, too, and when I've been in that condition in the presence of a new man, I've fallen in love. In about an instant.

By the late summer of 2001, when school started, I no longer denied my fairy beauty and its allure. I was not longing consciously for a lover, after my recent divorce, but my massively unknown self was planning intimacies and pleasures for me, the action hero. Like Wallace and Parker, I leaned into love and like The Fool in the tarot deck that sat in a box above my desk, I walked, with a light step, right off a cliff. One of the forms that love the infinite emotion took was a relationship with the fairy lover, a man whose fairy beauty enlarged my own and led me to write a performance piece that I titled The Aesthetics of Orgasm.

How long it takes to trust your heart.

What else can you rely on but love? Death, some say. That declaration generally complies with a morose, world-weary, or jaded posture toward life; a posturing that neutralizes and even negates Hummingbird's power, which is the supreme love-conjuring medicine. I think of Peggy Lee singing, "Is that all there is?" I think, too, of the characters in cowboy movies who say, "It's your funeral," when someone seems determined to commit a stupidity that is easily avoidable. Dad loved westerns. Especially High Noon and Shane, whose heroes, respectively played by Gary Cooper and Alan Ladd, serve Hummingbird because they trust their hearts. Like Mel.

Fairies are not inclined to say, "It's your funeral." They have the sense of humor to parody the Hollywood cowboy, but since they see the fairy in him, they do not want to attack him with irony. Or in any other way. He is a brother, another bearer of the green brooch. For a fairy to say seriously, "It's your funeral," would be to communicate a toxicity. Fairies differently appraise the world-weary.

— Before the fall semester began in late August 2001, I traveled to Canyon Ranch in Tucson, as I did the year before. Earlier in the summer I lost a bit of the weight that I gained while witnessing my parents' sickening and dying. Also, my skin brightened some. Yet I could tell that I kept on mourning, because my body continued to be heavier than my spirit knew itself to be. I hoped that the spa would lighten me, soul-and-mind-inseparable-from-body, indeed, that I would exude light, like Aphrodite, whose radiance beams as brightly as a fairy's daring dazzle.

More than anything else, the spa provided time for me to feel comfortable doing nothing, being still, as it had before. So I observed people and listened to them, in an acute yet tender mode, which is the way that fairies teach themselves to see the spines, the lines, the lungs and tongues of human beings.

In a spa yoga class I observed a woman whose discipline was her cross. Her posture and vocal tone insisted that she knew not only what was right, but also that a right existed in a situation—the class—whose variables gave us practitioners the latitude to succeed no matter what our strength, grace, or flexibility. The teacher was strict, but she was not a martinet. She loved preciseness, and she believed that we could strive for perfection. But the woman whose discipline was her cross had trouble bending—in her spirit. Being too strict creates stricture. Too much rigor becomes rigor mortis of the heart. Too much discipline makes one a disciplinarian, an authoritarian of the soul-and-mind-inseparable-from-body.

An authoritarian cannot love, and neither is she loved. She stems flows of emotion and may believe, in the heaviness of her dark heart, that the body is a machine. So she acts, both deliberately and unconsciously, as if she can fix breakdowns by using the right tools—as if yoga, for instance, is a mechanics shop—and she disowns the body's luxurious sensuality, although she may be unaware of this turn of her being.

There is no mechanics shop for the human being. It is not fixable. We can mend the spirit—repair its exhausted condition; we can improve it. We can heal the spirit—bring it to a wholeness that might have been impossible a year or even a week earlier, a wholeness that had been unforeseeable during that week or year. Wholeness is a kind of stabilization; but the stability does not last, because we cannot fix human being. Its form refuses to be permanent, definite, or certain. Is the chocolate-red iris permanent? Is an orgasm? Beautiful as each one is in its stages of flowering, neither keeps its "proper" form. In order to fix her spirit, someone might try to properly arrange it or to restore it to its proper condition after emotions and events have damaged it. The result soon would be immobility, not stillness. Immobility is a state distant from that of petals—which flex with the breeze and turn the other cheek in a storm—and from that of orgasms, which move at a pace that people in the swelling and subsiding of orgasm cannot predict.

The proper arrangement of the spirit leads to self-chastisement, a fixing as in the statement "I'll fix you." When we try to fix ourselves, we punish ourselves. Pushing for security creates stress, and in our straining, we deform ourselves. The woman whose discipline was her cross, like the person who believes that the body is a machine, fixes herself into false security; both she and the person who believes the body is a machine clench their jaws, tighten their sacrums, squeeze their eyebrows together, stand stiffly rather than with comfortable and composed pride. They are trying to determine their fate, but they succeed in creating a predicament, because they have impaired their ease; and nothing can defend you against the stars. Maybe fate does befall us sometimes, and surely the stars, like fairies, know more than we humans usually do. Yet, we can both follow our fate and bend with it, as heroes do. To bend with fate means to bend its parameters and specificities, because fate is not fixed. Like the body, it is malleable.

If one is open to fate, the way that petals are open to rain, sun, and little animals with wings—in other words, with no agenda—she can learn that wanting to fix things, that being fixed, that finding her daily fix of surety in the cross of discipline—which she pays for in pain, whether or not she recognizes that exacting payment—are all obstacles. Fixing and fixedness hinder change, which, excruciating as it can be to accomplish, loosens intuitions, organs, and joints as well as the digestion of foods, emotions, and ideas. Change accomplished has a greater chance of radically re-forming soul-and-mind-inseparable-from-body than does change undergone and then dismissed. Change accomplished requires consciousness and faith, which are two aspects of the hero's constant self-training in the bending of fate, or the patterns that constitute *shih*. *Mel, even you could not re-form me. I trained myself in malleability.* In that training, I found fat changing to muscle and grief transforming into a sensuous contemplativeness whose openness brought me green brooches and a man who was a fairy lover. *Let me pelt you, Mel, I pelted you with irises and honeysuckles from our garden, I punched you lovingly, the way that men do with one another. My arm, straight as a ruler, was as ready as my fist, the two inner knuckles poised to meet your undressed upper arm.*

Change accomplished is less excruciating than a life of pain — backache; gas that bloats the belly; a scrawny voice, starving because it's given so little breath that it comes mostly from the throat; a continually aching heart that breaks more often than it heals. When we try to defend ourselves against the stars, it is pain that becomes predictable — not security, and certainly not freedom. When we try to defend ourselves against the stars, we literally get bent out of shape, because we cannot force freedom. Freedom comes, or it does not, like people who make love the way that irises gather sun. Aggressive seeking does not bring freedom, which comes from the stillness that lets us fly. Hummingbirds at nectar are still while flying.

Although the disciplinarian may be an assiduous student of spiritual practices that are mind/body training, such as yoga, she may little understand the swooning beauty, one of whose aspects is being in love with life. Being in love with everyday living — the cup of tea or coffee in the morning, alone or shared with the partner with whom we have slept through the night; hand watering the petunias; caressing oils into our skin and then caressing our skin; wishing good morning out loud to the robins and the hummingbirds. The authoritarian does not know how to sing a fairy song, and if she could hear one, it likely would not sink into her; because she believes in obedience, which is belief in the predictable. She may not know that fact about herself.

She may feel that yoga or a Botox treatment or a vegetarian diet makes her free. But nothing can *make* you free, can *make* your freedom — which is freedom of the spirit. Your desire cannot obligate your spirit to be free. Obligation, like stress, deforms and strains human being. Obligation means that orgasm does not happen. *Orgasm* derives from the Greek *orgasmos*, to swell with moisture, swell with lust. When we fuck, our genitals plump, and when we're full of pleasure—from fucking, from enjoying our morning beverage with a loved one, or from watering flowers whose pinks are twinkling in pots on the deck—our spirit is beautifully plump.

Freedom is not planning, not having an agenda. (Of course, who knows what the massively unknown subject has in store for itself? what it has "planned"?) How easy it is to try too hard, like the woman whose discipline was her cross. We make ourselves crazy, trying too hard. We madden ourselves. *Demented* serves as a synonym for crazy. *Demented* originates in Latin, and literally means out of one's mind. We can madden our bodies just as we can madden our minds. A life of backache, heartache, and a voice starved for the air that feeds its plumpness signals the fact that someone has made her body crazy, that she has *decorped* herself—maddened her body by being out of it, perhaps by trying its patience with disciplines that turn into crosses. Trying too hard, we become hard, and our discipline, which is our pleasure, becomes our unpleasure. Our freedom becomes our unfreedom when we push for a security that human beings can never find. Yogi T. K. V. Desikachar implicitly speaks to this problem in response to an interviewer who asks, "Can you say something about the concept of structuring your yoga practice intelligently?" Desikachar responds:

First I must ask: What do you mean by "intelligently"? You are probably familiar with the argument that doing the headstand brings more blood supply to the head. Somebody who has the feeling that the blood supply to the head is not good enough then comes to the conclusion that the headstand is the best asana. But first we should think this through. Do we all suffer from a deficient supply of blood to the head simply because we stand and walk upright? Suppose that someone is haunted by this idea so much that he begins to practice the headstand every day, if possible first thing in the morning, perhaps as the first or only asana. Our experience in working with all kinds of people has taught us that people who do this eventually suffer from enormous problems in the neck, that then result in great tension and stiffness in that area and a decreased supply of blood to the whole musculature of the neck—precisely the opposite of what they hoped they would achieve.

Aggressive action produces incongruity, for we become the opposite of what we wish to be. In stillness, we have a good chance of singing fairy songs.

Mel, you interrupted me with song all times of day. You awakened me with singing any time of night, even if I happened to be sleeping soundly. You taught me fairy songs, which are love songs, which means that they supported freedom and that they lingered in this learner who was listener and singer—and sometimes even muse—like the perfume of a lover's body, permeating every tissue and every organ—every cell—into wide-awakeness. Mel, you did not leave me alone, asleep.

And so you sang to me till I joined in:

O Joanna, my sweet rose
Let me help you rock and doze
O drink me, rose, I heal the sick
Joanna, I have seen you cry
Sweet rose, keep rocking, don't be shy
Sweet rose, keep dozing, don't you cry
Sweet rose I love, you're quite a guy

Mel and I wore pink together. I knew and desired so many pinks, which requited the disquietude of death and divorce. Like the roses, from buds to past full bloom that I floated in a large gray Russel Wright bowl—heavy, low, and elegant—and in a John Baldessari vase incised with the words "Pure Beauty". (She knew how to make things beautiful.) I wanted sheets the color of the nudes in Picasso's *Les Demoiselles d'Avignon* or tinged just like the glossy fabrics worn by aristocrats who converse in Watteau's parks. I wanted Grandma Ida's cosmetics to be my remedies. Ida, my mother's mother. I wanted to apply Gram's pink lipstick, the one that smelled like lily-of-the-valley, and I wanted the pleasingly pink scent of her rose water and glycerin wafting from my medicine cabinet. I wanted the exuberance of M·A·C's Razzpa, the electric pink lipstick that hid out most of the time, unused, on a shelf above the one where my Gram's sweet scent should have been. I wanted to pull out Mom's shocking pink Rodier jacket from my closet, to wear it the first day of class, and on that day I wanted my feet to delight my own and others' eyes because I had glamorized them with my bright pink suede high heels, whose decoration near the toes resembles rosettes. Like a fairy, I wanted to be shimmering and screaming because I was in my pinks.

In the summer of 2001, I *was* pink in my garden. Sweaty wet—from a flush or from the labor of digging, planting, weeding, and pruning. Often I could not distinguish one heat from another, that of a flush from that of working in the garden or the gym. Usually in the garden I grew extremely hot, and I noticed that heat when I was tired and ready to end my gardening for the day. Many times when I was hot and tired and had been working in the front yard, I walked through the side yard to the shed in the back, carrying the last of my tools—already having returned the largest and heaviest ones—and unbuttoning the long-sleeved white shirt that I wore, without anything underneath, for gardening. I loved being nearly naked, then entirely naked above the waist. I loved seeing my very creamy breasts, my happy pink nipples. Sitting on the deck in the back yard, I undressed almost completely before going indoors. I didn't quite scatter or pile my socks, shoes, and jeans before stepping into the living room. I was hot pink with happiness, gay when I noticed the tender white and light-gray haunches of Violet, the neighbor's cat, who spent many hours sitting, hiding, and playing in my yard, dancing through the irises, prancing among them for her pleasure, which became mine as well.

Although lipstick, clothing, and garden pinks brightened me during the years of my parents' demise and Russell's and my separation and divorce, I was a complex of contrasts in brights and darks. My unconscious could not help itself. Mom's and Dad's imminent deaths lured it into creating dark circles under my eyes. Many people think that dark circles under one's eyes are a marker of aging, as if one were growing into a permanent exhaustion. Dark circles are seen as symptoms of ill health apparent on the body and indicative of attacks on one's well-being that the exterior body does not show. Permanent exhaustion and ill-being are not necessary conditions of either aging or maturity. Rather, they signal discontentments and disillusionments; they reveal that a nexus of discontentments and disillusionments has secured a place in soul-and-mind-inseparable-from-body. But that locus of pain can dissolve, like calcium that makes a crunching sound in our knees and which yoga movements can dislodge. Dark circles, like weight gain, dull complexion, and inflexibility, tell someone that she is so wounded that she is becoming disembodied, absent from her feelings. Not totally and not all of them; but sufficiently not-there for herself that numerous sensations and emotions can be articulated only unconsciously, through a corporeal manifestation.

The body acts out—with undereye circles, unwanted weight, and aches attuned to inflexibilities of heart and psyche. Many times I've heard and read that language lies and veils, that sentences, no matter what the syntax, can never tell the truth. I don't say that words, in themselves or just because they're linked together linearly, tell the truth, let alone work miracles of love. Neither do I say that language is always in compliance with superficial reality. Sentences do not fix reality, they open it, so that the almost inexpressible—such as the feelings between me and Russell during our separation—can see the light. Which shines between the lines . . . and between the lines and between the lines, like the shimmering and screaming pink at the heart of fairy songs.

The ultimate disembodiment is death, and we fear that our (perceived) symptoms of aging are slowly, painfully, and unaesthetically depositing us in the grave. How many invisible signs of discontentment and disillusionment had my unconscious given me? What was happening inside my body during the month after month after my mother's death that I received Medicare mail in regard to her? I'd open the envelopes and read, "This is not a bill." Yet each piece of Medicare mail dunned my heart, which was tired of paying an apparent debt to death.

Over the month following Mom's death I reread the condolence cards and e-mails from friends, acquaintances, and students, and they broke my heart again and again, even though they inspired me to the tears that, in expressing the almost inexpressible, were healing my heart as well. Many more students wrote me after Mom's death than after Dad's because she died during the school year and he did not. Only one male student wrote me. He was Norwegian, which struck me. No young American man could find the words, or none had the cultural or familial training to do so. None could be that heroically full of sentiment.

Young men, I am in sympathy with you. Be with me, in feeling, in my pretty dire pathos. Use your ability—unsure, hidden—to enter me . . . through compassion—yours—and through suffering—not only mine, but also your experiential knowledge of that condition which appears to be unavoidable. Use your unsure and hidden gift of affinity. We can vibrate to each other's etiquette of openness, an etiquette that helps human beings guide the dead to a restful place in suffering hearts. In affinity we create a resuscitation, of your heart as well as of mine, which is a revolution, in your heart as well as in mine, because openness lets the spirit move and revolution is letting the spirit move. Little resuscitations and little revolutions happen all the time: they come from and result in deeper, freer breaths, unlabored exertions of our limbs, and prayers that the entire body makes because another's body has vibrated to our own, like voices vibrate when they sing in unison. Such prayers are unconscious, yet they earnestly ask for more of what initially produced them, which is openness. Openness is the source of prayer. Openness, with its resulting resuscitations, revolutions, rejuvenations, and renaissances, is a network of expiation that is also the heart's stronghold. Openness fortifies the hero. It is his brave heart, which tells him when he has wronged himself. Young men, open up, have a heart. Be a hero.

The Norwegian man also brought me Norwegian chocolate later in the semester. He said as he handed me the bar, whose gold wrapping I saved, something about how I had to try the Norwegian variety if, in my life and my writing, I truly cared about quality chocolate.

A card accompanying Peggy's gift of irises, her condolence gift, read, "Dear Joanna, there are no words. Love, Peggy." I understand why people send flowers when a loved one dies. It is not only that flowers are a living beauty. They arrive at your door in the condition that gives you an immediate lift; they are a gift of life. Also, flowers make words unnecessary, or they relieve people of the task of finding the "right" words. Yet, there are no right words with which to console someone whose loved ones have died; as there are never the right words for expressing anything. Sweet words, lovely words, soothing words: give them to me when my heart is growing hard from grief or, rather, is protecting me from grief. Daring and direct words: give them to me anytime you want to tell me truths, and mix them with some lovely, sweet, and soothing words if all of them are what you mean; what you mean from your pure heart, that place and time and space that discontentment, disillusionment, and self-disgust have not plundered; that place from which words that love each other have not been expunged. Words that love each other are the truth. Between the lines and between the lines and between the lines. The linearity of words — from lips, on paper, and in the air — is only form, which can shuffle content this way and that. Peggy's note surprised me, because she and I love words.

Mel, you did not leave me alone, asleep, and you did not leave me without words. Mel, a man. Mel, a man who gave me sympathy, who felt with me and told me that he did. Mel, a hero of my heart because your own heart was full and unafraid.

Santa Crea, our family's housekeeper when Ren and I were children, sent us a condolence card that reads: "A warm and heartfelt message / to comfort you, and say / That sympathetic thoughts / and prayers / Go out to you today." On the front of the card white roses—one budding, one flowering, and one readying to drop its petals—look as though they're floating away from the words "With Sincere Sympathy." Below them, at the card's bottom right, words from John 14:1 convey a wish: "Let not your heart be troubled."

Now and at any time, I would like to be able to satisfy that wish, for it is my own as much as it is John's. Untroubled hearts are not easy to find, and people's bodies constantly betray their troubled hearts. Like the disciplinarian. Like the woman I noticed in a restaurant where I enjoy going to lunch alone, to eat a salad and carrot cake, drink three cups of coffee with half and half, and relax while observing my fellow diners. Some people look just plain mean. That's the way their troubled hearts reveal themselves. One day in the restaurant a woman whom I'd met a number of years previously was standing in line several people in front of me—you order, take a seat, and someone brings your food to you—and then she sat down fairly close to me. She had looked mean in the past and she looked mean to me as I waited for my lunch. I was surprised that she didn't look milder or happier; I was surprised that she hadn't changed. Because she'd had time to change, just as I had, and any time is enough time to change. Being aware of my own change, I was expecting others to be changing too. Russell's mother, Alice, with whom I continued a relationship after her son's and my divorce, told me that I changed after my parents' deaths, that I became "warmer and more human." In stillness after death, whether of people or of relationships, we become more truly human.

I know that change isn't easy and that it can break your heart as it simultaneously mends it. And I know that without changing, which is often a matter of becoming richer and less mean—less petty, less selfish, and less ill-tempered—we lose heart and sicken in spirit, we tempt fate or the angels to fuck with us real bad. I used to tell my best girlfriends that I loved them because they were nasty; so I was implicitly praising their bitchy senses of humor and their highly critical perceptions and assessments. I've changed my mind; or, my heart has changed my mind and my language. What I love is my girlfriends' acute intelligence. Why fix my love for them in my own meanness? In words that described it? If I had become warmer and more human, which means that my heart had become less troubled, then my language needed to change along with my being. When the heart is "fixed," what once worked as words and ways of being becomes an obstacle. In the realm of soul-and-mind-inseparable-from-body, there is no till death do us part. I parted from my unconscious defensive agenda, from assuming the mask of a nasty girl and arming my friends with it as well.

Santa, who was acutely intelligent, though not conventionally educated, wrote her own words inside the card.

3.23.2000
My Dearest,
JoAnn and Renee
I am terrible sorry in 8 mo. to lost both parents to me both are been grand person the sound of the piano always his in my head.
I am glad they last at age over 80 years of life I shall miss them on the next Holiday not to be able to send my greeting.
With lot of love always remember you at young age and always love both of you.

Santa Crea Reilly

As I reread Santa's sympathies two and a half years after Mom died, their healing touch helped me again, even more than it did in spring 2000, and I reminded myself to "Chill out and see what happens," advice given to me by my friend Barry in summer 2002 after I broke my wrist in mid-May, had surgery, and did not yet know what means I wished to use to take care of myself, psychically more than anything else, over the weeks when I could neither type nor drive. "That's my mantra for the summer," I told him as soon as I heard "Chill out and see what happens." The only way to follow that mantra was to drop some of my defenses, to open, like a flower, in unwavering vulnerability. "She's blossomed," goes the cliché about young women. A midlife woman can flower too, with the healing touches that come to her in the posture of "Chill out and see what happens," which is a posture of stillness. The disciplinarian operates counterintuitively, so does not receive many of the healing touches that are abundant in her prosaic activities — her breakfast oatmeal's lightly toasty flavor, the colors that she painted the walls in her house, the oak floor's support as she lies on it, the birdsong in her back yard, the lovely and sometimes amazing things that happen precisely because she did not push for them either to come into existence or to live in the intimate spaces of her home or body.

I was pushing against death, pushing for my mother's life when I gave a noon-time lecture for the Women's Studies Program at my university a few days before she died. I was pushing, because I chose to give a lecture that focused a good deal on what I called "the passionate daughter" and her mother. Characteristically, my presentation was intimately autobiographical as well as scholarly. I was pushing, because I'd called Ren the night before and told her that she should get herself to Reno as soon as possible because Mom was dying. She'd stopped eating, and in the afternoon after the lecture I arranged for hospice care.

I was speaking in my lecture about the difficulty and the necessity of girls' and women's loving their mothers and of the difficulties that impinge on doing so. I wore a white wool pantsuit. The jacket looked like it was made in the 1940s, the decade at whose end my mother gave birth to me. In my lecture I was offering the purity of my love for Mom both to the audience and to her in Washoe Village, five miles from campus. I was performing the innocent absurdity of keeping her alive, through speaking about her and through loving her in public. I told the listeners, very briefly, about the ongoing crisis. I cried a little at least once and fought tears other times. I felt almost like an idiot, but I wanted to display my love — or maybe my dutifulness, as both a daughter and a scholar, fulfilling my personal and professional responsibilities. I cannot say that I was completely pure, and I wanted my audience's healing touches.

Several days after Mom died, I received an e-mail from Joseba, a colleague in my university's Basque Studies program.

Joanna, I hear your mother has died. Accept my sincere condolences.
I attended your extraordinary lecture the other day. I found it very moving and beautiful and compelling.

Joseba Zulaika

I felt exquisitely and extraordinarily real giving my lecture. Sun Tzu advises, "Use the orthodox to engage. / Use the extraordinary to gain victory." Let it roll: I revel in my crimson lipstick; I order two pieces of carrot cake at the restaurant where I often like to eat lunch alone. Let the spirit move: I luxuriate in myself. I hadn't known that my lecture was extraordinary. Although I had heard before that my lectures and performances were moving, beautiful, and compelling, this time, with Joseba's healing touch, I began to know the truth of such responses.

— Part of the Canyon Ranch routine includes meeting with a program coordinator right after a guest has gotten settled in her room. Along with a questionnaire about herself that the guest has mailed in, the meeting determines her course of spa activities and treatments. Because I'd gone through two parents' deaths and a divorce in such rapid succession, my program coordinator suggested that I meet with Sue, the nurse who initiated Canyon Ranch's Healing Touch therapy. Healing Touch was developed by Janet Mentgen, a registered nurse who had been practicing energy-based care in Denver since 1980. In 1990 the American Holistic Nurses' Association sponsored the Healing Touch certificate program; they certified it in 1993. Canyon Ranch's information card about Healing Touch reads: "*Healing Touch* helps your body heal itself through a variety of gentle touch and subtle energy techniques used in hospitals and alternative settings. Performed by a registered nurse, this nurturing approach enhances natural restorative processes by influencing the body's energy field and creates a sense of deep relaxation."

Healing Touch is not massage. The receiver lies on her back and removes only her shoes. The information card suggests that guests consider nine possible benefits from Healing Touch. Five applied to me: "Reduce stress & anxiety," "Create peace of mind & connectedness," "Rejuvenate your spirit," "Restore balance of energy," and "Process grief."

While sitting across from me before the therapy, Sue asked if I adhered to any spiritual practice. I told her that I was spiritually inclined but did not practice any religion and that orthodoxies put me off. What did I believe in? she wanted to know. I replied that I identified with certain goddesses; but that, being a scholar, which trains one to be a skeptic, and being a feminist scholar, which too easily obliges one to question past and present icons of femininity, my identifications often embarrassed me and I frequently felt that they were retrograde. Sue asked which goddesses I identified with, and I answered, "Goddesses of beauty, love, and sexuality, like Aphrodite. Aphrodite in particular. And more than any other. I've dedicated my most recent book to her." This, too, embarrassed me: who did I think I was, anyway?

Suddenly I knew that my most recent grief, over the divorce, manifested desolation over my own beauty, love, and sexuality. They had not disappeared, yet Russell's and my prolonged indecision about ending our marriage had especially assaulted my aphroditean qualities. Sue's questions, presence, and voice, her physical and psychic touch, soothed me, while I sat during the interview and while I was lying down and feeling my body brighten and lighten in some places where her hands and understanding of soul-and-mind-inseparable-from-body released blockages. "All of your chakras are blocked, except for the legs—purpose, moving forward, action, direction," Sue informed me. Out of seven chakras, only Chakra One, which is the lowest, the base—groin, lower extremities, legs—was open.

If I was a fairy, I was as light as Aphrodite. If I was a hero, then every chakra opened. Lightness. Openness. What deep and corny possibilities for myself. I pictured my body radiating light, like Aphrodite's, and all of me opening to the love that some call narcissistic. I saw me standing firmly, barefoot, naked, arms to either side and palms up, like the resurrected Christ in a Renaissance painting. I saw me standing, legs strong, shoulders back, away from my ears, neck and spine long, palms together at my heart in yoga's *anjali* mudra, soul-and-mind-inseparable-from-body integrated in a gesture that embodied the yoga instructor's calm direction, "Lead with the heart." A corny gesture is worth a thousand, and probably a million, words, and corny words point to at least a thousand sincerities of love.

I was holding onto Russell as well holding onto grief, making myself unavailable to other men and to my aphroditean and narcissistic love. "Femininity" and "availability" left Sue's lips several times. My left side, which she called the feminine side, was weak compared with my right side, the masculine side, she said. My right hand was "cool and gripping"; my left hand was "cold" and the arm "limp." Although the naming of a human body's left and right side respectively "feminine" and "masculine" has never sat entirely well with me, I chose to let go of my skepticism. "I want to let go of Russell," I said, weeping, then quickly succeeding in stopping the heaving in my abdomen that would have happened had I not tightened my abdominal muscles and more. Sue also let me know that I was controlling. That was no surprise, but hearing about that trait in the context of my Healing Touch session loosened my attempted grip on life, which I imagine was already looser than it had been in a while because I had chosen, by making the Healing Touch appointment, to relax into ideas and techniques that were unfamiliar to me.

Sue told me, too, that the curve in my lower back was exaggerated and that my front ribs ought to soften into my belly. Her news about my posture, my block-ages, and my withheld femininity did not make me happy, not consciously. The whole "feminine left side" and "masculine right side" designations didn't play well to my feminism. Nonetheless, her news thrilled through me, and I knew, in my chakras, that my removed femininity soon would be moving, within me and outward. "What do you want?" she asked. "I want to attract men. I want to be available." I may have said those sentences more than once, because speaking the words, I heard them intensely. They were my realization of a change in myself. Sue listened tenderly and brought to my attention that I was saying, "I want to attract men," rather than "I attract men," or even more significantly, "I attract men who are . . ." She suggested that I state my wishes beginning with "I attract men who are. . . ." Indeed, she implicitly suggested that I live through faith rather than wants. Without analyzing anything, I knew, in a state of discovery and revelation, that what I wanted need not be phrased indecisively, as a postponement of purpose, action, and direction. To postpone, through the phrasing that disclosed my fear of movement, had been leaving me in a state of desire, and in my books *Erotic Faculties* and *Monster/Beauty: Building the Body of Love*, I've created theories and presented experiences that counter much feminist scholarship in which women have been theorized as not having our own desires, our desires being only the reflection of men's. I concede that desire is a pleasure; but it was neither the one nor the kind for me.

I realized that "I want to attract men," like "I want to stand up straight, graceful and balanced," "I want to be open and light," or "I want to forgive Russell," was static and that wanting can be stated as a process of I am doing or I am being.

I am jumping with joy.

I am coming out of hiding.

I forgive Russell.

My hair is soft and beautiful to the touch. My hair is shiny and sensual as hell.

I am open on my right and left, in my front and back, and in my masculine and feminine.

I am leading with my heart.

I am available.

I am blossoming.

My friend Carolee wished for and prophesied my blossoming in her condolences, dated March 9, 2000:

Joanna,

I'm so sorry your Mom died. Persephone transition from below to above, invisible to visible. Welcome the energy and blessings — she will surround you with her love. . . . as you wander, dig, retreat to shadows and blossom for us . . . for her . . .

My love,
Carolee

The medical intuitive Caroline Myss asserts in her books and lectures that an individual can change in an instant. Change is a matter of choice. It is letting go, like the fairies do, letting go of past wounds, and it is acting purposefully, like heroes, moving clearly, though with no foreknowledge of an outcome, in the murk and chaos that life so often appears to be. Changing in an instant sounds romantic, but it is as practical as can be. For what purpose do wounds serve, asks Myss, except to mire us in the misery of our own (apparent) incompatibility with the circumstances of our lives and, thereby, our (apparent) incompatibility with the cosmos's plot for each of us? A plot isn't necessarily a story worked out in every detail, like a finished novel. A plot is most simply an arrangement — one that can be rearranged. A plot is also a piece of land; it can be a small area of ground specially set aside for sacred or decorative purposes — a cemetery plot, a garden plot, someplace to wander, dig, retreat, and blossom — a place to die and be reborn.

Cemetery derives from the Greek word *koimeterion*, sleeping place. My abundant irises in particular helped put to rest my grief for Mom, and in my entire garden, I bid Dad's restless soul to find repose. Mom, the lover of irises, and Dad, the gardener: maybe they, like Iris herself, come often to my plot, so dense in summertime that a boy of twelve or so, seated beside his father, who slowed the car that he was driving to a standstill in front of my house late in the summer of 2001, exclaimed to me as I took a moment from pulling weeds, "It's like a jungle!"

What a compliment! The plot thickens: my garden grows.

"The plot thickens" was a family catchphrase, spoken in mock seriousness whenever a sudden emotional twist or a newly revealed fact simultaneously complicated and shed light on matters for the characters in a TV show or movie. The plot of my life has thickened since my parents' deaths and Russell's and my divorce, thickened like a chocolate pudding on the stove, like chocolate cake batter in the oven. The plot is rich, delicious, and in the making.

Some of me changed instantly under Sue's deft touch, and some of me changed instantly during the hour with her because I literally changed my mind. The body is itself a kind of plot, it is a ground of being. As such, it can be a cemetery, a graveyard of our unactivated wants, and it can be a garden, a sanctuary from which to act.

Myss neither writes nor speaks about the body as a cemetery or a garden, and neither heroes nor fairies appear in her talks or writings. Yet to me, heroes and fairies are in the making in her sagacity. They wander, dig, and blossom in her counsel to straighten up and fly right.

Summer 2000 was the season of dragonflies, and hummingbirds loved the yuccas in front of my living room window in the mornings of summer 2001. Another animal that flies right on its fairy wings visited me throughout the summer of 2002. Butterflies were just about everywhere I looked or turned. Often they simply caught my attention: several arranging themselves for a few minutes in a backyard apple tree; one flying to be with another in the lilac, whose flowers had faded weeks before; a number of them scattering through the air as I walked out onto the deck. Other times, I needed to pay attention. In my garden, I'd quiet myself, hear the birds before I'd hear the cars on a relatively busy nearby street, see the yellows, blues, and purples, the greens and whites and pinks of blooms and vegetation, and then the butterflies seemed to appear, magically, like white or multihued petals, fluttering and landing, then sometimes settling on a stalk or branch. Butterflies were in my sight line and in my path—to my right and left, in back and in front of me, above me and near my feet—more often than my perception brought them to my awareness. For instance, one evening my friend Ariana and I were walking home, downhill on a trail in Rancho San Rafael, a park in our neighborhood, and her observation caught me off guard: "Butterflies are all around you!"

I learned to pay closer attention to many things, both in myself and outdoors, over summer 2002, when my wrist was healing and I spent many hours at home alone in a stillness that allowed the world to simply move around and with me and allowed me to simply move with the world. In that stillness, which some might call meditation, I began to learn about alignment in a way I hadn't known before. Alignment is continual transformation, such as knowing while in an asana that adjustments, of my breath, my bones and muscles, and my mind and being, are always ongoing.

It is common knowledge that butterflies symbolize transformation. *Medicine Cards* advises:

> To use Butterfly medicine, you must astutely observe your position in the cycle of self-transformation. Like Butterfly, you are always at a certain station in your life activities. You may be at the egg stage, which is the beginning of all things. This is the stage at which an idea is born, but has not yet become a reality. The larva stage is the point at which you decide to create the idea in the physical world. The cocoon stage involves "going within": doing or developing your project, idea, or aspect of personality. The final stage of transformation is the leaving of the chrysalis and birth. This last step involves sharing the colors and joy of your creation with the world.

Medicine Cards also advises its readers to use the courage that Butterfly represents—the courage to change oneself and then to live joyfully in a world that is entirely different from the cocoon and that demands that she use her lovely wings for flying.

I have a hard time separating egg, larva, and cocoon stages. When one is finding alignment, both the massively unknown subject and the occasionally known self are too complex for me to easily single out a predominating stage in my work, my relationships, or my spirit. All of those areas, like all the stages of Butterfly development, impinge on one another.

And in all of those impinging complexities of soul-and-mind-inseparable-from-body, pink became my color of comfort. Sheets as softly pink as the nudes in *Les Demoiselles d'Avignon* appeared in Bed, Bath, and Beyond. I bought them. And I remembered, in June, July, and August of 2002, when my broken bones were knitting and I was mostly by myself, words exclaimed by my fairy lover in lust, appreciation, and respect. He spoke them in the cold of January, and their sweetness penetrated me once more, as acutely as did the songs of birds all summer long that shared my garden with the animal who was the hero whose broken wrist had stilled her. "Your radiance, your joy!" I heard it as lucidly as I heard the birds.

3

Lost Loves of a Little Girl

Chocolate sundaes were my preferred dessert throughout childhood and into my teens, and my father often made his delicious cocoa during the frigid Chicago winters that I loved all through those years of my life. Often after school, during junior high and high school years, my best friend Suze and I walked to Gsell's, the downtown Highland Park drugstore, and picked out chocolate bars, usually Hershey's milk chocolate, alone or with almonds, less frequently Nestle's Crunch. When Mom and I clothing shopped at Marshall Field's, a landmark Chicago department store, the most fun items we selected were chocolate-covered donuts at the store's terrific bakery. Each time, we bought at least half a dozen and ate a lot of them on the spot. I keep Mom's brownie recipe, in her handwriting, on her stationery, smudged with chocolate and simply framed, in my study. She often served that homey dessert with vanilla ice cream and sprinkled it with powdered sugar while it was still in the baking pan. Mom's brownies were cakey rather than chewy. I like them that way still. When I make brownies, hers is the recipe I use. I take it off the wall and lay it on the kitchen counter.

Pleasure is the absence of lack. Self-love is a necessary plenitude. Vigilance in love brings us freedom. Yogis say the self that is not ego is free. That self is the spacious heart, the spacious mind. Freedom, then, consists of being in space — or *being* space — rather than filling a void. When we fill a void, we succumb to everyday life as a withering whirlwind of activity. The smoking, the partying, the eating more than we want or less than we need; the buying yet another dress or DVD; the more than one too many lunch and dinner dates; the watching movie after movie with their massive visual and emotional impact that simultaneously sedates and disturbs us in our massively unknown selves; the searching online for hours for a dream, a date, some data that will never turn up: the urgency and the regret created by the whirlwind intrude into our space. Withered already, we nonetheless try to grow; but we have planted ourselves in the ground of depletion. Our space: it is the simple being and simply being that houses love, as nothing special.

Special is the whammy of romance, how it endears us to it and how we fear its flight, the ways that it creates longing and ultimately nowhere to place our passion, even though romance appears to be the perfect place for that. Romance is a flighty pleasure, but even it, like more permanent pleasures, requires a participant's permeable heart. Love that does not get lost in the whirlwind or in our depleted space requires, like those permanent pleasures of which it is one, the most permeable of hearts. "I don't love you anymore" is an absurd statement. If you've loved somebody, you don't stop; because love doesn't stop. Human beings can block, contain, and restrict love. But we cannot stop it. Love is plentiful. Human beings are stingy with themselves. The stoppage of love is self-deceit and a hardening of the heart. The stoppage of love is a romantic myth that human beings keep believing in order not to feel loss.

If I were a less passionate person now, and had I been a less passionate child than I was, my statements about love and freedom could be the beginning of a homily.

I'm not a preacher. I'm a girl, forever, caring for my psyche as best I can. As a girl, I wooed my soul-and-mind-inseparable-from-body with chocolate, books, and masturbation; I wooed myself away from the psychic grief that families bestow on their children. My parents weren't cruel or punishing, and my sadness and loneliness were little, caused by our interacting sensitivities' misfits and misperceptions — neuroses, one could call them; mine in a developing state and theirs full blown.

Mom's grand piano filled a corner of the living room. Almost every day before dinner, for one or two hours, she sat at the piano, playing like an enraptured angel. I walked by and Mom didn't see me. I became invisible. When she touched the keys, I felt as though I did not exist for her. Her music made me unearthly, like she seemed to me, and only the music existed for her. Maybe a divinity had sent the heat into my mother's fingers. Her music was beautiful enough to melt ice, like fire from an angel's wing. Unable to sleep because the music kept her awake, Ren sometimes lay down under the piano and cried. "I couldn't not listen," she told me recently. "And it was so beautiful." My incorrectly remembered image of Ren under the piano is this: she sat cross-legged, propping her chin up with both hands, as if her head weighed many pounds, elbows jabbing into her thighs, crying as silently as she could.

Like many fathers, Dad often kept his emotional distance. He said, "I love you," but the words embarrassed me, as if, for him, they exceeded father-daughter propriety, or as if an unbearable depth of feeling from which they came, and at which I felt them, would set us both to sobbing. I appreciated his "I love you," and I wanted it more than he gave it, or perhaps with less of the possibly overwhelming emotions that I intuited—misperceived?—might threaten our equilibrium.

My mother's body educated me in femininity, and it took, big-time. Mom's femininity enmeshed her beauty. Her femininity hooked me. All I had to do was to glance at her. Why wouldn't I want the graceful glamour that wove a glowing materiality from her fair skin, black hair, brown eyes, and petite figure? Why wouldn't I want to imitate that glamour? If I could. If I thought I had a chance of coming close to its magic.

Not so easy. Not so fast. Becoming feminine doesn't just happen, as if it were a matter of cause and effect operating only in the unconscious; and as feminists know, femininity is certainly not natural. One takes to it or one doesn't. Mom *trained* Ren and me in femininity, and her body *was* part of the training—her tailored, tasteful clothes, her eloquently and generously ladylike movements, her makeup, minimal though it was: red lipstick, powder, Vaseline emphasizing the shine and streamlined shape of her eyebrows, lashes curled occasionally and mascaraed even less. Her body *was* cause, and my imitation *was* effect. Yet girl children need training if they are to succeed at femininity, because femininity is work. It is a discipline: how and how often do you file your fingernails? What one of many ways do you want your hair cut? Bangs short or to your eyebrows, thick or layered? Hair parted in the middle or on the side? If on the side, then which one? Do you want your hair to convey the image of a butch or vamp, a pixie or pin-up, a girl-next-door? When you imagine yourself in pearls, what outfit suits the strand's length and the beads' size? How quickly or how far can you transport yourself from the animal state of hair and dirt and smell? What is the distance from earth to heaven?

When I was a little girl, I put on Mom's lipstick, her high heels, her jewelry, her mink coat. I see myself alone in the house reproducing her femininity and testing my own and luxuriating in it, even though I don't know when I was by myself in the house at age five or even eight. But the artist needs solitude in which to dream and in which to hone her talents into skills, and I was becoming an artist of femininity. So maybe the rest of my family was outdoors, or reading, or making dinner, and I remember solitude because it was my necessary state of mind. It was the space of my being. I loved wearing Mom's mink coat without any other clothing. I delighted in the touch of silky lining on my skin and the coat's opulent weight on my sturdy body.

One recent afternoon in my Reno home, I heard a tune, suddenly loosened from my throat, my diaphragm, my heart, that made me happy. Maybe I was happy already and that's why the tune sounded itself. I didn't know if I'd ever sung that tune before. It has no lyrics, so my voice moved up and down the notes using only one syllable—da. The tune is classical, and it's buoyantly melodic. I wasn't sure who the composer is, but it's probably Mozart. I knew that I was singing the tune for Mom.

I couldn't assuredly identify the composer because, although I heard an enormous amount of classical music when I was a child, from the sonatas Mom herself practiced to their recorded versions to chamber music and symphonies, my unconscious made a point of not learning who or what I was listening to, neither the composers nor the musicians nor the works. I, as the self that is the essential me but not free of ego, must have made an effort not to learn, because I absorbed the names of authors and visual artists without even trying to. As a girl younger than ten years old, I admired and read the art books in our home library, and images and their creators' names became part of my world, part of the vocabulary of a girl destined to be an intellectual. As soon as I began reading literature, like Little Women, which was my first novel, writers' names lived in me like magic words, like an abracadabra to open my own soul-and-mind-inseparable-from-body. I remembered the names of writers whose essays I read in the Saturday Review, to which my parents subscribed, and I remembered the names of the art, architecture, and music critics who wrote for the Chicago Tribune, the newspaper delivered to our door every morning. A naturally early riser, I was usually the one who brought in the paper, at around 7 A.M., took off any plastic protecting it from rain or snow, and set it on the kitchen table ready for reading.

Sometimes I wonder why my students don't remember the names of the art critics, art historians, theoreticians, and philosophers whose work they read in my classes. Then I realize that those students' brains may be good at keeping other company and that one person's magic is another's boredom.

I called Ren to find out who composed the happy tune. Ren is a musician, like Mom and Dad were. Dad played clarinet and saxophone in the big band era. He loved Bix Beiderbecke's playing and he knew the McPartland brothers. Dad played with local bands in some of the big Chicago ballrooms, and he enjoyed combo work as well. The Lawrence Welk Band and others scouted Dad, but he detested Welk's music and he didn't want to travel. Ren started with clarinet in grade school, fourth or fifth grade, and with saxophone in seventh grade. She learned the classical literature. She taught herself guitar in eighth grade and learned claw-hammer banjo in high school. She played in bands — jazz and rock 'n' roll. When Ren was in her early twenties, Mike Bloomfield, the famous blues guitarist, asked her to join his band on tour. She didn't because of her faith in Sun Chalice, the band she played in. Ren earned a bachelor of music degree at Roosevelt University in Chicago, a school renowned for its music instructors, some of whom played in the internationally esteemed Chicago Symphony Orchestra. One of them was the violist Karl Früh, our uncle. (He kept the Swiss German spelling of Papa Früh's name. Papa Früh was Ren's and my grandfather, the one we never met.) Mike Bloomfield was a cousin whose distance Ren and I have never figured out.

In my preteens I took piano lessons, but not for long; long enough to hear my teacher say that I played "with great feeling," but not long enough to become a serious musician, like the rest of my family. With my unconscious as my guide, I avoided that path. Mom was as acute a critic of Ren's playing as she was of Dad's writing. Many times, they asked for her opinion, but often it felt harsh to them. I avoided the pain of my family's interlacing — no, interlocking — musical charisma and craziness, the misfits and misperceptions of their interacting sensitivities. I holed up in the library, reading, as I heard Ren or Mom practicing their instruments or fighting, terribly, about Ren's playing, about musicianship.

I heard the fights on the many weekend afternoons when I read on the library couch all afternoon. I wanted Dad to stand up for Ren, but I don't remember him doing that. I didn't want him to defend her against Mom, to take a side. I wanted him to assert his elegant rationality, in harmony with his love for them both, in order to establish balance. I believed that he was capable of doing that. I didn't want him to be the "man" in the family, but I was longing for him to practice an admirable patriarchal authority. My father was a gentle man and a gentleman. I wanted our gentle patriarch to claim and stand his ground in the fray of extreme female temperament.

Mom had all the magic of a fairy when she performed, in Highland Park, on Chicago's North Shore, and sometimes in the city itself. I'd love for one of the dresses she wore on such occasions to be hanging in my closet, in between the Betsey Johnson dresses that the professor teaches in when she's feeling brave and wears to art soirées and dinners in Reno, London, and New York. If it were hanging in my closet, I'd wear Mom's dress to the opening receptions of art exhibitions. The length of both the skirt (midcalf) and the sleeves (three-quarter) suit me. (As do the clingy fabrics, low-cut necklines, and sheer fun of Betsey's clothes.) Or do I choose those sleeve and skirt lengths because Mom wore them and her femininity still provokes mine—because her style continues to stimulate my style, and I am still an assimilationist, now fashioning myself after a phantom?

Fairy dress, most likely as much a phantom as my mother in her late forties is to me. Fairy dress with its fitted waist—how I enjoy the slight pressure of a dress or jacket whose waist conforms to mine. Fairy dress with its fullish skirt. Fairy dress whose big, white satin collar, just below Mom's collarbones, adorned the black moiré below. Fairy dress of white and black, flirting dramatically with her red lipstick (only red touched her lips). White, black, and red: fluidity and fit-tedness. That combination of sweetness and severity is just plain smart. Mom sparkled so in her concert costume that I'm seeing a diamond brooch on the phantom's dress. But I think that actually she wore pearls.

I was the singer in our family. I didn't consider myself a musician. I sang folk music and rock 'n' roll. No one else in my immediate or extended family had a voice. By high school, I'd discovered my rich alto. With my three best girl-friends, Suze, Sharon, and Ruby, I formed a folk music group, which became a rock band a couple of years after its inception. I was the lead singer, and when we were juniors or seniors in high school, we cut a record with Mercury, which was a big label headquartered in Chicago. One of our classmates was the son of a Mercury executive, and the boy thought that our girl group was terrific. Someone at Mercury or in one of our girl-group families came up with a name for us — the Sugarhill Four. I disliked it. It sounded too folksy and dumbly cute. I didn't object to *Sugarhill*, because it's girly and sexy: O my sweet mons veneris.

Mercury provided a drummer and both a rhythm and a bass guitarist, and we recorded a single. The A side stunk, though it became successful in Atlanta. It was one of those cute, dorky songs that sometimes became hits in the sixties, like "Yellow Polka Dot Bikini." Young male voices sang the ditty's sexy silliness with a flat prurience. None of Elvis's dark, rending sexuality in "Don't Be Cruel." None of the vivacious passion of the Beatles' "I Wanna Hold Your Hand." Even at a young age, when I tried on my mother's femininity and played with the eros of red lipstick and mink, before I ever heard Elvis or the Beatles or "Yellow Polka Dot Bikini," my sexual tastes did not encompass the bland or the juvenile.

The B side of our Mercury recording should have been the A side. I wrote it, lyrics and melody. "My Lonely Room" was a perfect teenage ballad of misery and romance. No surprise, since I was a depressed teenager, and my empathy with folk ballads like "Silver Dagger" and "Geordie" — which ache with, respectively, hostility and melancholia — created an updated love song. "My lonely room is the place I live / When I have no one who has love to give / To a lonely me . . ." I don't have the record, but I'm sure of those words, the first in the song, and I'm sure of most of them in the last verse. Preceded by a chorus which asserts that the subject will leave her loneliness for a better place, provided by romantic passion with a male, the last verse declares, with perhaps more resoluteness than joy: "Then my lonely room will disappear / And my love and I will soon be near / The birds that sing and the flowers that bloom / The tears will leave my lonely room." I'm glad to say that not once in the song did I rhyme "room" with "doom," and I'm relieved not only that I demonstrated faith, but also that happiness entailed song and flowers, not just a guy. Distinctly flavored by British-invasion groups such as Peter and Gordon and the Beatles, "My Lonely Room" was a ballad to myself, that helped me to secure a bit of space within depression's desolating contraction of being.

I love the line, "The tears will leave my lonely room," partly because it lessens the almost unredeemable corniness of songbirds and blossoms, even for me, who takes pride in her sentimentality, which is a passion, fairy-deep.

The tears will leave me, in a room that's pinkening like cheeks whose color improves with exercise.

I let more breath into my body and strengthened the little pin-up's creative solitude, so that it filled the room and energized it, just like my happy tune brightened all the space inside my house.

When I was a girl, sitting by myself in the deep shade of our Oak Knoll Terrace home's backyard, I found myself staring at the darkly pink bleeding hearts that Dad planted. (We moved from Chicago to 145 Oak Knoll Terrace, in Highand Park, when I was one, and moved to 90 Riparian Road when I was eleven.) He also created a rock garden that I adored. Plenty of pansies, which, these days, I plant in pots. Looking at the pansies from my bedroom window that faces the deck, I breathe more easily than usual. (We are almost always catching and holding our breath, slightly suffocating ourselves.) Young girl, I felt like a funny flower lost among the rocks in the garden's beauty. Funny flower, I tried to hide myself. So I chose the deep shade, among the bleeding hearts, and I grieved in that part of the garden, for some broken or benumbed part of me, and I wanted to pinch the flowers' plumpness, but I let them be. My beloved bleeding heart.

I was still a plant
I was as still as plants seem to be
I saw rain and through the rain as I walked into and out of storms
I was not storming
I was drizzling on myself and I was lily of the valley, drooping in the shady
    necessity of downpours
I was dianthus, named by the Greeks: dios, divine, anthos, flower.
Plants of the pink family belong to the genus Dianthus.
Carnation is a pink that grew in my back yard near two pink flamingos that
    never wintered indoors
The flamingos froze, they saw the rain and through it as they stood in storms.
I was still as lilies of the valley in the garden of my girlfriend Sharon's parents.
Smelling superbly fragrant like the lilies

Asking not even for a nose
I was the carnation budding into a further fragrance
That would have besotted and intoxicated the Greek gods.
Smile-loving and sweet-smelling Aphrodite, spicy pink like carnations, I too
    reeked of clove.
        Flesh-colored, carnal, incarnation: those are the territories from which
            carnation comes
        Hail you
        Hey you
        Hell, you, Aphrodite, are my divine flower

— Sometimes I sing in my performances, popular songs like "True Colors" or "Blue Moon," or more esoteric numbers like Nick Cave's "The Ship Song," or my own lyrics. Recently Peggy surprised me by saying that I sing like Chet Baker, the jazz trumpeter whose voice she loves because he used it, as she says, "purely." When I was in my midtwenties, Everett, my voice teacher, told me I have a "golden" voice. I have not been quick to take compliments, to let them sink into my self in such a way that they open up more space. My slowness did not proceed from modesty, but rather from lack of faith in my ability to follow my talents, gifts, and skills, such as singing or femininity, into their most spacious, golden forms.

Golden was the epithet used more than any other by the Greeks to describe Aphrodite, the most golden girl of ancient Greece. As I feel my goldenness, more and more since my parents' deaths, I'm able to hear and hold, within my golden core, facts about myself that people tell me. I shied from such facts before, deflecting my recognition of them as congruencies with my soul-and-mind-inseparable-from-body, deflecting them as though they were spears rather than being arrows of eros.

Difficult battles, against the decline of my parents and my marriage, instigated self-protection, which led to war weariness. The Old High German werran, to confuse, is the root of warrior. I spent time confusing myself, and fatigue was both the method and the outcome. My goldenness dimmed like a soldier's who has marched too long, bathed too little, seen too many comrades killed, too many entrails of enemies and friends, too many auguries of future failed missions. Soldier derives from the Latin solidus, a gold coin of the late Roman Empire.

My golden Aphrodite, soldier of fortunes determined by longing, less capricious than the Greeks needed you to be, thank you for having resuscitated me.

Ironic, how we cringe from compliments or psychically jump out of their way, as though they will wound us, kill our ability to continue disbelieving and even thwarting our talents and skills, our artistry in having created beautifully some part of ourselves. An erotic arrow melts the heart, melts into the heart. It is our own richness coming back to us and causing our acute understanding of congruency: "You sing like Chet Baker." Thank you, Peggy.

I'm glad that I was able to hear Ren ask me, three days after I broke my wrist, "How does it feel to be a singer and not to practice your singing?" I heard her, a real musician, asserting in that question, "Joanna, you're a singer," and her faith moved me. For decades, she knew that I'm a singer, while I'm beginning to know that. I thought that my singing was too simple, so I didn't take it seriously. Singing simply, Chet Baker is eloquent.

The tune for my mother that I sang at home is eloquent. I felt like I was singing my mother's skin. I wasn't singing to it or for it, though I was celebrating and yearning for it. I was simply singing because I loved her skin, its beauties and its teachings, and I knew that they were not phantoms.

Imitation of her mother's femininity may be a young daughter's submission, the only way to go if you want to survive, in your family, in a gendered world; or imitation may be passion, a leaning toward the adventure of dress-up. Femininity did not make Ren submit to it or love it. She hated it and was happy being a tomboy in jeans and moccasins. She wears jeans and cowboy boots today. She's worn them for the past thirty-five years.

I loved my femininity, but it's a trait from whose intensity in my appearance I sometimes suffered, the way someone can suffer from a dream that can never quite come true. I've been one of those women to whom the armor of femininity gives a sense of power akin to self-protection.

I've worn my leather bustier, skirt, gloves, coat, and jacket as armor. Especially in my bustier I remember the leather corselets that protected Mycenaean warriors. Leather proves that human beings are predators not prey. But the ways that people prey on one another gives them the opportunity, if not the degraded pleasure, of calling one another beast. Here's how I'm a beast: my hairy legs and underarms, my animal desire for certain men. Although these qualities—so unfeminine—have pained me—how ugly I am! (a nagging misperception until my early thirties) how transparently sexual!—they do not designate me vile. I do not prey on my kind, man or woman. My beastliness, when unloved by me, has hurt me far more than it's hurt anyone else.

Who *was* that witch in my recurring childhood dream? She looked like the Wicked Witch of the North in *The Wizard of Oz* movie, and she flew on her broomstick, high, in an almost monochromatically gray sky, and low, in the Oak Knoll Terrace home's back yard. She terrified me. And why as a girl did I dream recurrently of a torture in which Nazis were readying to pull out my toenails? Or maybe they'd done that already. Black and blue, chartreuse, and other colors of bruises pigmented my feet and lower legs, both of which were the dream's visual focus.

I identified with Porter's hammered toes in *Payback*. He was my proof that the soul, always undetermined, rescues itself from agony. When Porter endures the torturers' evil, we could think that he is determined, by which I mean that he has the will not only to survive the horrendous present but to live on in a different present that includes some degree of happiness with Rosie, his girlfriend. Perhaps Porter is determining—precisely calculating—the locations of his fortitude and how to employ them. But the requited soul, which is every soul, has no limits, and its ways and means—its fortitudes—are unpredictable. The requited soul always has the ways and means of breaking free. Many souls suffer what human beings feel to be a holocaust, and surely Porter's hammered toes are a soul-beating that could be called a holocaust, which threatens to burn out the soul. Ever since I can remember, I've told people that I don't need proof that the Holocaust happened, and I don't watch films about it or read about it.

Was I the witch? Was I the Nazi? Why did I think, until several years ago, that I rammed a knitting needle through one of Ren's fingers when we were little? Why did I bear a torturer's burden for over forty years? Was I dreaming my damaged soul? Finding a way to heal it? The dreams did end, long before my "memory" of mutilating my sister did, a memory that itself had been a dream or the keenest fantasy. Dreams and fantasies serve a purpose. The soul finds a way to heal the beast by asking her, through images, to consider or to reconsider a section of her massively unknown self, lit up a little by the dream or fantasy. The beast's self-consideration released her into fairyland bit by bit.

I was a hairy child. Dark hair on my legs, from ankle to thigh, on my forearms, on my cheeks and chin near the jawline, and over my lips embarrassed me.

I bleached the hair above my mouth, and when I was in seventh grade, Mom took me to an electrologist in Chicago to begin ridding me of the other facial hair. I swear that I could have started shaving my legs when I was eight, but in actuality I must have been older. I thank Mom for her attentiveness to her hairy little beast, Joanna, who, in the many novels she read before and into her teens, never encountered a hairy heroine. Unsurprising as this was, considering that my little beastly self was reading mainly nineteenth-century novels, whose heroines did not examine the corporeal particulars of their animality, I still wanted to identify with the heroines' beauty. I wanted to identify with a femininity based in creamy skin that was as hairless as it was acne-free.

As a young adolescent, I looked in the bathroom mirror and it told me that my face was full of pimples. I also considered myself fat and made a point of proving it in the shower. I raised my right leg, turning it so that the inner thigh faced up. I saw a huge expanse of flesh and, slapping it, said under my breath, "Elephant thighs." I look at pictures of myself at age eleven, on a family vacation in Charleston, South Carolina, and my depression is more vitally evident than anything else is. Embedded everywhere from my greasy, sallow skin, whose continual breakouts don't appear in the snapshots, to my feet that look as though they haven't the energy to carry me a couple of yards in order to smell a nearby wisteria, depression fashioned my body from the inside out.

However, in photos from our stay in Stowe, Vermont, when I felt so depressed that I declined to go on an outdoor outing, I looked as glamorous as the Italian movie star that I conjured up, at age eight, in the mind of a male my parents invited to a dinner party. Standing across the table from him, the fairy magic that was my young pink self radiated glamour, as my young pink self continues to do today. In Stowe, I was at my most introverted, and I felt at my most hideous. I remember Mom commenting outside the motel room, as part of her kind affirmation that I wished to be by myself, that I looked like Sophia Loren.

In Stowe, I was around sixteen. In the Tucson pictures of me and Ren on horseback, we were respectively five and six and dressed in jeans, plaid shirts, and cowboy boots. We wore the same clothes in Red Rock, Colorado. In the many snapshots taken in Miami, when Gram and Gramps and Aunt Sylvia (Mom's sister) and Uncle Lawrence (Syl's husband) vacationed with the four of us, I was seven. Ren and I wore identical, happy-colored, horizontally striped bathing suits. In mine, I see the girl belly whose slight roundedness I carried into adulthood. Mom looked like a movie star playing on the beach with Ren and me in Miami.

Our family traveled to every state east of the Mississippi. We drove to most of them. We visited Nassau, which, likely, is where I first took to tropical weather and vegetation, and we vacationed in Toronto, Montreal, Alberta, and British Columbia. In big cities and in resort locations, we stayed at lovely hotels: the Chateau Frontenac in Montreal; Chateau Lake Louise, whose dining room looked out on the gemlike water, a color between emerald and aquamarine; the Warwick, in midtown Manhattan. In New York, Dad threatened to buy a Braque. I wish he had. Being able to see his idol's actual art work every day would have given Dad great pleasure. We toured Civil War sights — Savannah, Appomattox, Harpers Ferry, Gettysburg. We walked the homes and grounds of presidents' residences — Mount Vernon and Monticello — and plantation owners' mansions. Ren and I received more lectures than we could stand from Dad about architecture and American history, and she and I got grumpily bored when he and Mom spent what seemed to us girls like hours in antique stores. Our parents were building their collections of art nouveau glassware and American paperweights. Occasionally they purchased Sandwich glass or lustreware. We sisters went into the shops, took an admiring look around, then headed outside to sit in a New England town square or to wait in the car.

I never felt like just a tourist — a picture here, a picture there to prove that one's physical body had left its dedication to the grueling torpors of work and domestic life. Even when I was bored, depressed, sullen, or restless, I felt that we were traveling heart first. As an adult, only once did I take a camera with me when traveling — my first time to Europe, when I was twenty-one. The camera broke early on. I didn't replace it. I kept a journal, to trace my heart. Experience — I am an actor — rather than memories — I am a blunt and passive instrument — has been this traveler's pleasure: having to use a White Only public restroom in the South, the pine scent at night in Dor County, a leaking roof in a motel dining room during a hurricane in Biloxi and Dad's joking about the storm, the textures and variety of flower petals in Charleston's Magnolia Gardens, the tastes of foods, from Howard Johnson's chocolate malts on the road at lunch to Perdita's shrimp bisque at dinner in Charleston. (Perdita's no longer exists.)

I'm glad that my father knew what he was talking about when he told Ren and me about art and about our country. I'm glad that he had strong, informed opinions about politics and culture. I'm glad that his words are embedded in my heart, as are the color schemes in Braques on display in Upper West Side galleries, the turquoise green of Emerald Lake, the exotic shapes of saguaros, the fairy colors and designs of Tiffany lamps and vases, the humid smells of southern soils, the humidity of the West Indies, the breathing-easy beaches of Martha's Vineyard, and the high waves off the coast of Maine, so much more furious than those along the shore of Lake Michigan, where my parents' ashes found their home.

We heard that a shark had killed a newlywed American man during our stay in the Bahamas, and on a highway in the West an automobile accident stopped traffic, and my parents, like the drivers and adult passengers of other cars, offered assistance. My girl belly tightens when I think of Mom, shocked and horrified at the death of a guest who was staying at our seaside hotel, when I think of Mom or Dad giving a blanket to a critically injured or dying fellow traveler; for we are all fellow travelers in this sensuous, enspirited world. (In director Oliver Stone's *The Doors*, the family Morrison witnesses the aftermath of a highway accident in the American West. In order to assure Jim that everything's okay, his mother speaks softly and assuringly, "It's just a dream, Jimmy. That's all it is. It's just a dream.") How my garden grew as I experienced the unpredictability of the actions and the love of requited souls. Like my father, I'm a dreamer and a gardener, a lover of myself when I'm grimy from the garden that I beautify.

I was always in the girlish and womanly process of beautification—sometimes gripped by it, sometimes coddled—and my success could be contained by misery and chemistry, which worked together in the depressive's soul-and-mind-inseparable-from-body. (Before I consciously beautified myself, Mom took care of the concepts and details of the process.) Mom and Dad told me that they had worried about my appearance during my early adolescence and that they had referred to my limbs as "piano legs." I like my legs better today, in my fifties, than ever before. Spoken or unspoken, the judgments of one's parents can be like a hangover that never ends. Or like a hijacking of our hearts. The unspoken is not unknown. We know what we don't hear, for feelings from our loved ones can't be hidden. "The Shadow knows," Russell and I said jokingly when someone's behavior mystified us. "The Shadow knows" is a famous line from the *Shadow Radio Show*. The shadow that knows is the unconscious, which sucks in the sounds made about oneself but not made necessarily in one's presence.

— My mother thought I was beautiful. My mother thought I was ugly. Other people thought I was beautiful. Other people thought I was ugly. I felt sensual and sexual. I felt repellent.

Mom told me I was beautiful. How was I to believe that when, at age eleven, I was situated by her on the toilet seat in the bathroom that Ren and I shared and made to submit to her attempt to beautify my skin, which had begun to break out? The breakouts continued into my early thirties, though not with the eruptive force or frequency of my teens. Dermatologists and popular knowledge regard facial breakouts as a normal though unfortunate result of adolescents' chaotic hormones. I accept the scientific prosaicness of that explanation. Yet, just as we know what we don't hear, we see what we're not conscious of — my breakouts making visible my inflamed escapes from the conflicts generated by pin-up and animal occupying the same soul-and-mind-inseparable-from-body. As I sat on the toilet seat, Mom tried to extract blackheads. I say "tried" because whatever proof she showed me of her success registered as failure. I looked in the mirror afterward and I didn't look any better after having undergone what became a ritual torture that lasted sometime into my teens. Mom positioned her diamond and platinum wedding ring on my face so that she could see a blackhead between the entwined double bands. Then she pressed and twisted the ring, reporting that a blackhead was being extracted. The procedure hurt a lot, and in my adolescence I was sure that the scars on my face were left by Mom, not by acne. Every time Mom insisted on her "beautification" of me, I protested, but Mom won. I don't remember if I cried, but the extractions did bring tears to my eyes, and I asked Mom to stop, which she never did until she was ready to. Through beautification, I saw myself as hideous.

Yet the fastness of my unconscious protected the best of animal and pin-up. Far more than a remnant of one particular event lived boldly in my being: When I was eight, Mom and Dad gave a dinner party at which the guest of honor was a renowned pianist. I wore a black sweater with thin, multicolored, horizontal stripes. It had a cowl neckline, and I pushed up the long sleeves to my elbows. (I still push up the sleeves of sweaters and T-shirts, or buy ones that have three-quarter-length sleeves. I guess I wear my heart high on my sleeve, on the biceps perhaps.)

I felt sophisticated in my sweater. The guest commented on my beauty as I and my parents sat with him at the table after eating. The adults drank coffee, whose aroma acted on me like an aphrodisiac. I felt as though a perfume imbued with heady florals, found in the tropics, was encircling me and the guest, who was telling Mom and Dad that I resembled a gorgeous Italian movie star. The pianist smiled softly as he and I held each other with our eyes.

I broke the embrace because I wondered why he didn't tell Mom that *she* was beautiful. The pianist's compliment separated me from Mom, and the pain of that separateness brought me close to tears.

I didn't understand why I, the child, the girl, received praise for my appearance. I felt the desire in the pianist's admiration, and I sensed that his desire could enable a power in me. Very likely, I had never felt that particular power over someone before. The power was sexual, and it was large, and I loved it. Just as orgasm enlarges us, so does the desire that puts us on the verge of the verge of orgasm. And there I was, on the brink.

I'm trying to remember if my power over the pianist frightened me. I think I knew, right then at age eight, that I could control people through sex, through sexual beauty. Granted, my later suffering with acne, weight gain, hairiness, and piano legs that created the hideous pubescent and adolescent may have prevented my developing skills of flirtation. I hid the fullness of my sexual beauty for decades. I recognize now that its fairy magic is a welcoming love both to myself and to men and women. Now I let my sexual beauty twist and shout, as the Beatles used to sing. Twist and shout with a man who's ready to do the same. "Twist and Shout": what a joyous song! My mother is dead, so I let go of protecting her from my beauty and sex, of indulging her own insecurities. I give myself to myself, I give my sexual beauty to Joanna the fairy, the hero, the thinker, the chocolate lover, the masturbator, the human being who loves to fuck and loves to read.

The Sturm und Drang of femininity can produce neurosis in girls and women. It doesn't matter if you enjoy feminine drag, like I do, or if it plagues you, as it does Ren. Femininity is a taskmaster, and brilliant women who play the game, willingly or under pressure, may become more or less crazy. (Some feminists would say that no woman brought up in modern Western civilization has been able to choose femininity, because cultural systems force it on females and they themselves enforce it.) Feminine drag is demeanor, from its roots in the massively unknown self to its flowering as dress, from the uninhibited to the subtle ways that our culture structures feminine demeanor into everyday life so that femininity as drag seems to disappear. Aunt Sylvia was a good drag performer, as was Jeanette, who Ren and I called Aunt, but who was actually Mom's and Sylvia's cousin. Like Florence, Sylvia and Jeanette were physically beautiful and they were brilliant artists and intellects. Sylvia was a writer. She wrote I, *Madame Tussaud*, a biography of the waxworks genius, and coauthored numerous travel books with her husband, Lawrence Martin. They lived in New York, above the Hudson River, and I loved visiting them. I think that once I even met their literary agent. Her writing career encouraged me in mine. Jeanette was a harpist. Mom, of course, played a passionate and expert piano, and from Ren's and my childhood into our teens, Mom studied with Rudolf Ganz, a renowned and glamorous figure in Chicago's music world.

"The beautiful Pass sisters," Dad called Syl and Mom. He called them that when they were all in their twenties and he fell in love with Florence. Beautiful women, does our madness differ from that of our sisters less blessed with physical loveliness? The beautiful Pass sister Florence suffered from black and silent depressions in her fifties, when I was a teenager. The beautiful Pass sister Sylvia, with her French bangs and red lipstick, her list of book titles, her travels to Europe and sojourns in Mexico and Sicily, her enthusiasm experiencing the ocelots and the bubbly drinking fountains in Central Park, tried to kill herself. The beautiful Frueh sister Renee played down her physical beauty by not glamorizing it. Who needs the sadness that comes from submission to femininity?

We all know the stereotypical equation of artists with madness. I don't believe it, for the more gentle and sane that I become, the richer and more fluid my writing grows. However, women of my mother's and aunt's generation had neither the cultural nor familial support that I have had, and that lack helped them to fail. Not in skill or artistic ardor, but rather in the confidence to be as masculine as they were feminine. I'm being facetious, for the essence of art lives beyond gender. Yet, to move professionally in a public sphere, assertions of self appear to be necessary, assertions that do not have much to do with being in a pink state of mind and image.

In truth, pink is the heart of favorable outcomes—pink, the color associated with love. Because love is the ground and goal of art and acts that are most favorable to sentient beings.

Many modern women artists failed to move into a public recognition that confirmed those women's brilliance. Honor Moore comes to terms with her grandmother's failure in *The White Blackbird: A Life of the Painter Margarett Sargent by Her Granddaughter*. Because of the Sturm und Drang of femininity in Margarett's life, her inability to negotiate her brilliance and talent in terms of feminine drag, she went crazy. Which devastated Honor. The philosopher Christine Battersby's *Gender and Genius: Towards a Feminist Aesthetics* details, from ancient Rome through the 1980s, why women failed at being artists. As Battersby says, it's great to be like a woman but not a woman. In other words, it's great, and expected, for male artists to display emotion, sensitivity, and exquisite perceptiveness, but when female artists do it, they're just women, crazy women. Thus Margarett, born in 1892, Florence, born in 1912, and their genius-kin Sylvia and Jeanette. Femininity is dangerous to its female performers because it may produce extreme temperament. You cannot do what you want to do, you cannot go where your brilliance is leading you, you are so vigilant in gender that you cannot be vigilant in the (self)-love that brings you freedom.

Syl accused Mom of being crazy or told Ren and me that Mom was crazy. Mom feared that I was going to go crazy after Syl attempted suicide and was in critical care. I would be arrogant to judge her suffering, and yet I sense that a self-attacking rather than a self-loving attitude was one of the bases of Syl's suffering. We mount attacks against ourselves, we're hard on ourselves, when we tighten our hearts into a mad hardness. Mom was so worried that she called my psychoanalyst—I was in my late twenties—and asked him if I was okay. I was depressed from around sixteen into my late twenties. Gram told Ren, me, and Mom how Jeanette, who had visited Gram and Gramps from Toronto, where she lived with her husband, Max, and their children, packed bags of flour in her suitcase. Gram saw them.

I was surprised each time a female student of mine, in her twenties, told me that her mother "used to paint" or "loved to make things with her hands" and stopped doing it. Like Margarett stopped painting. The pain of the daughters' regret sets me mourning for all of us daughters whose mothers failed as artists, failed at that avenue to freedom. Mourning fills me, so I breathe deeply and my tears flow. I keep breathing through the drizzle into downpour, and then, in long aspirations, I give my sisters, who are maybe crazy and maybe not, my love.

Ren's craziness took the form of rebellion against feminine drag. When we were kids, the almighty stiffness of a crinoline aroused my sensitivity to the particular forms and movements of my legs, hips, and buttocks. Ren detested crinolines. Crinoline claustrophobia, crinoline catastrophe. While I always looked the feminine part, I haven't always been able to act it. For decades I didn't consciously use my sexual aura or *sillage* to court men or women or to help them court me. I was a bulldozer with men as well as being hostile toward them, though that latter aggressiveness diminished considerably in my early thirties. The bulldozer now is gone. My psychoanalyst in Chicago, whom I saw three or four times a week from my late twenties till I was thirty-three, and my therapist in Reno, whom I began to see once a week the autumn after Russ moved out of our house, helped me become kind to myself and to others, especially men. (I was angry with men for attracting me and for being attracted to me. More acutely, I was angry for not letting myself twist and shout with them. In the years between talking with Dr. Fajardo and Larry, I saw no other psycho-counselors.)

Now, in my fifties, I'm flirtatious, a quality that I associate, in my maturity, with lightness. These days, my lightness augments my high femininity and vice versa, and even though my femininity caused me suffering, it also saved me from craziness; because femininity is a home for my creative energy. As masculinity now is, too. In my fifties I am deeply confident in the playfulness that is my feminine style, and I enjoy the fact that I display my authority, as an artist, a scholar, and a woman, in the fun of femininity. Now, in my fifties, I am light. Though maybe I was light when I was eight.

I look at photographs of me in that cowl-neck top I wore when the young pianist noticed my feminine beauty, and I look light—sparklingly sexy, luscious—my deep eyes, full lips, gleaming hair, my shining being that created my voluptuousness. Like a lot of little girls, I was diva delicious to myself. However, my power may have frightened me—the force and clarity of my response to the pianist's compliment excites me even today—for what avenues are open to a young girl who wants to explore her sexuality? Sometime before that dinner party Mom educated Ren and me about sex—sex, which fascinated my mind as much as it enveloped my being. And I knew, as a little girl just as I've known throughout my life, the ever-presentness of sex for me, my love for it. Still, I did feel awkward in my own skin and my own eros.

That discomfort surfaced when I'd watch TV, with the family or only with Dad, and a couple would kiss, embrace, or become even more sexually explicit with each other in a weekly drama or a movie. Dad often reacted to such TV scenes and moments as though sentimentality was their primary aura. He said something like "Schmaltzy," or "Get on with it," meaning the narrative or the "real" drama. I wanted to savor the sexuality more than the romance between women and men, and I resisted my feelings, assuming what I thought was a mask of disengagement. Whether or not he verbalized his feelings, I sensed Dad's embarrassment, and it embarrassed *me*. Whereas I sensed "Oh, no, not this again" from him, I wanted more, because the broadcast entertainment wasn't giving me enough.

I've usually wanted more sex and eros. For instance, when I loved the people I slept with; because *enough* is not the measurement of pleasure: abundant satisfaction, which we provided for each other, is that footage, yardage, mileage—space. The TV love scenes gave Dad more than he wanted, a rising within him of emotions to be defended against, which guarded the architecture of sexual standoff that my parents had built between them. Mom asserted to me when I was in my early teens that Dad "was good in bed." I have no idea why she did that; yet a psychic nudge urges me to honesty: I think I drove her to it with my more-sex, more-eros yearnings. They were evident to her from books I was reading. Some I checked out from the Highland Park Public Library, like Grace Metalious's bestseller *Peyton Place*, published in 1956, and other contemporary novels of less notoriety but of similar value to me. Those frankly sexy, not very literary novels nurtured and expanded my imagination as much as did books whose language and thinking intoxicated me with the poetry and mystery of life. I read many nineteenth-century novels from girlhood into college, and I read the Modern Library edition of Freud's works in my early teens. In the 90 Riparian Road house the Freud sat among numerous books—an entire wall of books—in the room that we called the library. The library was one of the four rooms on the fifth and top floor of the strikingly beautiful and modern split-level house that my parents had built in 1959.

Mom knew my sexuality because she saw me masturbating in the bedroom that Ren and I shared in the Oak Knoll Terrace house. I was eight or younger.

My back was toward the door and she opened it during my sexual pleasure. In an orgasm or near it and in my aqua nylon nightgown with its puffed sleeves and scooped neckline, my pleasure, which rendered me delectable to myself, impelled me to continue it. I *sensed* Mom at the room's entrance, because she didn't interrupt me. And she didn't mention the incident later. Neither did I. Today, I thank her for appreciating her daughter's sexuality and the private heaven of such intense pleasure. Today, I thank her too for saying to me, "You're sexy," after seeing the Sugarhill Four on Chicago's PBS station when all of us in the group were sixteen years old. Mom declared my sexiness when other people were around, maybe Suze, Sharon, and Ruby, maybe Dad and Ren. At the moment that Mom gave it, her compliment stunned and befuddled me. Because she knew my deepest being, she saw it manifested in my appearance and in an extremely public manner; she unveiled my love of sex and eros. I was a shy teenager who didn't talk sex with my mother. Hearing a most particular intimate and obvious truth about myself from her, I verbally did not respond, or I stuttered a thank-you. I closed my emotion- and thought-packed self within the erotically charged shell that I delight in revealing and removing in my performances and my writing. While that shell is my fairy femininity, I was a girl who was charged erotically as deeply as I could be.

Watching TV together, Dad and I always seemed to be in our familiar space of almost exceeding father-daughter propriety. By the time I was in my thirties, I made a point of neither breaking my gaze from the TV image nor cajoling my father's discomfort, say, with a laugh. In my thirties! And I never felt entirely at ease in my own sexuality when I was in his presence.

When I was a little girl, I loved sexual pleasure—I always have; but as a little girl my intense sexuality embarrassed me more often than during the TV tensions with Dad. My sexuality encompassed knowledge and clear consciousness of my own fairy opulence and my own sexual pleasure, which I discovered through masturbation quite awhile before the dinner with the pianist.

I explored my genitals, my beautiful dark pinkness, while looking in the big mirror that faced my parents' bed, in that bedroom where I surprised them fucking one time and where I celebrated myself in my mother's clothes and makeup. I looked attentively at my genitals, my fingers slid into my vagina, and they practiced pressures on my clitoris. My hands embraced my labia and mons veneris and lingered over the various and variable intensities of pleasures that were and are my body. I enjoyed myself visually and sensually.

I masturbated in every room in the house. I played with pink and I loved myself. The looking and the masturbation weren't a *trying* to love myself or a *learning* to love myself. I simply loved myself.

I loved the aesthetics of orgasm. Me, a swooning beauty.

I've been told that pink is the color of love and happiness and that if you wear pink, people will be likely to find you appealing and amiable. I love pink. I've loved it since I was a little girl. I don't remember any pink clothes that I wore as a girl, except a tutu for ballet class, but I remember a humiliating grade-school incident whose visual source was the pink knee socks I wore with a dress that showed the whole sock. Vivian, a girl in my class, teased me about them in a very nasty way. The way that people mock fairy men, calling them sissies. Her language attempted to dishearten me—and I mean dishearten like disembowel, to remove my heart. Pink, being one of the primary colors of valentines, is, along with red, associated with the heart. I didn't retort with words, I held back tears, and I've defended pink ever since, by wearing it and by telling people it's my favorite color (which it often has been), a primary color for me.

In junior high, when I was best friends with Suze and Sharon, a girl named Sally, mean like Vivian, tried to break my heart. She said, "Sharon's the pretty one, Suze is the cute one, and you're the ugly one." I believed her and I didn't believe her. How curious that in the year after graduation from high school, an acquaintance from there told me that a friend of hers at college, looking through our high school yearbook, said I was the most beautiful girl in the senior class. As with Sally's statement, I believed the newer one and I didn't believe it. Sally and Vivian hijacked my heart—which they couldn't have done had I not been susceptible, had I not been that sad and sullen, not only funny, rock garden flower.

When your heart has been hijacked, you probably don't look or sound so good. You slump in your chair, stick your neck out when you're walking, arch your spine so that your buttocks punctuate the excessive curve that gives you back pain, raise your shoulders as close to your ears as possible, and stiffen your muscles into an armor that can never adequately protect you. You contract your vagina and anus, you press together your lips, as if to shield some of your orifices from penetration; you internally grip your abdominal organs as if always anticipating a punch. You breathe shallowly, sometimes so lightly that your voice softens to a mumble that quivers slightly or to a feeble wave. Maybe your voice becomes prickly with a passion that drives people away; like the rose, you produce thorns in order to guard your beauty. But unlike the rose, you may never even show the beauty that is yours.

The stolen heart continues to live in its original soul-and-mind-inseparable-from-body. But its space grows cramped and heavy.

You very likely don't know that you're barely breathing, that you're dimming and crushing your goldenness. Defense mechanisms don't announce their targets; and, as I often reminded myself, "the subject is always massively unknown to itself."

When a hard heart exerts its force on a softer one, the latter must pay attention to the source of pain; which is, of course, its own softness. And if the soft heart is wise, it remains in a disarmed condition. But when the soft heart is very young or inexperienced, harshness tempers its tranquility. The tranquil heart is large and light.

Harshness and horror that penetrate us hijack our hearts. Hijack means to steal something in transit by force. In the continual flux that is life on both grand and banal scales, our hearts are always in transit. As a corporeal fact, the heart is stable: it lives in the human chest, and if we're healthy, our hearts beat steadily, whether speeding up with exertions and excitements that can be happy or tragic, or whether slowing down with relaxation and peace. In this stability, the heart takes care of itself. However, as an emotional, spiritual, and psychic reality, the heart is in continual passage from one state of love, understanding, or trauma to another. As we grow up, we develop the ability to care for our own hearts in those passages, which range from the subtle and almost obscure to the blatantly cathartic. When harshness or horror has penetrated us — sexual abuse, spousal abandonment, emotional absence; infidelities of myriad sorts; death, whether expected or not — that harshness and horror have hijacked our hearts. In its passages, individuals and events can steal a person's heart.

We call the resulting condition heartbreak, which may last forever after it has occurred and which may reside in our crumpled posture, our tight mouth, the surly tone of our voice.

Every cell of our bodies grieves under the duress of heartbreak. And festering hearts hurt other hearts. I acted to ensure that heartbreak didn't last forever. Confident in the renewal of my massively unknown self, I noticed a lightness in and around me, an atmosphere or aura that students, colleagues, and friends noticed too. Without self-love, we diminish our proximity to freedom.

I was a fairy.

— Chocolate sundaes are one of the gaudiest yet most beautiful chocolate desserts. I haven't eaten one for years. Of all chocolate treats, cake excites me the most, then truffles. (Hairy little beast who loved her cake remembers Ren watching an episode of *Ben Casey,* a TV show starring a very hairy man playing Dr. Ben Casey, in which a sick boy child had to throw up the chocolate cake he had eaten. Maybe this memory is as true as the knitting needle incident.) Ice cream dishes are low on my list. From childhood through high school, when chocolate sundaes ranked highest of my chocolate pleasures, I also loved chocolate malts. I ordered them on the family road trips and western travels we often took during spring break and during summer vacation. Cheeseburger, fries, and a chocolate malt: that was my lunchtime order. Sometimes I ordered a chocolate sundae or a hot fudge sundae for dessert at dinner after we'd checked into a motel. The contrasting textures, temperatures, and flavors in chocolate sundaes provide erotic spectacle and sensation; and I'm not even including in that the addition of a maraschino cherry, whose flavor always seemed frivolous to me, but whose appearance I enjoyed as part of a sundae's showiness and visual fun. Maraschino cherries are ickily sweet, and unlike every other ingredient in a chocolate sundae, including pecans or walnuts, they lack richness. The most important ingredients in a chocolate sundae are, of course, the vanilla ice cream and the chocolate syrup. Whipped cream — never from a can — provides extra lusciousness, a third kind of melting softness in the mouth, one that is lighter than either ice cream, which is the high note in the concoction, or chocolate, the bass note, which becomes even lower and sexier when the topping is hot fudge. Hot fudge sundaes have a rare lightness, like the rare lover with whose body your own feels fairy light.

As I redecorated the house after Russell and I filed for divorce, I followed the lighter side of my heart, the growing fairy side, which led me to paint most of the rooms a pale yellow green accented by an almost imperceptibly more saturated trim. My bedroom and study became the richest cream that I could find, so they have a peachy cast. Bright yellow green on two walls in the kitchen turned them the color of a thick leaf held up to the sun and penetrated by its brilliance. The warmth of oranges makes me happy: Dreamsicle orange upholstery in a velvety chenille on the 1950s living room sofa; a Fiesta teapot in a shade between salmon and Asian poppy; two of my parents' Gallé vases, whose translucent glass glows from burnt orange to peach where they sit on the living room's front windowsill; a couple of Mom's and Dad's Beidermeir-style dining chairs, whose seats they covered in an orange vinyl the color of the citrus fruit.

The interior had been beautiful before—colors that, in my newer state of mind, seemed brooding—scarlet and a darker red, bluish gray, sage and hunter green; and they changed from room to room. (Did I need those reds? That bloodred beauty?) A gorgeous eggplant called Black Magic once clothed the bright yellow green kitchen walls. The mysterious depth of highly saturated colors moves me. In the Oak Knoll Terrace house I often drank grape juice. I loved the color as much as the taste. I remember walking down the long hallway and accidentally spilling my grape juice on the white walls. What a striking contrast!

Unlike Chicago, Reno is not graced with deep winter. While I love desert sun and dryness, I miss snow angels, sledding, and ice skating. I miss the coziness of indoors when the cold outside turns my cheeks bright pink and a little icy. I miss my father's cocoa, and I miss his Christmas cookies. He and Ren and I baked them together. Dad was the lead chef. We used the Spritz Cookies recipe in Mrs. Simon Kander's *Settlement Cookbook*. I own a copy, given to me by Alice, Russ's Mom. It's the twenty-ninth edition, enlarged and revised, published in 1949. The book looks like the one that my parents owned, and I treasure the cover. The title, in a sturdy typeface, appears in the middle, and tiny female chefs, wearing poofy hats and long skirts and aprons, all peering into their open cookbooks, parade from the lower left up to a big heart at the top center. "The way to a man's heart" runs across the heart. One way to fathers' and daughters' hearts is through their baking together. Baking together feeds their hearts, unites them.

Spritz Cookies are basic and rich, like love.

Gleefully, the three of us squeezed shapes—magical to us—from the cookie press. Hearts, spades, pinwheels, Christmas trees, and camels were my favorites. We decorated them with red and green sprinkles. We added cocoa to some of the dough, and the chocolate camels delighted me with their absurdly naturalistic color. Baking Christmas cookies with Dad and eating the yummy results of our fun released endorphins.

I miss the comforts of my childhood.

I remember the Noguchi coffee table in the Oak Knoll Terrace living room, the table that my parents painted tomato red. At some point after committing what some people would consider that sacrilege against classic design, Mom and Dad regretted it. But their playful boldness in painting that table and their general daring in interior design—high modern with art nouveau, stunningly clean and sensually minimalist—marked my dressing of both myself and my homes. I walked down the hallway clasping the grape juice glass with red fingernails and drinking with red lips—having experimented with Mom's lipstick and the nail polish with which she occasionally colored her short nails. (I, too, keep my nails short, and I haven't polished them in decades.) Grape juice purple with paradise reds—the table, the lipstick, the nail polish: how they color my spacious heart!

I preferred a different kind of uplift during my change from wife to fairy hero. So continuity and a floating quality characterized my fairy oasis. I replaced the drab Formica and tile in the kitchen with bright white, and chose a tile named "bamboo"—a soft but substantial and nuanced green—for the bathroom walls. The bathroom's whitish vinyl flooring vanished, and the new, large black tiles felt deliciously cool and smooth to my bare feet. Black repeated in my study's enameled wood desk and chair, from McCobb's Planar Series; the vinyl of my father's desk chair, designed by the architect and painter Bob Tague, a friend of Dad's; the oblong Eames coffee table in the living room; an American Indian pot that belonged to my parents for decades; the goofy spheres that serve as feet for the soothing gray leather bedroom club chair; the legs of the Herman Miller dresser and nightstand that lived in my parents' bedroom as long as I can remember and now lived in mine; and in much of my clothing, from lingerie to jackets. Fairies often like the sexy elegance of black. It reminds them of the many ways that nighttime is the right time for love.

Although I grew lighter, almost every piece of clothing that I owned armored me, even my bright pink organdy gown with its spaghetti straps and low back that exposed my skin, soft from body creams, and my muscle, strengthened by weight training. A sheer, matching capelet to just below my shoulders, spangled with sequins, completed the look: fairy princess—a fantasy materialized with the help of Betsey Johnson, whose designs appeal to the girl-at-heart. From leather to organdy, my feminine costumes provided pleasure as both strength and gentleness.

When people bother to think seriously about pleasure, they often misunderstand its lightness. Hatha yoga instructors remind their students, "Lead with the heart." In terms of physical alignment, this means open your chest and move your shoulders away from your ears and your shoulder blades down your spine. When the student accomplishes this, her body feels longer and lighter, because she has created more space in it. With practice, that lightness fills the space around and near her, fills more and more space, creates the spaciousness that invites the openness of others.

Spaciousness is a home rather than a destination. Spaciousness is a place that is anywhere at all and no place in particular. The earthworks artist Robert Smithson, quoted from a 1969 interview in Lucy R. Lippard's *Six Years: The Dematerialization of the Art Object from 1966 to 1972*, speaks about his choice of places "where the disintegrating of space and time seems apparent" as "nowhere in particular," in which "the ego vanishes for a while." He called those places "non-sites." Spaciousness is a non-site.

Without opening the chest—leading with the heart—we turn in on ourselves. That lessens, restricts, and even crushes our internal space, and we create our own confinements, our own body as prison, when, in our rounding of our shoulders and sinking of our chests, we weigh ourselves down by unconsciously attempting to protect ourselves. The protective ego hides the self beyond it; while leading with the heart, by opening the heart, reveals the self beyond ego; so that we feel strong through vulnerability, able to take care of ourselves, yet not on-guard as we usually are. The human body as confined space is the void that a person's drive to partying or merciless shopping attempts to fill.

When people bother to think seriously about pleasure, they often confuse it with frivolousness. That is one way to consider pleasure, but it gives pleasure no respect. It makes pleasure into avoidance, amusement, an easy way out of life's ordinariness and pains, and a bad habit. But even the void-filling cosmetics junkie and beer guzzler are not being frivolous in those pursuits. They want; for their own space is an absence. So they force pleasure, because they want the space of the open heart as much as do consciously self-attentive students of yoga. Pleasure is the heart's requisite; it is not a waste of time. Spaciousness is the non-site of unforced pleasure.

Paraphrasing the nineteenth-century writer Novalis, Where are we going? Always home. The self's homecoming in the spaciousness of pleasure is lily-of-the-valley light, which is light as a fairy; and it is light as a fairy princess.

I woke up remembering a dream: BRAVEHEART appeared like the word HOLLYWOOD does in the Hollywood hills. In other words, it was huge. California landmark and a symbol of human beauty and glamour that are larger than life, HOLLYWOOD points to a mythic and iconic scale, a dimension that is larger than Everyman's and Everywoman's supposedly and comparatively paltry existences. HOLLYWOOD: the space of hopes and fantasies. BRAVEHEART, however, designated that Joanna, the Everywoman, was growing a larger—more spacious—heart, in which faith and dreams come true were tempering the weeping daughter and divorcée, dissolving her in healing tears. The heart is an icon—in Catholicism, the sacred heart, and in romance, the Valentine's Day image—and the heart is a myth, for who but saints replenish an apparently heartless world with love?

Braveheart is a dumbfuck movie. "Are you ready for a war?!" Wallace exhorts his followers. Their answering cries rally in jubilation, for war is as romantic as the passion of women and men who couple in the Western world's excruciating loveplay that requires heartbreak. Lovers repeat the tales of Tristan and Iseult, of Romeo and Juliet. Feeling pallid in an apparently heartless world, today's lovers do not actually die because of their romantic passion, as they do in the iconic tales of romance, but mortality enters real life as the very death of romance itself.

The love stories between Tristan and Iseult, between Romeo and Juliet paint romance in a morbidly adventurous palette. Too many reds, not enough pinks. As a girl, my romance with images abetted my adventures in pink. In first grade the brother of a girlfriend introduced me to playing cards adorned with pin-ups. I identified with them, they aroused me sexually. Desiring their desirable bodies, I desired my own body. In my preteens and teens, I masturbated while looking at the nudes in *Playboy*. They looked as soft to me as I felt to myself—all of me that I loved to touch, from cheeks and lips to neck, breasts, shoulders, and arms, to belly, buttocks, cunt, and legs, from my brunette hair to the curves of the bottoms of my feet. Wearing Mom's makeup—and then my own—and her mink coat and high heels, I was my own burlesque star or porn amour, I was the Italian heart- and cock-throb of the young pianist's fantasy.

Several years ago I bought a four-by-five-inch book titled *Early Erotic Photos: 30 Postcards*. The cover nude resembles Courbet's *Woman with a Parrot*, dated 1866. In both, the subject is lying on her back, her hair spread out around her head, on the floor, in an aching opulence that I felt in my own body, that I felt to be my own—when I looked at well-appointed female nudes that increased my appetite for sex, when I was entirely unclothed with a lover and we hadn't yet fucked but were about to. The photo, by Jules Duboscq-Soleil, predates the painting by a decade and a half. My lust and love for myself predated my viewing photographs of erotic female nudes, as any artist's passionate celebration of her own body, or shame about it, predates her painting or photographing the human body. My passionate celebration of my very young body generated my receptiveness to photographs of erotic female nudes and helped me to perceive myself as an erotic female nude.

When I was a little girl, my mother sat on the bathroom stool while I bathed and played with plastic toys. She kindly instructed me to wash between my legs, which I did not take to mean that my genitals were uncommonly dirty or smelly. I might even have heard her words as an invitation to put my fingers into my vagina, which squeezed them, first involuntarily and then with my consciousness of the pleasure produced. By the time I saw a human male's penis—a little boy had asked me, a little girl friend, to his house for lunch, and I stood with him as he peed in the bathroom before we ate—I was lavishly invested in the pleasures and presence of my vagina. His penis attracted me as a curiosity. I had already looked intently at my vulva, made easy by the floor-length mirror in my parents' bedroom, and I kept looking, in various mirrors, as I was growing up. Looking was neither a preoccupation nor an inconvenience. Our culture, which glorifies the phallic while being embarrassed or shocked by even the word *vulva*, leads girls and women to believe that it is difficult, a nuisance, to see their own genitals, that the physical effort—as if one must contort her body—is too much work, as is the use of a mirror. In her *Vagina Monologues*, Eve Ensler recounts an interview with a "high-powered businesswoman" who felt that looking at her vagina took too much time and trouble. Why bother to look? Especially if the ugliness seen by our phallically conditioned culture awaits the effort. Knowing myself from the inside out, I saw and felt the beauty of my pinkness, and I pictured my vagina from the way it felt, unto itself and to my touch, and I pictured the skin outside it as much from my tactile intimacy with it as from reflections.

Four images in Early Erotic Photos especially drew my heart to them. All are dated between 1850 and 1854. The ancestor of one of them is Praxiteles' Aphrodite of Knidos. Russell photographed me as that Aphrodite, standing in a meditative self-consciousness that welcomes the viewer's gaze but does not toy with it. The photo of my nineteenth-century sister is attributed to Bruno Braquehais. The other three photos are attributed to Auguste Belloc, the famous photographer of erotic female nudes who found his subjects in New Orleans bordellos. (Bordello—the romantic name for brothel. Courtesan—the romantic name for prostitute.) One woman reclines and reads a book. (Ah! Reading and masturbating, thinking and fucking.) Another one faces us, propping herself up on a forearm, raising her other arm behind her head so that we can delight in her small breasts and nipples and the curve of her hip, over which a garland of flowers and fruit undulates—just above her pubic hair. The last one looks at her face in a mirror as she leans into a few cushions, creating a nearly Ingres-like contour from her left buttock to her hand. Arms to either side, right hand ever so gently pressed to the mirror, she is about to kiss herself. I thanked her, I thanked Auguste, for an inspiration in positive narcissism, for aiding my ability to feel myself as the loveliest of courtesans.

My romance with images has been an adventure in such inspiration. Earlier than my preteens, I drew an angel. I paid no attention to the reproduction from which I was copying, and I have no idea where my drawing disappeared. In my twenties, studying the art and writing of the Pre-Raphaelite poet and painter Dante Gabriel Rossetti, I saw the angel that I had drawn. It looks like an androgynous child, and it appears in Rossetti's The Girlhood of Mary Virgin, which was the artist's first completed oil painting, dated 1849 and produced when he was twenty. Just as I identified with erotic female nudes, I also identified with Rossetti's fantasy of woman. At age ten or twelve, I probably connected with the angel, whose intense gaze, sensuous lips, and simultaneously earthly and heavenly presence appealed to my soul-and-mind-inseparable-from-body—my similar features and my soulful sexuality. I wrote my dissertation for a Ph.D. in history of culture at the University of Chicago on what I would now call soul-and-mind-inseparable-from-body in Rossetti's visual and literary work, and I titled the dissertation "The Rossetti Woman." That glamorous creature of an artistic vision that fired and founded my own is, like me, forever a child-angel. No wonder I loved Hannah Wilke's self-portrait drawings that feature her as an angel. How daring it is to reveal oneself as an angel — or as an Aphrodite. The year after Mom died, I fantasized Mel's and my initial meeting in front of one of Rossetti's paintings in Tate Britain.

When I was a girl, I myself painted for a few years. I took oil painting lessons with my friend Barbara from an instructor named Jerry Vález in his small corner studio on the immediate outskirts of Highland Park's downtown. That began in around third grade. Many years later I found my canvases of cats with big eyes, ballerinas after Degas, and landscapes after Van Gogh in the large chest that housed old family art works — Dad's and mine — in the 90 Riparian Road basement. During the Oak Knoll Terrace years, Dad was enrolled in night courses taught at Moholy-Nagy's Institute of Design. Moholy was one of the many European modernist masters who emigrated to the United States after World War II. Dad loved Braque, and Dad's oils often elegantly followed Braque's analytic cubist monochrome palette. Dad painted lots of still lifes, and he loved abstract art. His collages, begun many years later — during my college years — and continuing into his old age, were love poems for and about Mom, Ren, and me. The pieces included items primarily from three sources: Mom's and Dad's travels; cultural events, restaurants, and sites in Chicago; and fragments of classical music.

The collage that hangs in my study combines purples, Braque browns and tans, and a lime green ticket that cost ten drachmas and contains text in both Greek and French. "Joanna" appears below a huge "L'ARTE, above which is a "J" that's at once quiet (the font) and vibrant (a very pinkish magenta). Dad is subtle in this collage, as he was in most of them, so they are full of the gentle man and the gentleman, the scholar and the artist who became a businessman, the vice president and then the president of a textile-manufacturing company owned by Gramps. Multireferential words and images interlock with beauty, together demonstrating his simultaneously cool and ardent intellect: reproductions of drawings of the Chicago water tower and of a chateau; the names, from cards or menus, of two restaurants in Tucson and of that city's venerable, casual, and luxurious Arizona Inn; the directions *a piacere* in the bars carefully torn from a sheet of classical music; a newsprint "volatile" on a diagonal beneath the music and almost upside down; torn papers of different colors, sometimes enlivened by Dad's ink markings. His love of Paris, my love of nineteenth-century French literature and art; my living for a while in Tucson and his and Mom's visiting me there; a basis of art in ancient Greece and my captivation by its intoxicating skies — joyously blue — and its very dramatic light, both like Tucson; "a piacere" directing the musician and "volatile" in a diagonal that is nearly upside down; ART over all.

Tell me, Daddy, how well you knew me. Because you did. I loved hearing from you about our love of food and about our midwestern roots. I am so comfortable with the colors that you chose. I loved the ART in you, the ART that you were. "For Joanna" you wrote, and "Frueh '89," when I was forty-one and still could be contrary with you and Mom: volatile. "For Erne," I say. "A piacere": literally, at pleasure, and for the musician, meaning "at liberty." You and me, Erne, at liberty to say, "I love you." For Erne, forever. Did you write in pencil? Hard to believe, but if you wrote in pen, it's faint. Too faint for me; don't disappear.

After William Wallace's father dies and Wallace's uncle acknowledges that the child didn't want that to happen, the uncle adds, "But it did." You died, Daddy, into the sunlight that was holding you as your breath left, and into Lake Michigan, where Iris told me you'd be safe.

Daddy, my soulmate. The word soulmate once came to me in or after a teenage dream: you and I were meeting in Marshall Field's, and I was watching you on the down escalator. Marshall Field's, at State and Wabash, the luxuriously spacious department store famous for Chocolate Frango Mints, candies that melted in one's mouth. Daddy, my soulmate, I have a romance with images because you did.

And how could it surprise me to know — which is to feel in my soul-and-mind-inseparable-from-body — that catching a glimpse of you and Mom making love — an amazing image — most acutely inspired my romance with images?

I was experienced in masturbation by the time that the pianist at my parents' dinner party complimented my beauty. I translate the pain engendered by his compliment as an effect of embarrassment as well as an effect of my separateness from Mom.

I was a hero: to withstand his desire and my embarrassment without crying, to stand in the beauty of my mother's own beauty, to love her beauty as I loved my own, to passionately protect her beauty in my mind and heart. As the hero, I learned to know where I stand and I learned the art of existing on the verge of the verge of orgasm.

Like the sage commander addressed by Sun Tzu, I both stood my ground and moved beautifully within shih's whirlwinds, whirlpools, and fluid unpredictability. I give myself too much credit by calling myself the sage commander, because I wasn't as relaxed as the sage commander is. But children deserve to be named heroes when they stand their ground.

Did my fairy lover love in me whatever the pianist saw? Could it have been the ruthless beauty that little girls have without knowing it? Was it my red Mary Janes? Was it the pagan cry that I released when my lover and I were fucking and I didn't know if I was him or me? Could it have been my unadulterated enthusiasm — for chocolate, sex, and learning? "You're so sexy," my lover told me, many times. Could it have been that I am sexy like little girls who stand their ground and catch, then hold, the gaze of lucky men? Men who cannot control the look that's meant to lure a girl into a tighter nexus of desire?

We girls are innocent, yet we've got a lot of wit, like Isabetta, the subject of a 1936 painting by Alice Neel. Isabetta, a naked beauty with big dark hair and wide-open eyes, plants her oversized feet on a striped rug, holds her arms akimbo, and just plain looks at us. No shame or embarrassment, no taunting sexuality. "Here I am," says her body, with an emphasis on *here*.

I've always liked early morning and the beginning of the day. "Here I am" with particular clarity at that time. I liked getting out of bed between 6:00 and 6:30, reading the paper before anyway else in the Riparian Road house, liked walking Duke, our neurotic Shetland sheepdog when we lived on Oak Knoll Terrace, liked morning drinks and breakfast foods, the quiet and the good cheer of a new day. Russell was not a naturally early riser. I got out of bed before he did, made coffee, and woke him to its aroma. When we first lived together, in Tucson, I brought him coffee in bed. After our divorce I drank green tea, usually the kind called "gunpowder." I drank a pot of it, sometimes two pots, while I looked at the hummingbirds outside the front window; or enjoyed the winter sun from the chair, in my living room, that Dad used to read in; or listened to Morning Edition on NPR; or wrote at my computer.

On weekends, Dad made breakfast. Saturdays it was often oatmeal. Dad's oatmeal was special. He made it with milk, whole milk, no water, and we complemented its creaminess in a couple of ways. Dad liked to add cheddar cheese to his cereal, and he regularly asked us if we wanted any. The cheddar's sharpness tasted great with the oatmeal, and its melting sensuousness impressed me.

But I usually opted for butter and sugar, as did Ren and Mom. At Oak Knoll Terrace, Dad made waffles and we covered them with jam. But waffles didn't become a staple, because the batter usually stuck to the waffle iron and none of us cared enough about waffles to insist that the chef become more skilled at making them or that Mom and Dad buy a new waffle iron. Sundays Dad made French toast or, more frequently, scrambled eggs, bacon or sausage, and toast. Actually, Dad fried the bread, and we called it "mishi." He pressed the mouth of a glass into bread and fried the circles. Ren and I loved that buttery treat.

Meals could be substantially "Here I am" or means of escape. "Here I am" included delicious tastes and textures and conversations where I learned the erotic art of conversation through both observing and participating. Almost every weekend, we spent most of a Saturday or Sunday at Gram and Gramps's apart-ment (eventually condo) on Chicago's North Side, overlooking Lake Michigan. Although the TV might be on, the family talked. Sunday brunch and *Meet the Press* stick in my mind, along with games played by Chicago teams, the Bears, the White Sox, and the Cubs. (Wrigley Field, the Cubs' home park, wasn't far from my grandparents' home.) The politicians and diplomats on *Meet the Press* pro-voked political conversation among my family, and Dad and Gramps especially loved such conversation, just about anytime. Ren and I took after them. She also loved talking baseball and football. Dad played baseball with Ren and me when we were kids, in the Oak Knoll Terrace back yard. We played croquet there, too, and everyone joined in—Mom, of course, and Gram, Gramps, and whatever family or friends were visiting. Dad enjoyed playing baseball with his girls as immensely as he enjoyed ice-skating with us, even on the coldest winter days. One supremely frigid afternoon, warmed by his thermos of cocoa, we three were the only skaters.

Dad played football in high school, won skating races too, and Mom said that if he had played golf more often, he would have been spectacularly good at it. Mom loved to swim and told Ren and me about her and Syl swimming strongly in Lake Michigan when they were girls. The image buoyed me: Flo and Syl exercising their muscle and their grace in the waves. During the years that I knew her, Mom swam little. In her fifties or sixties, she used her membership at a YWCA to swim. Throughout midlife and into old age, Mom walked regularly on long routes through Highland Park, within several blocks of the lake. When I accompanied her, we talked a lot. Sometimes she performed a routine of yoga-like postures in the master bedroom. She never lost her graceful movements, although they became more and more restricted after the series of strokes that ultimately caused her demise.

Unlike Ren, I didn't follow my familial male models in loving to watch baseball and football and to talk about them. Rather, I loved sitting downstairs in the 90 Riparian Road family room with Dad—the air conditioning made the family room especially cool—when we watched the Cubs or the Sox and ate our lunch: ham sandwiches on rye with mustard, gherkins on the side. Dad also had a beer, sometimes two. Russ and I called that combination of sandwich, pickles, and beer the Erne Special, and we liked to celebrate Dad by making ourselves Erne Specials on hot summer days in Reno.

Summer lunches were the only time that Dad had a beer, a habit that touched me. Hamm's beer sponsored the baseball games, and the commercials, all in animation, touched me, too, resonating still with Dad's beers, the cool family room, and vacations in western Canada, New England, and Dor County. The commercials featured a friendly, anthropomorphic cartoon bear that the ballgame announcers called "the Hamm's Bear," north country lakes and forest, and a Hamm's beer can on which the sweaty condensation connoted erotic pastimes. The Hamm's beer jingle, an ersatz Indian song with tom-toms—a song that could never exist without irony or offense in today's political and cultural climate—featured the lyrics, "From the land of sky blue waters." On those summer afternoons, I shared that land with my father, and always, the land of sky blue waters enlivens my soul-and-mind-inseparable-from-body.

Gram made Thanksgiving dinners. All of us helped with cooking, setting the table, and cleaning up, except Gramps. Along with turkey and bread stuffing, mashed potatoes, and pumpkin pie, Gram served matzo ball soup, chopped herring, gefilte fish, and Sunshine Cake, a sponge cake. Gefilte fish disgusted me. Dad loved it. We celebrated Christmas at our house, with Gram and Gramps and with Syl and Lawrence if they were in town. Aunt Dorothy and Uncle Al, Gram's brother, celebrated with us at Oak Knoll Terrace. Rings for Ren and me were their gift one year. We received the same ring—gold in the shape of a serpent. Its eyes were our birth gems, and it held the same gem in its mouth: amethyst for Ren, garnet for me. The rings' glamour and sophistication had me emotionally wide-eyed. Ren exchanged her ring, and I kept mine.

A typical Christmas menu included: an appetizer of caviar that Mom spooned onto a brick of cream cheese—this was served with sherry in the family room, where Dad, Ren, and Gramps watched the football game on TV; a shrimp cocktail whose sauce was a curried whipped cream—this was served at the beginning of the meal, in the dining room with its large, round, early twentieth-century walnut table covered in a holly-patterned cloth and set with utterly simple white porcelain plates and, for my parents, ornate silver; a green salad; turkey stuffed with bread, celery, and onions and spiced with marjoram and thyme; gravy; buttery mashed potatoes; creamed spinach; a Jell-O salad made in layers of red strawberry, green lime, and plain gelatin enriched with cream cheese; a wine that was never anything special; water in very large, aqua-colored crystal goblets—which I filled from a modern pitcher after Ren or I placed them on the table; pumpkin pie, for which I whipped the cream, and cherry pie; and coffee, into which I freely poured whole milk and sugar. Everything always tasted good.

It was taste upon taste, both the food and the table setting. Mom knew how to make things beautiful.

I learned the enjoyment of laughing and talking with people at holiday dinners and at family meals. Current politics and culture provided frequent and sundry topics, and my family usually spoke about them from passionate and informed positions. No one tried to ram a position down our throats or convert us to a position with which we disagreed. So my own throat learned to open in the erotic art of expressing oneself. The adults accepted my ideas and opinions and welcomed my intelligence.

However, 90 Riparian Road dinners with my nuclear family could be horrendous. "Emotional tension" is a mild way of putting the silences and the shouting that voiced not really the emotional tensions of the day, but rather the emotional tensions of the years that arose during the day and that we blocked or expressed that evening. Keeping quiet was my modus operandi at those excruciating occasions, from which I left as soon as family etiquette allowed. At the kitchen table, where we ate our family meals, the pain of the people I most loved, including my own pain, closed my throat. Yet it threw me into the internal eros that explored emotions and psychic complexity. Family etiquette required that the dishes be washed before anyone headed out of the kitchen. To leave before the table dishes and utensils were in the dishwasher, before any large-sized or delicate utensils, cookware, or dishes were washed and dried, before the sink was cleaned with kitchen cleanser, and before the counters were wiped clean was extreme behavior, or more accurately, a sign of extreme distress. I fled to my room from the agonizing distances created by dinners' emotional tension. There, in my bedroom, I succored myself several ways. I played rock 'n' roll records — loud — or wrote (nothing that teachers assigned) or ate a lot of Oreos. Sometimes I used more than one means of relief at a time.

Despite the distances between me and my parents, they created emotional moments of everlasting loving brilliance. Dad made hot cocoa to celebrate my first period. The proportions of ingredients he used — cocoa, whole milk, sugar, and salt — always blended into luscious darkness, never too sweet. Sometimes we drank Dad's hot cocoa from a thermos when he and Ren and I went ice-skating together in her and my childhood. Mom decked me in menstrual gear — a sanitary belt and pad — in her and Dad's bathroom. I most remember my nakedness from waist to feet and her delicate, attentive touch, intimate as it was, easing my mild embarrassment. On that early evening in winter, I was just about to turn eleven. As I put on flannel pajamas, Mom told me that Dad was washing my bloodstained underpants. He was washing them by hand. His hands and hers embraced my soul-and-mind-inseparable-from-body while hot cocoa invigorated and soothed us all. That I felt loved as a daughter and learner whose vagina and what it exuded were recognized and celebrated — with chocolate — profoundly formed my sense of vaginal and general well-being, which were corollaries of a vaginal consciousness that was simultaneously aesthetic and erotic, a consciousness that knew the generosity of swooning beauty. My family fostered my ability to sheathe myself in chocolate.

So chocolate was my aura, my radiance, not only enclosing and protecting me, but also generating my embrace — of Ren and Russell, of eros, a dead aunt, and my students, of deceased grandparents and parents, of my girlfriends, of any fairy lover, of myself. Open-minded, open-hearted, open-mouthed for chocolate, we learn to embrace ourselves and others.

One of the most influentially pleasurable ingestions of chocolate occurred during ladies lunches. Throughout my childhood, some combination of Mom, Ren, Gram, Syl, and I gathered at Marshall Field's Walnut Room, the most formal and the fanciest of the department store's several restaurants. Mostly women dined there, with their girlfriends or with their children. I remember calm and spaciousness, dark woods, hunter greens, tablecloths and ample napkins of white linen. Surely flowers brightened the tables, and I'd like to think that they were real, not cloth, and surely, too, the gentle friendliness of water singing to itself from a fountain in the center of the restaurant also brightened the atmosphere. Always eager for the presentation of the pastry tray, I relished listening to the waitress's description of its delights, and I chose something chocolate. Most likely, my chocolate choice was mousse or an éclair or a napoleon or cake. We all dressed up for ladies' lunch, which meant, before my teens, a nice dress and shoes, a hat for the adults, and white gloves for all of us. Conversation was erotically light, though I don't recall any of its subjects. Ladies' lunch satisfied my soul-and-mind-inseparable-from-body, as it has throughout my life. And I especially like to frequent a place, as our family did the Walnut Room.

Here in Reno, it's the Cheese Board and Wine Seller. Students with whom I'm friends or with whom I'm friendly beyond classroom kindness and enthusiasm know that's where I like to meet for lunch, and some of them even tease me about it. Professional people of both sexes make up a large part of the clientele, and women and men by themselves appear to be comfortable there. My friend Rob and I have met there many times, as have Pam and I. My student Pete and I talked intensely about gender and about war at one of the Cheese Board's tall window tables for two. I cried with happiness about my fairy lover over lunch with Ariana. The Cheese Board infrequently offers chocolate cake, but I'm wild about their carrot cake with cream cheese frosting, which I eat with a couple of cups of coffee and plenty of half and half.

The Cheese Board and Wine Seller is not a romantic name. More precisely, while I have a romance with the restaurant, that does not extend to its name. Thinking about the magic of restaurants and their names initiates my deep breathing, frees the girl belly by knowing it from before its tightenings. In my girlhood and preteens, the four of us, often with Gram and Gramps, frequented the Chicago restaurants Don the Beachcomber and Shangri-la, both of which featured Asian cuisine. Without Gram and Gramps, we often dined at Café de Paris, whose bistro elegance could relax family tensions. Dinners out, especially at French restaurants, called for dressing up. Their gracious atmospheres provided sacred space, one of my favorite training grounds for femininity and for the erotic art of conversation. With its cushiony red booths, bright white linens, silverware whose weight balanced beautifully in my hands, waiters whose knowledge and attentiveness fashioned the calm and sophisticated environment as much as did the décor, Café de Paris consecrated the Fruehs. Soul-and-mind-inseparable-from-body, I became richer at those dinners. And I regularly chose a rich entrée. Chicken Kiev arrived like a gift or a surprise before me. Because butter has been rolled into the center of skinned and pounded chicken breasts, which the chef dusts with flour, brushes with beaten egg, rolls in dry bread crumbs, and deep fries till golden brown, a diner's first slicing into the meat produces a gentle flow of butter. Sensual to the nth degree, like sexual fluids. Seasoned with tarragon and parsley, chives and perhaps garlic, as well as salt and pepper, the butter tastes as exceptionally divine as it feels on its receiver's tongue and in her mouth, and the butter's texture also divinely complements that of the delicately crunchy crust and the extremely tender meat. Our family also frequented La Patisserie, often with Gram and Gramps, and L'Escargot, both located, when they opened, in parts of the city that were barely becoming gentrified.

In the northern suburbs of Chicago, San Pedro's appealed most to me. The architecture and furnishings were hacienda and Spanish mission, and I almost always ordered mushroom soup and Shrimp de Jonghe. I still compare any mushroom soup with San Pedro's, and none has measured up. Usually the seafood and the garlic flavors in the Shrimp de Jonghe beautifully balanced each other, although the garlic was occasionally a little sharp. The Deerpath Inn and Indian Trail: their combination of service, food, and décor—their atmosphere—didn't create as erotic an atmosphere as did San Pedro's, but their names recalled a history of Chicago's northern suburbs and displayed nostalgia for it.

I've been as nostalgic as I could be for Perdita's in Charleston, South Carolina, and for Ballato's, on Houston Street in New York. I may have been eleven when we first ate there, with Stamos, the painter, who was a Ballato's regular. The owner knew him and treated him, and therefore the Fruehs, with a humor and politeness that were both charming and raucous. Dad and Stamos became friends during Dad's business trips to New York. Lillian Nassau, who owned the Tiffany and art nouveau glass shop in New York, had introduced them. Stamos is pictured in the famous *Life* photo of 1951, the Nina Leen shot captioned "Irascible Group of Advanced Artists." The Irascibles included the fifteen self-determined foundational abstract expressionist painters. Stamos sits in the front row, across from Mark Rothko. Stamos was the only gay Irascible, and Hedda Sterne, standing, on a chair or stool, in the back row, was the only woman. Theodoros Stamos, known professionally and to his friends as Stamos: the first fairy man I knew. And in Ballato's, which was an intimate and casual Italian restaurant, the owner looked at me in a similar way to the pianist at the dinner party and called me "beautiful princess." "Beautiful," says Wallace to Murron during their first intimate time together by themselves. "Beautiful princess": those words and whatever was behind them, beneath them, whatever was hanging and hoarded between them, woke me up, as did the pianist's words.

Wake up, little fairy. Set yourself free. Liberate the fairy princess.

Most likely I ate chocolate desserts at Café de Paris, La Patisserie, L'Escargot, San Pedro's, and Ballato's, and I also ate crème caramel and desserts that my father chose, such as fruit tarts. Imitating Dad with our soul food for us soulmates.

Dessert: it spirited me to peaceful places. Even when I used it for security in times of escape. Like the Oreos. During major times of crisis, I kept packages of them in my bedroom. The large size. And I ate half of them at a sitting. Sometimes I devoured an Oreo variation, chocolate cream sandwiched between chocolate cookies. I think that the brand was Sunshine Hydrox.

Like the many hues of pink, the many flavors of chocolate, but milk chocolate more than any other, brought me peace.

Peace does not mean complacency. Peace is silence if you want it; AC/DC for fifteen minutes, until their relentlessly adolescent lyrics bore you; Bach's *Sleepers, Wake, A Voice Is Calling*, loud as you can bear it; making love with a smart and beautiful young man and fucking the shit out of each other; screening phone calls if you feel like it, while listening to your friends' or family's badgering from afar, "I know you're there"; dancing around your house like a dervish; raking leaves; drinking till you vomit; hiking around half of a mountain lake; baking oatmeal chocolate chip cookies for people you love; sleeping well for nights on end; talking with your parents, if they're still alive. Peace is the most everyday of pleasures, untrammeled by conditions that impel the psyche into alert; and out of the pink.

Baking chocolate cakes brought me into the pink. Like all the cakes I ever baked, the first ones, from the Oak Knoll Terrace kitchen, I made from scratch. I used a Betty Crocker cookbook for children, and I should ask Ren, but I think that the cakes tasted good. Though sometimes they looked pretty unappetizing — once I tinted the white buttercream frosting green. My family made some jokes about my color choice during the initial viewing or eating of that cake, but not till years later did anyone tell me how truly unappealing they found green frosting to be. The Betty Crocker children's cookbook included photos of heart- and crown-shaped cakes and instructions for creating them. I made heart cakes frosted pink, and I took the cookbook's suggestion to make the crown for Father's Day. I had my baking failures, which included cakes whose texture made them crumble. But my successes outnumbered failures; or my mother's positive responses to both the process and creations of my baking encouraged me to bake more, to enjoy it completely, and to feel, now, that my Oak Knoll Terrace cakes were treasurable.

My love of sexual pleasure, reading, and desserts didn't altogether save me from Mom the angelically hypnotized pianist or Dad the typically distant father or from their fights, whose sounds but not words I heard. Maybe I've just forgotten, or repressed, the words. Maybe the words specified parental emotions that caused me such pain that my defense mechanisms have forever barricaded the words from my conscious mind. Or maybe my unconscious softened the words a bit, or a lot, by constructing the primal scene—when I surprised my parents fucking in their bedroom—as pleasure.

One winter night when I had the flu and was so sick that the brightly colored hooked rug in Ren's and my bedroom spun when I got up from my bed to pee or throw up, I heard my parents' raised voices spewing unkindnesses to each other. We were living on Oak Knoll Terrace, and their voices carried from the front door or living room and dining room area—no walls separated the spaces—down the long hallway and into our bedroom at the other end of the house. Was she accusing him of spending too much time in New York? He traveled there every other week or so on business, and she got sick of all his trips, his time away. Was she telling him to pack a suitcase and get out? I think that happened once or twice during my childhood. If I hadn't been so sick, so floaty and dizzy, maybe I'd remember more now. Maybe I just can't bear to. The front door slammed, and I knew that Dad had left. I was scared that he wouldn't be coming back. Minutes or hours later, I have no idea which, he came into the bedroom, fedora in his hand, overcoat still speckled with snowflakes. I felt the cold of the outdoors as he sat beside me, and the wetness of melted snow, and he must have touched me or spoken. Whatever he did, his presence comforted me, although when he left the room my fear rose again. I wonder if I would have been as afraid as I was if I hadn't been ill. I worried that night that he and Mom would get a divorce, a concern that provided an undercurrent of anxiety throughout my childhood. I wonder how soon Dad made me a chocolate sundae after I recovered from the flu and the normal level of household discomforts pervaded the elegantly clean design of our house.

My father was usually not light in physical or mental tone. Yet he was very light with his young daughters, before our preteens. Mom asserted all too often for my taste, "Erne, you have no sense of humor." For years, I felt that her criticisms of Dad were excruciatingly hostile, and I cringed emotionally when she flung them at him. "Ask your father," she said frequently and disdainfully when I wanted money for buying a special piece of clothing. I silently sided with him. Her hostilities ensured my own similar inflictions on the men in my life when I was in my twenties.

Even earlier, my conflicts about males, my hostilities, surfaced in crude, clear emotions. In junior high school I was eating lunch at Suze's, in the conservatory of her family's large house, when her older brother and his friend posed—macho adolescent—in the doorway. Suze asked her brother something like, "What are you looking for?" and he said, "We want to see Cleo. Cleopatra." The boys chuckled. Suze or Sharon, my other best friend, or Suze's mom, or I in a consultation of amusement with any or all of them had come up with the nickname Cleo for me. We shared agreement about its suitability; mainly because of my hairdo and hair color, I thought—brunette, to the shoulders, short, straight bangs. Mom had my hair cut that way before I was in fourth grade, and even though I changed my hairstyle a lot from my preteens into my early thirties, I always returned to the "Egyptian" style. I relished the nickname Cleo, because regardless of Sharon's, Suze's, or her mom's association with the name, it resonated with sexuality for me.

Suze told her brother to get lost, and I didn't tell her how I felt. On one hand I thought that the boys found me ugly and that a cruel teasing of me prompted their laughter. But on the other hand, Suze's brother had stared at me, his eyes had touched me. I wondered if Suze had noticed, and I wanted to run after her brother and ask him what his response to his sister meant. Simultaneously I wanted to slap him and to stroke him.

Mom attacked Dad not only for what she perceived as his dourness, but also for his too frequent reluctance or inability to discuss emotions with her. She said that sometimes he was great at it and that they talked for hours about the ins and outs of extended family matters; but I guess that whatever the amount or quality was, it didn't satisfy her desires. Maybe the amount and quality of their sexual activity didn't satisfy her either. During my high school years they often slept in separate rooms, and though I didn't much ruminate on that fact, it profoundly affected me. The passionate pleasure that I witnessed, perceived, or construed in the primal scene had disappeared, and that reality saddened me. Mom and Dad loved each other deeply, devotedly, and perhaps despairingly throughout their lives: they tugged at each other, each close to immovable not in heart but rather in their sensitivities' misfits and misperceptions. I vowed that I would never lose sexual pleasure as they had.

I connect lack of good lovemaking with lack of a dynamically and playfully erotic emotional and spiritual connection as well — because the erotic is connection. Obvious as it sounds, lovemaking is foundational for fairy lovers.

I believed that Mom should have been more gentle and understanding with Dad. She pushed hard at him, which drove him into the kind of silences that women find maddening in men. Mom would have done well to treat Dad as a human being whose motivations and psychic territory differed from hers. Recently I began to do that with the men who were my intimates. It wasn't an easy lesson to learn. So I appreciated Mom's emotional aggressions on Dad. I always knew that Mom pushed at Dad, but not until my thirties was I ready to see Dad's communication failures, which were inadequacies in the domain of love. An acute example was his patting Mom on the head, which she hated, and calling her "little girl" and "Florencita." The first diminutive bothered her more than the second. She told him of her dislike, explaining her feeling of being trivialized and infantilized, though those were not her words. Still he persisted. The bad habits of intimacy are hard to break.

Countering Dad's aura of heaviness was his love of beauty: in my mother, in architecture of all periods, in jazz and classical music, in modern furniture, from Aalto to Noguchi to McCobb, in art, especially cubism and abstract expressionism and art nouveau glass, and in the facts of history, particularly the Civil War. Dad's love of beauty was so pure, it was fairy light, and it was contagious. Although he often launched into male lecture mode, a manner of talking that for many men suffices for conversation and is actually a way to avoid conversation's give and take through an authoritarian control of subject matter and content, Dad's enthusiasm about visual art contributed largely to my own love of it.

Must I undercut our shared enthusiasms? Must the unconscious, with its damned leakiness, tell me that I became an art historian in order to please my father, who did not easily praise his daughters with words? in order to follow in the footsteps that he would have liked to have made, as a professor of art history? in order to compete with him and surpass him because he didn't follow his love of art but became a businessman instead?

Massively unknown subject aside, I was sad that I didn't give Dad credit for being an art historian while he was alive. In his presence I leaned toward his learning, even when his male lecture mode irritated or bored me. I felt comfortable with art because of Dad. I never felt I had to whisper in front of it. I critiqued it with ease and said whatever I wished about it, good or bad. I readily formulated my own thoughts about art, even as a second-grader who copied Picasso's cubist portraits from books. Art was Dad's and my medium of communication, our way of being close with each other. At the funeral home after Dad's death, when the funeral director asked Ren and me what we would like in Dad's obituary, she said, "He was an art historian." I felt like crying and like an idiot daughter who had failed to see that fact plainly, as Ren did. Dad and Mom together wrote *Chicago Stained Glass*, a history of the subject published by Loyola University Press, and their articles on Gallé and Tiffany glass appeared in antiques magazines. Dad researched then wrote the drafts, and Mom edited them. (Their writing process became a horrendous bone of contention between them. Mom's literary sensitivity coupled with her immense talent for criticality meshed poorly with Dad's clumsier writing skills and ability to be crushed by her criticism.) Dad lectured in the Chicago area on his areas of expertise. He was an authority, and the fact that he didn't make a living from art history should not have determined my thinking of him as a businessman rather than as an art historian.

Erne René Frueh, my Dad, the modernist artist, retrieving the voice of his passion from the emotional silences he sustained, locking that passion into his paintings and collages so that any viewer's observation of them served as the key. He adored beauty, and I adored him.

Our similarities embarrassed us, although we adored each other because of them. *O Daddy, I want to talk with you now about any art at all.* A few years before he died, I sent him *Gardner's Art through the Ages,* the tenth edition, which was then the latest one; I knew he'd enjoy it so much. He was still using the first edition, which was probably the first art history survey book that I ever read, and the revised text and good quality color reproductions of the new edition would bring him peace, carry him away from his worries about Mom, both her health and her care if he died before she did. The first time I visited him after he received *Gardner's,* he couldn't thank me enough for it. What delight to give someone the gift that they want!

I regretted Dad's and my competitiveness and hostility about art. Who cares who was the better man? He responded to abstract expressionism almost as much as he responded to Braque, but most art after ab ex left him cold. When it became clear that contemporary art was my field, in my late twenties, he frequently railed at it—the incompetence of the artists, the lack of depth or beauty. Very late in his life, he said that he didn't understand art anymore; which was a reference to contemporary art. I think that he could have understood anything, whether it was art, politics, or the soul. Surely I became an art historian, an art critic, and a performance artist because they're my calling. I became a thinker about sex because that's my calling. I became a lover of beauty, in art, in souls, in bodies, because that's my calling. Surely I became a thinker, a beauty, and a lover of beauty because of Dad. (He knew how to make things beautiful.) My Mom and Dad, a couple of Sunshine Fairies in my life. (They knew how to make things beautiful.)

I remember—or is it imagine?—me, an eleven-year-old girl called to sex and beauty, sitting one morning in math class, noticing a sign posted high on the wall in the front of the room. It read:

Little men talk about people.
Big men talk about things.
Great men talk about ideas.

I had not seen the sign before. I wondered about the subjects of conversations with Sharon and Suze and my other friends. I wondered about my own thoughts. Often I couldn't tell the difference between a thing and an idea. Meat, for example, was surely both. In my mind I went over recent conversations with Suze, and I couldn't separate people from ideas. I knew that math was the science of numbers, knowing about numbers, gaining wisdom through numbers. Three kinds of men—little, big, great: I couldn't fit myself into the equation. People, things, ideas: I couldn't find the fraction of the world into which my own experience could be divided. I couldn't fathom that I was *supposed* to divide it. The sign angered and frustrated me. I couldn't divide properly, in the manner implied by the sign, I didn't feel manly, and the thought of becoming a mathematician or scientist or philosopher—someone who thinks deeply in nonartistic or nonliterary ways—didn't cross my mind. I knew that I was smart and that I thought and imagined uniquely, in ways that other people, whether adults or children, didn't. But art, sex, and beauty, my subjects—whose dissection from one another even then confused me because it did not make sense—didn't strike me as the lodgings of great ideas. My anger and frustration, however, means to me now that I wasn't wrong: the sign was wrong. Right now I remember—imagine?—the teacher facing the class seconds before the bell rang and calling attention to the sign with an arm pointed in its direction or an upward shrug of one shoulder and advising, "If you want to be great, don't be small-minded." I see myself, mouth close to Suze's ear as we left the classroom, saying, "Unless you want to see another side of infinity."

That sounds snide, like a smart aleck's comment. But my infinity comment was sincere. I wasn't a smart girl who acted like a smarty-pants. I was a serious chocolate lover who indulged in her attraction to cocoa and chocolate sundaes in particular and to art, sex, and beauty. Attraction precipitates one's knowledge of her calling. Chocolate, art, sex, and beauty: my calling was pleasure. I did not become a hedonist, a sybarite, a slave to pleasure, but rather its faith-hound and philosopher.

So I liked pink underwear, wore a pink tutu, and became the Sugar Plum Fairy. I joyfully mimicked her at the family Christmas gathering, which included Mom's parents, Ida and Sam. Dad loved the Sugar Plum Fairy and asked her to perform. As I pranced around and executed absurdly clumsy leaps and sloppy pirouettes, Dad laughed and laughed. Ha! He did have a sense of humor. Fairies laugh at fairy fun. The Sugar Plum Fairy made appearances for Dad into my forties, and she would be happy to perform privately today, if asked, by another spirit light as a fairy.

My first public performances took place in elementary school, where I starred in plays presented on the stage in Braeside School's gymnasium. In one of those plays, written by Mr. Rohrs, my fourth-grade teacher, I was a space traveler. At Elm Place School, when we lived at 90 Riparian Road, I played the stepmother in an eighth-grade version of *Snow White*. The costume, borrowed from a Highland Park woman whose clothing collection I longed to delve into, the way a mystic passionately explores her soul, consisted of a long, fluid dress, a cape, and a crown. Sequins or a piece or two of glittering jewelry lit up the fairy princess, even though she was acting an evil queen. Mom and I together with the costume collector picked out my garments of lavenders and purples. I felt at home in my fairy garments, and a friend of my parents, who experienced me as the wicked stepmother, said that I should become an actress, as I already was capable of projecting a powerful and persuasive presence.

During the Elm Place School days, I fell in love with both Sharon and Suze, as many girls fall in love with their girlfriends. Fairy friends, they were blonde beauties, so different from me in coloring and animal attributes. We three met Ruby in high school, and she, like me, was dark-haired, but no one called her "exotic," as they did me then and have since then.

Like Dad, Russell knew and loved the Sugar Plum Fairy, and like Dad, Russ, when asked, made us cocoa on winter nights. He drank a cup with me, then gave me whatever was left in the pot. Lemon, not chocolate, was his favorite flavor.

Mel, you made me cocoa without my asking. And you invited the Sugar Plum Fairy to dance and then laughed lovingly at her star performance, which was every single one of them.

The Sugar Plum Fairy was pink at heart in order to perform. Recently I purchased a lace thong in a deep, bright pink. I imagined that Aphrodite and the Sugar Plum Fairy selected the same lace thong for their lingerie collections. Aphrodite, whose flower is the rose and who, as an epitome of girly girlness, I imagined to be enchanted by the pinkest pinks. The Sugar Plum Fairy, whose spirit, to me as a little girl who watched *The Nutcracker* on television every Christmas that she could, was absolutely in the pink.

I grew up in darkness and in pinkness. I grew up watching Gene Autry and the Lone Ranger, each hero partnered with a male companion. I grew up on an upper-middle-class street, Oak Knoll Terrace, where a ragman hollered his wares through the neighborhood. Milkman and laundry man picked up and delivered in the early years of our family's living at 90 Riparian Road. My family raked and burned leaves at Oak Knoll Terrace, and when locusts came one summer, I sat on the sidewalk observing, as close up as I could, their fairy wings. I listened, with my sister, as we lay in bed before going to sleep, to Dad reading *Treasure Island* and *Winnie the Pooh*. I laughed and listened with my sister to the stories that Dad made up about the Lima Bean Kid and Chief Ookapoochee. I slept in the den of the Oak Knoll Terrace home when I was ill with chicken pox and measles. I watched our Shetland sheepdog Ebon killed by a car right down the street from 145 Oak Knoll Terrace. I saw his blood spreading, unfamiliar red on familiar gray. I slept in the utility room — off the kitchen, housing the washer, furnace, and water heater — with Duke, the Sheltie we chose to live with us after Ebon's death. I walked him at 6 A.M., and I went to him in the middle of the night, in the earliest morning, when he howled. I held him and petted him, as if he were my lover. I comforted him, I wanted to quiet him because Mom especially disliked him, calling him neurotic. Eventually we returned him to the Sheltie kennel where both he and Ebon had been born. When I was a little girl I sat on my grandparents' deep rose Chinese rug, in the living room of their apartment on the South Side of Chicago, and the rug, patterned with flowers, seemed huge to me. The rug's dark floral appeal continued for me as an adult when it decorated Gramps's bedroom in his and Gram's North Side condo. By then, the rug seemed much smaller. I inherited the rose-colored rug and some of the deco bedroom with which it looked so good.

I grew up sitting with my sister in the car by the railroad tracks in Highland Park while our parents dug up wild plants for their garden. I watched Mom arrange the peonies and roses from the gardens tended mostly by her husband. I grew up impressed by two large botanical prints — probably three feet wide by four feet high — which hung in the private quarters of Oak Knoll Terrace and Riparian Road. One print pictured a purple flower, the other a yellow one. Purple, the evil queen's regal attire. Yellow, Russell's favorite color. The organs and the blossoms of those flowers enchanted me. They excited me with intense, emotional pleasure.

Orgasm, from Greek *orgasmos*, from *organ* to grow ripe. *Orgasm*, akin to Sanskrit *urj*, *urja* nourishment, power, strength: swooning beauty.

I grew up believing that I saw a fairy spider, white with rainbow-colored stripes on its fat legs and body, in the back yard of the Oak Knoll Terrace house. Fairy spider, fairy gardens, fairy dogs and fairy stories, fairy parents, fairy sister, you wove me, fairy beast and fairy flower, wove me more and more, because of our fairy tales, into the nourishment and ripening, the strength and power that are swooning beauty. Swooning beauty stabilized me and moved my soul-and-mind-inseparable-from-body into new terrain.

4 ~

My Brave Heart and Mel's

Chocolate Cake Cockaigne became the dish I most enjoyed baking when I was in graduate school, and it's remained so. My friend Mandy introduced the cake to me, and we baked it together in her kitchen. I featured it at the dinners that I cooked for Mom and Dad at my apartment during my M.A. and PH.D. studies at the University of Chicago and my first years of being a published art critic. The recipe for Chocolate Cake Cockaigne, in Joy of Cooking, calls for two to four squares of unsweetened chocolate. An attractive feature—the baker's ability to adjust the intensity of chocolate according to her own or her lovers', guests', or family's desires.

My manhood amused me, and I was wary of it. I was happy in my female body, I didn't want a penis, although for many years I enjoyed imagining how orgasm feels for men.

I didn't want to associate my strength and bravery with those of the mytho-poetically created man of the men's movement exemplified by Sam Keen's *Fire in the Belly* and Robert Bly's bestseller *Iron John*. (Shepherd Bliss, a lesser-known leader of the movement, asserts that he brought to light the literary term *mytho-poetic*—mythopoesis is the making of myth—in order to remake or reenvision contemporary masculinity.) Published respectively in 1990 and 1991, Bly's and Keen's books sold the idea of the "deep masculine"—authentic manhood. Bly, especially, angered feminists who argued against his brand of mythopoetic viril-ity. They critiqued its belief that male anatomy is naturally a destiny of heroic courage. Men gain that destiny by releasing themselves from the everyday yet goddess-powerful grip of women. Keen claims that in women's haunting emotional and psychic bondage, men's knowing the mysteries, the divine and esoteric secrets, of their sex lies fallow. The mythopoetic men's movement appeared to feminist critics, both female and male, to be a sometimes whiney but, more important, a dogmatic reinstatement of conventional masculinity after feminists in the 1970s had challenged it. Men's-movement spokespersons charged those feminist challenges with feminizing men. Many scholars have written about a contemporary "crisis in masculinity," the academic phrase that encapsulates white, postmodern Western man's having fallen off his high horse of social and gender superiority. The men's movement was attempting to address that, yet have we needed another hero like the heroes of a fairy tale or folklore or some imagined past life? Can we even find or fashion one? *Braveheart* was, of course, an extraordinarily successful answer to those questions.

Feminists derided the men's movement for poeticizing the hero's journey necessary to becoming a real man, that journey being a vision quest away from women's demands and desires and into moral courage, self-reliance, and the ability to nurture oneself and others. Perhaps I was on a hero's journey and am continuing it in my ruminations about chocolate, Mel, and fairies. But I could never be all man, a he-man, or only one kind of man or hero, and I did not want sanctuary from women. I was the sage commander, I was Narcissus and Manjushri, I was lightning gods in a good mood. I was an eight-year-old girl, a femme fatale, and a lady. I was an action hero and a fairy man.

Maybe my parents' deaths precipitated my entry into a phallic well-being that was previously unavailable to me. I took charge of many practical matters as Mom and Dad became more and more ill in their old age, from helping Dad with his banking to paying Mom's Medicare bills to arranging for Social Security benefits to seeing that Mom lived as well as possible after Dad's death to tending to her cremation. Taking charge stunned me emotionally, for I was simultaneously heartbroken and in renewal, and both conditions exhausted me. Of course, women take charge during family crises as much as men do, but the dire losses I anticipated and then experienced over several years expanded my spatial effect, swelled my bodily competency and pride. In Western culture, those qualities have been largely men's estate, part of their phallic well-being, which is located in men's real and mythicized ability to move assertively and decisively in the world.

The phallus: central to manly being and sometimes synonymous with the centrally located penis of a man's body. According to the psychoanalyst Jacques Lacan, no one actually has the phallus because, as the ultimate signifier of authority, it transcends the material body. In its abstract power, the phallus, in Lacanian theory, is the Law of the Father, and from its ideological grandeur the phallus has ruled the psyches of women and men. Part of this sovereignty plays in people's minds as a penis/phallus conflation; so, contrary to Lacan, men enjoy a close relation to the phallus and women end up lacking—both prick and power. Supposedly, men lack the phallus, but their connection to the phallus is evident in historically male-dominated social structures and institutions—war, medicine, visual art, higher education, to list a few—that assert phallic influence: man has laid down the law in his behalf.

For centuries in the West, the phallus has represented virility with a simultaneously lovestruck and fearsome glory. Loftier than the penis, the phallus is monumentally beautiful and silly, and as a symbol of a sex's and a gender's power, it is without a female equivalent. The phallus can swell a man's pride in his virility, whereas the phallic woman may be a lost soul and body. I am not she, who's been missing in the action of Freudian drama; the mother, lost—slaughtered or abandoned?—missing in the psychic miseries of castrated men and women.

Webster's New World Dictionary gives the anatomical definition of *phallus* as "a) the penis or clitoris b) the undifferentiated embryonic tissue that develops into the penis or clitoris." It also tells us that *phallus* derives from the Indo-European base *bhel-*, to swell. Having a clitoris, vulva, vagina, and uterus, I am more than the phallus. Many contemporary feminist philosophers, scholars, and critics have argued that sexual difference is culturally rather than anatomically determined, that it has been inscribed in ancient and current myths; in popular and fine art; in narratives, images, practices, and behaviors throughout history and within our daily lives. I swell beyond the phallus's limiting and culturally limited boundaries. This is not simply sweet talk to myself, wanting to believe that I, as one lone woman who recognized that she was a man, can increase the positive symbolic volume of women's genitalia and think I can make it stick.

In my phallic well-being, I was a swell, kin to the fairy men in *Velvet Goldmine*. Like them and Mel, I was a phallically flirting array of corporeal pleasures.

I didn't always recognize my sexual elation and attractiveness so distinctly. Embarrassment and anger filled me when Mom discovered objects that I hid in my bedroom. Those items included preteen reading (self-help psychological studies about improving one's sex life and contemporary novels related to *Peyton Place* in both their suggestive and their direct descriptions of sexual occasions, bodies, and activities) and my diaphragm one summer, spring, or Christmas break when I was home from Sarah Lawrence College. I didn't leave those indications of my sexuality in plain sight, and I felt criminal when Mom told me of her "discoveries." "Told" neutralizes her emotional tone, which was heated but whose details my massively unknown self has chosen to hide from the gender observatory that I've produced as my lyric and my narrative of swooning beauty.

Men are hairy and bony, Mom assured me after finding the books. More vaguely I remember her affirming that sex with men felt good. Hairy young beast that I was, plump with both self-love and self-doubt, plump in the flesh of sexual desires fulfilled by masturbation but not yet with the mutuality of male desire, I tried to picture men according to Mom's descriptive dissuasion from sexual activity. I had never seen a naked man, not even my father, and her description rang untrue to me. My soul-and-mind-inseparable-from-body knew the goodness that Mom asserted after her desensualizing picture of men.

How curious was my massively unknown self, which after Mom's death created Mel, a hairy beast like me, to please me. Amazing animals exist in fairy tales and fables. Fabulous stories offer simple moral lessons: the hero, who is an animal or whose attributes are animal-like, is good — in bed and for the heart. Neither of my ex-husbands is hairy like me and Mel. No lover of mine was like him.

In high school I endured and enjoyed an agony of desire. Familial training to be a good girl in combination with the Western myth of romantic love that pervades popular culture, as well as the numerous nineteenth-century novels and poems that I read as a preteen and a teenager, kept me from fucking anyone. Captive to the impossibility of someday my prince will come, true for Walt Disney's Snow White but not for a budding fairy man and action hero; captive to the impossible demonic splendor of femmes fatales, whether in Baudelaire or the Brothers Grimm, I was my primary lover till I was twenty-one. At twenty-one I didn't suddenly become the femme fatale that I imagined when reading "Un Hémisphère dans une chevelure" or "Little Snow-White," nor did Peter, a short, moustached man my age, fit the image of a kind or gracious prince. Simple as this—my agony of desire outweighed good sense. I loved sex with Peter, but he was also the first of many men I slept with who lacked the luster of a braveheart shining in compatibility with mine.

Mom knew my sexual voraciousness and the passion of my thoroughly sensual intellect and body, and her knowledge, turned to worry in my college years—and continuing into my thirties, indeed, till I was thirty-six and married—impelled her to initiate my meeting with a psychotherapist when I was in my late teens or early twenties. I met with her at least a few times, and her only words that stayed in my consciousness disturbed me. I heard them as a kind of proclamation, and it provoked my ire as a feminist coming of age in the Sexual Revolution: "Men want to please and protect." My hostility toward boys, then men, had kept me from flirtatiousness and comfort with them. In my fifties, as a man, a woman, a girl, a fairy, and an action hero, I learned about pleasure and lightness from my rich milk-chocolate center, my flirtatious braveheart and behavior. I let them loose with the help of Dr. Fajardo, the psychoanalyst with whom I talked four days a week for several years between my late twenties and early thirties, and with the help of Larry, the therapist I cried with the first time we spoke, on the phone, as I stated my reason for seeking help—a marriage whose disintegration I could no longer bear. Stephen, an acupuncturist from whom I sought help, declared, "That doctor in Chicago let the genie out of the bottle and she's not going back in."

Men, my healers, I chose you in order to love, with unconfused affection, the sex that I am not anatomically.

The female psycho-counselor chosen by my mother was, I'm sure, excellent in her work, but I didn't want her understandings of either sex or gender. What I lacked—what I truly wanted, did not have—were men's understandings of those subjects. "Men want to please and protect." The young beast, in her budding, luscious feminism, believed in her own self-protection. It was, of course, the very thing that stood in the way of her flirtatious braveheart and behavior. It was, at the same time, a healthy belief in her ability to take care of herself and to be the agent of her own dreams come true.

Some might say that as a teenager I could have attributed my agonies of desire to hormones. Joanna in the desert, tormented by male demons. The hormone explanation simplifies eros, flatlines it. *Agony*, from Greek *agonia*, a contest for victory. Oh, to win my erotic freedom from the clutches of American femininity before the Sexual Revolution, to be the protagonist in a self-created narrative and lyric of erotic freedom. My agony was my pleasure—both the beauty of masturbating to orgasm again and again, sometimes several times a day, and the abundant sensuality of my soul-and-mind-inseparable-from-body. My agony was my ignorance. It appeared as my fantasies of me and a man partnered in a wholly heartwarming eros of both sexual and mental intelligence, and my dreams far exceeded the capabilities of teenage boys. It appeared, as well, after one of my few teenage sexual adventures, when the boy I'd been with in the back seat of another boy's car was telling people that Joanna "didn't know her ass from her elbow." Maybe I didn't, maybe my stroking of his smooth and golden back was naive, maybe my languorous, excited exploration of his smooth, hard cock with my fingers and my hands was too slow. Long before I entered midlife, my experience of his body brought to mind the midlife movie star Alexandra Del Lago's love of young male bodies in the 1962 film version of Tennessee Williams's *Sweet Bird of Youth*. Del Lago, played by Geraldine Page, is about to be in the sexual company of a preternaturally beautiful Paul Newman, traumatized, as Chance Wayne, the ever-climbing, ever-stumbling hometown hero of a sort, by his failure in the world of fame. She states her love of young, hard, and golden bodies. (Perhaps I played the older woman beginning in my youth.) I remember the boy's body as golden, even though our interlude took place at night. My hands must have heated up from the glow like gold beneath them.

I am the lookout stationed at the gender observatory of my creation. Outstanding sights and small no more than tall stories from that position consist of romantic crises and devastations in my combined aesthetic and erotic health. Yet, being an action hero and a fairy man, even though I hadn't yet armed and brightened myself with those names, my beauty and my eros grew. In graduate school a male peer, Tony, described me as "one of the most seductive women I've ever known."

Seductive though I was, I did not uncover my phallically flirting hips. That required a happiness that is relatively new to me. I attracted men, and they attracted me, but I feared them. What do you do with a man? Besides fuck him? Besides be kind in a not-too-distant way? Besides talk in a passionate intellectualism that leaves him stranded? Staring at your beauty, unhinged in his heart by your enthusiasm for ideas? I've chosen men whose hearts I could unhinge too easily, and without trying—without even knowing! I suppose I can attribute that power to my seductiveness. (More seductive at age eight than her mother at age forty-four.)

I loved my mother, even during my prima donna teenage years, even after I knew that she perceived my sexuality and sexual activity to be like some distended organ, not malignant, but toxically bloated.

I axed off her head in a dream that came during the years when I was talking with Dr. Fajardo. I tried to control my soul-and-mind-inseparable-from-body when I told him the dream. (It *was* a dream. *Nightmare* connotes a terror coming from someplace other than ourselves.) I dreamed my crime as long as a decade after her hysterectomy. I was eighteen that summer when she spent weeks upstairs in the master bedroom. Maybe she and Dad talked about the surgery and named it—hysterectomy—with Ren and me. If so, I don't remember that. And I don't believe that I was any more seductive than my mother was. Men have their preferences. I cannot account for them. But I changed in such a way that the preferences I draw to me for deepest intimacies are different. I've changed, so that I can converse compassionately with the eighteen-year-old girl who sat on the stairwell, heart darkened by the drawn curtains in at least the master bedroom, heart begging for the light, crying or in too sad a silence for tears.

Why tell yourself that you remember it all wrong? Why tell yourself that you should have bridged the silence between your parents and yourself with the sage commander's equanimity? Why tell yourself that you failed? Stay with the clarity of good sense and compassion: I was eighteen, my parents kept quiet about the medical information and their feelings, I did all that I could.

Who doesn't love a hero? Her grief and isolation are compelling. Only an emotional deviant, someone afflicted with dire heartlessness, doesn't root for Captain Karen Walden in *Courage under Fire* when, wounded in the stomach, she faces her troops—all men who are saps compared with her—with the devastatingly animal intelligence of a mother: "I gave birth to a nine-pound baby, asshole, I think I can handle it." But how does a woman who's a mother handle a probably unnecessary hysterectomy? A surgery that plagued women of my mother's generation if they bled a lot during the years leading up to their menopause.

Captain Walden cries in battle and makes clear the meaning of her apparently inappropriate emotional excess: "It's just tension, asshole. It doesn't mean shit." I interpret that as a command: Don't misread me! Misreadings and misreadings. Inbred in human beings, like a disease that dulls our generosity and compassion, both vital parts of understanding. The seductiveness of heroic singularity and solitude: we find the movie hero alone, making her own memories and decisions, quickening our seduction through the hero's own honor, integrity, and love of family tried by the fires of cowards fueled by false consciousness and fraudulent crusades. Till now, I have misread my tears and silence on the stairs. The daughter mystifies herself with wanting to have been a saint. Or the man who could please and protect her mother. I did all that I could.

Gibson's heroes seem transparent. Being men of extreme emotions, they perfect the hero's obligation to the film and reading public to dispense what the audience cannot feel. They redeem us through their emotional fortitude, which may not have range, but rather operates at the edges — suppression and excess. A Gibson hero displays apparently inappropriate emotional excess — what a gal! — and he also remains an ultimate outsider, unable or unwilling to communicate with anyone else, whether for strategic or psychological reasons. A Gibson hero appears to participate in normal human communication. Wallace eats and laughs with his men and cries in front of them. He talks from the heart with them and with Murron and the princess. Police detective Martin Riggs, played by Gibson in the *Lethal Weapon* series, jokes with his partner Roger Murtaugh and with Murtaugh's family. Benjamin Martin's deep melancholia clouds this devout family man and citizen. The cloud speaks more tellingly than does Martin when he talks, so that we who watch him ask ourselves, without knowing our own desires, how might I penetrate this mystery of a man? How might I redeem *him?* Mystery though he is, a Gibson hero is also extraordinarily expressive. Mad Max's near aphasia captivates us. What *is* this man thinking? What *does* he feel? *How* does he feel? In other words, where do his thoughts and feelings move in that simultaneously harrowing and redemptive fluidity of human being? The leader, of men in battle, of women's hearts, of countries in their founding, keeps his own counsel. So does the wise businessman; who was my father, who advised his daughters, "Keep your own counsel."

In confused counsel with myself, despite the frequent good sense of my girl-friends, with whom I talked a lot, I proceeded in my sexual forays, waving, over my heart, like a white flag, the antique standard of romantic love.

In literature, such as the story of Tristan and Iseult or Shakespeare's Romeo and Juliet, romance is doomed love. Denis de Rougemont's *Love in the Western World* is a landmark study of the phenomenon of romance, which he calls "the passion myth." Want, lack, futility, suffering, obstacles, insecurity, and insta-bility: most of us have felt these hallmarks of romance's apotheosis of pain, as if we have drunk a love potion that draws us into a passionate love of love itself. Tristan cannot have Iseult, nor Romeo his Juliet. De Rougemont calls the lovelorn female "the faraway princess," for she is impossible for the pining male to reach in any prosaic way. The Princess of Wales is certainly faraway for Wallace, even though *Braveheart* shows them as lovers. But that is only once, and furthermore, she dwells in enemy England and, yet more perfect for the passion myth, in the castle where king and prince (feckless though Gibson as direc-tor portrays him) plan carnage for the Scots. Murron too is Wallace's faraway princess, dwelling in the heaven imaged in his psyche for most of the movie. In the passion myth, the lovers must die, and then they can be together in heaven. Even though Gibson the director forces his audience to endure Wallace's grisly torture-death, Gibson also indicates, during the drawn-out details of Wallace's suffering, that Murron awaits him in heaven; for she appears to him in the watching crowd, as a sign to him of his own divine courage and of her readiness for him to be her celestial companion. De Rougement uncovers twelfth-century connections between troubadours' songs and Christian mystics' writings: the language of love is the language of prayer. "I'm in heaven when I'm with you!" the lover exclaims to his beloved.

A number of times I've been told that one's fantasy of sleeping with some-one is better than the reality, and I always disagreed. Distance, which cloaks the soul-and-mind-inseparable-from-body in an excitement that puts its martyr beside herself in love, is the ether of a crazed desire for perfection—locking the lover into a false paradise. I disagreed in practice even more than in theory that fucking is a fuck-up. My disagreement rested in the experience of flowering rather than falling when I fucked someone I loved, of rising rather than falling in love, of melting, opening, and lifting the heart. Though in my twenties the phenomenon of loving-fucking-flowering rarely occurred, sexual activity itself, especially vaginal intercourse, only *differed* from fantasy. Reality didn't *disappoint* fantasy. Rather, it offered the aesthetics of corporeality and its pleasures, which the passion myth pushes aside. Reality also created a *together*, whereas the sexual contact of the passion myth relies on *apart*. Together and togetherness are not the same. Togetherness is a family-values accountability that viciously tweaks love into law and order, as if the domestic unit can exist only under bureaucratic control. In *Against Love: A Polemic*, the media studies professor Laura Kipnis goes so far as to call the togetherness of coupledom the "domestic gulag."

I am only yours, and you are only mine: those staples of the romantic love suffered by Chance and Heavenly, Chance's sweetheart who is his age, support the lyrics of a myriad love songs, the I'll-always-be-trues that overlay the likes of Peggy Lee's "Fever" and Bruce Springsteen's "I'm on Fire." Heavenly and Chance and the clichéd rhymes of popular romance represent the "rights" of true love that create guilt (gee, I'm attracted to other human beings) and heart-break (if I follow my desire, I break my vow of truth to love). Such rights ensure that love becomes a shut-in.

Love is not the hindrance to happiness, but as a shut-in, love transforms into a breed of emotion that insinuates itself into conflicts between spouses, partners, and short-time lovers, so that they grind each other into hot seats of humiliation and recrimination. The emotion bred in the prison of romantic passion answers to chance and heaven as whims of lovers who know little of equanimity. They turn ups and downs into highs and lows, then yearn for those extremes. Trained to punish human beings for knowing, seeking, and satisfying their pleasures, love changes its name to flounder, humiliate, get lost.

Love is large and easy, largesse and ease. What could be happier?

I am happy in it together, in my cunt. The penis is not alone in the vagina. When I loved, my heart was in my cunt as much as was the heart of any man who was my lover.

Heaven is here, in my body, in my home, in its every room and in my garden. People can found heaven in the pleasure and the beauty of our prosaic imper-fection. The prosaic is necessary for true love. The prosaic is not boredom, but rather the beauties as well as the frustrations and revelations of everyday life with a partner. Love always takes courage. In the passion myth, the lovers'—the heroes'—courage turns into the self-absorption of their pain.

Humility makes way for others, unlike self-absorption, which isolates a person. Humility is not self-effacement, a humbleness that makes the person housing humility a victim. Generosity belongs to humility, and so does the indulgence that is generosity to oneself. I have been men's Iseult, isolated by the self-absorbed deception that led them to disregard the reality of their pleasures with me. One man could not get his words out smoothly, and he tripped over two of them—*fantasy* and *fantastic*. The sentence that he formed nonetheless was probably this: "You're fantastic, fantasy." Or it may have been this: "You're fantastic, my fantasy." Fantasy kept him far away from me, even though our fucking was so very close.

Mel knew that I was firm and earthly. He, like me, attested, "Love, confirmed by earth, is not illusion." And our refrain, which was a prayer, was this: "I am heaven, here as I am."

Classically, romance is about compulsion, about emotions so intense that we have no control over them. People most often use *self-indulgence* in an uncomplimentary way, to denote excess, a going overboard. A friend e-mailed me, "love . . . the thing I'm drowning in." Shipwreck. Open sea. Rescue probably not impending. The pause in his thought, which the ellipsis indicates, was the lover attempting to align or coalesce some mental and emotional resources before going under or before realizing the implications of that sinking (and most people never realize those implications). The pause may also have been the deliciousness of that sinking into the romantic myth, whose fangs and gaily painted fingernails have, for centuries, been embedded in the very flesh of lovers' hearts. When we have no control, we indeed have *fallen* in love, as if some force had punched us in the gut and we had dropped at least to our knees in agony. On our knees, we abnegate ourselves to the beloved, as if she or he were an unprincipled deity, a sadistic god or goddess who demands obsession, which is composed in part and paradoxically of the lover's narcissism. That self-absorption goads the lover to ignore the beloved by foregrounding the former's own feelings—or, more accurately, the lover's own predicament. Tristan *tristesse*, missed and missing, trysts and twistings in our fantasies of a heaven that is never now.

Mel and I renounced the suffering of unisex and sexed-up fantasies, the ambivalences of heaven can wait.

I resist the romantic ambivalences of Elizabeth Smart's *By Grand Central Station I Sat Down and Wept*, described on the back cover of my Vintage paperback like this: "hailed by critics worldwide as a work of sheer genius." I am tired of the "genius" of women's suffering and masochism. Smart's short novel details and cloaks, in stupendously gorgeous poetic prose, her mad love gone to bad love with the poet George Barker.

I am with Diane Wakoski, who writes in her poem "Breathless" that the men in her life leave her in that condition. (I read "Breathless" to a class of mine. It so moved the students that one young man was nearing tears and all twelve looked awed by beauty.) It is possible to be breathless . . . and to breathe. "Madly in love," "crazy about him." Those phrases squeeze our hearts into the box of romantic compulsion. Believe that they are just a couple of ways of proclaiming passion, and you'll fall ever farther into the fairy tale of erotic elixirs, faraway princesses, and no defense. We may think that such lack of defense disarms the heart, but it is an armor, against the true colors, bloodred and pink. I see the *madly* and the *crazy* of romantic love in light of Alphonso Lingis's discussion in his *Dangerous Emotions* about the "value terms. *Great, beautiful, strong, healthy, delicious, wild.* . . . The value terms . . . find their meaning . . . in exclamations: How healthy I am! How strong I am! How happy I am! How beautiful I am! How good it is to be alive! We say these things because we feel them, and by saying them we feel still better." The value terms can make us what we are, and they can be negative as well as positive.

"How crazy I am!" Smart seems to exclaim. It is her constant theme. Love does make her feel large, beneficent, magnificent—altogether unusual. "Be reasonable. Be usual," she cautions herself, cognizant of the impossible. Love is unusual. It is Martin Luther King's not filing charges against a man who hit him during one instance of King's nonviolent resistance. King said that love is courageous. Throughout *Dangerous Emotions* Lingis harnesses the hero's energy, demonstrating how we can elongate our hearts each time that we risk loving. Neither King's nonviolence nor Lingis's erotic philosophy draws the burning silk of love gone as bad as it can be around their shoulders and over their chests, to sear their hearts, to inhale the smoke that leaves one breathless without reprieve. When I use the word *erotic* I do not mean necessarily or only genital sexuality, although that may be a component of radical loving. The erotic is rich, profound, and complex connection with the reality of another person. In my prayers and in my heaven on earth, eros encompasses *philia* and *agape*. *Dangerous Emotions* is erotic because it *connects* its reader, it *connects* us to *corage*, the Old French word for heart and spirit.

One of Barbara Kruger's best-known photographs addresses the viewer, "I can't look at you and breathe at the same time." Her *you* is not the lover but the enemy. The *you* who leave us breathless in Kruger's terms, full of shame and insecurity, add more pressure to the many people with sad shoulders. One's shoulders may round severely forward because of old disasters, in a continuing attempt to protect the heart, to make it invulnerable. Consequently, the chest caves in, and the breath does not have clear passage to the heart. The chest caves in, the heart caves in, collapsing rather than yielding. We rarely see an open, unprotected chest—and though I am not telling you, the reader, as you breathe the best you can, that all cave-ins indicate the closure of a heart or that all open chests are signs of erotic wonders, I am aware that when I elongate my spine and draw my shoulder blades down it, in an alignment and a tuning that lift my heart, courage is preparing me then and there for true love.

"How free I am!" I sang with Mel. The *madly* and the *crazy* stayed away from our lips, as did the lunatic love that lays siege to courage, because we asked heaven to come everywhere with us.

"I love you" can be a gratuitous phrase, a passive statement that, unconsciously voiced, maintains a partnered syntax of avoidance, hostility, and misunderstanding. Romantic love is a paradoxical and poisonous antidote to "I love you" as a gratuitous phrase.

"I am dying for love," Smart languishes, and claims in the next sentence, "This is the language of love." "Ugh," I wrote in the margin. A page later she suffers some more: "O the language of love. The uninterpreted. The inarticulate." I am as clear as I can about the meaning and the lack thereof in the interstices of spoken and unspoken I-love-yous. I, like Smart, am articulate about the grammar of romantic love, used in daily abnegations by women and men I know. "The language of love, which nobody understands," she bleeds again. Her poetry is remarkable, but how unremarkable is her plight, to which she appears to pledge herself. She is the romantic as victim. The victim holds onto her wounds, to her lovesickness, and in that state, she cannot relax. Maybe she spoon-feeds herself the stomach-cramping confection of an unrequited, high erotic tension. Maybe she has a heart attack.

I resist Smart's language of love as the language of woe. In *Saddle Sores,* the artist Vanalyne Green's brilliantly acute and humorous 1998 video about herpes, one section title asks, "Is romance a sexually transmitted disease?" The STD romance is the lovesickness suffered by Smart and by my drowning friend, who talked with me about "access" and "resistance," words that kept recurring in our conversation about his illness. He said that in any love, no matter how old, no matter how passionate, no matter how opulent, no matter how deep, "there is always resistance." Protection, resistance: woe is always somewhere in the caved-in heart.

In the clutches and the clinches of romantic love, we believe that its intensity will give us access to the high lights and deep darks that generally elude us. High lights and deep darks measure the mysteries of our own unconscious and of life itself. We believe romantic love will rescue us from dullness, both our own and what too often feels like everybody else's. In those clutches and clinches, we decrease accessibility to the heartwarming that we are searching for. In those clutches and clinches, we learn the coldness that repels me in Smart's masochistic woe. In those clutches and clinches, we are dying for love, killing our ability for erotic connection with another human being.

I do not deny the effectiveness of unconscious resistance to love. The heart expands and contracts without our knowing it, as the lungs fill with air and empty themselves of it. I do not deny my susceptibility to openings and closures, expansions and contractions that may be wanted or not, warranted or not. I do not deny my resistance to courage, humility, and generosity. At the same time, I am equally aware of conscious, brave resistance. Like my having said to my fairy lover, who rejected my love while desiring it, "I'm tired of resisting my feelings." Like my intolerance to Smart's plaint, which reminds me of folk songs whose poignant melodies and melancholy lyrics I loved to sing. Such as "Silver Dagger," in which a mother tells her daughter that men tell lies that sound like love. My friend Peggy's term, "the charming bad boy," fits the rotten lovers bemoaned by the singer of "Silver Dagger."

No longer can I alter either clothes or men to make them fit. Once I outgrow them, I look elsewhere for the aesthetics of love.

In the desperate disconnect of classic romance, lovers believe that they can alter each other. That mistake demands the absence rather than the presence of the loved one. In other words, it requires a soporific dose of fantasy that puts us in danger of being asleep to the uncommon yet so possibly prosaic bouquet of courage, generosity, and humility. Asleep and adrift, we have fallen for a fantasy, fallen for feeling that is overwhelming yet simultaneously is a travesty of eros. We have fallen in love with love, because that state feels more real than reality—that dullness that passes for life.

I would not describe any of my over fifty years as dull, and during that time, boredom didn't waylay my spirit. However, malaise took hold of me a lot during my twenties. A few years ago I would have used *depression* rather than *malaise*. But I always ate, slept, socialized, and worked; I didn't exhibit the classic depressive symptoms. I suppose that someone other than myself could say that I became Dr. Fajardo's patient because I was depressed, but the poetic specificity of my mental state interests me more than do clinical names for it.

As I recount romantic forays, in a nonchronological order and in the midst of ruminations about heroes, I see my past self, who both endangered the hot spring of me and let it, a little, be my source of ease.

I called Peter, the first man I slept with, after a long hiatus, and on the phone I heard him yelling down his dormitory's hall, "I guess I'll have to fuck her." The first man I slept with didn't love me. I didn't love him, either. I obsessed about him, so the fullness of his cock in my mouth, the power of my cunt, to draw his kisses and his cock to me, our sweat and every other wetness produced by heat induced me to return to him for more. Peter and I explored and exploited each other. I fucked him once again after that phone call. I wanted to know the part antagonism plays in fucking, or so I convinced myself.

Looking for love, but inhibiting my freedom, my own love for myself, I garnered disappointment. I acted out many dramas of love lost in the play of bodies caught in faulty sacraments. I believed my goal was clarity, but mostly I learned chiaroscuro as one man after another told me, without my asking, that I was sensual. Addicted to that response, which proved my desirability, but not enough, I sought more evidence. I knew that I was sensual, I loved that I was sensual, but I rarely knew or loved my sensuality enough to free it in the safety of a man who saw—who I would let see?—the materials and the process of my weaving that created the sensual tapestry to which they responded. *Lover*, a euphemism for the starry-eyed lost souls I attracted. Oops, my misreading. The latent fairy was herself a starry-eyed lost soul. Yet, through all my obsessions, my rejections of men who didn't fit the charming bad boy theme, and my ineptness at freedom, fucking drew me to men because my plentiful orgasms and other erotic pleasures kept afloat my faith in love. By my late twenties, antagonism receded—it's been long gone—because more love, for me, for men, defused my enmity.

I rejected an attentive man, studying at Princeton to be a doctor, whose confidence made unnecessary any showing off of his tender, deep intelligence. Howie, too nice for me when I was twenty.

A nineteen-year-old guitarist, seven years my junior, infatuated me. I drank gin and tonics with him, and a lot of wine. Violence against me entered my dreams about him, disturbing my heart during my many nights alone. Or . . . he dreamed about me and a knife or knives. He didn't appreciate the gourmet dinners that I cooked—a practice of mine only in my midtwenties to midthirties—and one morning, hungover from the night before, I either ran into him in downtown Chicago or hallucinated that I did. That actual or mental encounter stopped me from seeing him again.

A blind date in Boston, when I attended Boston University my first year in college, took us to one of the city's deservedly famous restaurants. The food was better than anything else about the date, although most memorable was my red-haired companion's desired kiss. I couldn't kiss him. He didn't excite me sexually. At Boston University I lived in a dorm, which was a row house near the Charles River, and I closed the dorm door, repulsed.

I carried on my love and sex life under the spell of the charming bad boy. I suspect my younger self of false pretenses: believing that I loved men. I loved them some, like Jason, whom I met through my sister and who was the first man I lived with. Jason played trumpet in a band that Ren organized. He was certainly not the demon lover who tempted me from my teens into my late thirties. But I was mean to him. Not often, but in a way that caused me to cringe. I'd call him "dummy" or something similarly hostile, imitating my mother's dumping on my father because he didn't satisfy her. For what, exactly, I'll never know. Maybe it was a solitude that she read as a distance void of love. I learned her alienating language. Not the exact words—my own spilled out of me with a surprising quickness—but rather their stingy and bad-tempered tone. Erne took too much of her guff into his heart, where it brutalized him, despite his utter devotion to her. (Maybe, in a masochistic magnanimity, the brutalization helped to shape his devotion.)

Like Dad, Jason was gentle. I do love gentle men. Their ability to love grounds them in tenderness. Jason and I loved each other gently. He taught me yoga. His humor delighted me, and his sweet disposition, cruising and laughing into my hostility, alleviated it more than a little. Smoking dope, eating ice cream cones—we'd walk blocks from our apartment to Baskin-Robbins—spending the little money we made on dinners at good restaurants, often with other couples, like Ren and Ken (whom she married when she was twenty-two) and Curt and Ginger. One summer Ren and Ken and Jason and I lived together. Our camaraderie, amidst the Rice-A-Roni, the kitchen cockroaches, Ken's rude waking us to Alban Berg's opera *Wozzeck* on weekend mornings, and the Puerto Rican neighborhood (long since gentrified), grew out of hippie culture's communal living arrangements, drug sharing, and politics of peace but not passivity.

Dad closed the door in Jason's and my face when we showed up in Highland Park one afternoon to befriend my parents as the couple that we were. The gentle patriarch shocked me. Yet he and Mom were at least ten years older than the parents of most of my peers, so the 1960s' extravagant changes in sexual mores and social behavior especially bewildered my parents' confidence in my ability to lead a stable, safe, or secure life. Through my twenties, my intellectual talents, skills, and aspirations provided the means through which my parents loved me unworriedly. Despite my demon lovers, save for Jason, I excelled in graduate school at the University of Chicago, began writing art criticism for *Art in America* and *Artforum* as well as for local and regional publications, and worked as director of Artemisia Gallery, a not-for-profit, woman-run alternative space. Jason called me a workaholic, not resentfully, but as what appeared to him to be a statement of fact. Every man I lived with found his own words to describe my passion for my work.

It was safer than my passion for men. Crazy me, crazy men. More likely, crazy me? Crazy men? Misreading after misreading.

During Jason's and my relationship, we tried a threesome with his best friend, Curt. The men's mutual sexual activity was nil, and I teased them about that. They loved each other, but I was the focus of their touch. Even so, their tentativeness suppressed the high passion roused in me by the situation.

Curt and I slept with each other after Jason and I broke up and I was living by myself. I sensed an undercurrent of violence from Curt, as I had with Jim, the guitarist. Maybe it was Curt and not Jim who dreamed of knives. Maybe one of the three of us imaged a whip during our sleep, separated by blocks or miles. Maybe this and maybe that. I robbed myself of reality. I replaced reality.

I did all that I could.

Larry, my therapist during and after Russell's and my divorce, reminded me, as I spoke of misreadings and misreadings, that a man dreaming of a knife could mean something different from my interpretation of violence. Superstition, a source of misreading, abounds in the realm of sexual relations. Cultural superstition — knife as penile and phallic metaphor. My superstition — men as threat, not to be trusted with precious me. I use *precious* without the sarcasm that some might misread into it. Sarcasm turns words of love into unfriendly arrows.

"Loose!" cries the English commander, ordering his archers to let their arrows fly. Fly, and hit or miss the Scotsmen led by Wallace. We think we hit or miss with love. But our superstitions pick the person we can count on to appease them. "Loose!" Frame after frame, arrows fill the entire screen, which is the blue sky. Beauty moving, flying free, beauty undeniable. Damage moving, damage flying, damage undeniable. Stephen jokes to Wallace as they crouch, with all the other Scotsmen, all raising their shields above their heads as protection, all forming a gorgeous pattern of vulnerability attempting to be invulnerable. "The Lord tells me he can get me out of this mess, but he's pretty sure you're fucked," offers Stephen, as if his sarcasm is a prayer for safety, backed by the force of his hysterical laugh. "Loose!" A fairy's caring admonition to let go. To let the arrows that Aphrodite knows so well meet the flesh and open it to possibilities, unwedding them from superstition.

A woman bases her love of a man on superstition. "So I was afraid of sex with men?" I asked Larry. I could have asked, just as well, and been equally or more reasonable and compassionate, "So I was afraid of men's desire for me? Their passion for me? So I was afraid of receiving love from men?"

So I most often chose ones who provided it insufficiently or not at all. The funniest examples were a hippie in Boston, "King of the Hippies," whose apartment was filled with farting cats, and a religious guy in Chicago who, when we were naked and about to fuck, exclaimed, "I'll go to hell if I do this!" "Are you serious?" I asked. "I'll go to hell," he repeated. I laughed in his face and at our ludicrous interlude, and then, without asking him why he had taken off his clothes and was lying on top of me, I voiced two words whose tone filled my small apartment with an order that was equally a request: "Get out." I wondered, did his misreading of women's cunts make them hell for him? Did he think of both cunts and hell as "down there"? "Down there": the blunter and the more poetic words with which I've always named my body charged it with earthiness and rhapsody. Hey, boy, the underworld was not in me, but rather in your head. I laughed after he left, but was he any more ridiculous than I was?

I slept with one of my professors in graduate school, and I told my mother. I sound like a little girl saying that. "I'll tell on you," and maybe that's what my massively unknown self intended. But Mom horrified the conscious me when, in her love and her concern for me and in her moral rage against the professor, she threatened to contact the University of Chicago, which was her alma mater, as it was my father's too. "How can someone be so brilliant, and so dumb about her own life?" she asked me sometime in my twenties.

Women gave me comfort and more safety than did men. I let them. I didn't let men give me as much. In her fifth-floor walk-up on West 94th Street, my best friend from college, Serena, and I became lovers. We easily pleased each other: talking about art and sex and parents, eating delicious food at New York restaurants and in her brownstone apartment — pastas, seafood, spinach cheese pie that we prepared together, sharing a bottle of wine — sipping it as we cooked — or a pint of Haagen-Dazs chocolate ice cream. Her bedroom faced a courtyard, trees, and the back windows of brownstones. Serena's windows with their lifted shades allowed any neighbor who was looking toward her bedroom to witness our venturing physically, for the first time, into the soul-and-mind-inseparable-from-body of a woman who mattered to each of us.

Mandy, baking partner for my first Chocolate Cake Cockaigne, also became my erotic partner. At a café table Mandy fascinated her small audience of young intellectual women by telling them that men preferred sexual intercourse with some women because of the way that their vaginas tilted. She'd recently read that news. The fascination centered, I'm sure, on every woman's wanting to determine if she had a pleasing cunt, but Mandy couldn't remember the feel, fit, or position of the most desirable female anatomy. Maybe I asked, "What difference would this make to a lesbian? What you say seems only to apply to cocks and cunts." I don't think she replied, "I don't know. Probably none. Funny that we're all focused on cock." Rather, I think I am focusing now, in my fifties, on my determination, in my twenties, to learn what cock could teach me about love.

One night when Mandy invited me to dinner at her and her husband Potter's apartment, we all slept together. We did that a number of times, always at their place, and Mandy and I also met by ourselves, to bake, smoke marijuana, and make love. Chocolate chip cookies or chocolate cake often focused our attention for a while—beating and tasting the batter, probing each other intellectually and emotionally as our treats were baking, trying new frostings that we stirred on the stove or mixed in the blender. On one of the many afternoons that Mandy and I spent together, I observed her eating sugar out of the canister she kept it in. We head for too-sweet when lack of love is trying soul-and-mind-inseparable-from-body, for somewhere away from the reach of prescription medication. I looked for too-sweet with Mandy and Potter. He wanted sex with me, just us two. I didn't like his smell, and the sexiness that Mandy saw in him missed the tunings of my eros.

When I watched Mandy and Potter fucking, I read a woman's body jerking like it had no rhythm of its own. I read a woman lost, in a world of a man's creation, and nausea overcame me when I heard, as if from another room, Potter's appreciation, "Joanna, you were hot." Often during sex, with Mandy and Potter and with others, "out of synch" described my state. For several minutes after penetration, I shared a man's rhythm, and orgasm came easily, as soon as my cunt embraced his cock. Then I disengaged for a while, until an emotion unknown to my consciousness reconnected me, to the man or to the sensations that he provided for me, I'm not sure. In disengagement I rarely reached a level of excitement that propelled or eased me into a cadence that suited both my partner and myself, a cadence free of his control while also freeing me to be a lyric in the mutuality of our radiant energy, our hips linked in a poetry of pushing and passivity, acting and pausing, a poetry of all my intertwinings—of limbs, of visceral unrestrictions—given, giving leeway to the pinpoints and the spreading of orgasm undulating and unlocalized. I told my friends I loved to fuck. Cunt engaged with cock, a situation meaning that my unconscious unlinked some element of psychophysical enslavement, brought me so much to my senses that I screamed, in an undoing of any vocal impediments to pleasure.

I unblock the organs of my enlightenment. They exist in soul-and-mind-inseparable-from-body. Men love me and I love men. Today I know that, *with* the simplicity in which I just stated it and *from* the delusions, deprivations, and dishevelments that I endured in my twenties and that I sorted through and sorted out since then. I love men and men love me. Contingencies have disappeared, the ifs and only ifs, the whens and the whatevers, the conditionals and the false futures; because my brave heart is refiguring a past that adds up to a whole whale of a different present. The heart holds our memories, and in my heart's reconstitution I cried with understanding for the fairy woman who cringed at her own hostility to men; I cried for the sage commander who misread her close encounters with men, misread their *shih*, over and over, as if she were making first contact with an alien species.

The action hero with his brave heart is often the romantic hero. While Sean Connery's dapper and deliberately seductive James Bond epitomizes that equation, even Bruce Willis's melancholic detective John McClane in the *Die Hard* films, caught up unexpectedly in saving the public from terrorist horrors, cast a spell on me with his ingratiating bad-boy macho. I watched all the *Die Hard* films between Russ's and my separation and divorce. McClane is a pain in the ass to everyone, generally including his wife. She is his only romantic connection, and the three *Die Hard* movies mostly depict the two as partners in a troubled marriage without ever showing them as lovers. McClane's body seems to be vulnerable only to fast and furious battering, not to the pleasures of sex. Yet in *Die Hard 2*, when asked what he's going to do as he heads out on an altruistic, self-imposed mission that's obviously doomed to failure, McClane responds, "Everything I can!" That startled me, despite the fact that action heroes' modus operandi is to do all they can.

How long can one do "Everything I can!" before lockup in the domestic gulag or the breakout of divorce?

Chance Wayne's hometown girlfriend, Heavenly Finley, played by the blonde and beautiful Shirley Knight, sighs to him after they've made love, "No one in love is free or wants to be." Now there's an idea whose time has long passed. That idea should reside in a Museum of Romantic Memories, filled in at least one wing with an infinity of chains, at once familiar and ornate, that keep so many people in the bondage they call love. Heavenly, with your head in the clouds, close as it can get to the ethereal dementia of divinely dopey romance, you are proof that having fallen in love, the company we keep inside us when we fuck helps us feel like hell.

The title of Aretha Franklin's hit bangs the nail on the head: "Chain of Fools." Chance Wayne, embodiment of the waning chance, for him and Heavenly, for any of us fools, to know a true lover when one appears in our path.

Of course, the fool is the wise one, disguised not only to others but, as the enchained lover, disguised to herself. Fooling around, one may be fooling away one's time and one may play the fool. Then again . . . an enchained lover, enchanted like a loony fairy princess locked up in a Museum of Romantic Memories, may reshape herself into nobody's fool by reshaping her misreadings.

In Dr. Fajardo's office, when my soul-and-mind-inseparable-from-body told him about axing off Mom's head, I laughed and cried at the same time. I tried to control myself, the wise woman in disguise, but I could not. Heavenly, you loony fairy princess, you sycophant who flatters fucked-up romance, I prefer freedom because it's happiness, so I did away with my captivity to my reading of Mom's perception of my sexuality as toxic. The head holds ideas, so I cut off her head.

Stroke by stroke, we reread the pasts that our misreadings have misshaped.

Since I first visited the armor collection at the Metropolitan Museum of Art in New York, the beauty of shields and weapons—less so, the beauty of metal suits—has awed me, like the paintings of Caravaggio, the unconventional baroque master, and of Dante Gabriel Rossetti, a nineteenth-century Londoner who also went his own way. As does Wallace, as do Jack Fairy and Curt Wild in *Velvet Goldmine*. Standing in the aura of armor, an aura penetrating any glass encasing lances, battleaxes, swords, and daggers, I have wondered, since I was a girl in the Met, how men felt to swing or lunge or jab or hack with such a sculpture, how men felt to simply carry it around, to take its beauty for granted or to be oblivious to it. How would such a sculpture feel to me—five feet four inches tall and weighing 125 pounds? Watching *Braveheart*, especially the first time, when the extremely fresh memory of my mother's death claimed much of my attention, I wondered, during the cinematically long and famous battle scene with its strikes and stabbings, gougings, stinks, and tramplings, how it felt to fight. The Scottish troops wear no armor, no chain mail. What did it feel like to run into battle? Gibson the director magnifies and thus aestheticizes sound—the

Scotsmen's feet as they speed up, the hooves of the English soldiers' horses, the yells of force and effort, of surprised surrender to a sword. Turn, twist, spin, fall, lunge, dive, ram, whack. Lickety-split, not fast enough. Editing creates a dance of expressionist extremity, and, of course, strokes of red adorn the pictures. True red, real red, bloodred, dead red.

Stabbings, gouging, stinks, and tramplings . . . not to mention . . . beheadings. Fighting to be free. Tom Petty wails about this necessity, in his usual persuasive way, when he sings "Refugee." In my dream, where I knew the weight and movement of a weapon, I took a stroke. Like Caravaggio and Rossetti painting a new canvas. I wonder, standing in the aura of their paintings, how did they do that? Take an infinitude of just-right strokes. In my dream, I took a stroke for freedom. Like Wallace and his compatriots, and watching Braveheart's fictional reenactment of the battle of Stirling times far beyond my counting, I wondered about medieval European soldiers, how did they do that? Take the strokes that saved their lives.

One stroke after another, we create our freedom.

My freedom with women climaxed in a relationship, longer than the one with Jason, almost as long as my first marriage of around four years, with an amazon—a tall, strong, big-boned, blonde artist named Veronica. "All natural," she once quipped to someone as she flipped her shoulder-length hair with her index fingers. Her excitable passion altered the atmosphere around her. Veronica's irrepressible—often uncontainable—passion flooded her Prismacolor self-portraits, portraits of friends and lovers (including me), and fantasy environments housing lovemaking women couples. In her first solo exhibition at a commercial gallery, paintings featuring the last subject caused a stir in the Chicago Tribune review of the show. The critic, who gained Chicago artists' disrespect through his own disrespect toward their art and his general ignorance about it, declared that Veronica's work belonged in the "erotic dustbin." I use quotation marks because, even thirty years after the fact, I think that my memory of his phrase is true, and even if my memory misreads that part of my past, it correctly reads the cruelty of the critic's phrase. Living together in a big apartment where we painted every room a different color, I remember our astonishment, as well as some laughter, when we found out—from an artist friend, or perhaps Veronica's art dealer (who was a good friend of mine), or from the paper itself—where Veronica's work had been relegated. I had entered the Chicago art world, as a critic, a little before Veronica did, and we were in the thick of things.

Calming pink bedroom, chocolate brown living room, white hallway and painter's studio, black bathroom (with its gray tiles); dining room done in Chinese red, pantry and kitchen painted cantaloupe, writer's study a steadying sky blue. The colors in which we lived, like the colors in Veronica's drawings, looked like jewels. She pressed hard when she used the Prismacolor, making the marks dense, the tones rich.

Gladiator, from Latin *gladius*, sword. *Gladiolus*, from Latin, sword lily, small sword, diminutive of *gladius*. Gladiolus, any of a genus of iris family plants. *Glad*, the colloquial variant of *gladiolus*. *Glad*, from the Indo-European base *ghel*, to shine. Shining, golden, like some sweet bird of youth, Veronica increased my happiness, like the irises that grew wild, three flights down, in the alley under my study window. Shining, golden gladiator, cream of the crop of colors, dropped her armor when she danced, breathless, smoke in hand, flying like an overly excited bird out of its cage. Shining, golden gladiator, in a flurry, in a fury to cultivate bright blooms on the plains and in the hollers of misogyny and lesbophobia. Two of her lovers gleam in luxury: she called the piece *Love at the Ritz*. In *Angry Bunny*, or some similar title, she pictured a rabbit and a plastic knife that she painted camouflage colors. In my possession, then through now, is a small black painting studded with a plastic knife she painted gold and encrusted with sequins. Gladiator, that knife was her heart worn on her sleeve.

Before we became lovers, Veronica's self-portraits and her portraits — always of women — included flowers, like Dante Gabriel Rossetti's tributes to the female sex. I wrote my dissertation, "The Rossetti Woman," when Veronica and I lived in our many-colored home.

I loved being semidressed for sex, as much with Veronica as with any man. Jeans and panties tugged just below my cunt, a skirt hiked up above my hips after a lover removed my panties, complete nakedness from the waist down: all heightened my desire and my sexual satisfaction.

I was in love with my cum. I passed my fingers, covered with it, over Veronica's and my mouths and we licked it off. I masturbated with her finger in my cunt, amazed by my juiciness. During one slow and vastly deep orgasm, I said I seemed to be hallucinating, for I was lying in a garden moist with flowers, pink and red. I see the silliness of cunt as fruit and flower, that cliché, yet there I was, my cunt a huge rose, petals opening wider and wider. My multiplicity of lips was luscious, as was all of me, from flesh to reason.

Yet I loved men sexually more than I loved women, and, as I didn't hide that to myself or to anyone else, it propelled me back to men. After breaking up with Veronica, I heard through the grapevine that within the gay community of the Chicago art world, I had become a traitor. To be maligned is to be human.

So the hero learned to keep her own counsel. I understand Dad's advice to "keep your own counsel," as doing so preserves one's energy and even increases it. Dad also knew that people malign other people for no good reason. His maxim for expressing that, "Some people won't like you because of the way you part your hair," usually made me laugh. I appreciated the aptness of Dad's words, maybe even more so because I've parted my hair in the middle for most of my life, whether it was fashionable or not. "Don't explain yourself, don't suck up," advised Dad with "Keep your own counsel." Most important, "Be brave."

The retired U.S. Army lieutenant general Harold G. Moore, who called his soldiers "precious" during a National Public Radio interview, stated the obvious to his interviewer: fear ill serves you on the battlefield. (Moore and Joseph L. Galloway coauthored *We Were Soldiers Once . . . and Young: Ia Drang; The Battle That Changed the War in Vietnam*. Published in 1992, the book served as the source for *We Were Soldiers*, released in 2002 and starring Mel Gibson as Moore.)

Most of us are familiar with the battle fatigue of romance. On that battlefield, we forsake many opportunities to pay attention to *shih*. In one kind of battle or another, maligned or not, people take the counsel of fear. Fear makes people tentative, and it is a slow and dolorous road to freedom. Too much fear, and freedom eludes us.

Bravery and attack are different behaviors. The sage commander can back off, can befriend. Using a sword to thrust one's way into victory—with physical violence, with words as a weaponry of accusation, flattery, or manipulation—diverges from the hero's front line of wisdom. Wallace's glaive—a double-edged sword that slashes—has its purpose, but as we learn early in *Braveheart*, a man must learn to use his head before he uses a sword. Wallace's dad asserts to his very young son, "I know you can fight. But it's our wits that make us men," and after the boy's father dies, his brother, Wallace's uncle Argyle, reiterates the message. Pointing first to his nephew's head, then to the sword that Wallace wishes to learn how to use, Uncle Argyle affirms with loving, firm alacrity, "First learn to use this, then I'll teach you to use this!" No matter how daft—from my current perspective—some of my actual and desired sexual pairings were, I always chose smart men.

Wits before weaponry. What was my weaponry, other than the powers of seduction that my hostility, riding my well-trained fear, had disabled? Fear, the racehorse that runs like hell and always loses. Even though Tony, my fellow grad student, experienced me as profoundly seductive, and he, among both men and women, was not alone, much of my sweet allure eluded my own recognition. Seducers may lead astray or they may entice in playful ways. Giving the fairy as free a rein as we are able, our beauty rides on love.

Wits before weaponry. Wallace adheres to Argyle's wisdom. I adhered to it in my own way, through the decade of my many sexual misadventures. The seductive scholar spent lots of time alone, both loving it and feeling weird about it. In a culture that sighs over the Heavenlys, while dumping on them for putting all their eggs in the basket of romantic love, a woman, especially a young, attractive, sexy woman, shouldn't be so devoted to her work. Go to a bar, get laid, have fun! The smoke and noisiness of bars always obviated their being fun for me, and as I like to fuck as much as to be fucked, getting laid—by getting men to want to do it—struck me as a lot of work (my hostility toward men aside) for nothing much.

On a Friday or Saturday around 7 P.M., in the comfy living room of my Boston University dormitory, I was reading and absorbed in a story or a train of my own thought when another student stuck her head in, looked at me like I was nuts, and asked me if I had plans for the evening. Reading, that was my plan become the reality that I was enjoying. Get up, go out and dance, get drunk, do anything but your devotions to your vocation—which is your avocation and your calling—which makes you happy. As an undergraduate at Sarah Lawrence College, I discovered Havelock Ellis, father of sexology, in the all but empty library. I spent hours at a desk in the stacks, embarrassed by my bliss, hoping that no one would see me or search for a book in my hideaway. I relaxed in the company of thousands of books, feeling at home and secure. My Havelock Ellis retreat occurred between a Friday morning and a Sunday night. On weekends a lot of the students left for New York City, only fifteen miles south of Sarah Lawrence, located in Bronxville, or for another campus, like Wesleyan or Yale, where their boyfriends attended school. On another Sarah Lawrence weekend a couple of years later, I was lying on a couch where I lived, in the second-floor living room of one of the mansions that served as dormitories, reading *Anna Karenina*, stopping only to eat. Reading was my frequent weekend passion.

From my preteens into my forties, before Mom and Dad moved from our 90 Riparian house, I read all afternoon in the library on the top floor—when I lived at that address and when I visited there, as a student residing on the East Coast, then in Chicago, and as a professor in different cities. I varied my positions on the sofa, napped occasionally, thought a lot, and let the fairies take me anywhere they wished. No wonder that I found freedom in the Sarah Lawrence and University of Chicago libraries. In those libraries, at 90 Riparian Road, and at schools, I learned the names and the ideas of Ellis's contemporaries and descendants—such as Sigmund Freud, Alfred Kinsey, William Masters and Virginia Johnson, and Shere Hite—and of art critics and art historians and of nineteenth-century painters, poets, and novelists. I felt at home becoming a philosopher of sex who sighed in the aesthetics of orgasm and other signs of life. Sometimes Mom found me in our library and, always polite, asking if she could come in and waiting for my Yes, sat down beside me on the sofa or, by herself, on the wing chair, the deco desk chair, or the light ash, molded-plywood Eames dining chair with metal legs. In the library, she opened some of our most intimate conversations, often about her or Dad's family. A small anxiety or annoyance accompanied my switching from the eros of books to the eros of mother-daughter relations, from one kind of enchanted concentration to another. I loved the state of absorption, so moving from one to another, despite the pleasures of each, demanded a deliberate waking up, as if from a dream that I wished to prolong.

In the 90 Riparian library, the fairies and I listened to summer winds and thunderstorms, anticipated delicious meals from the aromas of the stewing, roasting, or grilling meat that Dad was preparing, and heard his calls to Ren and Mom and me that dinner was ready.

The family library lingers with me, like Mel's sweetness and exemplary freedom. At home in Reno during the summer and autumn of 2000, I re-created the pleasures of that library, one of the most important places where I learned the aesthetics of love. I relived and renewed my bookish pleasures, which the sage commander used for achieving victory without battle.

To use one's wits is to be attuned to *shih*, so that, as Sun Tzu counsels, one can achieve victory without battle. The sagest commander outwits self-destruction as much as he outwits destruction of towns, lands, and bridges. Being brave requires the action that is stillness—observing details, recognizing patterns—so that the sage commander does not misread the contiguities and contingencies of the moment through preconceived, misshapen goals. In a sense, the hero wants nothing. Like Shane, the hero in the eponymously titled western. Joey, a boy who worships Shane, witnesses his hero's interaction with a bad guy. Joey asserts, "Shane, I know you ain't afraid." The bad guy asks Shane, "What do you want?" "Nuthin'," replies Shane.

Wanting nothing, the hero does what is necessary. And doing what is necessary, he wants nothing. Attuned to *shih*, hair parted wherever it may be, the hero can do nothing but what is necessary. Shane's and the sage commander's "nuthin'" precludes fear. "Nuthin'" makes freedom possible.

Velvet Goldmine is simultaneously a tribute to personal freedom and a tragedy about the failure of personal freedom to change the world. Just minutes from the film's end, Curt gives Arthur the green brooch, Haynes's recurring symbol of fairy freedom. Arthur finds the jewelry in his beer after Curt leaves the back room of a bar where they have been conversing implicitly about freedom. Ten years after his glam rock escapades, Arthur the journalist has been attempting to track down Curt in order to interview him about the mysterious disappearance of Brian Slade from the music scene and from the lives of everyone who knew him when he was the glam idol. During the glam years, Curt and Brian had been infamous lovers. Infamous lovers, infamously free. Curt and Arthur, the fan, had been lovers too, but only for one night. In the bar's back room, which is empty except for the two men, Curt gives no obvious sign to Arthur that he remembers him, although an image from memory of their rooftop lovemaking—whether Curt's or Arthur's or both men's isn't clear—indicates that Curt may recognize Arthur. Then, with a poignancy that gave me chills, Curt bequeaths the emerald brooch to Arthur.

Arthur smiles wide with amazed glee on discovering the pin in his beer and looks up in the direction of Curt, who has left. The gift reminds Arthur who he is, what he can be, no matter how gray and unsmiling he and his world have become, and, in voice-over, Arthur remembers: "He called it a freedom." "He" is Curt, and "it" is infamous fairy sex. Next, looking into his own past, Arthur sees himself happy—full of an easy grin, stretching out on a mattress on the rooftop. The image sparkles, with the city sunlight and with the sunniness of fairy freedom. Back to the bar, where we witness the reawakening of Arthur's fairy consciousness, which includes his words (in voice-over): "A freedom you can allow yourself. Or not." Any freedom is just that kind of freedom.

Earlier in Curt's and Arthur's veiled yet intimate conversation, the journalist draws out a confession of disappointment from his once (and maybe still) dream lover: "We set out to change the world and ended up . . . just changing ourselves." But that is where changing the world begins and continues, in the bravehearts that open up to their own kind and others, after having first opened up to themselves.

Who *was* that witch flying around our family's backyard garden in my childhood dream? That garden was *mine*. It was me, my sexuality, and she invaded it and terrorized it. Who *were* the Nazi torturers who sorely bruised my toes in the other dream recurring when I was a little girl? So sore, but I could walk if I tried. I could walk in my garden. Let me be. Be in my garden. Be my garden. Let me be the entire territory of my paradise. I say paradise rather than utopia. I say paradise in contrast to the dystopia that I experienced after the Sexual Revolution. The witch looked like a stereotypical Halloween hag; so my unconscious appropriated her big nose. Nosey me. Dad liked describing me as "curious." I nosed into sex, inadvertently when I surprised my parents fucking in their bedroom, with deliberate delight when I masturbated in a robe or in my mother's furs and lipstick, when I looked into mirrors to see the garden that I'd grown. Despite the witch, despite the Nazis, despite my parents' beginning to sleep in separate bedrooms sometime in my teens.

Like a Nazi, like an evil witch, I attacked. In my thirties, assessing my sexual and romantic history and at some of my continuing ways with men, I called myself a bulldozer. The bulldozer backed off a lot in her forties, and I no longer use the name. For years, however, I compensated with manly boldness for my inability to flirt. I was "too direct" for a woman. I showed my honesty and my integrity, not only sexually—I spoke my attraction to a man before he spoke any attraction to me—but also intellectually and emotionally. Maybe I flirted just fine, and maybe I was light—for a while. Then I forged ahead fast, I forced, and that caused failure after failure. "Nuthin'" was pretty much a mystery to me.

One night, in the throes of my curiosity, I looked from Mandy and Potter's bed at my clothes on the floor as though they belonged to another woman, one who had not bothered to be herself. Even then, my eyes softened and almost closed when I heard Potter's voice, "You're like a pillow inside. Not all women are that way, and I feel like I can ride on and on forever." Ah . . . a woman whose vagina tilted in the direction most preferred by men?

Ah . . . a woman whose cunt was full and rich and soft and welcoming.

Painful example after painful example of my simultaneous desire and dislocation from intimacy occurred after Jason and I decided to marry, then decided not to, and I lived alone. My motif of misery in my twenties worried my parents, who saw their daughter as a drifter from one lover to another.

The straw that broke this camel's back, this sexual beast of my own burden, fell after I invited a smart and lovely looking classmate to my apartment to study. He showed up, and my only memory of our evening is my failure to sleep with him. Around that time I experienced rages, few and quickly passing but effective in their ability to show me that seeking help made a lot of sense. I raged only in my apartment. One time I threw an umbrella down the hallway, then got pissed, then laughed because it bent so that I couldn't use it again. I might have thrown things a couple of other times, but nothing breakable, like china. One day in the tiny hallway of my apartment, between the living room and the kitchen, next to the bathroom entrance, across from the front door, a craziness enveloped me, a whirling cloud from within that then enwrapped me. Dizzy, spiraling, I may have placed my hands and forearms against the cool wall, to steady myself from falling further into my atmospheric funk. In that position, I could have as easily banged my head against the wall. I may have started to, but pressed my crown or forehead very hard against the wall instead. Out of my panic and my frantic muddle, words repeated many times. What am I doing? What am I doing? I knew that I was questioning my actions with men. Very soon after that episode, I called Dr. Fajardo.

I loved my healer Stephen's metaphor for the release of my heart in Dr. Fajardo's care—that he had let the genie out of the bottle. Stephen's comment surprised me, and I agreed, "Yes, he did." I began to know, Here I am. Here I stand. The genie with a freer heart liked to walk barefoot on the ground. She liked to move.

Women's containment of their gestures and postures is not a new idea. I've been intrigued by considerations given to it by the feminist philosophers Iris Young and Susan Bordo, but I first came across the idea in my early thirties.

Soon after I read about women's ways of taking up less space than men, I was sitting on a couch leaning forward, my feet about a yard apart on the floor so that my legs were spread. A man said to me, "That's an aggressive position." I assumed from his comment that I was projecting manliness, but I was simply being comfortable, inadvertently displaying phallic well-being in an extremely feminine self-presentation: lipstick, long hair, garnet earrings, my gold birthday ring wrought like a serpent, a sweater and pants that fit me snugly, shoes with a short, curvaceous heel.

I have attributed my increased phallic well-being, in my fifties, to the regularity of my bodybuilding over the previous two decades. My muscles weren't big, but the pleasure I felt and saw in their evident denseness caused me to swagger in the gym. Yet, that reasoning was unsatisfactory because obvious; the swaggering belonged to a larger complex of manliness that my parents' deaths enabled me to articulate. Also, I began to swagger while walking city streets or shopping or entering the classrooms where I was teaching, to move with a joyfully masculine rhythm. My hips swayed too, in a more than simplistically feminine pleasure. My phallically flirting and feminine hips said, Fuck me if you dare. Because my stride made it clear that I was the one who wanted to initiate the fucking, that I was the dominant male. *Swagger* probably derives from Norwegian dialect *svagra*, to sway in walking, and *Webster's New World Dictionary* defines swagger in masculine terms: a bold or lordly walk. I swayed with the intoxication of being a man. I never thought of myself as sister to the models who strutted the catwalk, though all of us were consciously displaying our sensuality.

In the summer of 2000, as I walked to the gym drinking fountain and toward the mirror behind it, which were forty feet away, I noticed that I was Braveheart. In the gym I pictured my long hair ornamented with braids like Wallace's, and as I swaggered toward my reflection, I admired my defined jawline, the beautiful bone structure of my face, I admired my pride.

In order to protect my pride, I pleased myself. *Hero* derives from the Avestan *haraiti*, (he) protects. The hero protects his beliefs, which include his family, his country, his soul-and-mind-inseparable-from-body. The hero pleases because he offers erotic inspiration. Not by giving us lovemaking methods. Rather, by being brave, beautiful, and crazy, as Auntie Entity describes Mad Max in *Thunderdome*. The hero is the patriot of eros, a new man's and woman's land of possibilities for being truly human. The hero's craziness stems from a sacred independence:

he is outstandingly noble of character, he has the skills for killing, and he still can doubt himself and cry obvious tears, which distort his generally placid, yet expressive, beauty, when members of his family have been killed or he suffers betrayal. Such sacred independence should put to rest the convention of a hero who is violent, cruel, and stupid, who is anything but a gentle patriarch.

Mel, you were my patriot, my fellow countryman in eros.

Heroes please us when they are as big as they can be. I admired Martin's erotic charge, though I was appalled when he appears, a gory ghost, from the waist up, shirt more red than white, someone else's blood revealing to our massively unknown selves the extent of a hero's suffering and the mess that even he can make of his wished-for-but-gone-wrong redemption. (After the French and Indian War, Martin's compatriots lauded him as a hero, but he despised himself for massacring fellow human beings. Ever since, he has kept his self-hatred as secret as he can, but no longer can he manage that when called to fight in the colonists' war against the British.) Martin in his reddened shirt is a mess—of sweat and dirt and trauma. In another scene, he subtly backs off, in a gesture resembling a turning of the other cheek. Gently, gently, he resurrects his faith in himself. In *The Road Warrior*, Mad Max has been badly hurt and his untrustworthy sidekick—nothing like a Pancho to a Cisco Kid or a Jingles to a Wild Bill Hickok—is flying our erotic compatriot to relative safety over enemy territory. Wow! Max's magnificent and bloody face high above a desertful of the manic enemy's vehicles stunned me. Porter, as manly as can be, walks up an outdoor, urban stairway with a gait between malaise and nonchalance. He's heading for a heroin dealer's hangout. Smoking a cigarette, he takes a drag, then tosses it. James Brown is singing his poignant ballad "This Is a Man's World" as Porter ascends, in a stark light and with an understated fierceness. "Something fierce": that's how Dad described weather so passionate that it could stop a person in his car or in his tracks. Fierceness and stark light elevate a bleak urban scene of several seconds, in which a criminal hunts his more criminally evil prey, into a fairy crossroads that startled me. I caught my breath, for, a man's world though that scene may be, Iris, messenger of the fairies, wearing her high heels and nothing more, could as easily have been walking up those stairs as Porter.

I noticed Martin's perfectly manicured hands. He's sitting in a forest militia camp, and the citizen soldiers have been away from their homes for long enough that we could expect their dirty, ragged fingernails to loom in close-ups of their hands. Martin's manicure is better than the ones I gave myself.

Big heroes, because they're glamorous, can act like femmes fatales, whose erotic dazzle proceeds not only from self-trained gestures of allure but also from fastidious grooming. So like the heroes of the big screen.

Mel, I loved your scent. I absorbed it into an animal vision, the irresistible array of a stinking hero.

When Wallace meets the princess for the first time, outside a tent, I imagined that his odor wafts around him and to her. Bathing would not seem to be a regular amenity of fighting Scotsmen, including their leader, who, awakened by the alarmlike voice of Hamish's father announcing the approach of a royal cortege, did not likely perfume or bathe himself before greeting his visitors. When Wallace follows the princess into the large tent, I imagined that his alluring stink all but fills it, depending on where anyone is standing in relation to the air that enters along with him. The princess may be stinking just as much as he is, and scented up the wazoo in order to veil her body's odors. Man and woman, ripe with the erotic currency that only their own bodies can provide. Stinking pretty, they like what they smell, perhaps more than what they see, without even knowing it.

Bellodgia, a hero's scent, my scent. Created by the House of Caron, 10 Rue de la Paix, in 1927. Like musical compositions, perfumes are composed of notes—top, middle, and base. Caron categorizes Bellodgia as a single flower scent, and carnation is Bellodgia's top note. Other categories of perfume contain more than one top note. We may react, as if enchanted by an aphrodisiac, to the narcotic intensity of some florals, and Caron calls Bellodgia's carnation "dazzling." *The Language of Flowers*, a book first published in Great Britain in 1928, gives red carnation the meaning of "Alas for my poor heart," but the scent of carnations lightens my heart. Caron emphasizes that Bellodgia is a "warm vibrant fragrance" inviting us into "fields of carnations drinking in sunshine." A bottle of Bellodgia surprised me on Ren's dresser in my twenties, when I began to wear the scent, which I'd never smelled on her. Mom had given the Bellodgia to Ren, who told me, shortly after Mom's death, that Bellodgia was Gram's signature perfume. I don't remember it on her either, yet every person's own scent makes a bottled one into an original rather than a huge edition.

Bellodgia, a "burst of light," promises Caron, raising the spirits of heroic maids and their progenitors. Bellodgia, an action taken by originals to recharge their fairy spirit.

Mel, you bought me bottles of Bellodgia, each stopper cut just like the "rough diamond" of Caron's description. Cut glass bottles match the sunlight with their reflective splendor, so, Mel, your gift of sunny scent raised me into radiance.

Top notes are the most evanescent of a perfume's composition, although they reach our noses before the middle or base notes. With their strength, top notes seduce us into the body of the perfume — the middle note is known too as the heart note. Base notes, which last longest on the skin and deeply blend with the body's chemistry, also help prolong the other notes. Perfumers often use musk as one of several base notes. Musk comes from male musk deers, small and hornless, native to central Asian uplands. A pouch on the animal's abdomen contains the musk, which has been used by human beings for centuries. Musk is one of Bellodgia's base notes.

Base note on base note, skin to skin, like Mel to me and Wallace to the princess. All four of us stinking with musk's staying power, a few centigrams of it said to fill a hall for years without any failing strength. It is said, too, that sunlight shining on some famous mosques brings out, in the interiors, the musk that builders mixed with mortar over a thousand years ago. *Mel, my musky legend, graceful as a deer in the high country that is home, you smelled like a real animal.* Today most of the musk in base notes is synthetically created. Even in the 1860s authors wrote of the extinction of the musk deer. Some say the deer can live after a hunter has removed its pouch, and I've read that costly perfumes, made by masters of *haute parfumerie*, use musk from the real source — a secret guarded like the erotic provocation that Wallace and the princess cause each other.

Recently, a man I sat next to on a plane was wearing a scent that provoked me to ask him what it was. We'd been talking for a long time already, flirtatiously, and the first thing he said after I asked was, "Is it too strong?" A woman's question more than a man's; but this man knew his fairy self. "No, not at all, it's lovely," I complimented him. "Boucheron." I breathed its gentle, manly glamour as he spoke its name.

Certainly, Gibson's heroes throughout his career protect an ultimate manliness glamorized in Western civilization's gender designs. Consequently, Wallace, Porter, Martin, and other characters through which Mel made his appearances are in danger of the emotional and aesthetic deficiency that signals kitsch, which is a simpler pleasure than camp. Mel could have dazzled me simply, with a beauty that was mere manly charm. Mel *was* penis/phallus extraordinaire, like Nick in *What Women Want*. A coffee shop counter girl played by Marisa Tomei asks Nick if he's ordering a Tall or a Grande, and he responds, "Grande. At least, I like to think so." Yet Mel also protected as if he were the embodiment of motherhood, by providing and sacrificing. That can be as kitsch as masculinist phallic grandeur. However, because Mel's in-the-bodyness exceeded gender designs, he was as much a poem as he was a fictive person played in my mind by a grandly attractive man. That poem was the cognitive body, which persuaded me to fall in love with Mel and to heal my hostilities with men. Healing was my mission.

Action heroes have missions. Indeed, they need missions and feel restless, even nuts, without one. An arresting example is Martin Sheen's Vietnam hero Captain Benjamin L. Willard in Martin Scorsese's 1979 *Apocalypse Now*. Willard's desperate drinking, smashing of objects in his Saigon hotel room, and wildly panicked appearance result from the fact that he has not yet been assigned his mission. Clearly, he's crazy enough to begin with because soldiering in Vietnam has become his obsession, but not having a mission sends him over the edge.

Willard's simultaneously heart-stopping and heart-revving mission is to locate and kill Colonel Walter E. Kurtz (an exceptionally enigmatic Marlon Brando), whose brilliance and whose torment over the war led him to lead himself, away from his superiors' orders and into mythic status as a charismatic and brutal guerrilla commander—for the enemy. Before Kurtz turned against his country, his status in the minds of the army officers who give Willard his orders was good-boy action hero. However, when Willard finds Kurtz, the decorated action hero has become a Buddha-like figure. He sits by himself, he barely moves. No action. And a Buddha would not condone or order killings and mutilations as Kurtz does. No action and no enlightenment.

I began to comprehend Dad as an action hero when I watched *Gladiator*. Maximus finds his wife and son dead, hanged by Roman soldiers. A passionate and devoted husband and father, his emotional breakdown on seeing their blackened bodies conveys the dire vulnerability of paternal and spousal love and of some men's absolute motivation to protect their loved ones, whose death motivates avenging phallic power.

"You killed my brother, Jerry." Dad gave us that line, his parody of the motivation of heroes in westerns. Dad loved westerns, so his parody came from appreciation and identification, and he told a story, every once in a while, about defending his younger brother Karl from bullies when they were kids. Don't hurt my brother, Jerry. Don't mess with my family. That theme recurs throughout action films. To please my family, I protect them. Ren and I agree that *Shane* was Dad's favorite western, then *High Noon*. In both films, the heroes display uncommon moral fortitude. More than Wallace does. But not more than Mel.

The fin-de-siècle femme fatale of symbolist art and literature and the cowboy of western movies, both fabled and larger-than-life outsiders, each embodying a gender extreme, respectively drew me and Dad to identify with them. The woman's woman with her red lips and carnivorous flair for seduction, the femme fatale is also a gentleman's lady, perfectly mannered when she pleases. The male's male with his leather sexiness — holster, jacket, vest, chaps, boots — is also a lady's man, the kind and generous icon of patriarchal politeness, who pleases women with the grace of his protectiveness, whether his lust or courtship is bold or bumbling. Plugged with holes — from gunshots — he becomes a bloodred beauty.

Within seconds of *Payback*'s opening, Porter's bloodred back fills the screen, except for his bullet-split shirt that frames the two gunshot wounds at the center of the composition. A dubiously prepared doctor removes a bullet and plops it in a glass, where Porter's blood mixes with whiskey. Much later, when he bleeds from his toes, Porter's blood again adorns him. Wallace's most stunning adornment is his own and others' gore. Blood is a fugitive pigment as it dries, cracks, and lightens. Lingering on the skin, it leaves a trace or can be rubbed off. But either we are not aware of these states or processes or we never see them in Gibson's films. High gore, like a carefully chosen and skillfully applied rouge or lipstick, makes the body of many of Gibson's heroes more expressive than they would be in their natural state, maximizes their effect as both terrors and seductions.

Bloodlust can lead to overkill, which may be war. But overkill may also be cosmetic excess or intensity, such as unrelenting red, a look that succeeds, if it does at all, through intimidation. I imagine that Mel's bloodred cosmetic overkill magically defends him from death, and that it turns him at times almost into a war god, like Mars, or into the destroyer goddess Kali, archetypal Mother (who gives birth to human flesh and then devours it). Kali's worship demanded blood sacrifice, and the Mahanirvanatantra tells us that because Kali "chews all things existing with Her fierce teeth, . . . a mass of blood is imagined to be the apparel of the Queen of the Gods at the final dissolution." The *divine* Wallace, worshipped in *Braveheart* by his fellow Scots, is also the divinely campy queen of bloodred beauties, who are not only bloodied, real-life warriors but also the femmes and hommes fatales whose scarlet lipstick signals that they may be hunters of sex action or other forms of erotic vivacity. Mel knew how to wear his reds, and he was a lovely predator, like the femme and homme fatale. He looked as dauntingly tantalizing as the homoerotic spectacle Jiro Sakamoto, a bloodied beauty, in Pierre et Gilles's *Les Plaisirs de la forêt*, a 1996 series of photographic works enhanced by paint, works that meld the horrifically haunting qualities of both fairy tales and Sade. Pinned in the center of a vignetted forest that sparkles as if covered with spider webs or sunny droplets after a rain, the young, well-muscled Sakamoto appears to be immobilized by vines that twine and cross in front of him. Rivulets of blood decorate him like flowing garnets from head to knees.

Blood and smoke; fire and yelling. Beautiful men, dying men, weeping men. Dead bodies. These are the apocalyptic and aesthetically thrilling viscera of cinematic success, and we love them because they make up narratives of calling, mission, and passion, stories embedded in conditions and directions that many people feel are minimal or missing in their own lives. The narratives of Ridley Scott's 2001 spectacle *Black Hawk Down*, as well as those of *Gladiator* and *Braveheart*, create catharsis, dispelling our emotional tensions until daily life resumes its pressures.

Braveheart worked cathartically for me after my mom's death, and its hold on me was rooted in the film's visually and emotionally aesthetic moments, the kinds of moments that compelled me, too, in *Black Hawk Down* and *Gladiator*. In *Black Hawk Down*, helicopters punctuate gray blue sky over a dun-colored Mogadishu from which biblically magnificent pillars of smoke are rising: the melancholy beauty of that image stayed with me more than did anything else in the movie. One of the most exquisite and powerful beginnings of any film I've seen is the first twelve minutes of *Gladiator*. A man's hand glides through a wheat field, tenderly touching the tops of the stalks. Next we're in an Imperial Roman military camp with soldiers preparing for battle, and we learn that the man whose body so gently loved the natural world is Maximus, the general who will soon lead his troops to victory. The atmosphere is cold, wintry blue, a light snow falls now and then over the brutalities, and the magic of these opening scenes, replete with the anticipation, longing, and despair of the hero or of the troops to whom the hero belongs stirred in me the beginnings of an altered state that is the warrior's.

Those ecstatic feelings existed in tandem with discomfort, because the site of longing and despair is home to the indigenous enemy, the barbarian Somalians and Germanians, the North Vietnamese in *Apocalypse Now*. *Barbarus*, from which *barbarian* derives, is Latin for *strange* and *foreign*. The barbarian is the stranger to the empire of the West, be it Rome or the United States. The stranger bleeds, yells, and dies, but the empire sees the stranger as part of a grisly landscape or a desolate city. The stranger blends into the world created by the empire, while the hero stands out from it. The stranger is camouflage—and chaos—but his camouflage does not protect him from the empire's representation of its own as human and of the barbarian as a lesser being. Imperialist film portrays barbarians as exotic fauna, most valued when dead, waiting for an autopsy that will never happen. *Braveheart* presents the barbarians' story, so it normalizes their ruthless militancy, and following the convention of the "You killed my brother, Jerry" imperialist film genre, the enemy are exotic fauna.

The mayhem of smoke, blood, and death in action films dispirited me—even though at times I wished to travel to wasted places when Mom, Dad, and my marriage were dying—but it simultaneously motivated me to caress the rose and iris petals in my garden.

Maximus bleeds, yells, and dies. However, his weeping scene stunned me more than all the gladiatorial showiness. Sobbing as he gazes at the corpses of his wife and child, who have been savaged by Roman soldiers, Maximus becomes heartbreakingly human—because his loss manifests not only in tears but in the mucus that leaks from his nose, that he does not wipe away. The memory of his wife and son drive his later gladiatorial brilliance: You killed my brother, Jerry, and I am the hero as avenging angel.

In the end, Wallace, like Maximus, dies, yet filmic action heroes succeed again and again at escaping death, the vulture. This is a large part of their romance, for preceding their escape they intensively lower their guard to the vulture. They seem to welcome her, sometimes even to salute her. The sign of the vulture meant *mother* in ancient Egyptian. Such salutations leave Wallace and Maximus emotionally ragged, though (almost) always in a state of preparedness. They are so damn good, the best of Boy Scouts: be prepared. Unfortunately, in that state one is a refugee, because no place on earth is safe from the vulture. But, as Tom Petty dares us, in his "Refugee," you don't have to live like one. "Refugee" is the perfect action hero's anthem: all of us are pitched for battle, fighting for our freedom. Maximus and his gladiator brethren could sing Petty's anthem before battle, and Wallace could lead his troops in a raucous rendition completed by their bending over, skirts flung up, buttocks bared to the English soldiers — an image that *does* appear in the film.

— Walden, Mel, and I, like Captain Kathryn Janeway in *Star Trek Voyager* — all up against the shitfire of gender norms. I wonder why I had trouble being Captain Walden when she was mowing down Iraqis or Janeway when she was negotiating with the Federation's most monstrous nemesis, the Borg. I'm with Kathryn all the way when she stands up to Borg threats, stands her ground, knows where she stands, and I'm with Karen all the way when she orders one of her fear-fried soldiers, "Give me my weapon," after she's been wounded and he's assumed a control to which he has no right. I'm listening when she yells, "We're gonna make us a perimeter. Rip out everything from inside [the helicopter]."

I wanted Karen to make me a perimeter, too, so I could isolate myself inside it. Then I realized that all the movies I watched over the summer following Mom's death were a perimeter. I realized that, more than anything else, weariness from my sorrow, a seemingly irreparable exhaustion that my parents' deaths flung from my heart onto the surface of my consciousness, surrounded me in a pathetic but necessary protection. I didn't feel comfortable in Janeway's or Walden's body because "Do it" from their lips, while obeyed, conjures up an enemy — temptress, mother, nag — for a culture afraid of women who say what they want. Usually one defies enemies, even if one respects them. In my hostility to men, I defied their desire for me. I feared that they would misinterpret any friendliness as a sign of *my* desire. *Mel, no one could question your motives.*

Martin Riggs is the lethal weapon in the four *Lethal Weapon* films. Gibson's manic Riggs, maddened by his wife's death in a car accident, turns deadly, overly happy to throw himself, literally, into excessively dangerous professional situations. With a ripped-up soul-and-mind-inseparable-from-body that doesn't allow for much perimeter building, Riggs is decidedly out-there, a man whose boundaries are dangerously permeable. Or maybe he's all perimeter, one crazy bundle of unconscious self-protection. But he's actually not crazy at all. At the end of *Lethal Weapon*, the first of the series, Riggs confesses to Danny Glover's Roger Murtaugh, the cop who is Riggs's partner and friend, that he, Riggs, isn't really crazy. (In my twenties I asked Dad if I seemed crazy. His "No" disappointed me, because I thought you had to be crazy to be an artist. At the same time, having Dad confirm my sanity flooded me with relief, at least for the time being.) Murtaugh responds that he knows Riggs isn't crazy. The interchange between the two is one of their many intimate moments in the four movies, and it acknowledges the likelihood that Riggs has consciously built a convincing facade of craziness in order to keep people out of his emotional life. A couple of months after Mom died, I wondered if people went crazy if they didn't or couldn't deal with a loved one's death because the perimeter of soul-and-mind-inseparable-from-body is so fragile that you have to find new ways to constitute yourself. Reconstitution as a man may seem unnecessary, but it helped me to be more solid, less permeable. I preferred to sit and chat with Iris on a rainbow, not throw myself off one.

Men's bodily perimeters are more solid than women's. While women armor themselves with femininity, such as makeup, form-fitting clothes, distinctively coiffed hair, and sassy sandals and Mary Janes, such accoutrements may only shield women from the unwanted vulnerability that living in a female body brings, a vulnerability that ensues from a cultural condition imposed by men's fantasies about women and by men's desire for women's bodies. This vulnerability is operative regardless of a woman's age or whether people evaluate her as beautiful or not. Feminine paraphernalia has given some women, like me, a sense of power akin to self-protection, the idea that they have control over men; because we women have a pleasurable control over some aspects of an all-too-lovable and all-too-punished, both fearsome and fulsome sexuality that resides more in myths about the temptress's magically animal flesh than in the reality of individual women's magically animal bodies.

The princess in *Braveheart*, like all feminine females, is a woman in spite of herself. Because looking that feminine is an art. Some women endure femininity only under pressure, like Ren, and their animality develops differently from the princess's and mine, for femininity appears to cover up the animal, while masculinity appears to let it exist more loosely; even though masculinity certainly styles facial and head hair and the etiquette of grunts, belches, alcoholic indulgence, and horniness. Women, of course, fart, drink, and lust, but femininity forces, or perhaps lures, men to search for female animality and for female masculinity. When a female's animality and masculinity radiate through her femininity, which might happen because she enjoys an interplay of essence — animality — and artificiality (structures civilizing that essence in highly mannered ways), then the erotic climate of her bodily perimeter, like Mel's, is extensive.

In a deli where I was killing time, I watched men in their twenties exercising their bodily perimeters. I laughed just a little at their gloriously prosaic show of masculinity, and I shook my head a bit, so that no one would notice it, in an acknowledgment that was also mind-boggled disbelief: the young men's gestures and facial expressions manifested a sex's history. The customers' activities distracted me from an inadvertent meditation on gender. They were imbibing beer and soda, eating sandwiches, and rooting for players in a baseball game on an overhead TV. The customers were all male, as the workers were too, and trivial though the young men's gestures and facial expressions could seem in that working-class Long Island hangout, I suddenly perceived all of their articulations of corporeal masculinity to be mimicking those of elders. The bodies of male elders educated the sons' bodies, indoctrinated younger male bodies in masculinity. Obvious as that appears to be, it gave me a chill, as if I'd been invaded by a spectral horror which was also a material truth that will never die. The process by which that indoctrination happens is mostly unconscious. Likewise, female bodies indoctrinate younger female bodies in femininity, like Mom with Ren and me. The horror of those indoctrinations is that no gendered gesture is trivial, because it has a history passed not only from one generation to another but linked, I was contemplating, to centuries if not millennia past. If that is true, then the young men in the deli moved like the young Scots who actually fought alongside William Wallace or in gladiatorial groups in the Roman Colosseum or like a macho Caravaggio. (How did Hatshepsut walk when she was pharaoh? Was it different from the walk of other royal women in the Eighteenth Dynasty? Why have Margaret Thatcher and Hillary Clinton incited such dislike? Surely their politics are not the sole cause.)

The conclusions that I was drawing from my meditations in the deli over lemonade were probably wrong. Men across time and cultures couldn't all have similar gestures and expressions just because they were men. Costume and custom differ too much. Yet the history of a severely gendered sex is surely embedded in its contemporary progeny. Men are surely a living history of their sex, of its moribund ways of being, which are often its self-flatteries. In the Long Island deli, this living history of the heterosexes entranced as much as terrified me. I saw, transcending the ages, a majestic and heartbreaking story, a true romance—of the dopey fairy princess kind—a romance set in so many of our bodies, composed of gestures that became necessary and are still so for people's psychic survival and for the survival not of the species but rather of the severely gendered sexes.

My mother's body educated me in femininity, and it took, big-time. However, if gender can be performed, as Judith Butler and other queer-theory scholars have philosophized, then I could mimic Mel as convincingly as the next guy, who was mimicking his dad. I could de-gender and re-gender an elemental aspect of my appearance. Elemental—the word interfered with my faith and inhibited my fantasy of de-gendering and re-gendering. Elemental: basic, foundational, primary—embedded. I could never be Wallace, or my husband, my student, or my Dad, none of whom had to (so) deliberately learn expressive masculinity. For me, it could only ever be an overlay if not an imposition. Still, Mel, my thoroughly modern muse of masculinity, I settled so comfortably into your body, as lightly as a hummingbird into my honeysuckles' nectar.

One of Mel's laughs was very big, it was as open as a child's. I liked laughing with you, Mel, when your soul unsealed so joyfully. My favorite laughing episode in a Gibson film occurs in What Women Want, his only romantic comedy. The scene takes place after Gibson's Nick Marshall has gained the ability to read women's minds. Nick and his business associate Darcy McGuire, played by Helen Hunt, are falling for each other, and when, in the office, she finds her eyes at his crotch and silently admonishes herself—"Oh, God, I just looked at his penis!"— Nick's genial hilarity enticed my soul-and-mind-inseparable-from-body.

Laughter flows, like the speech of a professor on a logorrheic roll. Nurse derives from the Greek naien, to flow. Mel, my muse, you nursed me to a new health, one I never knew before, the one that is only possible for midlife people who have experienced the recent death of both their parents. Mel could have been a femme fatale, cold as could be to damn his enemies, and the femme fatale as muse may encourage eloquence in obsessed lovers because she has driven them—who may be enemies, who *are* her hosts — into a hellish ecstasy. But Mel was mostly a sweet hero, the muse who helped me open my study curtains the July after my mother died so that I could see the birds, the junipers that I'd freshly pruned, and the yarrow, whose Latin name is *Achillea*, a plant with the same name as the hero Achilles. Mel helped me watch the bees at the daylilies, something I'm sure Dad did while having his late summer afternoon scotch on the rocks while he sat on the white metal bench that circled a huge oak at the bottom of a little hill near the kitchen of our 90 Riparian Road home. Me, I sat the summer after Mom died with sage tea or un-iced water and a lemon slice, observing the lilies or soothed by other observances that I'm sure had pleased my father in his own garden; and Mel activated all of those ritualistic pleasures. He also helped me to discover a meaning of *old maid*, a meaning I thought up that pays attention to the oxymoronic aspect of the term. A maid is radiant because she is full of life, and that vitality creates her beauty. My invented old maid is a midlife or older woman who possesses that vivacity, like Catherine Deneuve in *Indochine*, like me as I came back to myself.

In this revivification, young as well as midlife Mel's beyond-gendered gestures and my own were corporeal cohabitants. We shared my manhood and my new old maidenhood. Moved by *The Year of Living Dangerously*, Gibson's 1982 film, I realized that his character, the journalist Guy Hamilton, smokes a cigarette the way I would if I smoked, that he slumps in a chair the way I did; and the sexual innuendo of his movements and postures astounded me because it is mine. Or, even if it wasn't mine, I wanted it to be or I felt that it was, because Mel's body — derived from Gibson's — was so present in my own. The sexual innuendo of Mel's doing and being excited me and highly eroticized and aestheticized my self-perception. Late in the movie Gibson plays the classically feminine body, passive and vulnerable. He's been wounded in one eye, a bandage covers both eyes, and he lies flat on his back, arms at his sides, naked to the beltline of his pants. He asks the person whose footsteps he hears, "Are you here to kill me?" But Hamilton is in a position to be taken or kissed as much as killed, and the first two options interest me. (Without bandages!) I loved sitting on top of a man who was flat on his back, I loved to watch his arms reach over his head — of his own accord or at my request — to pin him down with my strength, palm to palm, my back thighs to his groin, and then to fuck and kiss him.

I loved to do that with Mel, even though he was stronger than I and much more muscled than his younger self. I loved to be his man while he was simultaneously being mine. In that state of gender, we were each other's gladiator, shining, free, not fighting for anything.

With an amusement bordering on sarcasm, Bordo challenges *Braveheart*'s theme of freedom. She doesn't believe that freedom comes in the package of romanticized inspiration—the recently deceased father's guidance to his son William in the latter's dream, "Yer heart is free. Have the courage to follow 'er." Bordo critiques Wallace, the icon of macho moral stamina, when he preaches, screams, fights, and dies for freedom. She doesn't believe that freedom or agency is so simply chosen as we are led to feel by either *Braveheart* or other vehicles of popular culture, such as advertisements for self-improvement products. I agree with her that free choice is a complicated matter, that individual psychology along with social imperatives—to be fit, beautiful, and go-getting, to just "Do it!"—interfere with any absolute or free-and-easy freedom to do as one wishes or to be a hummingbird in nectar. Yet Wallace must *fight* for freedom and must *convince* troops not yet willing to sacrifice their lives that freedom is worth the risk and struggle just to move toward it, let alone attain it.

Of course, *Braveheart* is a corny epic, which means that Wallace's emotions are ridiculously, embarrassingly huge. For me as a viewer they were almost unendurably so. But his emotions' embarrassing epic display reeled me in. My passion when I taught often embarrassed me, as did my direct expression to friends and acquaintances of my love or sexual desire for them. Such expressions could cause trouble. Some people received what I thought was a compliment with such surprise that they didn't speak with me again. I learned to curtail those expressions, but it pained me to do so, to understand that spoken enthusiasm or passion could provoke anxiety in its human object, as if the expression itself called for action, for a performance of equal unrestraint. Admittedly, my unconscious motivation for embarrassing declarations and "confessions" probably consisted of the wish for my object's equivalent response in form and content, which equivocated the free choices made by my passionate personality.

Forceful, confident, or brave expression asserts, "I am." It evokes and carries the lightness of freedom, whether momentary or prolonged. So when Wallace asserts, "I am William Wallace," before the classic, Gibson-directed battle of Stirling in the Sons of Scotland speech, he is a stunning embarrassment. Deities assert, "I am," and in his embarrassing presentness, Wallace, I imagined, could rattle both his troops' and many of his viewers' composure and complacency. "Sons of Scotland," he addresses us all, and his call can encompass daughters as well as sons, for hasn't everyone at least tried to fight for a homeland? Their country, their job, their family, their body, their integrity?

If the psyche is the essence of home, it houses an individual's freedom, or rather her ability to pursue or to unblock that state of soul-and-mind-inseparable-from-body. Wallace, Porter, and Mad Max have no home. Max's postapocalypse Australia is a bleak terrain, a lost homeland. In *Mad Max*, bikers kill his wife and child. In *The Road Warrior*, a group of cynical good guys accept him and welcome his bravery, which Max employs for their benefit; then they betray him. In *Beyond Thunderdome*, a band of children worship Max and provide him a home, but he leaves them. In each movie, he goes it alone, becomes the wanderer or continues as one. After being left for dead by his wife, who shot him, Porter recovers from the wounds and returns to the apartment formerly shared by him and her. Pronto, she's overdosed on heroin. In a succinctly arresting ritual of divorce, he "nails" his wedding band to the wall; her "phallic" instrument of destruction, the needle, penetrates the "vaginal" space created by his ring. He finds a cheesy hotel room. Not only does he know that the room is crappy, but he soon discovers that the henchmen of Bronson, Porter's nemesis, have wired explosives underneath the bed and that they're designed to blow up if he answers the phone. Constant agitation and danger, not to mention imminent disaster and death, shape Porter's psychic habitat. Wallace doesn't have it any better. He tells Murron, before they marry, that he wants to create a family, and he tells older men of the village that he wants to farm and to stay out of "the troubles" with England. He fails. Bereft of wife — and of father and mother long before Murron's death — Wallace fights for Scotland to be for the Scots; he fights in behalf of a state that will be his home, unmarauded by the English; but they capture and torture him before the cause is won. After the first quarter of the movie, most of which takes place in the village or environs where Wallace grew up, we never see him again in the geographic comfort of home. Even Benjamin Martin, the patriarch patriot, must fight to protect his home — house and family. His eldest son ends up dead, and Martin's house burns down, both victims of King George's troops. And Riggs, in the first three *Lethal Weapon* films, is more at home in his partner Murtaugh's house than he is in his own trailer by the Pacific Ocean.

Dead wives and material and psychic homelessness frame the narrative details of Gibson's action heroes' lives. The characters are so deeply male-bonded—Wallace with his troops and his closest friends among them, Riggs with Murtaugh, Martin with the Revolutionary militia—that dead wives prove the characters' heterosexual virility. With marital obligations nonexistent, the characters become freer territory for audience fantasies while implying, for women probably more than for men, that Wallace, Porter, and Riggs are capable of committed devotion to women. Even loners Porter and Max need dead wives. Max the road warrior has been juicy fantasy material for gay men, as Michael DeAngelis elucidates in *Gay Fandom and Crossover Stardom: James Dean, Mel Gibson, and Keanu Reeves*, his study of those stars' appeal for gay audiences. Indeed, Max's leatherman allure contributed to his receiving the gay magazine the *Advocate*'s 1992 "Sissy of the Year" honor, awarded in the June issue. Gibson's hostile comments about gays in a December 1991 interview in the Spanish newspaper El País also won him the *Advocate*'s tongue-in-cheek honor. "Do I sound like a homosexual? Do I talk like them? Do I move like them?" Gibson asks in the interview; and the *Advocate*, which ran a photo of Gibson on its cover, shirtless and pressing fingertips to nipples, responded, "Frankly, Mel, honey, you do!"

Still, Max's history as a husband protects him. Porter's caring attempt to stop his heroin addict wife from using demonstrates his lingering love for her, even after she has screwed him over royally. That, along with the mutual love between him and Rosie, a prostitute, shows his tender side. If he were only a guy out for revenge against the mafialike criminals, "The Outfit," his brutishness, which is both strategic and driven, could repulse a female audience. In Donald Westlake's *The Hunter*, on which *Payback* is based, the protagonist is unredeemed by any intimacies with women, because none exist. *Mel, you had the capacity to hold a woman, in your arms, in your heart, in your soul-and-mind-inseparable-from-body, all of which provided a home for love.* Providing a home for love is often the male movie star's job.

My psyche saw to it that Mel fulfilled his responsibility. But the recurrent dead-wives-and-homelessness motif in Gibson's films disturbed me. I hoped that action heroes needn't be destitute of home, because part of my heroic mission was to establish a new psychic home for myself. The old one, of fifty years, suffered disturbance beyond my parents' deaths; for not only did Russell and I divorce a year and a quarter after Mom died, but less than two months later the government was cautioning Americans to be "vigilant" for any suspicious behavior and "on alert" to any suggestion of unusual activities. The large-scale sadness, loss, and devastation of September 11 compounded my own losses of the previous couple of years and called them into conscious play. In fall 2001, as a new and newly peaceful rhythm came to my life, the unsettling of my country unsettled a new lightness in me. For several weeks I acted the same as in the summer after Mom died and the summer when Russ and I divorced, the summer that had just passed: I often found myself wandering around the house aimlessly, unable to concentrate. Legally, I was dead as a wife, marriage extinguished while the fire of love between me and Russell continued to burn.

The hero of myth and legend leaves or loses his home, faces terrible odds against his life and happiness before he returns, if he ever does. The hero's peace is hard-won. The Greek hero Ulysses is luckier than most. His wife has waited for him, she still loves him, and she's been holding down the fort with mighty wits and will. Even so, home is a changed place on Ulysses's return from his voyage, which is the psyche's trafficking in the seemingly treacherous terrain brought by everyday life.

For everyday life may also bring us a belly full of grace.

5 ─

Iris's Interlude

Over and over during the summer of 2000, my summer of stillness, I felt inundated by a rain, coming from clouds so dense that their edges overran each other, creating a gray white sky. No storm. Just rain that Iris, posed like a fairy pin-up, was always laughing at. Sometimes she swung her top leg back and forth, and watched me. (To her eyes the clouds were transparent.) Maybe she watched *over* me, waiting to give me some divinity's message. I figured she was thinking that I needed to notice the rainbow, to identify with her body, and to hear her laugh, which was neither light as a feather nor tinkling like a tiny bell. Iris's laugh had the pitch and volume of church bells; and as she saw me reading and gardening, sleeping fitfully, and leaning against doorways, so tired by three or four in the afternoon that I could barely move, she kept waiting tenderly for the turning of my head toward her, waiting as a bridge between the earth and heaven to tell me where my parents went. If I'd ingested aconite, I could have flown, like ancient witches attested that they did. I'd have flown to the rainbow and joined Iris, I too dressed only in a pin-up's pumps.

Iris, my hero, who impelled me to action, just a turn of my head. Iris, my sidekick in fairyland.

Three years later, I flew to her side to hear her.

"My synopsis of *Braveheart*.

"Men and tears. The director likes to dwell on the morbid.

"The dead speak, they speak to the living. A hanged boy speaks, a father speaks, a wife speaks, all to the hero and all in his dreams. Like Wallace, who speaks to the living in the movie theater.

"Missing women, missing persons: a dead mother, a dead wife.

"The boy learns Latin, the language of priests and scholars. The boy becomes a priest, preaching to the living in the movie theater.

"Arrows fly, an image of direction — goal. *Flèche* meets flesh.

"'Hold! Hold! Hold! Hold!' commands the hero. 'Now!' Now take aim for anything that intuition and direst necessity tell you is true.

"The hero stands on top of a mountain, and onscreen his head is huge, so his face gives the audience a chance to be spirited away by beauty. He has not lost heart, he never does, but his suffering sets the audience wondering what might be the sufferings of the person in the next seat."

— Iris paused between synopses long enough to laugh with me and pour us glasses of champagne from the bottle she just opened. "A break from gloom," she advised, "even though brave hearts have wings." We drank more than a little and each enjoyed a chestnut truffle, too. Iris licked from her lips the truffle's cocoa coating and gave her synopsis of *Velvet Goldmine*:

"Love changes everything; unless you're a schmuck."

After champagne sprayed out of my mouth because I was laughing, I praised Iris: "Well, I wasn't expecting that!" "Neither was I!" my friend giggled, my down-to-earth messenger of the gods who lived in the soil and the water as much as she did in celestial quarters. Iris, the sexy, empyreal maiden, was also at home in underground and underwater digs. In Irish lore, barrows and mounds signal entries to fairy dwelling places. Fairyland literally isn't heaven. In its upper region, my irises grow, and its deepest subterranean passages belong to the subject that is massively unknown to itself.

I could have listened all day and all night to Iris talk, and smelled her stinking heart. During her synopses and her singing, her perfume reminded me of Tabac Blond, created by the House of Caron ten years earlier than it created Bellodgia. On Caron's Web page Tabac Blond is the "deliberately provocative perfume" that Caron "dared to dedicate" in 1917 to "those beautiful androgynes," the Parisiennes who picked up smoking from American women. The androgyne embodied "the height of elegance" when she "nonchalantly" brought to her lips "a long ivory and mother of pearl cigarette holder," then exhaled "billows of smoky, typically masculine mystery that sworled [sic] around her feminine charms." That androgyne, that fairy chick, that whorled and swirling flower of a man for whom Caron decided "to signal the dawn of women's liberation" by originating "a subtly ambiguous fragrance, that steals leathery top notes from men, and combines them with an eternally feminine floral bouquet." Thank you, Caron, for the scent you describe as "ambivalent sensuality of warm leather and suave flowers," of bedroom trust met with public lust. As Caron explains, "The difference between fumoir and boudoir was wiped out!"

Head note: leather, carnation, linden. Heart note: iris vetiver, ylang ylang. Base note: cedar patchouli, vanilla amber, musk. Like Bellodgia, carnation in the head and musk in the base. Caron exclaims that men love to wear Tabac Blond in its eau de toilette form. Tabac Blond, a scent for women and for men—for fairies—who like their hearts to purr and growl with love.

The week before I shared champagne and truffles with Iris, I ordered Tabac Blond from Jacqueline Parfumerie in San Francisco. I wore it to sigh and ruminate with Iris. Besides knowing the ins and outs of movies, she knew every word my parents ever spoke, and she knew, as well, my every word. Sometimes, uncommon knowledge intimidates its hearer. Yet Iris and I talked together about anything, like the most common girlfriends do. Mutually in the embrace of our own and each other's Tabac Blond, Iris and I agreed to enact a paradox—to love my parents by releasing me from their phrases, maxims, metaphors, and exclamations embedded in my massively unknown self ten thousand times more forcefully than lyrics of a song that one hears in the gym or in the car or in a restaurant some afternoon and then repeats for the rest of the day. Motifs held in the massively unknown self, which is the flesh in which the unconscious lives, so often without our knowing what to do with it because we don't know what it's doing to us.

Iris led me in an incantation whose repetitions I did not keep track of, and as we chanted, she led us too in a dance. Our heads and torsos were describing spirals. So was the design made by our feet, which grazed the ground and seas of fairyland.

Spinning and elated and close to vomiting, I sat alongside her on a rainbow, as she asked. "Close your eyes," she whispered, her suave, warm breath at my ear. "Let my words, which are Florence's words and Erne's, take you where they will. Go with them and let them go."

I closed my eyes.

"Breathe like you do sometimes to help you sleep at night, and I will catch you if you start to fall too fast to earth, and I will keep you seated if you rise too quickly higher than the few clouds overhead."

I slowed my breath, and every bit of her stink was filling me.

Then her church-bell voice sank into my cells to unfreeze emotions so that they fleeted from my body's memory.

"Get my goat. That's too much. A foregone conclusion. Hunky-dory. Neat as a pin. On tenterhooks. Keep your own counsel. Watch like a hawk.

"A month of Sundays. Threw for a loop. Wowie keflowie. Beat all hollow. Just a micket.

"Hot as blazes. Spread like wildfire. Pack a wallop. Something fierce. Hitting like a ton of bricks.

"A tome. Oh, boychikal. Not worth a damn. Like mad. Oh, boychik. Bellyaching. Tortures of the damned. Ye gods and little fishes. Not worth a hill of beans.

"Pipsqueak. Phooey. Ipsy-pipsy.

"Yippee."

I threw up.

That night in a dream Mel appeared, in a pink miniskirt and a jean jacket. His attire surprised me, but it shouldn't have. There he was, the fairy hero dressed for action.

6 ～

Fairy Beauty

My friends knew me as a baker in my thirties, and one of them, Katie, gave me a cake server. She thought it was fitting, considering that I baked cakes for guests, such as herself and her partner Ken when they visited me and Tom, my husband, and I served the cakes with a dinner knife. I loved the elegance of her gift, with its mother-of-pearl handle. Once I baked blueberry muffins and took some to Kate, and I baked chocolate chip cookies a lot as well. When I traveled to New York I always stayed with Serena, and in my thirties I often brought her a tin filled with my chocolate chip cookies. My favorite dessert for dinner guests remained Chocolate Cake Cockaigne. I baked it, too, for Mom and Dad when I returned home to Highland Park for holidays. Dad adored chocolate, so I loved pleasing him with our favorite cake, always made with the maximum amount of baker's chocolate recommended in the recipe — four ounces.

My home was full of fairy beauty. Fairy images and objects surrounded me in my creamy, sunlit habitat.

In the living room a piece of Russell's featured the appropriated photo of a prim and pretty woman, gloved hand barely caressing her cheek. He airbrushed the background the brightest sky blue, a blue like Iris's environment when she was naked on her rainbow.

Almost every night I turned on what I called the "pink lady lamp," a slender, foot-high octagon of glass embossed on four sides with a lithe and long-haired dancing nude.

The pink lady lamp lit up a small section of the living room near the bookshelf that held one of four dolls that I bought in the mid-1980s. Sorting through boxes during the summer of 2000, I discovered the stash of toys. Three of the quartet, in garish colors, brandish warrior gear. I had poised the heroic cutie whose wings span from neck to calves next to a row of art history texts. She looked comic-book brash in purple and pink and a touch of black. One of her sister fairies, a mermaid in silvery blues and greens, presided, from a glass shelf, over the bathroom. The other two stood watch above my desk at school.

In the bathroom over the toilet I push-pinned a white plastic square stamped with a female nude who raises a ball overhead.

A black-and-white photo of me by the photographer Frances Murray, a friend who lived in Tucson, faced into the bathroom door from the hallway. I'm nude except for a dark, shiny loincloth designed by Frances, my arms are raised, like the bathroom beauty queen's, and both my lips and my body are smiling brightly.

The other hallway fairies included Russell's photo on wood, an image borrowed from tattoo flash of a female head swallowing a simultaneously wavelike and reptilian form that suggests a huge and gloriously undulating cock. Equally sexy but less sexual was a photo, probably from the 1940s, of a chorus girl in scanty clothing, arms held high as she sports a set of enormous satin wings. To either side below her were silhouette profiles of Ren and me when we were respectively about seven and six. Below and between the profiles, on a niche built in houses the vintage of mine — 1947 — rested a collage by Marnie Weber. (The niche was built for a telephone and phone book.) Marnie's collage features a hybrid creature, a lovely, kneeling female nude with a book in her lap and a pink bunny head.

More fairies graced my kitchen: a postcard of Dante Gabriel Rossetti's The Holy Grail, with its voluptuously sweet, long-haired, red-lipped sex queen; two 8-ounce glasses decorated with decals of Varga-like nudes surrounded by big golden, pink, and aqua bubbles, some of which they use to coyly cover sexual territory. The seated nude balances one of the translucent balls in her crotch, while the standing nude uses one of the spheres to obscure her breasts.

In my study, I appeared in a photo, conceived by me, designed by me and Russell, and shot by him. With my back to the camera and my hair swept to one side by my hand, I'm naked with Mel. I'm wearing our garnet beads, and the curve of my bare and muscular shoulders visibly defines the sinuosity of my desire for the man in the shower on the television screen in front of me. In actuality, he was Porter in *Payback*, though in my fantasy, the man was Mel. I'm as sensuous as Iris dressed only in her high heels and seated on her rainbow.

Affiliation with my household fairies — showgirls, pin-ups, goddesses of war and eros, beauty queens and beastly nymphs — and love for myself pictured in some of their guises guided me away from parental deaths and the marital separation. We become the words and the images on which we both consciously and unconsciously focus. Fairy beauty: I named it and I repeated the words, and I saw it all around me, so I was wearing my heart on my sleeve; and here, in my book where words constellate images into my fairy being, I continue to enjoy and to display that costume — heart on my sleeve. It healed me. I am bloodred beauty, but my heart isn't bloodied anymore.

— In my teens, Mom described me with the phrase "Still waters run deep." Full to overflowing with the still waters that ran deep, I let go, as the fairies invited me to do. They told me then that fairy beauty, though it is light — buoyant, illuminating, radiant — fills its practitioners with the ability to release their belief in pain and their need to hold onto it. Fairies are so good at letting go. Their grasp of life and death is large, yet everything slips through their fingers. How are they so bold and free? Here is the answer: they flame and sing as they fuck and love. Lucky for us, they purify the human servitude to suffering by showing people how to swoon in beauty.

The fairy man and the action hero create sensations. These may be flames — the flaming queen of Oz-like allure — or filmic explosions — effects at whose peculiarly safe center we find the hero and which my friend Arlene said give her a feeling of release. Arlene is an art critic whose stellar aesthetic responses I paid attention to, so I began to see such explosions as a kind of action painting in process. (The critic Harold Rosenberg coined the term *action painting* to describe the abstract expressionist Jackson Pollock's drip method.) Wallace himself is a flaming queen of warriors, painted in the gorgeous reds of his own and others' blood, looking like an abstract expressionist canvas. In his Sons of Scotland speech he refers ironically to the tales and image of himself, to his own fairy magic circulating in a sensational legend, as he parades, exhorts, and gallops on horseback in front of his troops before going into battle. A couple of them have already voiced what appears to be a larger sentiment, that the Wallace on horseback is not the real thing. "Not tall enough." "William Wallace is seven feet tall." Wallace begins to convince and then inspire the doubters, who, like all the troops, are followers of Wallace the legendary fairy figure. Wallace convinces by acknowledging his flaming power: "If William Wallace were here, he'd consume the English with fireballs from his eyes and bolts of lightning from his arse." *Great balls of fire.* Wallace gets a laugh, for how can anyone resist someone who has lived up to the nineteenth-century art critic Walter Pater's urging to "burn always with this hard, gem-like flame?"

As a scholar of nineteenth-century art and literature, I read Pater in graduate school, and his words stayed with me, in my soul-and-mind-inseparable-from-body. Burning as best I could, I fell in love with a graduate student in my first tenure-track teaching job, at Oberlin College in the small-town fishbowl of Oberlin, Ohio. In 1981, when I became a professor, I was thirty-three. Tom, who became my lover in 1982, and in 1983 my husband, was eight years younger than I. He, too, was a scholar of nineteenth-century art, and he was a flaming beauty. I loved to watch him, from a distance, walking. Lean legs, black hair curling to his shoulders, hunched forward as he sucked on a cigarette.

Raised as a Christian in rural Ohio, Tom believed in the reality of the sacred. The holy flaming beauty of pagan goddesses, particularly Aphrodite and Astarte, goddesses of beauty, love, and sex, claimed my imagination when I was in my twenties, and Aphrodite lived on within me. Joanna the graduate student became as learned as she could about ancient European goddesses. Christ the Savior and Aphrodite the Locus of Love the Redeemer, both shining with their hearts of gold, both represented with the iconography of sacred hearts.

Wallace of the braveheart, the sacred heart, I imagined his anus shooting flames of garnet, my birthstone, the color of venous blood, a gem credited in the Middle Ages with the magic to heal wounds, including those that bleed. While flames from candles, torches, forest fires, and logs in fireplaces fascinate us with either their intimate or awesome beauty, they are all unsteady, because they can be compromised by natural elements, such as earth or water. Maintaining the hard, gem-like flame, which Pater defines as ecstasy, would seem to be almost impossible to accomplish, but according to him, that maintenance "is success in life." It requires a commitment to unceasingly seek sensations of pleasure, in art and life, to live from one *moment* of passion to the next. By becoming utterly vulnerable to passion in the moment, one's flame paradoxically hardens. In the famous words of Baba Ram Dass, "Be here now."

Mel, you crystallized me into garnet.

In the fairy task of burning with a hard, gem-like flame, which for many everyday action heroes — who are all of us — remains pretty much a desire or a yearning, we operate beyond the nature that we believe we know. Beyond the nature that we believe we know, we do not dampen or turn to ash, because, like Iris, we understand the universe to be a compassionate teacher. Unable to be compromised — dampened, turned to ash — we become uncompromising, not stiffly adhering to our principles but, rather, strong enough to bend and soften them so that our hearts don't fall into disrepute. Uncompromising, in the way that Wallace listens to the princess, sent by his enemy Edward the Longshanks, king of England. Wallace disabuses her of Longshanks's lies, and he trusts her through his intuition. The passionate but weakly flaming Robert the Bruce hears from his father, in reference to Wallace, "Uncompromising men are easy to admire." The younger Bruce longs to be like Wallace, and the elder's cautionary words are a beginning to the son's hatred of his father, who again and again poisons and dissipates his son's passion by advising mealy-mouthed compromise.

In contrast, on the night of his father's funeral, Wallace the child dreams of release, from both father and anything that would dampen the young Wallace's flame. As we know, the father urges his son, "Yer heart is free. Have the courage to follow 'er." This counsel could bind Wallace to the father, but it also invites the hero to burn as hard as he can. If the child burns hard enough, he can give himself to a freedom beyond the parent who lurks in the unconscious of sons and daughters throughout their lives. The hero can give himself to a freedom beyond the all-too-human belief that the unconscious binds sons and daughters to the long-held pains that burden their adulthood. When I first watched *Braveheart*, and when I watched it again and again between May 2000 and June 2001, I was in sympathy with the dream father's sappy advice. The dream father roused the Paterian flame in me, who had been a truant from love.

Mel, I eased a finger into your flaming and flame-spouting flesh. You taught me to be hot like you so that I didn't burn to ash but learned to grow large with fairy beauty, which literally incorporates maternal femininity, macho chutzpah, and femme-fatale sexual radiance.

In our early years together, Tom could comfort me maternally. He played a rock 'n' roll guitar with the edgy masculinity that came from his animal self. The long scarves he wore suited his elegance well, and he endured guys in shopping malls calling him a fag. When a man in a bar responded to the rhinestone clip-on earring that Tom sported on the pocket of his white shirt with "Are you a gay?" Tom retorted, "No. Are you?"

In Caravaggio's painting *The Incredulity of St. Thomas*, the saint is certainly queer. Christ is pulling aside his robe so that the doubting and curious Thomas can finger the wound, can feel his way inside divinity. The wound, the anus, the vagina — a visually compelling hole into heaven. I see neither the anus nor the vagina as wounds, but Roman soldiers *did* lance Jesus, creating a hole in his body. They *did* hurt another man out of their own lovesickness. All three holes — wound, anus, vagina — singularly oblige our gaze. In Caravaggio's painting, Jesus, Thomas, and two companions all stare at the divine hole, and although Freud asserts that the genitals are ugly, they transfix us, if we let them, when they are available to view. Our gaze is our love — frustrated, fearful, or timid though it may be — for the loci of pleasure that our bodies share, we the fuckers and fuckees; and we become obligated to love by the beauty of that common knowledge — pleasure — by the beauty of its site.

Mel, thank you for activating my great balls of fire. Wallace's signify his love for Murron and Scotland. Jerry Lee Lewis's, however, proclaim the frenzy of driving lust. He sings about soul-shaking, brain-rattling love that makes people crazy. That kind of craziness can give the rattled and shaken great pleasure — how divine! — but lovesickness feeds on an energy from which I freed myself.

So that I was out on a different limb of love, sparkling with the fairies, sparking my ability to woo myself into the stardom that belonged to the fairies' flaming magic that any person could perform if they chose to. Magic — simply, an extraordinary power, the ability to burn as crystal-bright as Pater tells us that we can. Magic — the glitter, stardust, sequins, and other fairy flakes that flame throughout *Velvet Goldmine*. Magic — the ability to flame like a star.

In *Velvet Goldmine*'s quirky spectacle, even a tear glitters. It belongs to the fairy man's sheer beauty, which is monster/beauty, a showy exhibition of sensuous presence and emotional effusiveness. (I develop the idea of monster/beauty at length in my book *Monster/Beauty: Building the Body of Love*.) Sometimes that beauty evokes my tears, such as a *Velvet Goldmine* sequence that I cried in each of the three times I watched it in the theater over the course of a week and a half. Sporting femme-fatale red lips, a whitish lavender feather boa, and tight pants that look like iridescent skin, his own face and entire upper body glittering up the wazoo, Slade sings a ballad whose ironic beginning cautions us about falling for a predatory lover—a "vulture." As he performs, he parades with a programmatic elegance that elucidates the absurdity of femininely graceful gestures. He is an utterly ridiculous sight who, like his mannerist- and baroque-inspired surroundings, stumps a viewer's attempt to decipher their rationality. Slade is bursting beyond the merely human in decorative scale. The architecture features masks and Michelangelesque sculptures, signs of both uninhibitedly exaggerated and voluptuous emotion and of people's ability to perform that and to hide themselves in the sensual luxuries of such performances. Obscuring oneself through performance can make one into a vulture, which describes Slade, who is a shit. The movie traces his own trajectory as a vulture.

My crying puzzled me. I couldn't locate an obvious origin. But watching the film at home one day, I realized that my tears began during the transition between the previous scene and the one I've been explaining. In that transition, the ballad's music has already begun and stardust from a rooftop sex scene continues to fall in the huge window behind Slade. I guess that the music began to break my heart. It's melodic yet plodding, and the way it moves down the scale, then stops descending right before the lyrics start had me imagining that someone was about to take an emotional plunge.

The sex scene, between Wild and Arthur the fan, is the loveliest scene in the film. A myriad of stars oversee their sweet pleasure, and Wild, the gentle master of fairy sex, suggests, "Make a wish." (His urging is like that of Wallace's dream father, a fairy father, whose words enhearten the hearer.) Stardust showers the two men and the camera pans out so that the fairy sprinkles, like snowflakes, fill the screen.

Fairy flakes or sprinkles garnish many *Velvet Goldmine* scenes, so varieties of stardust start to intermesh. It is lofting feathers that soon float down; sequined and other resplendent costumes; the glitter that Wild shakes from a canister at his crotch as if he were ejaculating gems; the makeup that transforms flesh into joyous sinuosity; the brilliant effluence from the spaceship that deposits Wilde on Earth; the confetti that Slade finds at a chandelier's brim and scatters by handfuls as if it were petals; a tear. The intermeshing of Arthur's and Wild's lovemaking, their fairy intercourse; music that is vivacious while dragging down my heart; and all the images and meanings of stardust that Haynes provides operated in my unconscious to provide a reading of Slade's skin as tear-covered. Although I saw *Velvet Goldmine* before Mom and Dad died and before my hot flushes and night sweats began in earnest, the unconscious, perhaps prescient, had me sob to the tune that featured a vulture—an animal that signifies death—and made me susceptible to opulently glistening weeping flesh.

When the vulture threatened my well-being by flying into my life as dynamically as Iris did, *Velvet Goldmine* startled me into magical aesthetic/erotic self-creation. You *can* be in the pink, its many dazzling, coaxing, captivating images reminded me. Images worth remembering recall us to ourselves, in forms that are familiar and in others that dare us into luxuriant self-invention. I fell in love with a luminous extravaganza, a cathedral of queer, the crew of beautiful men. I recognized myself as their twin in lust and gender, their camp splendor and tenderness. Like them, I was silly and deliriously gorgeous.

I embraced pink as the supreme fairy color.

I'm proud that pink panties and slips with a little lace suited my taste when I was a girl, and I'm glad that we girls gave one another pink undergarments as birthday presents. At one of my girlhood birthday parties, I opened a box containing a pair of panties. Following my suburb's custom, which was to show each present to your celebrants as soon as you handled it yourself, I held up the gift—which very likely was pink. I heard sometime later that day or the next day that I'd done a tasteless thing by displaying underwear. I don't recall that this was Mom's opinion, and I'd like to believe that it belonged to one of my friend's mothers. I'd like to believe that my mother didn't find garments that touched little girls' private pinkness, our sexual parts, to be nasty or too sexy to show to other little girls, or to be inappropriate articles of a little girl's excitement.

Pink carries the essence of erotic play. It is a dynamic color, it can be light and dense, froth and crystal, liquid like sweet or tangy juices, pliant like tongues and genitalia, ladylike and fierce. Pink refreshes us, as does play. Episodes of play don't freshen us forever, but they do point at ways to liberate us from the everyday devastations of the soul that can occur in one's family, at school, in the workplace, and most painfully, with the people whom we intimately love.

The erotic is depth, richness, and joy—which is one reason why people associate chocolate with eroticism. Play weds us to our deepest, richest, most joyous selves, our erotic selves. My calling, when I bravely and sensitively—heroically—followed it, impelled me to a pink place, where I was dancing as lithely as the Sugar Plum Fairy. Human beings often allow the pews of culture as well as our closest relations to shame our fairy selves and consequently to obscure our freedom. In play, we feel free, and play is an avenue to freedom.

Fairies are as good at playing as they are at letting go. Mel was playful with animals and in love, fairy sweet and buoyant and he looked damn cute in *Braveheart* braids and skirts. *Mel, I loved to see you in a strand of pearls. In your pearls I loved our making love.*

Tom admired the style of his good friend Scott. In the early 1980s, men rarely wore bracelets, but Tom went on and on about Scott's bracelet of satin ribbons. He also liked Scott's black cowboy boots, his T-shirts with the sleeves ripped out, and asserted that most men could never carry off wearing two earrings in one hole, like Scott did, that a stud and a drop—Scott's was a tiny silver cross—would look stupid. Tom dressed simply, often wearing jeans, a white shirt, and beat-up boots. When I complimented him in that gear—"That's the sexiest stuff you wear"—he blushed.

Mel was a fairy, but Gibson is antigay, and as a director, he's merciless with the fairy men in *Braveheart*. The film portrays them—Edward's son and both his lover and retinue—as slaves to narcissism and incompetents in military strategy. Gibson colors the fairy men pink and the Scotsmen boy-blue. Narrative, plot, costume, and the choreographing of stereotyped contemporary gay posture and gesture work to designate the fairy men as counterpoint, and indeed, a countersex to Wallace and his cohorts, whom the film represents as the ultimate of phallic masculinity. The fairy men don't fight, and though we may assume that they fuck, it is not manly fucking because it produces no offspring. The princess's implication to both her husband and father-in-law, as Wallace is being tortured to death, that she and Wallace have conceived a child who will become king of England, draws looks of shock and consternation from the two English men. In *Braveheart*'s ideology, ladies are women and ladies are fairy men. Whoever directed the fairy men to act like ladies, and I presume that Gibson did so, may understand that ladies are big girls and little girls, of all ages and sizes. But the director doesn't see an oceanic picture, in which ladies can be girly girls and drop-dead butches and the many other permutations of masculinity and femininity that men and women play with every day as well as on special occasions. The action hero, however, is a perfect lady, meaning that Wallace is decorous when necessary and commanding of respect; and he wears his braids and skirts with style.

The prince's beauty and that of his companions resembles the princess's. The men are flawlessly groomed, and they wear long, fluid clothing that lends grace to their slenderness. Their faces are pretty, rather than beautifully rugged like Wallace's. The film represents the fairy men as unredeemable: they care about their appearance! Indeed, they are the only people in the film who observe themselves in a mirror. Loose hair, patterned clothing, and vivacious gestures paint a beautiful performance of fairydom.

Braveheart's derisive tone toward the fairy men damns them, as if they were simply silly. They are silly, but silliness, like pink, refreshes and liberates. Wallace is silly with Murron, but after she dies, no one else, no other relationship serves as a catalyst for his gaiety.

Promiscuous beauties Wild and Slade dispel my fear of inhabiting tartish style because they display it so gaily. My form-fitting tops of cotton, Lycra, and their combination, tops that show my naked nipples and my biceps; my Betsey Johnson outfits whose romantic sexiness and silliness appeal to the phallic presentation of my femininity; my collection of low-heeled ankle boots; my black spectator Mary Janes and my red Mary Janes by Robert Clergerie; my pink leather skirt with a ruffle of the same material; my lip liner and lipstick that together in highly saturated colors ask that my mouth be kissed: I feel more secure in both their splashiness and psychic comforts when I see Slade and Wild parading in their fairy gear. Slade shimmers like alien royalty, and Wild is a gothic aphrodisiac, fingernails polished and eyes rimmed in black, raggedy blonde hair true to his frenzied yet delicate allure.

Decked in high pink blush, Slade sings to a lily the color of peppermint ice cream. The petals expand as his breath caresses them.

Dwelling during the summer of my father's death within temperatures near one hundred degrees and flushes characteristic of menopause, I often wore a hot pink Betsey Johnson camisole decorated with even hotter pink flowers. Flushes, that's what I called my heat, because it felt pink rather than hot flashing red. Pink is a tart's delight.

On a salmon pink carpet filled with girls' paraphernalia, Slade and Wild, played by Ken dolls, consummate their love.

A schoolgirl tart's dark gold platforms remind me of my own flat and bronze-gold Mary Janes, the shoes I most loved as a child.

Tarts are fruit-filled, and I'm as tutti frutti as the next guy. "Tutti Frutti": a song that became a gay anthem, by the resonantly queer rock icon Little Richard, the fairy queen himself, and performed by Slade in a vignette from his childhood.

Tom and Scott and Andrea and I were feeling tutti frutti. Andrea, my close girlfriend, lived with Scott, and all of us lived in Tucson in the mid-1980s. I was teaching at the University of Arizona.

Fairy magic filled Tucson, making it a tutti frutti place. I loved the desert: its apparent severity purified my soul-and-mind-inseparable-from-body. In year-round daytime temperatures that ranged from the 70s to the 100s, the stripping away of clothing needed in the Midwest and the East freed my limbs and senses. The contours of my body became clearer to me, and my organs—indeed, all of me—lightened in the brilliant, burning desert and in my everyday familiarity with the subtleties within the apparent severity of unremitting sun, tremendous heat, sky as blue as anyone can imagine it to be, and striking vegetation. Immediately on my arrival, I was the lover of the nuanced greens of chaparral and cactuses, of the sandy browns and pinks of desert earth, and of the pink oleanders, poisonous if eaten, that grew in my own garden and in garden after garden. I was the lover of fantastic forms and unexpected lushness that poked holes in ignorant notions that the desert is a waste. I was the lover of a blue so huge that it broke open the heart. I was the lover of a sun whose unforgettable radiance touched my spinal bones and the soft tissues deep inside the front of me, touched the golden Aphrodite core of me with its own gold. I was the lover of mountains surrounding the fairy city on every side. Like Olympus for the Greeks and like the ziggurats for the Mesopotamians, the mountains let me know that divinity and the human heart are one. At school or at home, when I let some prosaic mishap cloud my heart, I stepped outside, saw the mountains, and my heart cleared. The Sonoran Desert, in which Tucson flames, gave me a lucidity that I had never before encountered. Desert hermits, desert saints, desert fairies: I knew that I was one of them.

Probably Andrea or I suggested that I make up Tom and Scott. Tom and I began to present performance pieces together in 1982, when we lived in Oberlin, and I'd tart him up for those events with gold eye shadow, black eyeliner—above and below the lids—light pink blush, and a mauve lipstick that looked a little darker than his lips. In Tom's and my cunt-pink Tucson bathroom, I beautified the men while we all hung out, sitting on the counter or the floor or the toilet with its lid down.

"You look beautiful," I exclaimed, and after tarting up the men, I, the Desert Queen, considered redoing my own lips red and pressing them to each man's mouth.

When the fairies Slade and Wild kiss lingeringly in a close-up that occurs in complete silence—this in a film full of rock music that the audience is directed, at the film's beginning, to hear at "maximum volume"—their breath in each other's mouths is palpable, and I was aware of my own breathing and that of the people watching the movie with me. In our shared breath, I became the fairies' kiss; I was the maximum volume of love.

That was a perineal experience.

Mandy, Slade's wife, jokes in front of a crowd, "You all know me—subtle-ty's my middle name. It's as subtle as the piece of skin between my vagina and my anus—ooh la! la! Now what's that *called*, I can never quite remember . . . No man's land!?" It's called the perineum, and men's is between the anus and scrotum. Sexual flesh shared by the bisexuals Slade and Mandy, the perineum is indeed neither man's nor woman's land. It is literally and figuratively pink, and it is fairyland. Like the pink fastness—Tom's and my bathroom turned into a fairy palace—where everyone said little, as if participating in a ritual of magic. Magic always requires the maximum volume of love.

Jack Fairy performs magic when he struts.

Young tarts, if they're lucky, become fairies.

When I was a girl in my gold Mary Janes, joyfully parodying the Sugar Plum Fairy at the family Christmas gathering, I performed like an antic ballerina. Dad loved to see the Sugar Plum Fairy, and she delighted in satisfying his requests to see her perform, well into midlife.

Velvet Goldmine is a fairy tale more than a fiction, a sugarplum fairyland.

The Sugar Plum Fairy has called herself, when pressed, "straight" and "pretty heterosexual." But one's true tune, the breath with which one sings it, floats into the world from childhood inclinations; which is why I began to call myself a fairy.

Mel, you asked the Sugar Plum Fairy to dance, and you laughed lovingly at her star performance.

The fairy self is a star.

The fairy self is more erotically compelling than is a movie star.

Velvet Goldmine's opening image is an infinity of stars—you and me in a fairy empyrean? You and me born—or born again—into luxuriant self-invention? Don't you wish?

Wish with me. "Make a wish," Wild suggests in the wilderland of an urban rooftop converted into fairyland by his and Arthur's lovemaking. Make a wish upon a star.

Oscar Wilde, who stars in the contemporary gay pantheon created by the needs and wishes of queers, descends to earth from the heavenly potential, the star-studded infinity. In *Velvet Goldmine* he asserts as a schoolboy, "I want to be a pop idol," which Wild, his virtual namesake, is, in a most emotionally unbridled way.

When feathers loft and float down, filling the theater where Slade presides, it looks like the star-studded infinity.

Slade is a rising and fallen star. Stuart is star-struck, and the stardust that showers him and Wild as they make love sparkles, like the jewels, confetti, sequins, and glitter that visually are starring everywhere in the film.

When we are stars, our own erotically compelling fairy selves, we experience the freedom to be queer.

I was Mel fucking Mel, enjoying orgasms in my vagina. I specify a vaginal rather than a clitoral orgasm, because the sensations are very different, and the former is more pleasurable to me. I was Joanna fucking Mel, delighting in our phallically flirting hips. The erotic etiquette of our cognitive bodies, behavior constituted by both of our maximums of femininity and masculinity, let loose great balls of fire. Eyes, anus, pupils, penis tip, vagina, ears, and mouth—our portals of sensation and divinity full of gem-bright flame, we were celebrating, like Jerry Lee in "Great Balls of Fire." Like him, we were exclaiming "Goodness gracious!" *Goodness* is a euphemism for god. *Mel, whore of heaven, our mission was to raze resistance to the perineal.*

In his great balls of fire speech, which is his Sons of Scotland speech, Wallace exhorts, "You've come to fight as free men. What will you do without freedom?" He ends with, "They may take our lives, but they'll never take our freedom!" In *Velvet Goldmine* Arthur has allowed "they" to take his freedom, "they" being the reality principle, the work ethic, the end of chronological youth, the antierotic, 1984ish New York in which he lives. "What will you do without freedom?" is a pertinent and poignant question that Haynes implicitly takes on. His answer, through Arthur's character, is, "You will become gray and depressed, one of those people who remember their youth as the best, the most glittering and magical time of their life. You will become the embodiment of melancholia." But the perineal resides in the renewing of passions; not in a resurrection, as of the dead, and not in a revival, as in a kind of cultism. And not in nostalgia.

When I told a gay acquaintance of about my age that I cried in *Velvet Goldmine*, he said, "Oh, that's nostalgia, for youth." His response first shocked and then dismayed me. I do love rock 'n' roll movies that fictionalize real rock stars or genres, even though I haven't loved listening to much rock music of any style or period for many years. Maybe I do relive my teens and twenties when I watch those films, the years when daring and eroticism seemed to least evade our beliefs and acts, when the poetry of rock lyrics, the flamboyance and loudness—in volume, costume, and emotion—appeared to have been constituted from our very muscle, bone, and blood. Rock music enables its fans to feel like heroes, so why not relive one's heroic youth?

Being an action hero, ever audacious and amatory, traversing, as ever, the eternal circuit of love, I don't deny the glamour of youth, but neither have I a lot of interest in glamorizing my own youth, when depression was dearer to me than my own sister, acne flared so fiercely that scars on my outer cheeks can always remind me of my adolescent ugliness, and boys stayed away from me as if I stank of a toxic femininity. At any rate, I cried during *Velvet Goldmine* not because I wanted back the peculiar beauties of Joanna's suffering—as if they could refresh me—but because the movie's soulful, sexy heart renewed my faith in freedom.

I raved about *Velvet Goldmine* in my classes. In the survey of Western art I was lecturing about Gothic architecture, explaining that the visual splendor of cathedrals was a material metaphor for the heavenly City of God. I described the visual splendor of *Velvet Goldmine* as a cathedral of queer, as the heavenly city of fairyland. While some scholars reserve *queer* to define gay men and lesbians, other scholars, as well as politically active lesbians and gays, use *queer* expansively, to denote and not delimit physical appearance, sexual behavior, or daily rituals and pleasures that exceed heterosexual norms. To my understanding, *queer*, *camp*, and *fairy* say Yes, to the whiffs of beauty that many people miss and to sensuous pleasures stigmatized by a culture that appreciates shame more than it loves beauty. Camp is articulately brazen artifice that manifests authenticity of soul-and-mind-inseparable-from-body. The camped-up person plans her look or actions, yet at the same time, the girl or boy can't help it: they're genuinely queer, stepping lightly, like fairies do, only to be construed by some observers as stylistically heavy-handed — too made-up, too sexual, too silly, too trashy, too elegant, too attention-grabbing, too simultaneously processed and unprocessed through a battery of cultural codes that grind down most people into Arthurs who have lost their color. *Lethal Weapon*'s Martin Riggs, for example, is so queer, so gorgeously decked out in his artifice of craziness, and though a viewer might experience Wallace as too righteous, ridiculously so, if she were open-minded she could reconstrue his bathetic preachiness. At first she might think he's a mythopoetic male yahoo; a pretty good legend but a pretty bad poem — the sing-song quality of his rhythm and rhyme. But she could change and call camp the concentrated expression of his being.

In either large or small ways, queers, camp practitioners, and fairies do not submit to privatization of pleasure, to minimizing sensual or erotic delight by getting stuck in the mazes of culturally approved sensory deprivations: older women should not look sexy or happily display their bodies; women should not become hypermuscular; men should not wear ruffles or obvious makeup; women and men should have sex only with each other; sexes are opposite rather than complementary, parallel, and multiple; individuals belong to only one sex, or they are unnatural; the natural is easily defined and clear to everyone.

The heavenly chocolate desserts that tempt us on menus and pastry trays, in cookbooks and gourmet magazines, are unnatural wonders, as queer as can be, like Arthur wanted to be but couldn't muster, like Wallace is. Because Arthur's a failed fairy, I sometimes judged him harshly. *Mel, you helped my compassion grow. I was with you, you were in me, because we were ingredients in a bold delectability, colorful characters as abundant in queerness as chocolate is.*

The treatment of freedom at the end of *Velvet Goldmine* isn't camp at all. (As a reminder, Arthur and Curt meet up in a proletarian bar over a decade after they've been lovers, and Curt ensures that Arthur will be the new owner of the green brooch.) Before Arthur's nostalgic and inspiring memory of his lovemaking with Curt, Arthur recalls, in voice-over, "He called it a freedom." After the erotic remembrance, Arthur remembers more of Curt's wisdom from that starry night-into-day: "A freedom you can allow yourself. Or not." Take it or leave it, Haynes tells us, it being the freedom of fairyland. Although his film is a pitch for freedom, this final promotion is so down-to-earth in its understanding—heroes inspire us to freedom, yet freedom can be a labor that is psychically costly to choose; thus the proletarian setting—that my resolve to follow my heart, like Wallace after his father's death, my movement to be free, was weakened as much as strengthened. I wasn't sure if Curt's gift of the brooch to Arthur is an invitation, a demand, or a dare, if Haynes invites, demands, or dares his audience to be free.

Mel, heart on your sleeve, the fairy way, you freed me. Heart on your sleeve, in the vulnerability and courage of your bloodred beauty. I ran toward it, I burned—with a hard gem-like flame—in empathy with you, my uncommonly masculine Mel.

Like Pierre et Gilles, Haynes creates a delicious homoerotic vision of blood. Schoolboys beat up the child Jack Fairy because he has already implicitly manifested his different masculinity, and leave him lying on the street. After brushing away dirt from a grate, he discovers the green brooch that the infant Oscar Wilde, according to Haynes's cinema fairy tale, arrived on earth wearing after being delivered to Dublin by a spaceship. Next we see a close-up of Fairy spreading his own blood from the assault on his mouth, as if blood were lipstick. Bright-colored lips strut fairy glamour, and suddenly I knew that the red lipstick I wore—red most suited me—was fairy blood.

Fairy always struts his bloodred beauty. From the dashing dandy in black—a long coat and wide-brimmed hat—to the swishy aristocrat in a glimmering green gown and jewelry galore, Fairy spectacularly monumentalizes eros. Fairy's swishing made me swirl. He moved me into a spiral of joy, an upward spiral of evolution that was the fluid poetry of self-love. A strut can be stiff and militaristic, but the Middle English *strouten* from which *strut* derives, meaning to spread out, swell out, let me linger over the phallic sensations and erotic implications—the orgasmic aesthetics — of my own striding like Jack Fairy. And striding, too, like Wallace. Unlike Thomas, I do not doubt. At my own height, I am as large as every sacred heart. Fairy, the originator of fairy glamour and heartthrob of women as well as men, is the most inspiring figure in Haynes's film.

When the child Fairy smooths his own blood over his lips, he grins with the joy that powerful self-loving recognition can bring. That kind of recognition leads to wisdom. Also, his blood-colored mouth recalled to me that lipstick began with blood. Besides painting their faces with menstrual blood, women have cut themselves around their mouths and tattooed dribble lines from lower lip to chin bottom to signal menstruation. The mythic *vagina dentata* injures its prey; and predator animals "bleed" from the mouth, sometimes with humans' blood. Both femmes and hommes fatales, both action heroes and fairy men, are called to bloodred beauty.

Wallace and Porter both wear dribble lines of human blood more than once. Porter's is his own, and Wallace's comes from battle slaughter. (Blood runs from the mouth of Kali, the Hindu goddess who destroys life and who gives it, and sometimes a red triangle, an apex under her lower lip, represents the fluid.) Porter and Wallace are scary because they're so good at wreaking bloody havoc. Just as Wallace creates mayhem for Edward I's England, Porter equally disturbs The Outfit.

Maybe action heroes and fairy men have stolen women's blood. But why be ungenerous with bloodred beauty? I don't believe that men are from Mars and women are from Venus, as John Gray professes in the title of his book, which I found depressingly popular. Wallace is no braver a hero than Fairy, and Mel and I both wore the emerald brooch, which owners use as a gateway to the emerald city of Oz-like beauties who are the heavenly city of fairyland, the encampment of the everyday. When people encamp, they dump the fatigues that bewilder individuals' freedom, that fatigue the soul-and-mind-inseparable-from-body into a stagnancy disabling to the fluid poetry of self-love.

O, Mel, red hot with fairy beauty, you swished over to my growing heart, so that our fucking love was flowing thick like hot fudge.

—The fairies sang more often than you think they might have. Fairyland surrounded me, and it fills or pierces us when we risk the fear of venturing between the world we know and worlds with which we are barely familiar. Haynes's spaceship surely flew to Dublin from fairyland. Fairies travel between human beings' everyday world and regions that the psyche experiences as both lighter and darker than the norm. The fairy turns blood into a cosmetic; the action hero creates—is condemned to?—situations in which his own or other people's blood decorates him. Because both fairies and action heroes are singing blood, are activated by blood, their names are interchangeable: a person who doesn't scare easy ups the ante of eros.

Just because human beings have difficulty hearing fairy songs doesn't mean that none are in the air. They penetrate as fairyland does, deftly, exquisitely, like the arrow that causes Bernini's St. Theresa to swoon. Fairy songs may follow or even pursue us. Sometimes listening takes a long time; but no effort once our ears are open.

Fairies sing about anything that enters their hearts, and their songs are unconventionally sweet—no sugary, fragile words or tunes, but sweet like the deep, dark forest of a Grimm brothers fairy tale or the sunburnt airiness of the Sonoran Desert. Similarly, fairy voices depart from any folk or operatic sweetness, any agreeableness that human beings are used to in their own vocal ranges. Fairy voices can sound like farts or croaking frogs or chocolate bubbling in a pot on the stove.

When the fairies performed, they expressed themselves erotically, in bodily and facial gestures. I recognized myself in them. Only since the death of my parents and my second marriage did I wholeheartedly claim that self-recognition, knowing that if I denied, even a bit, my own sexual expressiveness, or mentally occluded it, then pain would fill the places evacuated by my consciousness. Recurring headaches into my late forties, a pain in my lower belly beginning in my mid-forties but now gone, and all the "symptoms" following my parents' deaths—the ones I listed in the first chapter of this book—filled in those evacuated places. With the return of my consciousness, the self-recognition that was love opened my ears to the true statements that people made to me about myself. I heard Stephen, the healer, for instance, gently attest to my sexual expressiveness—in the clothes I wore, the movements I made, the entire ambience of me. I heard his words with relief and relaxation. Ahhh . . . this . . . is . . . me.

I let Tom's animal instinct open me to parts of myself that no lover had opened before him. He and I released and revealed much of the animal in our collaborative performance-art work. In 1982 we presented our first piece at Oberlin

College, and between then and 1987 we presented four pieces, including the first, in Tucson and Bisbee, Arizona, Chicago, and St. Louis. The animal: our focused passion, our muscular and graceful interactions with each other as we performed our music—I sang the lyrics that I'd written, and Tom, on electric guitar, played the tunes he'd composed. Tom: giraffe man, swan man, goat man. I, the ardent vamp, the girly girl. I look at photos of us and I see fairy rockers, full of passion—hauntingly, delicately, and dynamically beautiful. I spoke prose as well as sang, and my words were often indistinguishable from poetry.

I conceived the ideas for our performances, wrote the lyrics, and gave them to Tom so that he could create the melodies and arrangements. Except for the first piece, BRUMAS: A Rock Star's Passage to a Life Revamped, which I wrote in entirety before showing it to Tom, my prose came after our songs were materializing. In my lyrics, often dark compared to fairy song, the word alien and the feeling of being alien circulated in melancholy accounts of hard, lost, and cowardly hearts and through a narrator seeking hope, love, and heaven. BRUMAS, mostly prose, featured five songs. The first three are titled "Heroin Corner," "I Am an Alien," and "Alchy/Junko." In Justifiable Anger, performed in 1984, I railed at false friends and other people—from lovers to criminals—and agonized that, as the song title says, "Angels Beat Me Down." My lyrics focus on the survival and rescue of the heart, and reading them around twenty years after I wrote them, their turbulent anguish surprised me—my former turbulent anguish. Clairvoyance (For Those In The Desert), our last performance, ends with a song, as all our pieces except BRUMAS did, and how amazing it was to see that the song's final words are: "We're such aliens, aliens."

Yet, a counterpoint exists in my lyrics. A fairy counterpoint, which resides in my love affair with the desert and in the metaphoric relations between Tom and animals. Although I wrote the desert as a place of death and brutal sun, I also wrote it, and more memorably, as a savior and a sexual comrade, guide, and paradise. Tropical heat threads through my 1986 solo piece, A Few Erotic Faculties, along with desert heat. When I was writing A Few Erotic Faculties, which included thirteen poems and no prose, my directions to myself as I wrote were that each poem was to be like a jewel—unconsciously, I must have envisioned garnets—gorgeously faceted with graphic sex and romantic tenderness. When I performed A Few Erotic Faculties, I walked into the audience to give two cards to two people, one a man, one a woman. On each card I'd written an intimate though not sexually explicit declaration of my feelings. As I handed the woman her card, I gave her a rose; as I handed the man his card, I sprayed Bellodgia, from the cologne bottle that I'd brought from my bedroom, on the inside of his wrist.

Ground, mountains, flowers, water, sky, and weather conditions recur in my work from the 1980s, as do birds and other animals. So do androgynous human beings or my desire for them. At the turn of the millennium I called them fairies, who are lighter in being than anything that I imagined in the 1980s, although I was looking then for the hard gem-like flame. The chorus of *Justifiable Anger*'s "Esperanza Boulevard" gives an idea of my own severely sensitive pinkness:

If you hear me, I'll be frank,
My arid heart can't bleed
I'm wasting like some old dog's bones
On a sun-dried river bank
I'm waiting for a monsoon
To inundate my guts
To fill me up with liquid light
But all day is high noon

August is monsoon season in Tucson. Tucsonans anticipated the storms with excitement, and I, like any native desert lover, experienced the storms as one of the Sonoran's many excitements. Like the golden stud of a coyote that I witnessed crossing Speedway Boulevard. Speedway is Tucson's main drag, a six-lane road from what was in the early 1980s the undeveloped desert to the west of the city through the center of town and into the undeveloped desert to the east. In *Clairvoyance*, I sang plaintively for that animal and me in "Coyote." Here are two choruses:

Arizona blue sky
Swallow him today
Your sun comes down and picks him up
And carries him away

Arizona blue sky
Swallow me today
Your sun comes down and picks me up
And carries me away

Tom carried me away, from our first acknowledged erotic moment to his flaming ability to inspire me, to be my muse. Our first acknowledged erotic moment, in the slide library at Oberlin College. He'd cut his finger and I held his hand. Our bloodred beauty seeped and spilled into our performances, for instance, into the song "Be My Body" from *Solar Shores:*

Time to act time to love
Time to give the world a shove
Entry exit time to leave
See the ways we interweave
Blood and oceans, thought and deed
If we live we all must bleed

One night in St. Louis when I had my period, I climbed on top of Tom and felt the blood running out of my cunt, into his pubic hair. Later, as I walked to the bathroom, the blood trickled down my legs and spotted the polished wood hallway floor and the tiles around the toilet. Another night in St. Louis when we were fucking, Tom withdrew his cock and my menstrual blood splattered onto the bed and one spot reddened the floor by his side. We didn't wipe up the spot, and weeks later it wore away. Living on the third floor of a six-flat whose washer and dryer were in the basement, we rinsed and scrubbed the sheets in the bathtub, and Tom quietly remarked, "I didn't think there'd be so much blood."

In my thirties, I paid the best attention that I could to my arid, bleeding, stormy, and lovingly awakened heart. To my muse, I wrote "Cozy Man," which we performed in *Solar Shores.* It begins:

Gem and heart, he talks to birds
I don't know the words he says
He has a gift
With certain speech and snaky sinews

Climb his legs
Sometimes when he moans
In bed I stroke his hair
This cozy man
And then he dreams again

Tom and I were fucking beauties. I don't use *fucking* as a harsh word, but rather to express the interest that I had in the cognitive body activating graphic patterns of sexual beauty. Fucking is fairy intercourse, any of whose participants are simultaneously fucker and fuckee. Fairy fucking, like fairy beauty, can incorporate the maternal, the anal, the manly, the nipple, the vulval, the red-lipped; the Morgan le Fayish and Lola Montezish; the Little Richardesque to the Lord Byronish; Phryne-like nudity to Navratilova-like muscle to Nijinsky-like litheness; the fairy prince, the fairy princess, and both the canons and the decanonization of all of our my-heroes. A visiting artist lecturing in spring 2001 in the Art Department where I teach declared, "We all want the Empire State Building between our legs," but I silently disagreed. I'd rather have the fairy phallus, both as mine and as my lover's. The masculinist phallus — the Empire State Building — cannot engage in fairy intercourse.

Come hither, Mel, you loved my fairy phallus as I loved yours.

My favorite scene in *Braveheart*, besides the one where Wallace rides into the market after his wife has been killed, happens between him and the Princess of Wales. She has warned him twice about Edward's stratagems, which would ruin Wallace's plans to destroy the king. Considering the princess's political position as Edward's daughter-in-law, Wallace asks her, "Why do you help me?" Without waiting for an answer, he seductively repeats, almost in a whisper, "Why?" Previous scenes have made it clear that Wallace and the princess are attracted to each other, so when he grasps a beam in the hut where they've met and leans toward her, his action is not invasive. However, like the lover that he will momentarily become, he does intrude into the privacy of her bodily aura, the space around her that creates a comfort zone between people who are not intimate. That movement of his, into her smell, her breath and space, was overwhelmingly erotic when I watched the film the first time. *Mel, you breached with me that comfort zone of carnal limbo.*

Wallace and the princess are meeting unaccompanied by others, and the lovers feel very much alone, to me, in their romantic and erotic togetherness. Wallace has entered like an animal, with such instinctively quiet alertness that he seems suddenly to appear from nowhere in the back of the hut, less than a leap away from the princess. He must have been melding, in his dark and sensually hairy beauty, with the interior itself, the natural materials, the dusky light created by the structure. Like a fairy, Wallace moves through a forest as if he is an enchantment or has the power to enchant anyone and anything around him. Fairies may seem to be the opposite of animal, too ethereal, but fairies' lightness resembles animals' because both can move without being seen or heard. I'm reminded of the Count's wolves in Bram Stoker's *Dracula*. Also, many animals display fairy pink in dangerous and sexual ways. Pink tongues, lips, and genitals, those parts of animals that so fascinate human beings: they signal, as does fairy pink, vulnerability and power, tools with which to bite, kill, eat, attack, fuck, and reproduce.

The princess, who is as shrewd as she is lovely, having quickly become nobody's fool in a hostile court, looks like the fairy-tale princess in my childhood books. In other words, her gown and hair define her. The gown's long-sleeved, chest-revealing top fits snugly through the waist and the skirt flows to the ground; her hair hangs loosely to her hipbones in a neatness that a little girl or her mother might envy. The princess's style creates unfathomable grace, but she is animal too. Her response to Wallace's "Why?" is, "Because of the way you look at me now," which is the way he's looked at her before. The look is animal frank and fairy deep, and it excites her, as it has before.

Earlier in the film, during their first meeting, in a tent along with the king's henchmen, Wallace called himself a "savage." The label identifies him as an animal, and the princess perceives him as a very different one from either Edward, whose misogyny and cruelty repulse her, or Edward's son, whose involvement with a homoerotic entourage and a male partner—thrown to his death by the king from a high window—have left the princess to fend for herself. She wants a sweet savage, sweet to her at least. And Wallace is. He knows the tongue of love! At their first meeting, he demonstrated his French (as well as Latin). France is her native country, and French her native tongue. His linguistic abilities impress the princess, who on hearing his French smiles as delightedly as her diplomatic mission allows. His French is a matter of honesty: if Edward's ambassadors and the princess speak a language they presume Wallace can't understand, he wants them to know that he won't suffer their bullshit. The princess has heard from her confidante Sophie, who slept with an English courtier, that "Englishmen don't know what a tongue is for," and *Braveheart*'s audience sees that proven when the English soldier who sexually assaults Murron licks her grossly.

The princess's response confirms for Wallace that she sees him in his honesty, and so he leans farther forward, and they kiss. Making love with a man who knows the language of love lifts the princess in soul-and-mind-inseparable-from-body. *O Mel, you taught me the Paris I didn't know. You lifted me with the fucking fairy lightness of your sweet savage paws, your tongue forgiving every force and pleading in the amnesias and omissions I once called love.*

My fairy lover lifted me. In my desire for his sweet savage paws and tongue, I instinctively let him move toward me, anticipating his intention to align the pressures of our lips and bodies. And then he voiced a desire, "I want to be inside you," which Wallace very likely voiced to his princess. My fairy lover asked, "Do you want me?" which carried the same meaning as Wallace's "Why do you help me?" Both questions imply a man's knowledge of a woman's desire for him. For a loving animal, "Do you want me?" is an honest inquiry into reciprocal passion. He wants to put his finger on a Yes.

Wallace becomes Scotland's supreme patriot because the English kill his wife. Maximus becomes Rome's top gladiator because the emperor kills his wife and son. Avenging angels? Possibly. I name them avenging fairies, embodiments of the fairy phallus. In *The Male Body: A New Look at Men in Public and in Private* Susan Bordo defines the masculinist phallus as delivering conventional male force. In the culture we live in, which often presents the violence of male force—from war to entertainment—as sexy, action heroes typically represent the masculinist phallus, but Wallace is different. He is more than a sexpot; he is kind to women and gentle with them, yet not so gentle that he would be boring in bed.

Besides critiquing the masculinist phallus, Bordo also discusses the butch phallus, whose power one wields with feminist intent to heal and please women. Any phallus conceptually connects one body to another, the masculinist phallus extending, often hurtfully, from man to woman, the butch phallus bringing people, frequently woman and woman, closer together. *Mel, as your avenging fairy* sister and brother, I learned to give and to receive the fairy phallus, whose magic crossed and erased borders between sexes and genders.

Velvet Goldmine's Arthur loses the fairy phallus, which is why he becomes sexless, forlorn, drab, depressed, and cynical. Granted, he lives in the antithesis of Haynes's glam London filled with colorful, Oz-like beauties of costume, makeup, and interior décor. Haynes's New York squelches the fairy phallus, which, like fairy men, fills a lot of space because they make it radiant. The fairy phallus's beauty equals the radiance that the ancient Greeks attributed to their deities, Aphrodite more than any other. Her radiance is her goldenness, and, for me, golden girl Aphrodite embodied sensation while stirring this worshipper to live sensationally. According to Hesiod, Aphrodite becomes huge when she reveals her divinity to her mortal lovers.

Is she showing them too much love?

Too much love doesn't drive a fairy crazy. Indeed, "too much love" is nonsense to a fairy, an impossibility whose roots grow in the fear that humans have of never having enough—enough of anything pleasurable or good, including love. So people create an idea of love, the ultimate happiness, that is unhappiness—insanity. Romantic passion—the fire of desire in the lyrics of popular songs—as lovesickness holds no appeal to fairies because they are fearless about both love and chocolate. They are fearless lovers, fucking beauties, a reality that embarrasses people whose shame and whose pain at not being one of the sensual loves of their own lives the fairy evokes. Fairies are fucking anomalies in a world where we live as though love is a buried treasure to which we've lost the map.

Fairy beauties know that love asks that we surrender to it. Unlike the giving up of a loser to a winner and of the defeated to the victor, and unlike the "I give up" of a lover so frustrated with the beloved that the lover loses faith in love, the surrender of fairy beauties to love is a giving over of one's heart. *I offered my heart to you, Aphrodite. It was already yours, as every heart is born into the home of love—though sometimes people feel as though they're lost and they cannot remember the way home.*

I was wandering when I found you, Mel, and you helped me on my way home.

Before I watched *Braveheart* following Mom's death, Gibson's movies had never mattered to me, and, of course, Mel had not existed. I surrendered to my creation right away, without knowing what I was doing. He did not captivate me the way in which the Yul Brynner of two 1956 films, *The Ten Commandments* and *The King and I*, thrilled a preteen Bordo, through the sexual power of dominance. Like Brynner's full lips for Bordo, Mel's lips and penetrating eyes stirred my lust, but Bordo conveys her submission to the sexiness of Brynner's bodily exhibition(ism), his masculinist phallus, whereas I surrendered to Mel's ability to communicate fucking beauty, the fairy's captivating phallus. Even in my prepubescent sexuality, fairy beauty attracted me. Teen idol Ricky Nelson's prettiness, his lovely lips and eyes, were surface displays, features that drew out my fantasies about a complexity of corporeality and spirit, both his and mine, that could join with one another. Lips you want to kiss and eyes that invite you into intimacy: they were mine as well as his, features that allowed me to identify with a young man; they are Tom's in photos of him taken in the 1980s.

Ellen Fein and Sherrie Schneider, authors of *The Rules: Time-Tested Secrets for Capturing the Heart of Mr. Right*, advise women never to stare at men, because it shows that you're interested. In their 1995 bestseller, Fein and Schneider counsel their readers never to show a man their interest in him, period. "Let him look at *you!*" they exclaim in their usual adamantine righteousness. I don't believe in Mr. Right, who is a figment of bourgeois ideology, and if I must apply the archaic gender etiquette of don't-look-if-you're-a-woman, then the man in my gaze has no idea how to woo me.

I looked and looked at you, Mel, and you obliged my gaze, so bound me to you lovingly. You were anything but an obligato, and your fairy beauty obligated my commitment. Much obliged, Mel: O blow me with your satin, bloodstained lips; O blow me with your intemperate generosity and make me beautiful, as beautiful as a fairy.

Mel, I surrendered to the male gaze because I was a man looking at you soul-and-mind-inseparable-from-body.

The male gaze, defined by scholars as white and heterosexual, overwhelms what it sees through the viewing male's fixation, fixes its object by believing that controlling adoration is love. Since 1973, when the filmmaker and theorist Laura Mulvey critiqued the male gaze in her *Screen* magazine essay "Visual Pleasure and Narrative Cinema," scholars, educators, and artists have both blasted and standardized the male gaze. They've turned it into a cliché of sexual objectification and its practitioners into jokes, individual men and a male-dominant culture that literally cannot see beyond their own cocks, their masculinist phal-luses. From the later 1980s into the present, cultural critics have posited other gazes—of varied races, sexual orientations, ages, and subcultures—to have more wit and to be more considerate.

Here is my male gaze at work:

I loved to look at Tom beneath me when we made love, his arms overhead—no resistance. Once, in a combination of positions, what I just described among them, I saw gold stars on the wall behind him. Another time, in similar engage-ments of soul-and-mind-inseparable-from-body on an Easter night in Oberlin, Tom and I remarked about an energy that breezed around the ceiling. "Christ," he whispered. If it was my dreamy fairy Christ and my ears had opened more than usual, I could have heard him speaking: "I am the heart, I am the stars. I am the old blood and the new. I am the woman and the man, the fucking love that comes between you. I am the end when nothing is in sight. I am the seer in the night." Tom and I knew when the energy had breezed from our room to visit other lovers whose attention could be caught by fairy flames.

In Tucson I took photographs of Tom and Scott. In the pictures, they're cavorting. Men are boys sometimes, and that can be a delight. Scott yanks his own ponytail, and the two men seem to fall into each other, Tom's right arm crosses in front of him to point at Scott, whose right forearm thrusts against Tom's hip. Fairies are so good at playing. In another picture Tom pulls Scott's ponytail so that Scott bends backward, head upside down to the camera, and Tom is laughing. In my favorite photo Tom drapes his left arm over Scott's shoulder and presses into Scott so that their thighs touch and Tom's right hand rests on Scott's other shoulder. Scott crosses his arms and you can tell from the way his thighs meet that he's crossed his lower legs. The light brings out the muscles in his forearms. He leans his head to Tom's, looks angelic and in love, as if he's indescribably happy to be with Tom, as if they're lovers. Scott's pose accentuates his crotch, and along with the sweetness on his face, a leer appears—perhaps the male gaze turned on me, the photographer. The men's love for each other spills out into the desert and the photographic atmosphere. My love for them and their beauty spills out into the aura of each picture.

My heart did not turn against the male gaze. That gaze compelled me to talk to my friends about Mel as if there were no tomorrow. On and on I went, because my talking helped my heart to come alive again.

Mel, in our perineal conversations and caresses I spilled myself to you. You released a prohibition I endured until I met you, a fear of looking as long as I like at beautiful men.

My girlfriends gave me the freedom to say anything I wanted about Mel. Their giving assured me of their love for both my words and my moods. They didn't grant me permission to say whatever I wished. Rather, they were gifted in freeing me from my perimeter, in helping me be merciful with myself. So with Peggy, Claire, Pam, and Mary, I got logorrheic about Mel, who stirred my vocal cords and tongue into a pentecostal obliviousness to my own suffering. *Mel, my intelligible glossolalia shaped you into a divine whore, at ease to serve me as I wished to serve you, in a discovery of the laughter and conviction that it took to be a fairy, to spring to life, which was a leap for me as large as all the miles that Iris has traversed between barrows and rainbows.*

I took that leap of faith, the lover's leap, with my fairy lover, two months after my divorce. I could do that because I began to leap into an aphroditean world, into my own aesthetic and erotic self-creation, in unfamiliar ways. I was leaving my sickened love for myself, apparent to me, for instance, in my belly that I'd given many sweets and breads, making it larger than it had ever been in my adulthood. Or so it seemed to me. Maybe I created a shape resembling pregnancy, trying to keep my husband. More conventional women than I have tried actual pregnancy to bring a husband into a new marital intimacy. It didn't work — for me — because in that "pregnant" state, filled with gas and shit, filled with the waste of emotions going nowhere, I was an infidel to Aphrodite, whose alpha and omega are self-love. My massively unknown self created an embryonic glob out of heartache.

I'm surprised that a category of recurring dreams from my twenties into my thirties, which I called the Paris Dreams, didn't return during my lovesick pregnancy. Often I cried during and after them. They began in college, and in my thirties I wrote about the Paris Dreams in a journal that I kept very irregularly:

Love and enlightenment, the enlightenment of love, the love of enlightenment, lovelight, lighthearted love. I'm in the dark when it comes to love, always the stranger in the City of Light. I'm transparent, yet unclear, unable to understand my own vocabulary. I need a dictionary for myself, of light words turning dark as chocolate, of light words turning darknesses to light. I am the lexicon of ignorance, slow to translate *le français, la langue d'amour*, the tongue of love, for once I see the real story written in the images of the Paris Dreams, I'll have to create a new story, live a new life.

Swooning Beauty is that new life, in which I speak the language of love without compromising it.

— I learned a good deal about the animal from Tom. When we lived in Tucson, I watched him play with Jiggs, Peggy's Queensland Blue Heeler. Jiggs didn't love many men, but he loved Tom, who went to Peggy's sometimes just to play with Jiggs for an hour or so. At one point in St. Louis, Tom and I were living with three guinea pigs, two parrots, and a rabbit. I especially adored Marcel, our first guinea pig, named by Tom after Marcel Duchamp. Marcel could bite, but his plump silkiness and his generally sweet temper softened my heart into a more comfortable alignment with Aphrodite. Marcel was my fairy playmate, and when he died, after Tom and I divorced, Tom called to tell me. The death of a little animal who has been your fairy playmate is a large event at any age.

Marcel, a name originating in the language of love, like Café de Paris and L'Escargot, Chicago restaurants favored by my parents. From my late twenties into my thirties — until I began to teach at Oberlin — Mom and Dad often took me to dinner on a weekend night to L'Escargot (Café de Paris had closed). Because we frequented those French restaurants, French food became a language of love for me, a language shared with my parents. Dressed up for dinner at L'Escargot, I wielded my fairy glamour for myself and for the eyes of male diners, and I'd eat and drink with uninhibited pleasure. Mom and I enjoyed one brandy alexander each, and Dad would have two Rob Roys. Unsalted butter on little pieces of crusty French bread accompanied the drinks. Then, for me, came a smooth paté with cornichons, onion soup gratinée, crisp greens tossed with a light dressing spiked with mustard, tournedos (medium rare) or Coquilles St. Jacques, fruit tart — occasionally chocolate mousse — and three or four cups of coffee with cream. Dad ordered a bottle of wine, Mom finished one glass, and Dad and I shared the rest. The conversations were delectable, like each sip and bite of the meal, because the atmosphere at L'Escargot — created by mahogany booths with cushioned seats, shiny oak floors, low light, red-and-white-checked tablecloths, and walls decorated with unobtrusive prints — invited family reminiscences and insights whose tenderness and substance warmed me like a true lover's touch. Music, art, and gardening were conversation topics, as were relatives and my work in graduate school and as an art critic. When L'Escargot's owner, a native of Lyon, was overseeing the restaurant for the night, he stopped at our table and chatted a bit with the regulars, Mom and Dad. Often, as the three of us were finishing dessert and enjoying coffee, he served us a liqueur on the house. *Luxe, calme, et volupté:* I experienced that Baudelairean and aphroditean trio during our three-hour dinners at L'Escargot.

I didn't want to leave those dinners, for they aligned the animal and the flower. Those dinners balanced me in fairy beauty, which is the poetry of the flower and the animal aligned, allied, alive. In fairy beauty, a person is abundant energy, from receiving and radiating Aphrodite's love, beauty, and creativity. Abundant energy, like the pink peonies flourishing in the bed all along the east side of 90 Riparian Road. Dad, of course, planted them. Dad, my favorite gardener, from whom I learned all through my life so much about flowers. I see a lot of stingy gardens, as if the person who planted them believed only that he ought to put some other colors into the green of grass. Such a yard is not a garden, because convention rules it. The predictable choice of plants and their spacing creates an overorderliness that saddens the heart, for the openness of plants to soil and weather conditions seems stymied, as does the plants' will to be beautiful. Indeed, their will and their openness are one and the same. In the hands of a gardener like my father, his and the plants' will and openness become one, whereas the stingy garden suffers from a lack of human grace and giving. The person whose efforts result in a stingy garden has not cultivated the beauty of its inhabitants. In my father's fairy gardens and observing them, I knew bounty. I kept knowing it in memory. How good to have that bounty stored in my massively unknown self. *O, Daddy, keep leading me down your garden path, which is a steady beat of beauty.*

I wonder, did Stamos, when he visited 90 Riparian Road once or twice, see the peonies, the tiger lilies, the impatiens, lilacs, hosta? Did he eat the basil and the tomatoes Dad grew outside the kitchen window that faced Lake Michigan? Did he visit in the seasons when Dad's fairy artistry was in full bloom? Stamos, a fairy man identified by the name, "homosexual," given by a culture that could not bear the flaming of the fairy phallus. An erotically burnt-out culture, over-sexed with plastic spectacles that its pain has formalized into images that convey the ash of will and openness: blonde bunny goddesses with implanted breasts and surgically modified, depilated genitalia, builders of the body into a hardness lacking heart. Images of supposed pleasure, whose unbelievability brandishes a word made fascist flesh: *beauty*. Like the objects in a *vanitas* painting, which represent the transience of all things living, the plastic spectacles read as images of death. It is human beings' dead eros that burned fairy men when it burned witches, that murdered them both by setting faggots—bundles of branches, sticks, and twigs—aflame. Human beings' dead eros finds unbearable the gemlike flaming of fairy flesh.

Stamos was the first gay man with whom I fell in love, and Mom accused Dad of having fallen for him too. Dad's love for Stamos angered and frightened Mom, but I rejoiced in the mutual affection between my father and his friend, a love which let loose the fairy in my father, just like his gardening, his cooking, and his art-making did. *I was grateful, Aphrodite, that my Dad received and radiated your beauty, love, and creativity. I was grateful that my Dad so loved the fairy in me, that my Sugar Plum Fairy gave him such delight.*

The Sugar Plum Fairy had heart, like Wild does when he's performing. Eros and passion possess Wild in a song that's not on the CD of *Velvet Goldmine*'s soundtrack, Iggy Pop's and James Willamson's "Gimme Danger." Wild's dog collar, shiny silver pants, and wide, jeweled belt set off the pale and naked top of his body, which he now and then caresses in a seduction of the audience. I imagined that he is fantasizing being touched by someone else as well as by himself, and that he is surrendering to the abundance of pleasure.

Wild is sexy as hell, or rather, he is sexy as the starry heaven that is fairyland. On his knees, he seems paradoxically to implore and demand, and then promises that if his wish/command for danger is met, he'll heal the ills of the stranger who obeyed. The song's S/M implications do not undermine the fact that Wild is medicine for disease of the heart, which is lack of feeling. He embodies feeling itself, collapsing on stage, singing on his back in a to-be-taken posture, springing up, like an animal, clenching his hands, shaking as if in a seizure, repeating over and over his desire, his *need* to feel. He falls to his knees in a screaming prayer for feeling, and he cries pleadingly as if he's dying for feeling. But he's brilliantly alive with it, so much that when he invites and commands a kiss that's like an ocean breeze, I tasted the saltiness of lips after a sweaty fuck.

Wild took my breath away, like Wallace when he's riding into the market to avenge his wife's murder. Wild's daimonic possession is no less heroic than Wallace the avenger's. Heroism is not a matter of scale in deed, but rather of scale in soul and heart. By this description, Hedwig, the transsexual rock chanteuse of director John Cameron Mitchell's film *Hedwig and the Angry Inch*, is an inspiring and both literally and figuratively spectacular hero. Rivetingly acted by Mitchell himself, Hedwig has been done dirt. In her late twenties she was the victim of a botched sex-change surgery that left her with the mutilated genital flesh she calls "the angry inch." It is neither a penis nor a vagina or clitoris; and although I refer to Hedwig as "she," the currently correct term for a male-to-female transsexual, Hedwig is between male and female, masculine and feminine. She is in the fairy world, between dark and light, known and unknown. Because Hedwig is in-between, she is nothing and she is everything.

Hedwig's mother and Luther, Hedwig's husband-to-be, an American soldier, press the operation on Hedwig—a necessity for her escape from East Germany as his wife. Luther abandons her in Kansas. And Hedwig rises from the ashes of her dream of happiness with him: she falls in love with herself, which is an act of mercy, as positive narcissism, and of tremendous courage. In the trailer where Luther has left her, we see the transformation occur. Hedwig's extravagant makeup emphasizing eyes and lips, her luxuriously trashy costume, and her signature superblonde Farrah Fawcett wig add up to a fabulously camp and poignantly sexy phoenix. We are invited to identify with this heroic aesthetic and erotic self-creation and to participate in it by being phoenixes who rise from the ashes of our own devastations: as Hedwig humorously extols self-worth in song, a cartoon Farrah Fawcett wig bounces above the words for an audience sing-along.

Hedwig's practice of love adheres to the derivation of hero. She becomes the protector, the fairy watchman, of love and knowledge. She and Tommy Gnosis, her teenage lover, break up. *Gnosis* means spiritual knowledge. Hedwig has educated Tommy in the gnosis of his style, his rock history, his deepest self, his understanding of paradise, and Tommy has stolen the songs that he and Hedwig created together. He has become a star—which Hedwig hasn't yet. And as she tours America fronting a band whose every tune is a warrior's anthem—devotions, in a popular idiom, to bodily and spiritual fortitude and beauty—Hedwig in her huge, glittering red lips and her red T-shirt patterned with hearts, is a monumental angry inch. The East German doctor/butcher brought her within an inch of her sanity, if not within an inch of her life; and times of personal, professional, and planetary crisis may bring us to the same places. In these situations we easily feel tiny, outraged: we are angry inches. In these situations, as in every moment, we are simultaneously living within inches of love — calming conversations and intimate, desired touches: we are always within inches of being, like Hedwig, Valentines to each other, vigilant in love.

In my heart I began to play consciously with the fairies when I imitated the Sugar Plum Fairy. I've colluded with them ever since. *Collude*, from Latin, *com-*, with, and *ludere*, to play. How playful was my parodistic dance! Like Iris, the Sugar Plum Fairy was one of my fairy guardians. But unlike Iris, she could have been too goody-two-shoes. I read, in fall 2001, on the Celestial Seasonings box for Sugar Plum Spice Holiday Herb Tea that the "Land of the Sweets . . . is the land of the Sugar Plum Fairy, who is beautiful, gentle and kind. We created this tea to pay tribute to her." I bought the tea to pay tribute to her as well. Its color was so deep a rose pink that many would call it red. Whether red or pink, the color of the tea was one of the two main colors of Valentines. The tea tasted both sweet and spicy. Hedwig and Wild: their sweetness and spice registers as aphrodisiac power. So the Sugar Plum Fairy's lack of provocativeness worried me. I feared that her mildness made her a simpleton among fairies.

Then I opened to love, and I saw that being kind and gentle — compassionate, tender, generous, and sympathetic — belonged to fairy vision and that they were the only way to see another person's heart.

If you have lost your way home or your dreams, fairy vision will help you find them. In that cathedral of queer that is fairy vision, you will be like the salamander, a mythological reptile said to live in fire.

Who can live in fire but one who flames? The salamander, a fairy animal, also was said to be a spirit that lived in fire, originally, a spirit in the alchemical system of Paracelsus, the sixteenth-century Swiss alchemist and physician. The alchemists declared that they were turning base metals into gold, but what they meant, and could not assert for fear of persecution, was that they were transmuting matter into spirit. That is what flaming, singing, fucking, loving fairies do — like Wild singing "Gimme Danger" and Hedwig rising flaming from the tragedy of her marriage. Floweranimal, one body, become spirit — openness and will — through flaming, singing, fucking, and loving.

Fairy vision, from which any of us queers creates spirit, is the only passage to trust, because in the radiance and receptiveness of fairy vision, the heart feels unguarded and expansive, not pried into, flayed, surveilled, or invaded, as people's hearts so often do. Love welcomes us into a domain of connections, as the Sugar Plum Fairy welcomes children into the Land of Sweets.

7 —

Vaginal Action: Vagignosis

I ate chocolate ice cream during my performance Erotic Faculties: Red, *which I presented twice after my book* Erotic Faculties *was published in 1996. Displaying my blood-red beauty in a scarlet, off-the-shoulder, merino wool sheath, I enjoyed spoonfuls from a pint carton. A woman publicly eating chocolate, a lot of it and with gusto, is a spectacle, because women so often hide their appetite—for the pleasures of food and sex—or rarely revel in the fulfilling and fulfilled pleasure of their appetites. Women forbid themselves chocolate, or try to, or they succumb to their desire and suffer the consequences of protecting themselves against pleasure. Women talk and write about eating chocolate in private, as a secret ecstasy or evil, a violation of their bodies or their complexions or their happiness: I'll be ugly; I'll be damned—by my own pleasure. I ate chocolate ice cream without guilt or self-castigation. I smiled, I took my time.*

In my early forties, when Russ and I were living in Tucson, we spent a couple of hours numerous weeknights at the Helen Street Café, eating huge chocolate chip cookies, running into friends and acquaintances, and talking vivaciously with them and with each other. Cozy and low-key, Helen Street was home at night to many University of Arizona students who relaxed there reading or chatting with friends or studying by themselves or with classmates.

I was, I am, I will be. That sentence reminds me of the title of Gauguin's magnum opus, *Where Do We Come From? What Are We? Where Are We Going?* Gauguin and I each express a grand philosophical theme into which we place ourselves, and we both share an interest in past, present, and future. Yet, my words and their conscious origin differ entirely from Gauguin's. In 1897, the painting's date, he was contemplating suicide, so his piece, assert art historians, stands as a suicide note and a last will and testament. Gauguin asks questions which urge the viewer to ask the same questions—and his "we" implicates all humanity in his query. Here is someone who has lost his faith and who is asking—poignantly; pitifully?—all of us to follow in his doubt and lack. Gauguin's palette points me in that melancholy direction. I could call the blues and greens and browns mysterious, but I could also call them murky, or muffling of clear, affirmative thinking. Those colors want to clamber into my heart, and long ago they did do that, when I was a child or a teenager and I first saw the painting in its home, the Boston Museum of Fine Arts.

Then, Gauguin, to me, was gold. But now *Where Do We Come From?* spins a tale of poverty. It activates my memories of depression, which is the flatness that I feel in Gauguin's twelve-foot canvas—its huge and brooding flatness. Much appears to be going on in the painting: figures represent the human life cycle, two robed people are deep in conversation, a Maori deity bids us enter a realm of spirits, and Gauguin wraps the androgynous, monumental, and centrally placed nude, part Eve, part Christ, reaching for an apple, dressed in a loincloth, in dualities—of gender and ethics. What is male and what is female? What is good and what is evil? And ultimately, what is knowledge? What *do* we know? What *can* we know?

I can almost persuade myself back into this painting, because its beauty is familiar to me from memory. I've known the agonizing beauty that is the stagnancy of stifled emotions. Gauguin's painting is a garden, but one of aqueous and somber silence. Pink cannot live there. Gauguin's garden holds its breath, and I cannot live there either. I know nothing appetizing from within its breath-holding melancholia. "Exhale!" I exhort a dead painter who once was an idol of mine.

I was, I am, I will be. My words affirm.

If I were to let my affirmation generate questions, they would be these: Where was I? Who do I think I am? The first question I did ask in chapter four, apropos of my sexual misadventures, but in order to know ourselves, "Where was I?" insinuates itself continually into a re-asking. Usually, self-deprecating closure results from the way that people read or speak the question, with emphasis on the last word. However, in my asking—for knowledge—the second question opens expansive territory by emphasizing its first word.

Where was I in my forties? When I began eating chocolate treats in my performances and when I published a book of my essays, which are performance texts. When I met Russ, who was a graduate student in photography at the University of Arizona. When Tom and I divorced and I moved to Tucson to live with Russ. When Russ and I began collaborating on art work. When he and I lived in Rochester, New York, for a year, longing to return to the West, and then moved to Reno, where we've both lived ever since. When strokes started to weaken Mom, and my parents' doctor told Dad to stop smoking or die. When Ren separated from her husband, to whom she'd been married for almost thirty years. Where was I? I knew much less about love than I know now.

"How have I changed since my forties?" I ask myself, and I respond, "Let me count the ways." I take more action in my behalf. This probably sounds to some readers like selfishness, but rather, it's self-recognition—which opens me to a more compassionate recognition of others too. Self-recognition is self-love, which Aphrodite knows more than any other deity. The iconography of Venus, her Roman descendant, suggests to many interpreters that the goddess is a narcissist: artists have pictured her as the beautiful nude whose attribute is a mirror.

Women look too much in mirrors, we're told by a culture that is telling us to scrutinize the hell out of ourselves because we're *not* goddesses. Woe are we in our ugliness, but we'll keep looking, just to check up on it. We'll conform to negative feminine narcissism. We come to believe it through the cultural abuse that's heaped upon women's physical appearance.

The first definition of *narcissism* in my *Webster's New World Dictionary of American English* is "self-love." A semicolon follows "self-love," and narcissism undergoes a judgment: "excessive interest in one's own appearance." Looking at the definition numbered 2—and the *Webster's* gives only two definitions of *narcissism*—that word becomes more complex and problematic for anyone to whom it applies: "*Psychoanalysis* arrest at or regression to the first stage of libidinal development, in which the self is an object of erotic pleasure." How taboo is that pleasure! How undermined by the determination of arrest or regression! How do any adults learn to be the object of their own erotic pleasure when negative value charges narcissism? The definitions of words, which bear cultural meanings, can debilitate us by leading us away from self-knowledge.

To be the object of one's own erotic pleasure is simultaneously to be its subject. If we are not our own erotic subjects and objects, first and foremost, then how do we understand or experience being erotic objects in an intimately loving and sexual relationship? How do we know what our pleasure is? One way has been to indulge in the mystique of romantic passion, its seductions that remove us from ourselves. Another way, especially for women, has been to exist in perpetual querulousness.

Looking in the mirror, the goddess of love is recognizing herself, which means that she is knowing her beauty, through and through. When I was a little girl looking at my genitals in the full-length mirror in my parents' bedroom, I was knowing my beauty.

"How do I love thee?" asked the poet Elizabeth Barrett Browning. "How do I love thee?" and "How do I know thee?" share a lot in common. Browning answered her question, "Let me count the ways."

Several years ago, right before an endometrial biopsy, when I was in the lithotomy position and wanting to squeeze the nurse's hand if I hurt a lot during the procedure, she and the doctor stared suddenly at my cunt. Was it shrunken and dry like an old woman's supposedly is? Was it too colorful, more purple than pink, or its inside unusually rugose—both characteristics said to be indicative of a woman who enjoys sex and has had a lot of it? Was mucky mucus or dried cum decorating my orifice or lips? Were the latter, which are big, too conspicuous for the viewers' taste because I had trimmed off most of my pubic hair? Was my cunt looking vicious—greedy-mouthed, surely full of teeth—or victimizable, not quite ideally little or pretty enough, but so exposed as to make its substance, flesh, inescapable? Or was my cunt vaguely voluptuous, another possible effect of exposure as well as of lush lips? Was I the embodiment of synthesized sentiments about vaginas and vulvas, all playing both with and against one another to create a horrific sight?

I am beauty and its maker.
I am the meeting place of twenty million deficits.
I am the prize pig.

My name is everywhere, an unsung lesson.
Come into my clinic,
Clinic, from Greek klinein, *to recline*
Clinic, an intensive and concise group session of instruction in a field of knowledge
Come into my clinic and lie beside me.
We will sheathe ourselves in chocolate.

(Eva Keuls, in The Reign of the Phallus: Sexual Politics in Ancient Athens, states, "In the Classical Greek language the word for pig, choiros, . . . denotes the female sex organs, particularly the vagina.")

The controversial feminist gynecologist Christiane Northrup reports in her book Women's Bodies, Women's Wisdom: Creating Physical and Emotional Health and Healing, published in 1995, "Over the years, many patients of all ages and backgrounds have asked me during their pelvic exams, 'How can you do this job? It's so disgusting.'" Northrup also asserts that today "chronic vaginitis . . . [is] virtually epidemic." Vaginosis is anything but an aesthetic condition.

Bacterial vaginosis is a type of vaginitis distinguished by a foul-smelling grayish green or grayish white vaginal discharge. Although itching and burning may accompany the discharge, it is often the only symptom. The stinking, oozing vagina, a medical image of an abnormal state, is familiarly mythic. Ugliness, marked by specificities of disease, discomfort, and complaint, looms large in both cultural and women's consciousness of vaginas, and a woman is likely to have a more medicalized than aesthetic consciousness about her own vagina, unless awareness of ugliness can be called aesthetic consciousness. Northrup relates that "most women with chronic vaginal . . . problems have had them for years. These problems are usually associated with unexpressed complaints about a situation in their lives that have been accumulating for years." The problems may be troubled relationships, such as being married to an alcoholic or philandering man. On a larger scale, woman's relation to the wealth of history and tradition about the vagina, which include her suffering and her complaints about that suffering and which have been accumulating in the feminine unconscious certainly since ancient Greek civilization, impair her soul-and-mind-inseparable-from-body and decrease sensual pleasure in herself.

I did not that day in the examination room regain the relative soul-and-mind-inseparable-from-body comfortableness that I felt before the sudden stare of doctor and nurse — at what, I'll never know, but certainly not vaginosis; but my consciousness of the rich and sweet, active and articulate vagina disarmed the assaulting gynecological gaze.

Vagignosis — knowledge about the vagina — overcomes vaginosis — a myth of unremitting monstrosity. In Mantak and Maneewan Chia's *Healing Love through the Tao: Cultivating Female Sexual Energy*, better knowledge is better aesthetics. According to these Taoist adepts, "The best lover is a fully relaxed woman who understands what is going on inside her." The best lover for herself as well as for any sexual partner.

Who do I think I am? I was receiving Aphrodite's love, beauty, and creativity. I was radiating Aphrodite's love, beauty, and creativity. I was, like her, a narcissist. Love multiplies in self-recognition, because we observe, experience, and interpret everything in a gentleness emptied of the criticism of ourselves and other people. That kind of criticism depresses and depletes us, and it is the origin of *Where Do We Come From? Who Are We? Where Are We Going?* Love of oneself and love of others, from people to animals to plants to rocks to the vast holdings of our unconscious, which may know everything there is to love in the entire universe — which may know everything there is to love.

Gauguin, if you had exhaled, what could you have created?

— Russell and I met in January 1988. I was about to turn forty. He was twenty-six. In 1989, between Christmas and New Year's, I moved from St. Louis to Tucson — Tom and I having divorced in the autumn — to live with Russell. Between our meeting and our living together, we had thought about presenting a performance art piece together. *Breathing* is its title.

It would have been our first collaboration, and it would have been very different from our individual performance works, his incorporating climbing on walls that he built, mine incorporating text and voice. Born in Oregon, Russell became a rock climber in the desert and mountains surrounding Tucson. He moved lightly and daringly on the rocks and on his walls; he danced. Intending our performance to take place at universities and alternative art spaces, I wrote an unfinished description as part of an application package.

A restaurant table for two, with one chair on either side, sits center stage.
A vase holding a large, brilliant red or pink flower stands in the middle

of the white tablecloth. Audience seating is very close to the table. The performers, dressed for a date, enter from opposite sides, and each takes a seat. Dudley removes his jacket and Frueh sets the vase at the back of the table. The performers lean toward each other and begin to breathe, audibly, in variant rhythms. The performance continues as long as . . .

After the ellipsis and after fifteen years, I affirm: we began in bloodred beauty and fairy pink.

The vagina is rich and sweet.

"Move on me," he said.

It is entered through a rose.

My vaginal flora taste subtle on a lover's lips and tongue.

The vagina is a sheath. The female organ into which a penis fits during intercourse was called vagina, the Latin sheath, as a metaphor, by Renaldus Columbus in 1559 in his *De re anatomica.*

The sheath, so pretty in a simplistic pink, the color of cunt dressed up eternally in a virgin's purity, served to hold a sword.

Blades have entered flesh, blades of weapons, blades of speculums used in the vaginal examination. The health educator and performer Terri Kapsalis explains in her 1997 book *Public Privates: Performing Gynecology from Both Ends of the Speculum* that in the medical community many people have begun to use the term "bills" rather than "blades" in order to change the violent connotation of the tool that opens women's vaginas for gynecological examination. Using the traditional term highlights the vagina's defensive position, which remains the vagina's place, enforced by a culture that esteems the masculinist phallus.

Painful insertions experienced in rape and in gynecologists' exams remind me of other metaphors: vagina as bleeding hole (subject to the gore of menstruation); labia and clitoris as wound and mutilation; and female genitals in toto as no-thing (because the woman has been castrated by male genital narcissism). In these metaphors that belong to a unitary power and pleasure ruled by the masculinist phallus, to a model in which the vagina in particular has been "exalted" into pitch dark exile, that beautifully sensitive and delicious organ becomes emptiness—an unoccupied space; a cavity (perhaps decaying—that foul odor!); a hollow that is hollow (only air and, besides that, worthless).

I've been wary of Freud's phallic mastery over theories about the structure of the cultural unconscious. The marketplace of theory is stocked with considerations of castration complex and penis envy, and in the shopping mall a T-shirt features a joke about female no-thingness that entails male accusing female of her own lack. Adrienne, a student in my spring 1999 Feminist Art Criticism course, had seen the T-shirt, and she told me the joke: A little girl and boy, naked from the back, hands in front of them, exchange the following words as she looks at him and asks, "Can I touch yours?" "No, you've already broken yours off."

I've been as beleaguered by a simultaneously mythic and sacred terror—the great and terrible *vagina dentata*—as I've been by psychoanalytic theory. My vagina has never been a sphinx whose intelligence is wound around claws and teeth. Not toothed, but toothsome cells have fashioned my mindpower, my soul-and-mind-inseparable-from-body. "You're like a pillow inside . . . and feel like I can ride on and on forever," as Potter, in my twenties, complimented me. Maybe *he* was fucking Flora, the Roman goddess of flowers, who I imagined with a cuntful of blooms and petals in varying states of freshness and agreeably floral rotting. Men have surprised me by calling me goddess; but I have been leery of cunt goddesses—of the sacred vagina, whether dreadful or blissful, when celebrated as a symbol unto itself. Without conversion into contemporary needs, the sacred vagina—which, in action, sheathed Russell's cock in my love and eros—reads as platitude and mystification.

My sacred vagina has sheathed the cocks of men I loved as abundantly as Aphrodite's cunt has sheathed the cocks of gods and mortal men.

Aphrodite, thank you for having sheathed me in your love.

It should go without saying that the vagina is not the vulva and that each one is only part of the complete female genitalia; so that neither word is a synonym for the other, nor can one of the terms be used accurately to designate all of the female genitals. However, from scholarly to medical to fashion-magazine discourse, misnaming often occurs, with *vagina* being used when *vulva* is actually meant or with one of the two terms being used to designate all of the female genitalia. One of the weirder examples of this appears on the Web site of Dr. David Matlock, self-named "pioneer" of what is now, in popular parlance, the "designer vagina." He provides that fashion with his "Designer Laser Vaginoplasty" (DLV) in order to create what his Web site calls "the aesthetic surgical enhancement of the *vulvar* [my italics] structures (labia minora, labia majora, mons pubis, perineum, introitus, hymen)." While the vagina is my main interest here, I exclude neither the vulva nor female genitals in toto, because images and writing about the vulva and about the entire female genitalia often include ideas about the vagina and perceptions of it. For example, *cunt*, a generally denigrating term reclaimed in the early 1970s by feminist artists who wished to assert their own sexual and corporeal selfhood, means vagina *and* vulva, together. Feminist artists invented and named "cunt art." Because of errors in the nomenclature of female genitalia and its frequent inclusiveness, I'm very careful with my use of language that refers to them.

Vaginal and vulval beauty are related, integrally, but external flesh makes sight a ready determiner of vulval beauty, whereas internal flesh strongly calls other senses into play, the ones that require extreme physical closeness to the vagina in order to be pleased by it. Such closeness includes, of course, a woman's own vaginal experiences, like my fingers opening and knowing my vagina when I was a little girl, like my tasting my cum because my wetness, as a sensation and a texture, appealed to me.

Beauty, say the dictionaries, is that which provides the greatest pleasure. Because of the vagina's usual state of invisibility, its beauty is not in its appearance to me or to my lover—either of us could use a speculum—but rather in what the vagina can do, in what it does, and in what it can set in motion or make happen. My vagina's beauty has existed in pleasures felt—in soul-and-mind-inseparable-from-body—because of vaginal events and actions.

How you love this haunt of yours
Its scent and taste so often mild and mellow, like an herb that's said to
    heal the heart
Its gentle flavor and perfume sometimes spicy with the sweat outside its
    threshold
I know this full and piquant loveliness when it permeates my fingers,
    when my light lick brings me close as I can get to that sacred smell of
    me; and I know this loveliness from kissing you.
How I love this haunt of mine
Which exercises my desire as far as it will go, into the squishing perfume
    not created simply by a clinical friction of cock and cunt, just a pent-up
    rhythm, bodies graceless, vapid mechanisms lacking sacred weight,

but rather by the ways that we enjoy adjusting our corporeality, in
fucking intimacy, for pleasure.
When we apply those chosen pressures, something sumptuous occurs,
and something more than only sumptuous
The points and areas that have been haunted by bad judgment and bad
juju—the false consciousness that lingers in the Freudian icon of a
dark continent—become radiant: my clitoris, my G-spot, the very
back of my vagina.
It is not the size of your penis or my vagina that illuminates us
I shine, like a goddess, when we love this haunt of mine
My cunt gleaming
All at once

Even though the linguistic problem with cunts mystifies and even endangers female genitals by obscuring their structures, beauties, and pleasures through denying particularities that manifest the difference of women from men, that problem can also be annoyingly comical. Like the sacred vagina: "We shall briefly indicate that conceptualizing the vagina as a sacred object yields a perspective that appears to be of value in analyzing the vaginal examination." So wrote James M. Henslin, a doctor, and Mae A. Biggs, a nurse, in 1971. In their statement, the sacred has value as a device of absurd separation. Confusing a self-touching skin with an object—something apart from a woman's body—Henslin and Biggs separate the vagina from the integrity that is a woman's body. With her vagina objectified into sacredness, a woman's spiritual value is de-corporealized, and thereby de-eroticized. The vagina belongs to a woman's erotic life, even during a vaginal examination, precisely *because* the vagina is an integral actor in a woman's soul-and-mind-inseparable-from-body.

As physician and nurse separate themselves from the patient, through language and through analysis, they sterilize the profane and unhygienic vagina, culturally infected with disgusting odors, blood taboos, and unseen sensations of pleasure. As analysts, physician and nurse assert their rationality over the "irrational"—the vagina. The sacred is special, yet it is also irrational, because it is mysterious; and mystery scares as well as fascinates human beings. Erotic charge—smell, taste, touch, feel, sound, and orgasm—is part of the vagina's sacredness and "irrationality." Analyzing the vaginal examination cauterizes the vagina's eros with the heat of fake praise, all to beautify the unholy ugliness — to some — of vaginas in person.

The longtime feminist luminary Gloria Steinem, prefacing Eve Ensler's script for The Vagina Monologues, a play dedicated to fashioning vaginal community and culture, wishes that "my own foremothers had known their bodies were sacred." Having lived in India after college for a couple of years, Steinem remains especially impressed with the yoni, an abstract image of female genitals as a triangle, double-pointed oval, or flowerlike design that she saw in Hindu shrines and temples.

In Sanskrit, yoni means vulva and womb, and the yoni is the symbol through which the female divine in the form of the goddess Shakti is worshipped. In Tantric Hinduism the yoni must be worshipped by men because it is the sacred power spot of women's bodies. The Tantric ceremonial worship of the female genitals is called the yoni-puja, and according to the yoga scholar George Feuerstein's paraphrasing of the Yoni-Tantra's author, without cultivating the yoni-puja, liberation — realizing the divine Self, which is none other than the ultimate Reality — is unattainable. The vagina is essential to this Consciousness-Bliss because the vagina is essential to maithuna, intercourse between female and male practitioners in an enactment of Shakti's and Shiva's coupling. Besides being goddess and god, respectively, Shakti is Energy and Shiva is Consciousness. Preceding maithuna, sight is important. Anointed with sandalwood paste, the yoni looks like a flower. Its beauty is further beautified.

O Aphrodite, I received the wisdom of your Garden.

Maithuna itself produces the female's — the yogini's — sacred fluid, yoni-tattva, which the male practitioner, the yogin, must assimilate. This is sometimes done orally. In Tantric practice, the vagina's sacred fluid can only be beautiful; then, so too would be its taste and touch. Taoist sexual practice, which includes sexual exercises called "kung fu" (meaning discipline or concentrated work), knows the female body to be capable of producing three sexual "waters": lubrication on arousal (produced by the vaginal walls); ejaculate — the cum with which we're familiar; and an ejaculate, released by the G-spot, that sexual partners sometimes mistake for urine because most women do not produce it and many women and men are unfamiliar with it through either experience or knowledge. According to the Chias, the G-spot releases ejaculate, whereas the

Boston Women's Health Book Collective, whose members authored *Our Bodies, Ourselves for the New Century: A Book by and for Women*, states that some women may ejaculate—issue fluid from the G-spot—with continuous G-spot stimulation.

The viewpoint of *Healing Love through the Tao* is aesthetic, although never named as such. Like Tantric sexual practice, Taoist sexual practice aims to free pure spiritual energy, which engages practitioners in birthing themselves into enlightenment. Enlightenment is the epitome of a beautiful state, and on the path to it, through sexual cultivation, a woman learns to love her sexual organs. Necessarily, such love embraces these organs' emissions. Through love, the fluids become beautiful. With their ever-so-light texture, distinctly lush perfume, and almost-sweet to zesty flavor, the three waters are exquisitely aesthetic to the taste and to the touch.

Cultivating Aphrodite's Garden, I received the glamour of her famous cunt, whose juiciness indeed must be sublime. With lovers after Russ and I divorced, I was aroused, divinely, wet from the excitement that any Aphrodite knows. However, I noticed, during spells between the men, the sex, that sometimes my vagina didn't feel normal: dry compared to usual, let alone during the ardors of lovemaking and the passions of masturbation. Finger-fucking myself became unpleasurable because the very shapes and structure of my cunt, from inner lips to vagina, had assumed a guise of hardnesses and thinnesses and inflexibilities.

Gone, for a while, were any men I called lover, and my aloneness, in which I breathed and cultivated, in which I caressed myself as any Aphrodite would, let my hurts surface. I cried, and again and again my bravery led my fingers, guided by my heart, into my vagina, where the rising and releasing hurts—maybe men's own unresolved emotions absorbed by my body through their ejaculations and ejaculate—were relaxing my pelvis and easing my cunt. Rising and releasing from my massively unknown self, without the aid of Mel.

My hero, myself, took the best care of me. And if, in a past life centuries ago, I bled and wept because a medical incompetent treated me with antique tools and attitudes toward women's reproductive parts, or because a cruel husband beat me into having sex with him, or because I outlived men's fascination with my sexual performances—arrayed in diaphanous fabrics, belly naked, all my skin a magnet for males gazing in private clubs and opulent boudoirs: then in this life, my vagina became the best of action heroes. If you let it, vaginal action outwits the enemies of cunt, and those who are careless with it rather than malicious. If you let it, cunt forgives us women of former abuses against it—both those we know and those our flesh has not forgotten.

In Aphrodite's Garden her love, beauty, and creativity reshaped my vagina into softness, plumpness, and flexibility, and I am as wet as ever simply sitting here to tell you of my rebirth.

Steinem lovingly claims for herself and all women the value of knowing that their genitals are sacred. She especially revels in the fact that naves are vaginal. Feeling pride, she writes, "I walk down the vaginal aisle," as if she has wedded her own body and now loves and honors it. Her knowledge and sentiment moved and comforted me. Yet, reading Steinem, I felt restless, and I felt stuck in history, not because as a feminist and an art historian I'd known for many years that naves are vaginal, but because Steinem's passage is written as a discovery.

Poignant and joyful feminist discoveries like hers can result in revolutions of thinking and behavior that are inspiring and humane, and such discoveries can seem outrageous—outrageously good or outrageously offensive—to those who are unfamiliar with them. Steinem appreciates the voices in The Vagina Monologues—Ensler tells many women's stories—as "outrageous," and on the back cover of the book, Patricia Bosworth calls the play "a revolutionary piece of theater." Within the context of popular cultural motifs and acceptable public speech, Ensler's endeavor is revolutionary. However, for me, a girl, a fairy, a woman, and an action hero, who has loved and thought about her vagina for almost her whole life and who, as a feminist scholar of the erotic, has researched and written about women's sexual pleasure, The Vagina Monologues is neither outrageous nor revolutionary enough. Reading it, I felt a disappointment similar to that when I read the philosopher Elizabeth Grosz's "Animal Sex," in which she considers revealing her own experience of sexual pleasure and then, giving reasons, decides not to. Cunt-experience, written from the perspective of that brilliant feminist philosopher, would have deepened, enriched, and complicated her essay.

As I read Ensler and Grosz, my initial excitement turned to disappointment because I wanted more—more (self-)knowledge and more pleasure, both from the authors and for myself, and more revelations about the vagina's explicit sensuousness—which is both its beauty and its action. Replete with the truth of women's experiences, The Vagina Monologues is a feminist treasure, yet it hurts — so much shame and squelching, so much injury. Feminist revolution enlarges with every telling of women's truths, and trauma can be a tool for transformation. Yet, as a midlife woman who has called herself a feminist for over thirty years, I'm invested in *pleasure* and dedicated to it, to the erotic revolution whose possibility thrilled me when I read Marcuse's *Eros and Civilization: A Philosophical Inquiry into Freud* in college. Marcuse argues for Western civilization, as a system and as individual members, to raise the pleasure principle above the reality principle and to live by the former. Revolution is women focusing on their greatest pleasure — which is their beauty and its action — difficult as that may be.

I regret my often lapsed divinity. During those lapses I've wondered: perhaps I *am* an incarnation of Cunti, Yoni of the Universe, of Flora, whose festival the Floralia permitted celebrants to dance naked and to enjoy their lasciviousness; maybe I'm an incarnation of every fucking goddess ever dreamed up. Now delivered from those lapses, I ask, as avatar especially of Cunti, Flora, Shakti, Aphrodite, and Astarte, I ask, as simply a woman, I ask you, you gorgeous quintet, to remove the curse of reinventing the wheel. Then I can stop being called an ugly cunt, a silly cunt, a dumb cunt, because people will no longer have to pretend that the vagina is a trivial, idiotic, repellent, passive, and inarticulate organ.

I've seen through and around the tunnel of love, the birth canal, the toxic wasteland, the chamber of horrors, the stink pot and the honey pot, the resting place — the tomb — of man's desire; the adventurers and heroes who continue to explore the "dark continent" — a poetic Freudian phrase deserving remembrance but much less repetition; the detectives who investigate in theory and practice the crime of basic black — woman's elegant interior — in order to expunge themselves of too much poetic license; the no-man's-land until his flesh or the results of his seed make it into woman, which means make it his, which means make it into him. I've designed a vision from the actions of the inside out, from soul-and-mind-inseparable-from-body: from my vagina's folds and textures; from nuances, of slipperiness and stickiness and minute lubrication, of succulent fishiness and old roses; from pubococcygeal pressures; from itches and orgasms.

I've read too much about *you can't go home again*, how we're refugees from the mother's plenitude, lost within a misperception, "that hole you left behind when you came into the world" (so called by the feminist philosopher and psychoanalyst Luce Irigaray in her *Speculum of the Other Woman*). I did not leave a hollow, an emptiness. I did not leave some inconsequential conduit, defined in the *Webster's* on my desk as "the canal between the vulva and the uterus." The eroticized skin and space I moved through eroticized me. My mother's jubilant vagina transferred its joy to me, soul-and-mind-inseparable-from-body. The vagina's touch, which is an element of its action, the vagina's capacity for hugging and stretching, its ability to grasp and still be flexible, is always with us. If I were to leave behind my mother's vagina, I would be bereft of my own. My voracious and welcoming beauty.

Russell came right in. He photographed me for his own work and for my own. We collaborated on fairy nudes and portraits of me. I appeared in one panel of his huge black-and-white triptychs from the early 1990s; reclining on the floor of our living room or seated on one of our pink, vinyl-upholstered fifties chairs. Joanna, the pin-up in high heels or a stylish, silly hat and the gaiety of love as well as in the meditative gazes motivated by a more private plushness—the aesthetic and erotic confessional that photographs can be. I loved to model for Russell's photographs, conceptually and pictorially designed by him; I knew I looked beautiful in them. Occasionally I photographed Russell, and he looked beautiful in my pictures. I especially liked the one I took of him in my pearls, as if he were Aphrodite rising from an orgasm.

How have I loved thee? Let me count the ways.

Russell and Rossetti, who in my dreams once was my lover, and so many other men with mouths like roses, men who lived, like me, under the sign of phallus, who loved, like me, the sudden synergy of cock and cunt, How quick *was* orgasm when I was in your company? (Applying the lipstick to his mouth, it became as ridiculously beautiful as I made my own.) As quick as penis meets introitus.

Is that because my parents gave me an unusual gift? The ability to sheathe myself in chocolate.

J. Marion Sims, M.D., glorified as the Father of Modern Gynecology, the Father of American Gynecology, and Architect of the Vagina, asserts in his autobiography, "If there was anything I hated, it was investigating the organs of the female pelvis"—all of them. Kapsalis's analysis of Sims's procedural innovations and of what amounted to his experiments on African American slave women's vaginas shows that the vagina is perceived as an abjectly repulsive organ. Reinforcing that description are her readings of photographs of female genitalia in medical texts—"I discovered only one instance of a photograph of healthy, normal female genitalia"—and her critique of medical students' training in gynecology: "Medical students . . . have been indoctrinated into a system that privileges pathology." The medicalized and pathologized vagina is an unaesthetic one, and women unconsciously interpret the vagina's pathogenic qualities within an aesthetic framework.

I remember my shock when a very intelligent and articulate student of mine, in her early twenties, revealed during a classroom conversation that she had just discovered—through reading or through a gynecologist's explanation, I don't recall—that her vaginal secretions, which had disgusted her, were normal. She called herself a feminist, and she *was*: a pretty hard-assed and acerbic feminist. Here was one of my brightest students, one who I thought was well informed, and she didn't know an action of her vagina—its ability to secrete healthy lubrications—or the beauty of that action's product, the secretions themselves. My shock gave her a compassionate response and gave me the wisdom to know that, despite the feminist revolution that was a sexual revolution, beginning in the late 1960s and continuing into the present, young women—the very students I loved and identified with—wished for, longed for, and needed education about their bodies, their sexuality, and their eros. For my talented and thoughtful feminist student had feared that her secretions indicated vaginitis.

Ancient Aphrodite, you did not suffer from vaginitis, and as I became ever more at one with you, Love and Beauty grew within me. During the last couple of years of Russ's and my marriage and for longer than a year after our divorce, I suffered from a vaginitis coupled with distention of my lower belly. At the time, I attributed those discomforts to psychic and emotional pressures, densities, and constrictions—anger, heartbreak, grief, the corruption of intimate bonds—that had become embedded in my female flesh. I got "cured," through herbal remedies supplied by a practitioner of Chinese medicine or suppositories from my gynecologist; and then, within a couple of weeks or at most a month, the vaginitis and the pain returned.

It is not only time that heals all wounds. Indeed, time, without the assistance of healers we trust to move us into whatever sleeps uncomfortably in our flesh, may suppress wounds. Larry, my therapist, and Stephen, my healer, moved me deeply into my psychophysical flesh, which was another aspect of the massively unknown self. They took me into energies that went amok, from anger, heartbreak, grief, and the corruption of intimate bonds.

Aphrodite, I was grateful to be one with you, to have the fortune to recognize my union with your Beauty, Love, and Creativity. I see your imitators' adulations on the surface of their flesh alone. What nightmares ache to leave their home in the bellies and the hearts of glamour pusses, glamour pussies? I close my eyes and exhale; I hear my poignant chortle: funny to think of attractive celebrities, turned into sex goddesses — by a culture that sees Aphrodite from a distance, dislodged from Love, and dimly — with vaginitis. Once while standing in the grocery checkout line, I read a front-page headline in the Star or the National Enquirer that asked why men betray the most gorgeous women in the world. As if beauty so captivates men that they cannot escape its allure. Here we are, once again, in the absurdity of romantic passion, in which the princess's beauty generates her lover's eternal fidelity. O fantasies of perfection, in relationships, in bodies, be gone! How you ruin the beauty of reality. Rapunzel, Rapunzel, let down your hair and relax. Run from the tower of romantic twaddle and take with you the wisdom you have gained from your imprisonment.

The gorgeous women, the Rapunzels, were Jennifer Lopez, entertainment glamour puss, and Vanessa Bryant, the wife of the basketball star Kobe Bryant. I wondered if Vanessa Bryant and Jennifer Lopez suffered from vaginitis.

O Aphrodite, you let the luxury of your long hair mingle with mine. You let it be, for we were one. Gorgeous women, plain women: how do men betray thee? Let me count the ways. Aphrodite, you and I, as one, forgave them. How did I love thee, Aphrodite? Let me count the ways. How did I love me? Let me count the ways. This counting was an exercise in infinity.

Neither the infinitude of Love nor the infinitude of actual women's vaginal and vulval shapes conform to the measures of female genital beauty and action devised by Dr. Matlock. Just as Matlock's DLV creates the "ideal" vulva, so his Laser Vaginal Rejuvenation (LVR) creates the "ideal" vagina. According to Matlock's Web site, he and his team at the Laser Vaginal Rejuvenation Institute, of which he is the founder and CEO, are responding to women's stated desires: they want small, dainty labia and tight vaginas. How fascinating that these ideal anatomies correspond to today's beauty ideal for women, which is a fitness ideal: the body must be lean and streamlined — "clean." Excepting large breasts, the ideal must not exhibit any too-muchness. The clean aesthetic designates loose-ness and bulges as unsightly generosities of flesh—a mess.

Matlock's site differently markets DLV and LVR. DLV enhances the aesthet-ics of vulvas, while LVR enhances women's sexual satisfaction. Nonetheless, programs and procedures for the (impossible) accomplishment of ideal beauty are based in the concept of aestheticization as rejuvenation, thereby making LVR an aesthetic surgery. According to Matlock's site, LVR treats "the loss of the optimum structural architecture of the vagina," the looseness or "vaginal relaxation" that can result from childbirth, although some women are naturally looser—larger—than others.

LVR also treats stress urinary incontinence. Sims, too, was treating urinary incontinence in both his African American and white patients when he sutured their vesico-vaginal fistulas, small tears that can form between the vagina and urinary tract or bladder. Like the relaxed vagina, these fistulas could result from childbirth. Incontinence is not aesthetic—the discomfort, the smell. Sims operated on the nonoptimum structural architecture of vaginas. For both him and Matlock, "better" structure means "better" aesthetics.

Within both Matlock's and conventional wisdom, tightness means better sex for both women and men through more friction. Just as a small penis is sup-posedly (always) bad for a man's pleasing a woman in heterosexual intercourse, the large vagina brings pleasure to neither a woman nor a man. In this model of sexual pleasure, more friction brings about optimal genital sensation: "bet-ter" structure equals "better" sensation equals "better" (or even best!) aesthet-ics. How interesting that nowhere in *Healing Love through the Tao* do the Chias discuss let alone mention either females' or males' genital size. Newman K. Lin—the self-proclaimed "black-belt Sexual ChiKong (KungFu) Master, Dr. Lin"—exclaims, in his exuberant Web-site style, "The penis size is not impor-tant at all!" (Aphrodite understood that a good match or pairing of cock and cunt, a good fit, can sometimes overcome troubled emotional ties. The pleasure of fucking a good-fitting partner can provide an illusion of getting along well with each other.) Yet Lin does counsel women with self-described "loose" vagi-nas (and men with penises smaller than those men would like) to use his for-mulas, which, by ballooning the spongy tissues in the vaginal wall (and penile shaft), he declares, will narrow the vagina (and increase the penis). Lin asserts that "penile and vaginal sizes vary with the biological responses of the spongy tissues to the hormones and neurochemicals." Lin is anti-LVR: he does have his formulas to sell. However, the frictional aesthetic does not appear to claim his attention, even though he does not speak in behalf of large vaginas.

What a difference between the idealized small vagina and the nave as vagina, which is an architecture, an idea, and a symbol of monumental proportions: microcosm—vagina—is literally and figuratively envisioned as macrocosm, part of the heavenly City of God, represented in the actuality of a Gothic cathedral. Something might be *as* beautiful as that heavenly city, but nothing could be *more* beautiful. Nothing could be more radiant, more full of worldly or sacred splendor. And the vaginal nave is so big that, conceptually, it can hold the entire Church. Being fairy deep, the heavenly City of Cunt and the heavenly City of Queer have a lot in common.

Funny, in a frightening way: Sims also *enlarged* vaginas, but apparently only so that men could fit inside. By inventing means for enlarging the vaginal opening—through incising it or through hymenotomy—and its interior—through dilation with wedges of varying sizes—he attempted to cure vaginismus, the too-tight (!) vagina. Sims coined the term vaginismus, and as a self-labeled "explorer," his entrepreneurial remodeling of the vagina makes him an innovative architect, a term that might also describe Matlock. (Kapsalis writes that on "first using the speculum and viewing the inside of the vagina, Sims himself wrote: 'I felt like an explorer in medicine who first views a new and important territory.'") Although the "architect" epithet does suit Matlock, "Artist of the Vagina" might be more pertinent. A cover article in an issue of *Harper's Bazaar*, featured in the Media Overview section of Matlock's Web site, begins, "The way Dr. David L. Matlock sees it, he's the Picasso of vaginas." Artists such as Picasso have their "trademark" styles, so it is interesting, from not only an aesthetic but also a sales point of view, that Matlock has trademarked LVR (as well as DLV). Pioneers and explorers; masters, heroes, and messiahs: these words belong to what I call the language of war and the language of miracles, a rhetoric that pervades art historical discourse about supremely expert artists, the ones whose "trademarks" have distinguished the artists' historical significance, their greatness.

I am the artist of my vagina's health, its pink and bloodred beauties.

In her essay "Vaginal Architecture" Kapsalis critiques the medical rhetoric that fashions vaginas into vaults, chambers, and canals. She asserts that linguistically built vaginal architecture is "simultaneously utopian and authoritarian." So is the vaginal architecture built literally in women's flesh and of it. The artists Faith Wilding and Christina Hung's video *Vulva De/ReCONSTRUCTRA* (2001), which critiques the "designer vagina," comes from the same theoretical position as does Kapsalis, and it confronts today's medical styling of female genitalia, focusing on the vulva. Wilding is one of the originators of cunt art, and her collaborative video is at once humorous and cautionary. There, vagina as the structural source for nave occurs when a cathedral architectural plan appears supermimposed on the image of a real vulva. This image suggests that what's inside the vulva is the "foundation" not only of the nave aisle but also of the nave elevation.

Kapsalis's "Vaginal Architecture" elucidates the rhetorical paradigm that determines the medical—and popular—representation of vaginas. Thomas Laqueur, in his *Making Sex: Body and Gender from the Greeks to Freud*, pinpoints theories, events, and convictions, from Galen and Aristotle through contemporary feminism, that exemplify how aesthetic and scientific paradigms—not empirical or experiential facts—determine understandings and even illustrations of genital anatomy. Sex, he says—what is woman and what is man and what is their anatomical, metaphysical, and social relation to one another—is always being invented. Making sex, and thus what is made of women's genitals, is an art.

Irigaray laments woman's lack of representation of her own morphology and pleasure. Woman appears in the art of making sex as differentiated from man on his terms. Laqueur, who repeatedly demonstrates how female sexual organs are "attracted into the metaphorical orbit of the male," also tells us that Gregory of Nyssa imagined sexual differentiation "as the representation in the flesh of the fall from grace." Differentiated from man on *his* terms, woman's fall from grace is a fall from genital beauty.

In aphroditean embraces, I found grace. Like the female divine in the Gnostic poem "Thunder, Perfect Mind," whose rolling voice proclaims over and over *I am*, I say,

I am the baker and the baker's field
I am the enterprise after the dream
I am the epic, proportions given to a single female organ

I am the details in daily lives, muscles around it strong because
It caresses
not only cocks and fingers but every day its very flesh without a stop
I am the spine and diaphragm
I am digesting chocolate
cakes and truffles, ice cream, cocoa, hearts and flowers
I am red lips galore, pursed to ask for yet another big bite
I am a mouthful looking out for hunger
I am Mistress of Cunt Kung Fu
I am Cockaigne come to life

We do not need to make vaginas into art, but our making of representations as sophisticated, smart, and blatant, as full of ridiculous beauty and action as the phallus, would contribute to women's sexual, gender, and aesthetic parity that I believe women need for soul-and-mind-inseparable-from-body confidence. If the aesthetically deficient vagina were not culturally prevalent, Ensler would not have written *The Vagina Monologues*, and the first page of Germaine Greer's chapter "Sex" in her *Female Eunuch*, published in 1971, which I read to my 1999 Feminist Art Criticism class, would not have struck a chord with them, an experiential assent to the problems Greer describes: "actual distaste" for female genitalia stemming from modesty; women's lack of encouragement to sensorially explore their genital flesh, to identify its anatomy, to learn the processes of clitoral erection and vaginal lubrication; the ugliness of cunt— "the worst name anyone can be called." Women in their early to midtwenties composed the class, and the fact that Greer's words rang true for them speaks sadly and strongly of a largely unchanged perception of the vagina's ugliness.

I'm not writing about the vagina, selecting one of women's multiple genital and reproductive organs, in order to campaign for one part of a complex to be the unitary sign of woman, as the artfully penis-turned-phallus is of man. Rather, I make my choice because my vagina is a central pleasure in my body and life, as it is for other women, and because the vulva rather than the vagina is generally the subject of 1970s cunt art as well as more recent work coming out of that tradition.

Vaginal iconography, another term for cunt art, is really not precise, even though certain works suggest vaginal sensations. For example, while Hannah

Wilke's *Pink Champagne*, from 1974, a seven-foot-wide wall sculpture of overlapping latex rubber undulations studded with metal snaps, may be read as a plethora of labial "petals," it can be read simultaneously as both waves and multiplicity of orgasm—clitoral, vaginal, both, and more. (Wilke loved puns, so I understand the snaps to mean, Orgasm, it's a snap!) The paintings in Judy Chicago's *Reincarnation Triptych*, dated 1973, each of which displays a bright center from which sinuous forms radiate in every direction, likewise suggest the pleasure of orgasm, the kind that feels as if it's generated from deep within the body's core, say, the back of the vagina, called the "Epicenter" by Lin, or the uterus in tandem with the Epicenter. Yet another term for cunt art is central core imagery. Carolee Schneemann's performance *Interior Scroll*, performed the same year as *Pink Champagne*'s creation, is one of the few early cunt-art works that focuses on the vagina. Dressed only in her stunning nudity, Schneemann delicately unraveled from her vagina a ten-foot-long scroll and unfolded its "strange origami"—a phrase she used in a conversation with me—so that she could read the text that she had written on it. *Interior Scroll* understands the vagina as an articulate organ.

My focus on the vagina rather than the vulva emphasizes that a different, relatively unrepresented, and equally worthy feminist subject, the vagina with its wealth of metaphors and symbols, can be used to represent feminine sexuality outside of the maternal/reproductive function that, as Irigaray asserts throughout her writings, is the only sexuality that man has permitted woman. I assert my own function, which is the characteristic and normal action of my vagina.

—I sing to my vagina, without an interest in reasserting Freud's conclusion that the vagina is the organ of mature female sexuality (because woman's correct socialization demands her giving up the clitoris for the organ associated with man, reproduction, and thus family. That socialization is culture's pressure, not Freud's belief in an absolute social meaning of genitalia.) While the clitoris predominates in much feminist literature as the site of sexual pleasure, the organ is a mistaken notion with no basis in the complexity of female sexual anatomy or response. I sing to the vagina because it lends itself to representations of female morphology and of experience—both women's and men's—that are laden with multisensorial elements.

While Laqueur might agree with the philosopher Michel Foucault that "the gaze is not faithful to the truth," an aesthetic tradition, reaching back to classical antiquity, coupled with a gender economy that narcissizes the penis, constructs its visible "truth" into aesthetic truth: the phallus makes order out of the chaos of the male body, as art is said to make order out of the chaos of life. As many feminists have pointed out, the Western tradition has labeled the female body chaotic.

The phallocentric gaze doesn't sing to the vagina, and the masculinist phallus idealizes the penis into a shapely unit of ridiculous beauty. Artists of a later generation than cunt art's originators—who include Chicago, Schneemann, Wilding, and Wilke, all born between 1939 and 1943—have been creating such an aesthetic for the female genitals. Mayumi Lake's *Poo-Chi* series of photographs, produced from 1999 to 2000, transforms armpits or crooks of knees, often costumed in little-girl regalia, into trompe l'oeil vulvas. When the viewer realizes this trick of the artist and trick of the eye, she may smile or even laugh at the ridiculous beauty into which Lake has reconceived the sometimes sentimentally sterilized vision of sacred cunt. Judy Bamber's *My Little Fly, My Little Butterfly*, dated 1992, composed of two hyperrealist paintings less than ten by eight inches, scores a different kind of point for ridiculous beauty, a darker one. Each painting depicts a hairy vulva, one of which is covered with flies, affixed to the surface with pins, the other with butterflies, similarly attached. Same form, different connotations: one repellent, one attractive, their difference indicating the ridiculous beauty of oppositionally extreme notions about cunts.

Within the model of penis idealized into phallus, the intolerably invisible vagina is amorphous. In Renaissance terms man was informing and woman informable. He shaped her, and just as the artist, according to the philosopher Christine Battersby, "constructs a mini-world by imposing meaning and significance on formless matter," so the penis shapes the vagina. Its malleable contour conforms to the penile volume; fluid conforms to solid. The vagina gives, it stretches like fabric. It gets big—with a penis or a baby—does not or cannot remain stable. It is like woman as the sign of instability, and the vagina's "sloppiness"—its messy discharges and lubrication—augments the vagina's visual vagueness.

With the clarity that comes from aphroditean Love, I ask, How do I love thee? Let me count the ways.

At best, the vagina appears to be dull. Even for the contemporary performance artist Annie Sprinkle, in whose *Public Cervix Announcement* the female's internal organs become, in Kapsalis's words, "the pinnacle of beauty, the newest and bravest of fashion statements," the vagina is passed over because its visual interest does not compare to that of the cervix, which is Sprinkle's focus. As she says in an interview with Kapsalis, "the vaginal walls are kind of dull." The 1998 edition of *Our Bodies, Ourselves*, the famous women's health guide based in women's experiences, uses an anatomical illustration in which the vagina resembles a horizontally ribbed tube. This drawing, read as part of an idealized canon in anatomical illustration, is so simple as to be paradoxically abstruse. I do not "see" my vagina in this ridiculously dehumanized abstraction, for seeing is only believing when it belongs to a multisensorial complex. (The illustration has disappeared from the most recent edition, published in 2005.)

The vagina is all content—penis or baby—without form. We see this idea in an astoundingly creepy drawing by the surrealist Hans Bellmer for his 1957 book *Petite Anatomie de l'inconscient physique ou l'anatomie de l'image.* Depicted from the rear, a naked woman leaning over on her hands poses with her buttocks exceedingly elevated. Bellmer delineates the contours of her body, and the inside of it, too: from her waist to her anus, she is an enormous penis; or she has been penetrated by one. In other words, her vagina has become a penis.

When we were most together, Russ and I at one with Aphrodite, then our organs, in aphroditean expansiveness, which is embrace, have felt like one. Our forms were the function of erotic action.

Perhaps for the vagina, form equals function as use-value. As we learn in Christine Ammer's compact encyclopedia *The New A to Z of Women's Health*, published in 1995, "The vagina has two principal functions," which are "exit passage of the uterus"—expelling "wastes" and birthing babies—and "organ of sexual intercourse, into which the male inserts his penis." The vagina accommodates—the movement of blood, endometrial tissue, babies, and penises—and it is empty unless functionally full of something other than itself. More than being passive, it is almost apathetic—the "slack canal" described by the famed seventeenth-century French obstetrician François Mauriceau, whose writings informed nineteenth-century articles.

Slack: sluggish, idle, weak, careless, and lax. Not firm, infirm.

Free us, Aphrodite, free us women and us men from the sickening and sickly cunt.

Awake and awakened, my vagina is active and carefree, as dynamic, firm, and joyous as a fairy spreading her full wings. Buoyant as the female figures in Russell's photos from the mid-1990s, for which he appropriated images of pin-up lovelies, reconceived by him to look as though they are flying. He called them fairies, and his and my favorite, taken from a publicity photo for Houdini, unfurls her huge wings. Viewed from any angle, her gossamer beauty feels exuberant and comfortable. No upside down, no sideways, for Russell's fairy is floating in an aphroditean expansiveness, which decenters the viewer, like lovemaking and like beauty do.

Because the Greek *aisthesis*, from which *aesthetics* derives, means sense-perception, Western aesthetics' focus on visual perception, on material objects, restricts both the awareness and the study of beauty. Sight, like hearing, has been, since classical Greek philosophy, a higher sense, distinguished from smell, taste, and touch, the lower senses, which have been associated with the sexual and the body. Sight leaves the viewer distant from its focus, whereas smell, taste, and touch occur at intimate range. In Western aesthetic theory the higher senses are allied with reason and contemplation, which are morally and metaphysically superior to some corporeal seizure by sensation. Lower body and lower senses: the vagina threatens *and* lures with its implications and resonances of contact, including our own with our mothers during our birth.

The vagina also lures and threatens with its implications and resonances of infinity—the dark void from which no man returns. I sense this lure and threat in works by Lee Bontecou and Yayoi Kusama, artists who began practicing and exhibiting well before the invention of cunt art. So that term does not describe their work. Bontecou, born in 1931, drew the art world's attention in the 1960s with her wall sculptures of canvas, in stretched fragments, and metal, from wire frameworks to welded steel to saws. Projecting toward the viewer, composition centered by a dark hole, sometimes with forbidding "teeth," Bontecou's iconic, monumental "cunts" implicitly critique the military-industrial complex. At the same time, they bring to mind the truly menacing and awe-inspiring vagina—*dentata* or not—whose unavailable and seemingly never-ending interior may cause the psyche to spin. Decentered.

Infinity has been an ongoing concern in Kusama's work since the 1960s when she began exhibiting it, and many of her mixed-media sculptures have called attention to the phallus's ridiculous beauty. Kusama's *Fireflies on the Water*, exhibited from November 26, 2002, through January 18, 2003, at the Robert Miller Gallery in New York, was a spectacular experience of the infinite. An installation into which one person at a time walked through a doorway, closing the door behind her, *Fireflies* surrounded an individual—one was not simply an observer—in a completely mirrored space lit by what appeared to be a myriad of tiny lights, all tender tones of amber, blue, and red. Light—not at the end of the tunnel, but everywhere. A festal "architecture." That's what Karsten Harries calls for in his book *The Ethical Function of Architecture*. Festal architecture, he believes, would help people to feel community, to experience an ethos that includes the importance of literally and spiritually existing between earth and heaven. In *Fireflies* I knew above and underneath. I *was* them. Yet . . . upon entering, I was walking on a platform. It was shorter and wider than a diving board, but I feared that if the platform weren't strong enough or if I lost my balance, I'd be plummeting into infinity. I felt risk and longing, even though I also felt at one with the space, embraced by the gorgeousness that literally reflected me in a mirror facing the door. Here was bliss, the union of Energy and Consciousness. I didn't want to leave. And the piece haunted me.

How I love these haunts of mine.

If appreciated for its multisensorial haunts, for its multisensorially heady mix of elements, the vagina is protean. Its changing lines are subtle and dynamic gestures from which changing smells and climatic conditions cannot be separated.

Sheathe is a verb. Move on me, he said.

Radiance sheathes Shakti, sheathes Aphrodite.
Splendid metal sheathes the knight.
The salonnières sheathed soirées in conversation.
When we wish, we sheathe ourselves in perfume, just as the flowers do.
I sheathe myself in a chocolate-colored dress and shoes.
He sheathed me in love.

He, my husband Russell, loved my vagina, the temperature and texture, without latex covering his penis. I didn't experience his preference as an aggression in behalf of his pleasure alone because I loved the temperature and texture of his naked cock. Flesh loves flesh more than it loves rubber. He loved my vagina most when I wasn't having my period. He told me that during my period the quality of warmth was less inviting than usual and my vagina was too slippery for his greatest enjoyment. I understood what he was saying when I put my finger into my vagina during my period. His vagignosis was mine as well.

Flowers, sheath, and lips meet the compatibility of phallus. Like vagina and penis, they are intimate only at certain times. They are not ever-ready. I have not wanted opposite sex with you, Russell and Rossetti, and so many other men. (My father loved the smell of hawthorn blossoms. I love it too. They smell like cunt.) We are all more than opposite sex confines us to, a boring but romantic path from opposite to opposition. Where the difference of symmetry, analogy, homology, and complementarity is believable, sexual opposition is the battle between the sexes: he penetrates her, she surrounds him. We know too well the military terms of sexual encounters: he wins, she loses.

I'll bake Devil's Food Cake Cockaigne for all of us with exaggerated lips. In my copy of Joy of Cooking the well-fingered page with that recipe is smudged with chocolate. I look for chocolate smudges around the lips of female heads and figures in Rossetti's paintings, the figures that are as floral as their surroundings. I imagine me with those flowers at a party, us lovely cunts just eating chocolate to our heart's content. Profusely petaled, we may be fetishes for eyes that need the safety of visually exciting surfaces. Me, I am a lover and not a castrate. Me, I am deep. I identify with what I have—large, intensely colored lips above and below, flesh that's rich and sweet as roses; and that flesh leads into anything but no-man's-land.

Let no one sniff my pants for proof of a disaster that never happened. Looking at Rossetti's paintings, which he sheathed in chocolate, I smell sweetness and pungency, two tastes of vaginal fluids—they make the labia, the clitoris glisten—to which I add the balance of salt and sour.

Rossetti, Russell, and me and other men and women with mouths like roses, our delinquent genius is inventing a kinaesthetic alliance smart enough to know it is not opposites but intricacies that attract.

O, Russ, Rossetti, Mel, and fairy lovers everywhere, those I've known and those I'll come to know, How do I love thee? how have I loved thee? how will I love thee? Let me count the ways.

8 ~

Wisdom with Chocolate: Bride of Light

Chocolate cymbidium, a large, leafy orchid whose profuse blooms were the color of Chocolate Cake Cockaigne, flowered wildly near my mother's bedside the week that she died. I'd been bringing fresh-cut flowers to Mom when she was living in Washoe Village. About to buy an assortment of gently colored flowers, and perhaps yellow, that I'd selected from the walk-in cooler of the florist where I made my regular purchases, the orchid caught my eye and kept it. I asked the orchid's name, and hearing "chocolate" determined my decision to buy the plant. Florence Pass Frueh: D.O.B. 2.14.1911. D.O.B. Dear One, Beauty: born on Valentine's Day, born to be given chocolate.

At Red Oaks, the mother of an art-world acquaintance of mine lived on the same floor as Mom. Gwen's daughter, Karen, who lived in Chicago, visited Red Oaks often, and she brought delicious chocolates for her mother. Learning that my mother, too, loved chocolate, Karen brought her treats for Florence as well as Gwen. I enjoyed the relief of visiting with Karen and Mom at Red Oaks. Someone outside the nuclear family in which I grew up, someone who shared Mom's and Dad's love of art, someone, who, like me, had grown up in Highland Park, allowed my heartache to subside a bit during my hours at Red Oaks.

When I visited Mom, in Red Oaks and in Washoe Village, I was as sweet as I could be. That wasn't difficult, because I loved her. In Reno, I brought her chocolate as well as flowers. Dad had been the chocolate lover, but that changed over the last ten years of his and Mom's lives. In Red Oaks, Mom began to like any chocolate, from Snickers to the finest little heart-shaped luxuries that Karen brought. For Florence, chocolate was her favorite treatment

for a while, next to seeing Ren and me. When Mom stopped wanting chocolate, I knew she
wouldn't live much longer.

The tropical heat of a high summer night in Highland Park maximized my skin's oiliness. Tears seemed to adhere to my cheeks, rather than rolling down, as I walked alone, a sobbing beauty, caring only a little that I'd soon be seen by several people approaching from the other direction. Dad was dying in a room very close by car, and minutes ago I'd whispered to myself, "How can I live without this connection?" Without the light kissing of lips when we greeted or left each other? Without the massages I'd begun to give him in the last few months? Without the daughter's erotic bonding to her father's skin? I passed the people and nodded hello, and I remembered my friend Bill's comment to me when I was breaking up with Veronica: "Tragedy becomes you." Salutations, strangers! Politeness and generosity were filling me, nourishing my rosy complexion. Tragedy becomes you: it brings out the light.

If I were to perform this chapter, this is what my costume would be—a floor-length bridal gown and bare feet. A costume true to tragedies as well as love. Bridal white symbolizes the purity of love, and white's reflectivity can be dazzling, a quality indicative of love's enlightening qualities. Love is light. *O, Dad, your lovelight is traveling away from your body and mine.* White, so vulnerable to soiling, also signals the beginning of a drifting toward divorce. Tulle overlays the full satin skirt, and pearls adorn the snug bodice. My silver-streaked dark hair flows below the high neckline to just above my nipples and grazes my naked shoulders. My arms, hands, ankles, feet, face, throat, and legs (when I reveal them by pulling the skirt up and aside) are smooth, clear, and polished, a complexion not simply skin. Matte red brightens my soft lips. I sit on a plain chair, and at my feet I rest a bouquet of carnations that I've been carrying. I pick them up now and then to smell while speaking. I myself smell of a warm and not too sweet perfume whose rich seductiveness suggests that bridal white is not a motif of simple innocence. (I may be wearing Tabac Blond.) The overall effect is radiance—of groomed and gleaming surfaces, of a redolent corporeal interior.

The Bride understands the likeness of etiquette and skin-care, and she knows that in order to wed the light, which means to become the light, she must radiate politeness and generosity. So she grooms herself for goodness. Because refined people exhibit refined skin. (She knows the frequent falseness of that statement, but she's proving points to herself about life and death, and the process leads her simultaneously into truth and its disarray.)

Learning as a child from Mom and Dad to be a lady, and learning ladylike behavior and appearance on my own by reading charm books from my girlhood into puberty, my education in etiquette taught me to be human as much as it taught me to be feminine. For many years, I aimed to display ladylike skin, which, according to skin-care manuals, shows no signs of the oiliness I've grown to like when I now look in the mirror. Oily skin is problem skin. So say the skin-care manuals, the beauty etiquette books to which charm texts belong. Their authors type facial skin into normal, dry, oily, and combination, and they point out that the third category is acne-prone, large-pored, and greasy. A flyer packaged in a box of Clinique Facial Soap Extra-Strength, for oily skin, courteously reminds its reader that "oilier skins" are often the ones that "misbehave." The minced wording — oilier — amuses me, because my well-lubricated skin is anything but miscreant. Although I used to treat it as such, because pimples, sometimes cystic in my teens, and large pores embarrassed me.

Polite derives from Latin *polire*, to polish. Oily skin often exhibits greasiness more than polish, but the Bride is exhibiting the latter. The death of her parents becomes her. Within a few years she achieves the beauty that decades of applying skin-care experts' lessons could not. In her skin she embodies the impeccable and gracious behavior that displays a concord of radiance between a human being's depth and surface. The ayurvedic skin-care authority Pratima Raichur calls such behavior "bringing our awareness to all things." Skin, the screen of flesh and being and the projection of the latter.

Polished skin shines with taste and tactfulness, keystones of etiquette. "Good taste or bad is revealed in everything we are, do, or have," declares Emily Post in the 1922 preface to her initial etiquette book. Good taste is etiquette, and it far exceeds the social value of attractive clothing or household furnishings or simply good manners. Like her great-grandmother-in-law Emily, Peggy Post also makes clear the profoundly humanist value of etiquette in the 1997 revision of Emily's book: "Etiquette, very simply, is a code of behavior based on consideration and thoughtfulness. . . . thoughtful, unselfish behavior that enables humankind to persevere, with humor, love and grace" — in other words, with goodness.

Goodness requires slowing down. Moving with the pace of Mom and Dad, in their presence in their last years of life, calmed me after I quickly realized that moving at my regular pace, which was the speed of professional people, would have been rudely unloving not only to them but also to myself. First, I desired to slow down, then I consciously changed. Observing the lives of my friends, I witnessed the meaninglessness of everyday urgency that I experienced, which too much work and not enough love was generating. I saw colleagues, too, pushed and pushing, fatigued to exhaustion, and not paying attention to the growing aches embedding in their bodies. Flesh holds onto emotional and psychic brutality, even when we are paying some attention. The flesh is a teacher, because it tries to focus us on hurts of every kind, not only physical, so that we'll let them go. But usually those hurts become so familiar that we assume they're a permanent part of us, and mentally race over and around them, ever more fearful of a leisure that makes room for goodness to oneself.

Being good to myself, satisfying and agonizing though it was, had me feeling like an angel when I walked through Red Oaks to visit Mom. I walked very tall down the corridor to her room. The wood floors always gleamed surreally. Indeed, *surreal* came into my mind the first time I floated around the residence. Floated, like an angel, like a person who was losing the mind she'd once had. I hadn't asked myself, or anyone, for a word, but *surreal* came and it's never left. My confident posture and smooth gait contributed to the exceptional fluidity I felt, but my sense of unusual height and elegance of movement derived in part from the fact that almost everyone else in the rooms and corridors of Red Oaks was sitting in wheelchairs or lying in bed. In the winter I wore a long, roomy, black cashmere coat that swung gracefully as I glided. Once, when I was going to work at the University of Arizona and wearing a black dress of similar length and movement, a male colleague startled me with "You look like the Angel of Death." It was a compliment, and I thought of his words as I was becoming the Bride of Light, soul-and-mind-inseparable-from-body learning buoyancy — a counterpoise to grief.

How sweet an angel could I be? If I could have brought her death as easily and comfortingly as I brought her chocolate, perhaps I would have.

Divine and legendary figures stink. The Bride wants to stink to high heaven, the way that she imagines Nefertiti did. It's unlikely that the iconically beautiful queen wouldn't have used fragrance abundantly. New Kingdom aristocrats indulged in scented oils, emollients, and unguents. From ancient Egyptians to seventeenth-century Christians, human beings exchanged sweet odors with deities in a dialogue "of intrinsic essences," affirms Constance Classen in *Worlds of Sense: Exploring the Senses in History and Across Cultures*. Her scholarship probes and extends aesthetics beyond modern Western culture's fixation on vision. That exchange, she writes, "expresses and forms the highest ideal of interactive harmony." The Bride's wish to smell divine, to create a "scentscape"—Classen's word—to leave her *sillage*, her wake of fragrance, wherever she goes, is a prayer for dialogue with the light.

In medieval cosmology, heaven stank, and so did God and angels. *Reek, smell,* and *stink* have not always designated bad odor. In *Fragrance: The Story of Perfume from Cleopatra to Chanel*, the fragrance scholar Edwin T. Morris states that ancient Buddhists "described the transit to the afterlife as the passage to the 'fragrant mountain' (*gandhamadana*)." Saints who smelled of the sweet odor of sanctity and virgins who reeked deliciously belong to Christian "olfactory aesthetics," for which Classen presents a case. The fragrant virgin operates as a gender cliché in Patrick Suskind's novel *Perfume*. His "nose-wise" protagonist perceives that pubescent female virgins' celestially beautiful smell, and not their appearance, turns people's heads. Classen gives the definition of nose-wise, from the sixteenth to the eighteenth centuries, as "clever, conceited, or keen-scented."

The well-groomed woman, according to skin-care etiquette, should appeal to smell as well as sight, and perfume authorities speak of a perfume's radiance. The Bride's chypre scent clings brightly and caressingly to her skin, and she imagines its radiance embracing those who smell her and drifting lovingly into them. In 1917 François Coty created a fragrance that he named Chypre, and the family of fragrances called chypre developed from it. Chypre is a soft, warm, sweet, and sensual family of fragrance named for Cyprus, Aphrodite's birthplace.

In order to become impeccably groomed in the golden reeking of Aphrodite, the Bride forever is in training. As she transforms her skin into a complexion and maintains its glow, like roses, which are Aphrodite's flowers, the Bride receives the scents of her divine sister's garden. They enlighten her, again and again, in a soft, warm, sweet, and sensual process, when she surrenders, in many tingling recognitions of the light. Aestheticians, trained in the beautification of skin through cleaning, massage, and the application of scrubs, cleansers, masks, oils, creams, and lotions, distinguish between skin and complexion. The first is a covering, while the second exhibits brightness and clarity. Dictionary definitions agree. Skin is the integument of the human body, whereas complexion is the texture, color, and overall appearance of the skin. *Complexion*, from Latin *complexus*, past participle of *complecti*, to encircle, embrace: complexion is aesthetically complex; it surrounds a body in beauty. Skin-care advisers offer self-care systems that help the reader reveal her light from within—from the internationally infamous nineteenth-century courtesan Lola Montez to the charm promoters of the 1950s into the 1970s to the Hollywood star and beauty columnist Arlene Dahl, who published a beauty manual in 1965.

Many times the Bride feared that she would fail, that she would never emit light, only be able to invoke it. She feared the tragedies that become an acolyte.

So I have craved and eaten chocolate, more than any other sweet. From my childhood into my twenties, maybe even my thirties, I'd read that chocolate ruins your complexion. Who cares? When we are in the midst of tragedies, of our own making or of fate's—and what's the difference, anyway?—we obey the emotions embedded in our flesh. I've eaten chocolate in happiness as well as in sadness, to celebrate the known—a birthday, a wedding anniversary, the completion of a project—and to requite mysteries in the massively unknown self.

When I'm craving emotional nutrition, chocolate has supplied a false sweetness akin to false consciousness. I've eaten like that because I've felt like I'm physically starving. I understand "starving for love," which I was doing when my parents were dying and Russell was leaving me. Who was I? That creature bloated beyond beauty, like Rossetti in his later life. I am big and beautiful like Aphrodite is, but then I was bigger than usual through multiple strategies, originating in my massively unknown self, to protect Joanna. My body was being heroic. So my belly became larger and rounder—"pregnant," so that the man would stay in the marriage; viscerally guarding me from the closeness to another abdomen that svelteness allows. My belly hurt, too, from a dull to a severe ache, sometimes constant for days, often intermittent from one week to another. Doing its best to feel full because my heart was feeling empty, my belly was also letting me know that displaced heartache served best as a short-term solution.

"Quit bellyachin'," cowboys admonish the complainer in their television and cinema characterizations. (I wonder how many times I heard that phrase watching cowboy movies with Dad.) In contrast, my belly was asking me to pay attention to the aching angers and losses that I couldn't stomach, that I couldn't digest or eliminate. Overwhelmed with grief, for three intimacies were dying, I dealt with as much loss as my cognition could bear to do, and my belly cared for the rest. Some might say that my body's "complaints" were betraying me, displaying an emotional ineptitude, but I say that the body is brilliant, so that my bellyaching was a pretty gentle reminder: "Wake up, Joanna," "Stay awake, Joanna." Thank you, belly, for revealing mysteries to me about myself.

The tag on a piece of Prana clothing reads, "the never ending / and always expanding / harmonics of natural law." *Prana* is a Sanskrit word meaning breath. Prana is important to the practice of yoga, in which elongating the body is just stretching unless one breathes consciously, and Prana is the name of a company that makes stylish practical clothing for yoga and rock climbing. The belly expands in breathing, and my belly expanded in revelations, responding to the natural law of physical death. The belly follows Tao. Deng Ming-Dao, a student of Tao and bestselling author, implicitly attests to the light within the mysteries, the dark, of Tao. In *Scholar Warrior: An Introduction to the Tao in Everyday Life*, he likens the light that is human being (which is the light that is the limitlessness that is Tao) to a brightly flaming candle "smothered inside a steel lantern." Human beings rarely see the light, for they do not see *xuan*, the Taoist sages' word for the "dark mystery beyond all mysteries." Duality is nonexistent in limitlessness, thus dark and light are one. Deng states, too, that because the light simply is, those who follow Tao do not need to cleanse themselves, soul or body, in order to realize the light.

However, skin-care etiquette is strict and precise: cleansing is the foundation of good skin. And the followers of Tao who needn't cleanse themselves are masters. On the way to realization, the practitioner learns and practices purity.

Skin-care masters do not use the word *cleaning*. It doesn't connote inner purification or the degree of dirt-removal that *cleansing* does. In many skin-care guides, oily skin requires the most rigorous cleansing of any skin type. According to Peter Thomas Roth, quoted in the April 1999 *Vogue*, "When you have good skin, you wash your face in the shower," but "when you have bad skin, you buy everything available." Roth is cofounder of a skin-care-product company known for its aggressive targeting of troubled skin. He and other experts promote cleansing and its helpmates, such as methods of exfoliation and aids to circulation, as strategies for normalization. Skin-care etiquette presents normal skin as the ideal. In their definitions of skin types, Helen Whitcomb and Rosalind Lang, authors of the 1964 *Charm: The Career Girl's Guide to Business and Personal Success*, label perfect skin as not only normal but also "nice." Through the decades, the best-mannered skin has been described implicitly—or is understood by the reader—as resembling porcelain or peaches-and-cream. Marsha Gordon, M.D. and the medical writer Alice E. Fugate, who coauthored *The Complete Idiot's Guide to Beautiful Skin*, published in 1998, challenge the normal-is-ideal myth. While the fashion and beauty industries wish to instill in women the idea that a perfect skin exists but that none of us exhibits it, Gordon and Fugate may bring all of us abnormal women relief with the assertion that the perfect type is myth.

Undergoing her education, the Bride learned to prefer the concept of rosy to the myth of perfect or the pictures of peaches-and-cream and porcelain. Although skin advisers' use of *rosy* has designated a glowing Caucasian complexion, *rosy* means brightness as much as it means pinkness. The light should not be confused with whiteness. Classen reveals that white and black "are based on a similar sensation, as both are derived from roots meaning to gleam": a flame's light is whitish, and the flame's soot is black. Neither outgleams the other. Recognizing "the fact of blackness" in *Black Skin, White Masks*, Frantz Fanon laments that "there is a white song, a white song. All this whiteness burns me." Like "the fact" of "bad" skin, the fact of blackness has been a cultural marker of ugliness that the person of imperfect color or complexion recognizes. "I sit down at the fire and I become aware of my uniform," writes Fanon. "I had not seen it. It is indeed ugly. I stop there, for who can tell me what beauty is?"

In 1998 I talked with a black-skinned bodybuilder, René Toney, whose nineteen-inch biceps had been acknowledged by bodybuilding authorities to be the largest biceps of any woman bodybuilder in the world. René's complexion, from her face to her chest and arms, to her thighs and calves—everything that I could see—was a gift of rosiness.

The myth of blacks' ugliness, the myth of perfect skin, the myth of hideous aging. The night that Mom died, Ren or Russell commented on her beauty. I've heard students and others exclaim about the beauty of Georgia O'Keeffe and other women whose skin old age has "troubled" into creases, sags, and wrinkles. Usually I don't believe the exclamations. I think that their exaggerated excitement veils the fear-ridden wishfulness of the speaker, who wants to live as long as she can within the perimeter of an idea — perfect, which means young as well as peachy, skin. My mother indeed was beautiful the night she died — her complexion smooth and creamy, her face calm. Dr. Garland, who cared for Mom when she lived at Red Oaks, complimented her when Ren and I were asking him for a prognosis — how long she'd live. Out of the blue he remarked, "What a pretty woman!"

Mom cared for her body in a way that most people don't. I loved hearing her say when she was seventy-eight, "I'm interested in my body. Most people aren't." In her eighties, when she had lost most of her ability to speak words clearly and to communicate with language, her slenderness and clear, usually rosy complexion distinguished her appearance not only from that of people her age but also of people in general. Her light was shining, and it amazed me; because she couldn't dress or wash herself or brush her hair. Florence's fairy beauty shone even through her cognitive dysfunction.

How strong she was in her unchosen silence. The strong and silent hero of our friendship. Smiling when I broke off parts of a chocolate bar and ate them with her or when I fed her one after another piece.

Godiva chocolate appeals to the strong, silent type, to the action hero of any age or sex. A Godiva ad that appeared in the 1996 *Elle* assures the reader, "You don't have to say a word." That's because the pictured, signature gold Godiva box "holds the luscious chocolates that speak with greater eloquence than any words." Still waters run deep: I say that about my mother in her old age, just as she said it about me when I was a child. Neither a little girl nor an action hero necessarily speaks her passions, yet those passions animate their actions. Still waters run deep: a little girl's and an action hero's passions exist in excess of spoken language; they energize the girl's and the hero's body, so can be read by mothers, daughters, and by lovers. Cinematic action heroes' iconic eloquence, their vivid and forceful expressiveness that films convey more often in explosions, bravery, and bloodred beauty than in the hero's words, communicates a narcissistic richness, paradoxically (perhaps) inclusive of altruism, a richness purveyed by Godiva.

Richness of heart, courage, and passion have attracted my attention in Godiva ads, which have featured heart-shaped red boxes patterned in roses, heart-shaped truffles, and milk chocolate candies decorated with a lion or a fleur-de-lis. Lion: symbol of strength. Fleur-de-lis, an iris: Mom's flower. Godiva chocolates promise you the heart and strength to "say it like you mean it," which a *Mirabella* Godiva ad from January 1994 admonishes, in bold type, its reader to do. Full to overflowing with the still waters that run deep, like erotic currents that fire every membrane of new lovers making love, movie action heroes always say it like they mean it, and what they mean is always the same: I am an angel in trauma, a fairy overcoming defense mechanisms, a vehicle for sparking communion with the dead, which is the deadness that you, my viewer, feel within your own deep sea whose currents have stagnated with psychogenetic sludge.

Mom moved my sludge. She was my best friend when she lived in Washoe Village. Her arrival meant that I'd benefit from our closeness, heartbreaking though it often was in her six and a half months in Reno. "Why are you so devoted to me?" she asked me several times. Her words were perfectly clear. "Because I love you," I responded each time. "I want to live with you. Can I live with you?" she asked, too. Oh, Mom, all I wanted to do when you lived in Reno was to be with you, and at the same time I couldn't bear to see you.

I explained directly why she couldn't live with Russ and me. He and I had contemplated her living with us, during the couple of months between Dad's death in Red Oaks and Mom's moving from there to Reno. My house, which then had been Russ's and my house for about eight years, is a two-bedroom, one-bath dwelling, with neither basement nor attic. If Mom were to live with us, we'd need a bigger house for everyone's comfort and privacy, and we'd need twelve-hour-a-day if not live-in nursing care. "I'll give you my money," Mom offered. Ren and I already had her money, and by her bedside I kept myself from crying over the poignancy of both her proposal and her wish and over my refusal. Many times I explained the practical matters of space and having to buy another house and prepare it properly and aesthetically and the time that all of the preparations would take. I considered, too, how soon I thought she'd die — probably before the summer — and whether the short period in a new house would be worth the effort. I'm sure, as well, that my massively unknown self, full of clarity about Russ's and my disintegrating marriage, kept me from trusting our entry into a new responsibility.

Moving sludge: refusing my mother her request and accepting feeling terrible about it.

I wondered if she understood *everything* that I or anyone was saying. Sometimes I thought she did, and I cried over the anguish she experienced in becoming inarticulate. I knew that her mind did not hold onto information, and I knew that she remained brilliant and body-conscious. In my twenties, after Mom's parents died, she told me that she had nightmares about them. I asked what they were, but she never revealed their contents. As she generally wouldn't tell me thoughts, dreams, and feelings of hers during her last six months. She started, "I had a dream . . . ," or the expression on her face shifted, or I felt her melancholy mood, and in each case I asked, "What are you feeling?" or "What are you thinking?" and she said, "It's too sad." Often I held her hand or laid my head by her side. Sometimes we simply cried together. "I had a dream last night," she said one day, then surprised me with "Do you want to hear it?" Of course, I did. The dream was a nightmare, but it was one of those usual days when her verbal expression was murky and repetitive, so I asked, "What was the nightmare?" Then, with complete clarity she answered, "I was the nightmare." Maybe that was one of the times we cried, and maybe she hadn't been dreaming but had been thinking about the predicament in which she found herself.

Again and again my mother moved my egocentric sludge. I felt desolate and radiantly full.

Moving my psychogenetic sludge, Mom improved my circulation and my light, for after spending time with her one afternoon, while Peggy, who was up from Tucson, waited in the Washoe Village library, Peg remarked on seeing me, "Your face and neck are glowing!" I became beatific in Florence's fairy light. I was becoming a saint because of her. The closest that I usually am to saintliness is teaching.

Teaching is a state of consciousness, in particular the class periods, during which great and extended focus occurs. It happens without force. Mom's and my slow times together were like the best of classes, in which I learned, ultimately without forcing, a lot about the relaxed concentration that is love. I learned to receive her repetitious compliments with wholehearted cheer and thank-yous. "I love your bongs." Day after day she loved me with that remark. Mom knew that "bangs" wasn't coming out correctly, and sometimes she paused before that word, sometimes she said it more than once at the end of a sentence, as if to get it right. She also noticed when I was wearing a new pair of boots and told me that she liked them, as she regularly remarked on the beauty of two necklaces—one an amethyst pendant heart on a gold chain and the other an ornate silver choker featuring green malachite. I usually reminded her that they both were her necklaces, that she gave them to me, and that other people also found them beautiful, especially the choker. Mom's loss of short-term memory and her repetitive questions and statements irked Dad. His body gestures and facial expressions showed his annoyance, and he'd try to "make" her understand what he was saying as if the condition of her mind were normal. Early on, at Red Oaks, I realized that no one had anything to gain from struggling for normal. Let her condition exist in its surprises and its redundancies, I realized in soul-and-mind-inseparable-from-body, so that we can love one another in peace. So I continued to learn and to love, like I did when I was a little girl, her body-consciousness and mine. "Joanna, I love your bongs." Purple heart: the Teacher's and the Bride's bravery in their love of each other.

Purple heart. After Mom died and I was lingering over the possessions of hers that became mine, I smelled a purple heart when I opened her bottle of Chanel No. 5. She rarely used scent, and Chanel No. 5 is the only one that I recall her ever wearing. Classic, modern, fresh, yet sexy and sophisticated — Florence, Chanel No. 5, and Mom's brave heart.

The accords of head, heart, and bottom notes that the best perfumers create, each note composed of a number of ingredients, are meant to compose heavenly music. Accords between the human and the divine. The notes of Mom's brave heart still sing to me, siren-strong in their complex harmony, tenacity, and melody. The perfumed heart, like perfumed skin, is a symphony, and it is a garden yearning to be Eden; it is the desire of the mind, incorporated and thinking everywhere from brain to anus and from nose to big toe through the gravity of matter, to sing beautifully.

Current fashion magazine reports on skin care indicate that a woman should strive to make the entire surface of her body a complexion. Perfume aids in this endeavor, for rosiness wafts from the deliciously scented body, as if coming from deep within it. The perceiver experiences aura and organs, especially the heart, to be one. Surface and depth — which is the earthly and the divine — as one.

In their lack of concern for surface and depth operating in a moral unison of attentiveness and care, fashion magazines promote a "specific know-how" that Peggy Post declares to be only a small part of etiquette — manners. Specific know-how, featured in guides by Montez, Dahl, Raichur, and charm authorities, creates an illusion of beauty that, they agree, any woman can muster. Simultaneously they assert that radiance is not illusion. Illusion conceals, like

Maybelline's True Illusion liquid foundation and pressed powder. According to a True Illusion ad in the September 1999 *Harper's Bazaar*, the "formula floats on weightlessly, subtly concealing flaws." An *aura* of radiance is weightless, too, but its ethereal sweetness, whose presence witnesses both see and smell, reveals the light from *within* the skin. A radiant person exhibits radiant skin, which results from her own stewardship of her being and which signals beauty, described by Raichur as "effortless poise, grace, and vibrance: the individual totally at ease from *deep within the skin* and radiant from without." A rose's full bloom both emits and reflects light.

If an individual has followed beauty etiquette as a means to becoming the glowing complexion, the light, then she has used etiquette's techniques to bene- fit personal aesthetics through ethical practice. What began perhaps as a vain, despairing, or fear-inspired pursuit of beauty changes if one is to become the light, which is hardly a trivial endeavor. When depth and surface operate in a moral unison of attentiveness and care, purely cosmetic beauty is not the aco- lyte's primary motivator, for she has proceeded from I *want to look good* to I *want to feel good* to I *want to be good*.

What is *being good* when your parents are dying? I contemplated that question, and it lived in my massively unknown self.

If Dad had still loved chocolate, then baking him a cake would have been good. In *Cocolat: Extraordinary Chocolate Desserts*, author Alice Medrich calls a special chocolate genoise "A Gift for Dad." Indeed, it looks life a gift-wrapped object. Marbled chocolate ribbons decorate the "wrapping" of chocolate glaze over chestnut buttercream. The photograph's caption reads: "Rich masculine flavors—chestnuts and rum—make this a seriously delicious chocolate cake for Dad or the main man in your life." For a few years before he died, Dad was as much the main man in my life as Russell was.

Dad wanted his daughters' company and assistance, and he wanted death. One of the several times that Ren and I went to Highland Park because Dad's attorney and friend Mike called us to say that Dad was probably going to die, I asked him, once he seemed to be on a relatively even keel, how long he'd like Ren and me to stay. His answer took my breath away: "Forever." So soft in the heart, so bidding his daughters to enter it. I wanted to stay forever, and maybe I did the last time I visited him; because I sat with him while he died.

Months before his death he asked me if I'd help him die. I said, "I'll do anything you ask." I meant it, terrified though I was, having committed to acts whose dimensions of divine and earthly mysteries still cause my mind to seize up. The month before he died, he asked me again. We created a document. We refined it as he dictated to me and I wrote longhand. Dad signed it.

June 1, 1999
   Dad has talked with Dr. Garland about Dad's wish to die with Dr. Garland's assistance. Dad would like this to happen after Mom dies.
   On April 12 Dr. Garland told Ren and Joanna, when they asked him, that Mom would probably live 3-6 months. Ren and Joanna related this to Dad, and subsequently so did Dr. Garland.

                                                              E R Frueh

Dad wanted to die *after* Mom, because he wanted to continue to protect her. As the mysteries would have it, Dad died before Mom. I think that Ren's and my assuring him, many times and in emotional and practical detail, that we'd take care of Mom if he died first, helped relax him into the mystery that called him sooner than it called Mom.

Mom and Dad each had a living will, and both their charts included DNR orders. Dad and I called the document that he and I composed a "contract," and Ren and I called it "the death plan." It seemed so inexplicit to me, despite Dad's and my careful and precise phrasing. "Help Erne die with ease" — that's all we wished to say. I think that, besides me and Dad, only Ren read the death plan.

Mom wanted death, too. "Things will be better in the summer," she said many times. Or maybe I said it. Maybe we both said it. Actually, I'm sure she said it more than I did, because it repeats in my mind, a little less intensively than "I love your bongs." In the autumn that Mom lived in Reno, I took her for walks in her wheelchair around the Washoe Village buildings. Russell liked walking with Mom outdoors because looking at the mountains, the purple and white cosmos, and the roses usually animated her. He and I loved feeling her happiness.

Irises grew close to the residential areas of Washoe Village, and I looked forward to spring with Mom by verbally anticipating the irises blooming, not only at Washoe but also in my own garden, from which, I promised, I'd bring her all the different velvety purples, lavenders, whites, and reds. I didn't think that she'd live into the summer, and as winter progressed along with her waning interest in chocolate, I knew that she wouldn't live through the spring.

In the ancien régime, aristocrats liked to drink their chocolate in the boudoir at breakfast, preferably in bed while relaxing in a dressing gown or negligee. Chocolate helped people perform a ritual of transition from lying down to sitting up, so its ingestion belonged to an exercise of languid movement, an etiquette of refined leisure. Leisure being unoccupied time, Mom had a lot of it, and our chocolate interludes partook of the informality, even the fluidity, of a class that had time to tarry over chocolate.

Unlike the aristocratic connoisseurs of chocolate, Mom stayed lying down, for her transition was often from one nap to another. On certain medications or combinations of medications she could hardly stay awake. So I asked that they be changed. My main concern always centered on her pain, which I took to be indicated by her moans. "Where?" I asked. She didn't give definite responses. Was it her long-term back pain acting up? Was the pain in her organs? Was it a bladder infection? Was it mental? Every once in a while, the Washoe nurses told me, "Florence says she's been seeing Mr. Frueh," and she herself told me, "I saw Dad" or "I saw Erne": I'm not sure which she said. I didn't know whether to point out that he'd died. First, because I assumed that, even though she was seeing Dad, she knew he was dead, and second, because I thought that bringing up his death would be "too sad." I opted for the truth. Better that we share our rent hearts and learn more love from our tears. Only now do I know she was actually seeing her husband.

Recently I listened to a friend describe her old parents as "slow" and time with them as "boring." I imagined that "tedious'" would also readily fit into this descriptive vocabulary. Here's what's really tedious—reading skin-care manuals. A scholarly chore. I phoned Ren and complained, "I'm reading the same fucking book again and again. It's all beginning to sound senseless." As if no woman had the common sense to wash her face and moisturize it if necessary, to eat vegetables and fruits as well as pizza and chocolate cake.

Common sense unites intellect with sensory impressions and experience; in other words, with energies, effects, and eros existing beneath the skin. Consequently, according to beauty etiquette, the application in itself of products cannot produce the light. In her 1991 bestseller *The Beauty Myth: How Images of Beauty Are Used Against Women*, Naomi Wolf rails against "holy oil" and the "Rites of Beauty" that "sell women back an imi-tation of the light that is ours already." In her estimation, self-correction is unnecessary. If only women would simply see what they really are.

I do agree that radiance is readily available, but I don't believe that, in most cases, it is simply hidden. Radiance does not characterize most human beings. It is a possibility, a quality that year after year of living an ungroomed life has severely dulled. Peggy Post explains that etiquette combines "common sense, generosity of spirit, and some specific know-how." Fashion magazine ads and reports offer skin know-how, to which a woman may become dedicated, but without grooming herself in the look and the scent of love, which are foundational aspects of beauty etiquette discourse, she will exist as an aesthetic dimness.

Wolf understands women to be dimmed and diminished by men's inability to see women's light. Women's nonoptimum solution is to "make their beauty glitter because *they are so hard for men to see.*" Glitter can be the ambient radiance of fairy beauty—a force-field of allure that embraces people. More often, glitter is a flash, not like the enlightenment of satori, but rather, like a spurt that came and went, a surface performance of light. Radiance extends beyond a single body and leaves a wake. It is the sweet ether of a human being's intelligent and considerate sensuous arraying of her particular humanity. Radiance is the soul's charm.

Charm, like etiquette, resides in fluidity and flexibility. Beauty etiquette follows etiquette in general, and the latter, according to Peggy Post, is not a code of "'prescriptions for properness,' comprising rigid, formal, stuffy rules." Etiquette, she understands, "must be fluid" in its guidance for "doing things with consideration, gracefully and well." Skin-care experts would concur, for inflexibility makes skin-care practice an arduous formality; and that creates tension, which damages the complexion. Consideration applies to oneself. An acolyte of the light commits to practice without succumbing to rote, and glowing goodness originates in exercises that develop fluidity, in Raichur's words, the "capacity to be fully present at each moment." Beauty etiquette clarifies behavior as it advises how to clarify the skin. Etiquette structures room to move: a space for practicing clarity of consciousness and purpose, which reduces tension; and a spaciousness that engenders trust in flux.

What spaciousness of sadness I knew when Washoe Village left me a message at the hotel where I was staying in New York. I asked Russell to return the call. All I remember now from the information he gathered was that Mom wasn't eating and was losing weight. I knew that she'd die within the week.

I never liked to leave Mom, but I liked to live my life. "She's shutting down," I said to the nurse on duty at the desk near Mom's room when Russ and I arrived at Washoe Village from the airport.

I called Ren to say that she should fly to Reno, I arranged for hospice care, I taught my classes, I gave a brown-bag-lunch lecture for the Women's Studies Program, "The Passionate Wife, the Passionate Daughter."

I sat with Mom, as I had before, and listened. "I'm afraid." The time I most remember her stating that, she was sitting in a wheelchair, before I left for the New York conference trip, by the window of her room, near the table on which the chocolate cymbidium was coming into the full bloom of its many flowers. I held her hand, my eyes held tears. "I'll help. I love you. I'm here."

Mom laughed when she watched the parakeets and canaries in the lobby corridor of the wing where she was living, and she laughed when she played with Sophie, Russ's mother Alice's bichon, brought with her from Oregon on a visit with Russ and me. Mom and I laughed together, though I don't remember one thing that we laughed about.

Did I buy the chocolate cymbidium before I left for New York or when I returned?

How quickly the bedsores multiplied as her death neared.

Mom took Ren and me for appointments with her gynecologist, on North Michigan Avenue, when I was eleven or so. I was wearing a green-and-white-checked shirtwaist.

"Don't leave me. Don't leave me," I repeated under my breath one day at Washoe Village when I walked into Mom's room, she was napping on her back, and I stayed for a while as she slept.

In her old age, Mom railed against politicians who wanted to legislate women's legal ability to have an abortion. The first time that she did this — many years earlier — her righteous anger took me aback. She may have expressed her incensed position this way: "How dare they think they can control women's bodies!" Or her words might have been these: "Leave women's bodies alone!" I wish I remembered her exact communication of passion.

When Mom died, I was the only one with her. Ren had gone out of the room to call her partner, leaving Russ and me in a minimalist version of deathbed scenes in Western art. No display of extreme emotion. Colors serene, including the chocolate cymbidium blossoms. Russ touched her gently, as did I, and we knew she was minutes away from being dead. I wanted Ren to be with us because I thought she'd want to be with Mom, so I asked Russ to find my sister. When the two of them returned, I was crying and crying.

When Mom was in her seventies, she and I took walks around Highland Park, in neighborhoods, like ours, close to the lake. Gramps used to walk daily within sight of the lake, in Lincoln Park, across from his and Gram's eleventh-floor apartment.

How many times I left Red Oaks and Washoe Village crying! Once I almost ran out of the Red Oaks dining hall crying, and I often kept crying as I drove back to my parents' condo, empty of Mom, then empty of Dad. I knew the meaning of "beside myself," and returning once to Reno from a sojourn in Highland Park, my state declared itself in screaming moans and a verbal stuckness. Maybe I became more animal than usual in my expressiveness. Maybe my massively unknown self kept me from talking with a husband who was leaving me emotionally.

I tended to the details of Mom's cremation. Russ asked if I wanted him to go with me to Northern Nevada Memorial Cremation and Burial Society, and I said no.

The period of demise began in earnest with Dad's triple bypass surgery at age eighty-three. He insisted on having it in order to be with Mom, so that he could care for her. Ren and I each stayed with Mom for a while during and after the surgery, so that our visits overlapped for a couple of days. We walked with Mom arm in arm, from car to hospital entrance, through the corridors and in the cafeteria—everywhere. Her steadiness on her feet had weakened with succeeding strokes, so she needed our support.

The living room coffee table became my altar to Mom. For weeks it held candles of various colors, including the yellow shiva that burned continuously for seven days; a lustreware vase (collected on a family vacation to the East Coast) that I filled with the kind of flowers I used to bring her at Washoe Village; her death certificate; and the white cardboard box in which a plastic container held her ashes. For a while, her wedding ring and her brush, with strands of her hair, graced the table.

I imagined my parents' torments. Sometimes helplessness flooded me, because I felt inadequate in my ability to succor or heal them, to change the inevitability of their dying. I couldn't save them, and that played a particularly melancholy tune within me since Mom was living in Reno and more pointedly in my care than Dad was. (Mike was caring for Dad, and he did it well.)

Morphine was available for Mom the day she died. The bottle of liquid remained unopened until the Saturday morning that I twisted off the lid. A nurse from Washoe Village called to ask if I wanted to collect the unused drug or if I wanted Washoe to dispose of it. I chose the first alternative because I wanted to experience the morphine. It sat in a kitchen cabinet for at least two weeks, during which I asked Russ to take the opiate with me, we discussed the strangeness and danger of ingestion, and I often completely forgot about my desire, even when I opened the cabinet for olive oil or canned goods. In no way would I experience the state of being that would have been Mom's had a nurse administered the morphine to her; yet it symbolized mystical connection between her and me. A couple of hours after taking the morphine, Russ and I both became ill—horribly nauseated. Nothing relaxing or intoxicating, let alone mystical, occurred. I was alone with my sickness: we had guessed at our dose of the drug early in the morning, and feeling no effects or being unable to care for each other in the psychic pitch that was peaking as we carried out my desire, we began our separate pursuits. He left the house to keep a date, and I stayed in my robe, mentally restless and deeply unsettled.

My list of memories, before and after my mother's death, from my adulthood before her demise, and returning very unexpectedly from earlier years, may seem emotionally strenuous. However, as I observe my memories, two phrases come into my mind: much ado about nothing; ease the heart. Heart is filling my perspective, and I am full beyond measure.

A Taoist master would understand "much ado about nothing," more than Shakespeare would have. Easing her heart, the Bride saw beyond the projections that she called reality. Mystics, from William Blake to Taoist masters, know that mysteries, not "reality," are the Way. (Tao means "the Way," and it is always changing.) The body constricts with a human being's belief in the reality of projections: this is the way things are; this is the way I am — wedded to misery. The constricted body, energies blocked or in varying states of strangulation, begs us to open new neural pathways through which mind can smoothly move and generate new thoughts. My bellyache; your chest pain; their inflexibility. By name and more, the Bride began new ways, and they increased her radiance.

Mysteries were becoming to the Bride. So she spoke to her dead father in mystic prose, reminiscent of a solemn fairy song. *You bloom within me every instant. Still, I am lonely for your incarnation. Accept a gift, a nosegay, Dad, steeped in my carnal aching. You bloom within me every instant, so please receive these pink carnations.* Carnation: *from the Latin caro, flesh. In a language-of-flowers book dated 1913, pink carnation is "woman's love."*

After Dad died, I did my best to normalize my life. I felt like a mess, and everything seemed to be a mess. People who called to ask about my well-being heard from Russell, "She's doing a lot of cleaning." Housecleansing. Concurrently with that assiduous activity, I ate a lot of fruits and vegetables, an internally cleansing diet — recommended by skin-care experts. My father's unstoppable decline began in autumn, and during the nine months from then till his death, I ate more than usual and more sweets, especially when I visited Highland Park. At least one night of a several-day stay in Dad's apartment, I downed a bunch of cupcakes or Sara Lee cake, both left for me by Mike, along with more nutritious food.

I accompanied my internal and domestic cleansing with a change in skin-care: a facial once a week rather than once a month; a dermatologist appointment, when I hadn't had one for around thirty years; a shower in the morning *plus* a bath at night, and both times scrubbing with a bristle brush from feet to shoulders. I massaged pleasures into my skin — an unscented, thick body cream after the morning cleansing and a fragrant body oil after the evening one — from the toes up. The Bride was obedient: skin-care etiquette guides are full of rituals, routines, programs, regimens. I delighted in my new ones, and my complexion improved, so much that my aesthetician described it with *beautiful. Pretty* was the highest praise she had ever given me before.

Some may think that *mystery* doesn't apply to the death of an old man, like my father at age eighty-seven. For them, a predictable event, a given, cannot be mystery. In the most obvious of metaphysical statements, I could say that death is mystery, so anyone's death is mysterious. If only because death obscures the whereabouts of the departed, mystery describes everyone's death. The best that human beings can do is to be initiates, to sit with the dying and witness their light.

Mystery describes occurrences that astound the soul-and-mind-inseparable-from-body, and facial skin displays a person's attempt to know the unknowable. Mystery can shock and stress the complexion into eruptive soreness and weeping, into muddied and pasty hues. The disturbance of enigma finds a home in the pores after laying a foundation in subepidermal matter and in spirit. The darker side of Tao settles in the skin if the practice of etiquette does not prevail.

Skin-care etiquette advises that threats to physical health and mental well-being must be reduced or eradicated, because skin is a revealing organ. The fashion maven and jetsetter Luciana Pignatelli includes skin-care tips and observations in her entertaining *The Beautiful People's Beauty Book: How to Achieve the Look and Manner of the World's Most Attractive Women*, published in 1971. Facial skin immediately registers nervous tension, she asserts, disclosing too that her pores dilate when she's nervous. In contrast, when she's in love and feels cared for, her skin lights up. A good complexion is glad skin, relaxed by love.

Glad originates in the Indo-European *ghladh*, shining, smooth. Montez and Raichur relate skin disturbances to physical or spiritual stress. The courtesan warns that young girls need to learn that damaging their health destroys their beauty, and she calls the complexion "the index of the soul." She advocates keeping both skin and soul as clean, bright, and therefore beautiful as a girl can.

Raichur calls the complexion "an exacting mirror of the soul" that registers stress in the form of "*accelerated aging.*" Although Marsha Gordon and Alice Fugate's *Complete Idiot's Guide to Beautiful Skin* is a no-nonsense reference book, their advice for minimizing stress in order to beautify the skin resembles the chiding tone in charm books. Gordon (a dermatologist) and Fugate caution their readers to relax their facial muscles, to pay attention to habitually tight expressions that can render worry permanent in lines. In *Secrets of Charm* John Powers, founder of the Powers School, famous for charm training, and cowriter Mary Sue Miller also advise relaxation, because tension will ruin your complexion. Only serenity, being "charmingly unharassed at all times," they advise, can avert such facial afflictions as undereye circles and an overall wearied look. One outcome of tension is fatigue, which, believe Powers and Miller, dangerously strains a person's health and her perspective on life, not to mention her beauty.

They suggest that extreme tension may lead to "a crack-up." Obviously, that would be a severe dimming of any charmer's soul, the "fine inner qualities" that she has cultivated. Those qualities, presented by Powers and Miller as compassion, openness, humor, and generosity, surface from within a woman to envelop her in the radiance that is "an aura of irresistible beauty and charm."

That aura is a human being's halo. Maybe mine was showing when I didn't see it, during the minutes and hours of Dad's and my mysterious companionship, those slow times when my mind was neither wandering, fixated, nor obsessed. The Bride was learning a new thoughtfulness, consideration, and graciousness, a livelier and more resonant etiquette than she had previously practiced.

Clear-minded till a day or so before he died, Dad talked with me a lot. He went over and over money matters, whether they circulated around his and Mom's wills or amounts of money in bank accounts and investments or the auctioning of many of the modern and antique objects that he and Mom had collected since the 1950s. I'd wanted the Aalto dining table and the Mucha print of Lorenzaccio played by Sarah Bernhardt. I let them go, as I let go of the angry restlessness that his continuous talking used to produce in me. His repetitions indicated insecurities. Had he provided well enough for Mom and Ren and me? Had he sufficiently protected the capital? Weren't his and Mom's selections of furnishings and art glass evidence of their supremely good taste? Was he a good man? Was he okay? Could he die in peace?

I listened, I asked questions, I assured him that he was doing an excellent job of taking care of all of us and that Ren and I deeply appreciated his efforts, his practical intelligence, and his fortitude. I wished to convey that he was Mom's and Ren's and my hero.

One morning I helped him to his chair at the kitchen table, and he slumped. I was almost holding him as his body found the seat. His energy that day had been feeling fragile and sluggish, and I sensed that he might fall if I didn't assist him. Loved ones falling over: Mom found Dad on the floor of the master bathroom at 90 Riparian Road, and Dad found Mom on the master bedroom carpet in the condo. They both most likely saved each other's lives. Mom's discovery led to Dad's getting a pacemaker, and Dad's discovery led to Mom's living in Red Oaks. I'd imagined and considered those events to be traumatic for the discoverer, the person who had to take action, in each one.

Right after Dad and I sat down that morning, my concern changed to fear, because I thought that I could be witnessing his death any second. Ever so quickly, my loving and necessary actions if that were to happen unrolled in my mind. "If he dies right now, it's okay, it's good," I was thinking, because his suffering would end. In our companionship over the last few years of Dad's life—filled with his lecture mode; my listening to him and being with him; our talking about composting, gardening, and the names of plants and flowers, and our nightly TV watching while I did yoga—I observed that Dad's smoking, perhaps more than anything else, was doing him in, even though he'd stopped smoking years earlier. His breathing grew increasingly difficult and his pace to the lobby mailbox slowed. His robust body thinned and thinned as his interest in food lessened, and twenty-four-hour-a-day oxygen became a necessity. "Getting old is no good," he'd quote Gramps from Mom's father's old age. Dad quoted another old man, too, whose name he never mentioned, about how life isn't worth living anymore when it's too hard to tie your own shoelaces.

Always neat, clean, and well groomed, Dad stayed that way. A nurse shaved him and helped him dress on the days, in Red Oaks, when I went with him to his physical therapy. I sat quietly, perhaps pressing my lips together or massaging my hands in order to keep from crying, unconscious of either manner of touching myself, until, suddenly, I noticed—that my massively unknown self was trying to tranquilize me by guiding my physical gestures. It also affected my breathing, because I caught myself, over the week before Dad died, holding my breath as I sat with him and, usually, Ren, who arrived in Highland Park a day or two after me. We all were talking, or Dad and Ren, the baseball fans in our family, were watching a Sox or Cubs game. If I held my breath, I could hold time and keep death in abeyance. Sitting at the foot of the bed while he was sleeping and when he began to hallucinate intermittently—he asked if we saw blue—I caught myself holding my breath and told myself to breathe. My hot flushes, which had been mild, intensified in that room with Dad. Their frequency and heat increased, and the air conditioning seemed to amplify the slightly sweaty chill after the warmth spread through my upper body, turning my skin that I could see—my arms and hands—beautifully pink and moist. The heat inside, the light, was teaching the Bride the humility of radiance. In that state, she could best be her father's hero, protect and please him.

The charm genre of beauty etiquette addresses a female reader who desires to please—family, friends, co-workers, and men—by employing techniques of femininity. Dahl's title, *Always Ask a Man: Arlene Dahl's Key to Femininity*, couldn't be more apt. In charm books that slightly predate Betty Friedan's *The Feminine Mystique*, published in 1963, or that came on its heels, like Dahl's, from 1965, the supremely feminine model of the fifties housewife, dressed in a shirtwaist and pearls, superbly groomed, and attractively, never obviously, made-up, stands as an iconographical subtext. The career woman also appears in Powers' and Miller's book, in *Always Ask a Man*, and in Ruth Tolman's *Guide to Beauty, Charm, Poise*, which was reprinted three times in the 1960s. Dahl bemoans the career woman, along with the degendering of domestic chores and professional choices for women. Powers and Miller give the career woman a mere 4 pages out of 367. Tolman, while devoting 60 pages to the career woman — "Unit Six: Being Successful on the Job" — uses three-quarters of her foreword, titled "The Importance of Charm in Today's Business World," to "examine for a moment the feminine traits that will attract and hold a man." Tolman assumes that life's fullness for her reader includes more than a career, and she specifies a husband and children — nothing else — as belonging to that life. Nonetheless, she asserts that charm training, which is femininity training, is essential to becoming an elite worker. Skilled in femininity, the working woman can obviate the dimming tensions inflicted by her job or career combined with running a household and just plain running around on errands. Tolman declares the unequivocal value of femininity by citing a government survey showing that charm-trained women earn more than the woman whose business background is comparable but who lacks such training. Conflicted about women's nontraditional ambitions and successes, charm advocates believe that femininity cannot fail.

I think that my high femininity sometimes embarrassed Dad. Mom's training me in femininity produced a girl who grew passionately into the dramatic and glamorous woman who wears form-fitting tops, pink leather, red lipstick, and ankle boots with socks (sometimes colored, mostly black) that rise a few inches above a boot's top edge. Those are my professional gear, and *dramatic* and *glamorous* come from the lips of students, healers, artists, friends, and lovers, as they did from my mother. Mom loved my ivory-colored lace blouse, through which you could see my bra. When I wore it to Washoe Village, she complimented me each time. I sensed that the same blouse caused Dad consternation, as did the low-cut, comfortable Betsey Johnson dress, black with small, metallic gold flowers, that stretched clingingly over my body.

Not only did I learn femininity very well, but my sexual expressiveness radiated into that femininity. How radical for a midlife woman to keep free and to keep freeing her sexuality in ways that flex, meander, and leap away from the deeply instilled rhetoric that promotes aging as misery! How shocking for me to hear a twenty-four-year-old friend equate aging with his own expected "deterioration"! How bewildered I felt when a sixty-year-old woman friend several years older than I explained, "It must be my age," when inflexibility impeded her seated forward bend!

Having spent much time with Mom and Dad during their declines, I'm not a Pollyanna about growing old. However, I emphasize *growing*, and I use *old* to describe a fact of years. We can use *young* the same way. Susanne M. Thornley debunks the student's and the friend's beliefs: "It is a myth that pain is an expected, normal part of aging." I saved that statement from the fall 1994 issue of *The Silver Sage: Newsletter of the Nevada Geriatric Education Center* because it enhanced my faith in *growing*—in becoming more flexible and open in soul-and-mind-inseparable-from-body.

Just as ossification is not a given, neither is the impounding of self-love in a cultural rhetoric and production of *anti-aging*. Anti-aging products, services, and drugs—hormone therapy has often been marketed as anti-aging—wound the heart. The body, like the Tao, is ever-changing, so anti-aging, like anti-body, is illogical. Soul-and-mind-inseparable-from-body knows the logic of change, as does the massively unknown self. So the person who *fights* against aging is attempting to push down and push away the inevitability of the Way. That creates precisely the tension about which skin-care experts warn women. Being propleasure, through narcissistic self-exploration—inward, ever deeper into soul-and-mind-inseparable-from-body—eases the heart, perhaps into a femininity of new dimensions and radiance.

Several years ago, perhaps on the same trip when Dad slumped at the kitchen table, a friend of mine didn't find my femininity pleasing. I was costumed to give a lecture at Stony Brook University, in the clinging, black Betsey Johnson dress and in chocolate brown boots, a little above the ankle, that laced up the front. I especially liked the heel, the sexy curve, the lowness that made walking easy. My girlfriend, who gave compliments readily, kept silent about my appearance, but at one point she said something like, Older women who try to look young are ridiculous. Or that was how her words translated to me. Every once in a while since my midthirties, I've felt uncomfortable in my sexually expressive goodness. In each case, a particular situation, such as my friend's comment, brought my unease to my attention. Each time, of course, I was ripe for a new self-recognition, and vulnerable because of my life's circumstances. With my friend in New York, that vulnerability came from the tenuous conditions of my parents' lives and my marriage. I heard "Grow up!" in my translation of her words. When I was around fifty, my mother-in-law attested to women's leaving behind their desire to be sexy or their practice of sexiness at around age fifty-two. That seemed to be part of "growing up." Or maybe I was hearing in my friend's and my mother-in-law's comments the condoning of a female maturation that featured resigning oneself to erotic abstemiousness. Eros is fundamental to swooning beauty, eros being the rich and gorgeous complexity of soul-and-mind-inseparable-from-body.

I told my friend Robyn in an e-mail about the incident with my friend, who was my age, class, and race, and Robyn's reply eased my heart:

> I loved your anecdote about your outfit on the day you went to Stony Brook, and about the ways your relationship with your old friend maps the bodily and sexual differences between you. Have you read *Sororophobia*, by Helena Michie? The moment you described really seems to me to be a classic instance of the difference-between-women experience she analyzes (that is, when the "women" are in other respects categorically identical, i.e., white, heterosexual, middle-aged, middle-class, professional, etc.). Anyway, I wish I could have seen you in that Betsey Johnson dress: it sounds perfect for you (and perfect with those boots!).
>
> I don't remember whether I told you I've changed my "look" since you last saw me: went back to serious exercise, dropped about 30 pounds, dyed my hair back to its original bright-blond, went back to miniskirts & patterned tights (my old trademark). . . . I love . . . the built-mid-life woman's body (with, by the way, plenty of decoration in the way of makeup, clothing, hair color). I say, hooray!

The Bride grew up. Sometimes she very consciously renewed her faith in the erotics of light.

It is good to grow *up*, to focus on the *higher* education of soul-and-mind-inseparable-from-body. Goodness entails being good to oneself—gentle, calm, and soothing—so that one may give those qualities of goodness to others.

The Bride grew up by reading beauty etiquette books with love and skepticism, thinking simultaneously about the words *radiance* and *horseshit*. Occasionally *horseshit* threatened to overwhelm *radiance*, and she wondered if she was a better critic than she was an acolyte.

Maybe the Bride was lost, her skin and soul forever incorrigible. Those thoughts generally ended in a relaxation brought about by taking the advice of beauty etiquette: she smiled, a slight smile. It came from within and it lit up her entire face. The self-labeled lipstick addict Jessica Pallingston, author of *Lipstick*, counsels, "Most people's mouths look their best when the slightest smile hovers at the corners." Then she cutely asks, "Does yours?" The Bride smiled the same delicate smile when in her mind she saw her mother, sitting in a wheelchair—her mother could not stand for the last couple of years of her life—her mother, diagnosed with senile dementia, the sufferer of strokes, crying, telling the Bride how sad the death of Erne was. The Bride's mother described her pain. She touched the white-and-red-beaded pendant heart of the Bride's necklace and said, "On that order. But sharper." The Bride said, "I know what you mean." She was glad, in her most flexible moments, that mysteries became her, because as she grew up, she experienced more of them. Skin-care etiquette afforded the Bride means for processing the permutations and ramifications of "On that order. But sharper," so that they left no permanent injuries in her soul-and-mind-inseparable-from-body and thereby on her skin. Through skin-care etiquette the Bride saved her skin by learning *être bien dans sa peau*.

The Bride felt good with her father's skin. She massaged his feet, his ankles, his calves, his back, his shoulders—anywhere he asked for her touch. Once, when he was in the hospital, she saw the flawless skin of his naked buttocks.

Papa's mouth was as beautiful as Nefertiti's in Thutmose's painted limestone bust of her. In that famous art work, red pigment articulates a rosy tan complexion and sensuously wide and full lips shaped almost into a pouty cupid's bow. Papa was the grandfather who Ren and I never met, our father's father. Corrine, Dad's only and younger sister, called their father Papa when she saw the picture of him at the party Ren and I gave Erne the day after his cremation. Ren discovered Papa in the family photo album a few months earlier, in April, when

Dad was in the hospital with pneumonia and she was staying at our parents' apartment. I say "discovered" because not only had the image of Papa appeared where it had never been before, but neither Ren nor I had ever seen a photograph of him. Maybe Dad, knowing he would die soon, wanted his daughters to see where their own skin, their own lips had come from. Dad's mouth looked like Papa's, and so do Ren's and mine.

That April, Ren's and my visits to Highland Park overlapped, and one night, when we thought Dad would die within a few days, we sat across from each other in the apartment's living room. I was close to a hallucinatory state. One sees the light in that condition, and I saw Ren as my double. The thick, dark eyebrows, the lovely, large eyes, the high cheekbones and wide face, the strong jaw, the voluptuous lips. I relaxed in my new knowledge of the light. There we were, the Frueh sisters, *luxe, calme, et volupté.*

That well-known phrase from the nineteenth-century poet Charles Baude-laire's "L'Invitation au voyage" has entranced me since my late teens. As parental illnesses and deaths can do, Mom's and Dad's troubles beginning with Dad's bypass surgery were bringing siblings closer to each other. We sisters were accepting the invitation from the light to learn more about it not only in car-ing for our parents but also in tending to each other. Early on in Ren's and my continuing voyage, we talked on the phone for a long time, about menopause, marriage, insomnia, women, and ways to help ourselves feel good. Then or later, she told me that I'd changed, that my voice sounded different, so I didn't come across to her as a pretentious know-it-all. I felt her love, for me and for our parents, I sensed her emotional tightness too, coming from the intricacies of her relationships with Mom and Dad, which, from our childhood, had been much more fraught than mine. The cowboy and the princess: that was only one contributing factor to the tightness with each other that, in our fifties, we were unwinding.

Ren called the 90 Riparian Road house the "mausoleum," a more fitting description of entombed or entombing emotions than of a modernist sobriety. Her name for our house shocked me, and at the same time I found it very funny. I love Ren's humor. Loved it after being escorted around the funeral home "show-room" from which we were to select a container for Dad's ashes. All the designs looked ridiculous to us, especially, I think, because of our upbringing in two homes whose modern architecture and furnishings were the antithesis of the sluggish aesthetic of housings for cremation remains. Mausoleum of the heart though the 90 Riparian Road house may have been for Ren, its terrazzo and walnut floors, high ceilings, picture windows, Tiffany lamps, and Persian rugs; its garden of astilbe and daffodils, tulips and tiger lilies, hosta, peonies, lilacs, and impatiens; and its small forest left wild all sped the light of beauty into me. Upon leaving the funeral home, Ren said, "Just give me the plain paper bag."

We chose the sturdy, nondescript, dark plastic box that was supposed to serve as the interior container for a more distinct holder. The ashes themselves were in a clear plastic bag within the generic box. The glimmering morning that Ren, Russ, Mike, and I stood in Lake Michigan scattering Dad's ashes alternately drew us together as a group and spread us out yards apart from one another. By myself, I began to sing a folk song, one that Ren and I learned when we were teens. It celebrates the joy of flying away to land on a heavenly shore — God's home. The melody and words were themselves joyous, and we were standing at the shore. I sang softly and I cried as I sang.

I was walking toward Ren, and when we met, we sang together, in the pure, strong voices of sister doubles.

I saw what people see when they call me beautiful, and I told her what I was seeing. Our beauty astounded me. Ren, my action hero and my fairy beauty, I love you.

Unlike Ren, the Bride painted the luscious skin of her lips as brilliantly as Thutmose colored Nefertiti's most sensual feature. The Bride enjoyed the spectacle of lipstick, said by skin etiquette authorities and cosmetic know-how experts to resurrect, renew, enliven, and brighten a woman's spirit and complexion. The right lipstick enhances the complexion's color and emphasizes the mouth's expression. Tolman believes that the mouth mirrors the soul by disclosing a woman's temperament. Montez condemns coloring the lips, but she reminds her reader that because the mouth is almost as expressive as the eyes, women should think delightful thoughts in order to create a charming expression. Tolman advises the same path to beauty: "If you are jolly and friendly and approachable, your mouth reflects this fact." In other words, smile, a slight smile, like Mona Lisa, like Nefertiti, a legendary beauty since the discovery of her bust in 1926, a woman whose timeless beauty a historian or beauty expert may let triumph over the living skin of women. Philipp Vandenberg perpetuates the lore of eternal allure in his book *Nefertiti: An Archaeological Biography*, in which the bust "emits a fascinating, almost erotic radiance." *Beauty* and *beautiful* recur so many times in Vandenberg's book that they annoyed the Bride. On one hand the words feel gratuitous, on the other they confront the female reader with her own likely lack of such radiance. Easy to be timeless when you're a queen, luxury has no limits, and you're rendered to look like you're twenty-five. (Nefertiti was probably between her midtwenties and midforties when the portrait was executed.) Timelessness, however, is possible for mortal human beings. It is the light.

For a while the Bride felt bludgeoned by Nefertiti, who does not die. A timeless beauty always has her hooks in future generations of women. As a constituency of romantics about femininity, women want the rosy complexion of a feminine legend, even though they may be hard-assed career women and pragmatic both in the workday world and when undergoing treatments such as Botox, acid peels, and laser and traditional cosmetic surgery.

The femme fatale's reputation is based on her ability to devastate men, but she is fatal to women too. Nefertiti, the fatal beauty, determines from her tomb, from the mummified remains of her rosy skin, that femininity as a problematic fate is inescapable. Maybe she's not dead at all. Maybe she's a vampire—which is why her tomb has never been found. Beautiful Nefertiti, who sucks the life out of women without giving anything good in return. Bad etiquette.

Part of my good etiquette with Dad was to endure the extremely high volume at which he watched TV. Ren, Russ, and I joked among ourselves about the loudness, which required from anyone other than Dad, several long moments in which one's body adjusted. Ten o'clock with Dad brought our ritual of *Law and Order* reruns on the Entertainment Channel and my asana practice, which quieted the volume, within me, of the television as it also lowered my defenses against goodness.

I did my best to be good at Ren's and my party for Dad—a good daughter, a good sister, a good hostess, a good, long-lost niece. I ran down the hallway to greet Corrine and Jim, who Ren and I hadn't seen since our twenties. Corrine was a revelation, in her late seventies, similar in beauty to Mom—the grace and softness that drew one to them, the shape and gestures of their hands. Her beauty dazzled Dad's mourning celebrants, and as we looked at the photo album, she exclaimed over a picture of Dad in his thirties, "He looks like a Hollywood movie star!" She was right. One timeless beauty remarking on the light of another timeless beauty.

The Bride experienced some conflict about timelessness. She wished to gain the wisdom she suspected was signified by the timelessness of Nefertiti's red lips, the Queen's showcase and threshold of conjugal and other familial intimacies, of prayers and song. In their book *Read My Lips: A Cultural History of Lipstick*, published in 1998, Meg Cohen Ragas and Karen Kozlowski declare red lip color in and of itself timeless, "as appropriate today as when it . . . adorned Cleopatra's mouth." Or Nefertiti's. Was she aware that lip color is the finishing touch, the final polish for the complexion, as contemporary skin-care authorities assert? Did Nefertiti, or Thutmose, alter her natural lipline in order to fashion and display more fullness, to articulate a more alluring contour than the one she was born with? Or did she and the artist simply and boldly accent her radiance with red, thereby drawing attention to her smile, her light from within? Cosmetic and beauty etiquette authorities recommend corrective lining to effect the lips that most readily lure. Nefertiti, staring straight ahead, so confident of the future of your soul, the Bride wanted to believe that you were unimproved from the outside, by either your own or Thutmose's skills.

O Queen, did your husband, Akhenaten, like your lips? Cohen Ragas and Kozlowski warn that red both intimidates and invites. Bloodred beauty — scary and seductive. Did he mind that red lips made you a center of attention, a public presence, a diva of your day? Was your husband stinking full of pride and pleasure when he responded to your red lips? Funny to see in *Read My Lips* that husbands prefer their lovers in red lipstick and a wife's mouth bare or colored pink. Because I think that Dad loved Mom's red lips, and Russell fell in love with me, in part, because of my red lips — their clarity of form, their frank, bright sensuality, the iconic femininity of true red lips. I wore red lipstick for most of the time that I was his wife.

The Bride believed, as Dahl does, in the wisdom of letting a wide, generous mouth be your trademark. Papa's mouth is a family emblem that I chose to mark with a signature lipstick. Jean Danielson, BeneFit Cosmetics cofounder, advises women to find a signature lipstick in their forties. During that decade of my life I found M·A·C's True Red. It suited my rosy brunette warmth. Me and Nefertiti: the same type according to Powers in his and Miller's book. "True hues," he claims, "become every skin," though Cohen Ragas and Kozlowski alert their readers that everyone can't wear red lipstick because most women aren't a true red. In Dahl's chapter "Men Dote on Brunettes" I read that Nefertiti represents the quintessential brunette, who as the "the adventuress" and "the vamp" is also "the eternal siren." O Nefertiti, you lustrous, blood-lipped vampire, celebrated by the beauty doyens of my culture as recorded history's fabulous first beauty. Nefertiti, whose name means The Beautiful One Cometh, you must have been a perfume in the scentscape as you walked through Akhetaten's gardens. O Shining One Who Cometh, you can smell her a mile away.

Within a couple of weeks of Dad's death, I added two blossoming bushes to my rose garden. I didn't notice their names till I removed their tags after planting. One came into a second bloom soon after I cut off the dead flowers. Its name— Singin' in the Rain. I was afraid that the other, called Queen Nefertiti and known for its fragrance, wouldn't rebloom, but buds were covering it in late September.

When Dad was dying and dead, his skin was so unlike the apricot pink of the Queen Nefertiti rose. I watched his skin grow purple as his breathing became shallow and then nonexistent. He was gazing out the window for a while before he died. He was being in the light, which was the sun, and as I observed him in the sunlight, maybe he was being, at the same time, the Ground Luminosity or Clear Light, which, according to Buddhist belief, is the nature of mind, called rigpa.

Teacher and incarnate Lama Sogyal Rinpoche defines rigpa in The Tibetan Book of Living and Dying as "intelligent, cognizant, radiant, and always awake." Meditation is a method for receiving the Clear Light. In meditation, Rinpoche understands, "we allow our true Good Heart, the fundamental goodness and kindness that are our real nature, to shine out and become the warm climate in which our true being flowers." The Good Hearted resemble the person who learns through etiquette to be good— gracious, kind, compassionate, and generous— to be a radiant body, like goddesses Aphrodite and Lakshmi. The goddesses' subtle luminosity of being emits their superstinking goodness. Raichur equates that shining beauty to "an inner warmth that seems to emanate as light from . . . pores." My Rose, my Father, the Bride has been following the complexion of your mind.

I needed True Red during the few months of Dad's most difficult dying. In April, when I recognized my sister as my shining twin, I drove alone around the first Highland Park neighborhood that we lived in—Oak Knoll Terrace, Braeside School. Late at night as I was driving, I was sobbing, and a phrase surged into mind that witches use—so that the followers of Wicca may understand humility: what you put out comes back to you three times over. Uncontrollable tears released a longing, for loose ends to weave together gently. Only the unconscious could do that, guided by my wish. That night, or some other night determined by my massively unknown self as more suited for the weaving work that I desired, I dreamed about the old streets. I was there at night time, and it was very dark. Deep dark chocolate, deep dark forest. The dream felt like a fairy tale to haunt one for a lifetime. I felt fear, and I felt free.

Freedom comes to us as layers of obscurity melt, transmute, or wither over years and enlightenment, in unpredictably recurring instants, reweaves our lives by weaving loose ends together gently. So, despite new freedoms, my pores became more visible than usual in a muddy-colored field that felt both dry and greasy. My skin irritated easily, and no products aided its condition. "New lipstick for the springtime!" was my thought, my erroneous solution to being a true red in the rich abyss of mystery. I bought M·A·C's Cosmo, close to my own lip color, but drab. It dulled every feature, and with or without foundation, my skin color seemed to sadden even more. The contemporary makeup legend Bobbi Brown advises women to locate a magic-colored lipstick, one that looks great on their naked face. Bare skin, beautiful color: you'll know the combination when you see it, and it will make you happy. Cosmo could not correct my self-repulsion, which grief was generating. "Studies have shown that women who wear red lipstick smile more": that statement appears alone and unattributed on the page before the introduction of Jessica Pallingston's Lipstick. I returned to True Red, the color that my skin most loved, because it brightened me.

Blatant in hue, true red is subtle in its soul-and-mind-inseparable-from-body-altering performance. Experts agree that lipstick is the only cosmetic that can be simultaneously obvious and attractive. The Bride outlined and colored in her gift of Papa's mouth, of Erne's mouth, making obvious to herself her connection with two men whose timelessly beautiful feature she inherited. She chose red—the bravery of heroes and of fairies—for blatant display. Not of cosmetic illusion—a superficial smile of sex, sophistication, or simplistic color—but rather, of one momentous tiny detail of the universe—the lips—whose harmonies we see and smell as degrees of radiance, if we are lucky or we are close to wedlock with the light.

I saw the light of Mom's mind when I witnessed her pronouncement on hearing from her daughters that her husband had died. Ren and I had brought her into his Red Oaks room, and she sat in her wheelchair looking at him. "What a vacation." You'd think that her voice would have punctuated that with an exclamation point. But the truth of her statement required nothing more than her matter-of-fact articulation. I saw the flashing light of my fear when I decided to sleep in the master bedroom, where Dad slept before going to Red Oaks. The study had a sofa sleeper, and the living room had a couch, so the two twin beds in the master bedroom were the most comfortable sleeping situation in the apartment. I offered the room to Ren when she arrived the next night, and I saw the flashing light of her fear too. We laughed about our terrors: Who or what might inhabit us? Who or what might we inhabit? I saw the light of joy in a gorgeous autumn road trip from Chicago to Reno, driving home Dad's barely used Acura Legend a year after he slumped at the kitchen table.

One day between Dad's and Mom's deaths, I went to the Macy's perfume counter looking for the Bride of Light—on a little pilgrimage, the way I'd been searching for her, too, at the M·A·C counter when I bought Cosmo. I spotted Joy, by Jean Patou. When I sniffed the eau de toilette bottle a couple of days earlier, Joy smelled voluminous and floral, happily heady. I sprayed Joy on my wrists, my nose and brain expecting the elevation that I remembered. But my body changed the lift of Joy. Combining with Bulgarian Rose and absolute of jasmine, my particular nuances of the naturally yeasty odor of skin created a thinly sweet and noncommittal scent that reminded me of a bland, yet cloying, sunscreen. I need some gravity, some density when I want to reek of radiance, and that day I wanted a sensational layering of riches to coax my light out and to help it last.

Patou's interpretation of joy was too mild for me. These days, Tabac Blond holds the subtle powers that emanate from me in such a lovely way when the perfume's leather, linden, and carnation notes are mixing with the odor of my skin. Balenciaga's Quadrille used to be my Tabac Blond. Wearing it first in my twenties, I returned to it over the decades as I still return, for floral riches, to Bellodgia. Like Bellodgia, Quadrille was like an old friend whose scent and yours are such fast companions that you don't think much about the blending after it's been made. . . . unless a change occurs in the levels and the resonance of your own and your friend's light. Due to changes in heart, which may be greater ease or greater stricture. Quadrille: a knight's tournament, a square dance, the music for that dance. Quadrille: a structure, like etiquette, that makes joy possible.

Nefertiti, if you did die, save a dance for me in the garden that is heaven, a most radiant and spacious place. Other stinking beauties will join us in a quadrille, then a jig, a tango, waltz, and hula, and you'll teach me, please, the movements of mellifluously slinky women I see dancing in New Kingdom frescoes. We'll be naked, clothed in the sultry radiance of roses, leather, musk, carnations, Quadrille, Tabac Blond, and other perfumes, sweat, and skin.

Those French perfumes, resonant with love, fill me with their joy, something that, in order to improve my complexion, I'd been endeavoring to understand.

The perfume of chocolate that is melting, baking, or being unwrapped has always filled me with joy, like those French perfumes. While Ren's "mausoleum" may have housed somberly styled emotions, it also held perfumes of joy. The aromas of the hot dogs, hamburgers, and shish kebabs that Dad barbecued wafted into the dining room and kitchen from the terrace, through the sliding screens outside the sliding picture windows. Each holiday season, smelling the wax of Chanukah candles both relaxed and energized me into coziness, as did breathing deeply in the presence of our Christmas tree. Ren and I both loved the menorah, which she now has. I've been looking for one like it, looking with the faith and patience of the Bride of Light. That menorah's simultaneously modernist and ancient beauty is hard to find. I love the deep sweetness of my Quadrille and Tabac Blond; deep sweetness describes the tobacco that Dad smoked in his pipes.

It describes, too, the redolence of his Christmas cookies and Mom's chocolate cakes and brownies baking in the oven. *Death by Chocolate* offers recipes with names that conjured up melancholy circumstances for The Bride: Chocolate Demise, Chocolate Devastation, Double Mocha Madness, Death by Chocolate. Desaulniers titles chapter 5 "Chocolate Dementia." No flavor but chocolate could rightfully describe those states. Vanilla Demise? Lemon Devastation? Double Raspberry Madness? Death by Walnut? Coconut Dementia? Even Chocolate Wedlock, another *Death by Chocolate* dish, could have chilled the Bride's memories of radiantly baking treats, whose spirit, infused by a loving, parental chef, she was needing to nurture her heart.

The Valentines Days, the barbecues, the Christmas and Thanksgiving dinners, the birthday parties, the anniversaries all became a phantasmagoric Bridal history. In that history of chocolate, the changing scenes, events, and people showed the Bride the light, because, having borne protracted darkness, she could shine as she had never shone before. Would someone, she wished, bake Chocolate Phantasmagoria for her! Chocolate cake with hazelnut butter and chocolate ganache.

A student gave me an ad, from a women's magazine, whose subject was chocolate. I remember that it featured a recipe for No Guilt Brownies. Richness, like sweetness—which we all wish for, from family, friends, lovers, spouses, and life—stirs up guilt. According to the recipe, cottage cheese—no egg yolks—will make delicious low-cholesterol brownies. Part of me calls the cottage cheese an unheroic substitute for the full flavor of yolky brownies, while another part understands that eating low-fat and low-cholesterol foods can be heroic—restraining one's appetite and decreasing one's intake of substances that we've been taught are unhealthy. Well trained by our fitness and beauty culture, I've usually paid attention to my fat consumption, but not when it comes to chocolate. I don't believe that chocolate is *sinfully* delicious, so I don't feel guilty either when I'm eating it or afterward. What would be the object of my guilt? My own body? If sin is an untrue aim, reckless or unfocused, then depriving myself of pleasure is a sin against my history of chocolate.

Considering that heroes risk richness, I have liked to "taste the difference Land O'Lakes makes." The rhyme appeared in another unsaved ad. In our house, chocolate desserts were always rich with Land O'Lakes butter. Because of that, using butter for baking has been second nature for me, and it belongs to a chocolate protocol that I learned as a child: 1) margarine doesn't enter the baker's mind, unless she's going through a sumptuary phase—which Mom and I both did—in the short-lived belief that buttery home-baked goods will harm her or her loved ones' health; 2) the baker eats batter, which includes scraping the bowl with a spoon and licking it clean along with the beater attachments; 3) whether eating alone or in much company, chocolate lovers comply with chocolate's sweet insistence that it be given silent or spoken homage, that chocolate lovers consciously acknowledge how fortunate they are to be enlivened, and enlightened, by the substance that fills their mouths.

9 ⁓

Swooning Beauty: A Midlife Divorcée
Lets Eros Amaze Her

I am full of chocolate, full of love. In the past few years I've been receiving more chocolate gifts than usual, mainly from students. They've surprised me with chocolate lips of larger-than-life size, a big box of truffles, a choice of candies from a trip to Japan, and they've given themselves as well as me many treats in seminars: dark, milk, white, and bittersweet bars, home-baked cakes, brownies, and chocolate chip cookies.

The gifts I've been receiving are more than simply chocolate. They've treated my heart to love by healing the heartbreak that every human being has suffered. My childhood and adulthood, my womanhood and manhood, my selfhood have resounded with chocolate, which, as genoise, cheesecake, truffles, pots de crème, buttercream, fudge, and pudding, as mousse and candy bars, ice cream, custard, and ganache, is melodious in the throat, like cum, though texturally so unlike it.

My primal scene, the one that I remember: at around six or eight years old, I saw my parents fucking. I walked into their bedroom silently, which I must have done numerous times. (Was the door closed? Had I heard something that I wanted to see? Did I want to intrude? Was I pushing my luck and pushing my erotic limits?) A flash of skin; then a rush of action as my father (most likely) pulled the covers over him and Mom. (Did they speak? Did I turn around immediately and leave of my own volition?) I've always read and heard that young children who see or hear their parents sexually engaged experience the event as violent, especially as violence done to the mother; and that the psyche emerges scathed. I don't think so. Not for me. When the image has come back to me over the years, it has fascinated me every time, so I believe that it fascinated me originally and that it was one of my earliest initiations into a love of the erotic.

My primal scene is a kind of Proustian madeleine, recalling me throughout my life to the roots of my persistent love of sex. My remembrance of things past shapes orgasm in the present. It doesn't take a scholar to tell us that sexual desire and pleasure are mentally motivated; that orgasm is neither simply nor solely a biomechanical response. So the shaping power of my primal scene isn't an enigma. Yet the event holds mystery, my wondering in the grip of memory, whose preciseness is always in question, about the correspondence between the details of what actually happened in that bedroom among the three of us, and my own sexual tastes and fervors. For example, I've always liked orgasm best when fucking. Should I presume that this is because I saw my parents fucking—and maybe they were coming—and I have to repeat their pleasure?

I have felt anomalous: my primal scene provoked pleasure and fed my romance with thinking and fucking. As both image and experience, Mom and Dad in bed set me thinking, long ago, about sex as both a personal and an intellectual subject, and that subject was a lifetime occupation. Lovemaking is an untoward theme for a feminist intellectual. I couldn't help it: sexual bodies, sexualized bodies, bodies in sexual contact intoxicated me, as orgasm, a key high point of sexual contact, intoxicated me too.

My parents' real bodies have not stayed with me as spectral demons. Rather, they've been a source of my ability to fly on sexual fantasies and to invest my emotional intelligence in understanding sexual behaviors when I've seen and experienced them; and their bodies have been an engine of their daughter the scholar's ideas.

I e-mailed my fairy lover,

I want you to push me up against a building's wall, in some big city on a side street at night, push me up against it hard, your cock, hard, singling out my cunt for love. A wall where people can hear our pleasure but almost none can see it, unless they want to: from around a corner our groans and hyperventilation, our taking away of each other's breath and our giving our breath to each other—breathing into each other's mouths with kisses—seduces some voyeur, one who's supersensitive to sounds, or to sex in the nearby air, as if antennaed for it like an insect.

I want your cum running down my leg after we've fucked someplace in public or in a car, and you can lick your cum from my inner thigh or we can put my lace panties in place (if I'm wearing any) as we walk to dinner and they'll be wet with both our cum. I want us to taste your cum together, like we taste mine when we're kissing after you eat me. And at a restaurant dinner table you can put your hand between my legs and feel our wetness.

I'm on the verge of the verge of coming as I write you.

Those fantasies of public fucking, of coming in public with a partner: did they originate in the fact that I was the public to my parents' sex, so consequently wanted a public to witness mine? Was the very fact that fucking so thrilled me determined by an excitement that my parents' fucking provoked on-the-spot in me? Because my unconscious knows the position that Mom and Dad enjoyed each other in, did my unconscious decide my responsiveness, my quick orgasm when a man penetrated me from behind with my butt raised just a little? Perhaps a person's sexual predilections exist *before* birth. Maybe my mother's own desires, passions, and positions designed this daughter's passions, too, in utero. And was it there that I gave myself to my first orgasm?

I suppose that my primal scene could have precipitated an effect that differs from the pleasure I describe. I could have been scared of fucking or felt diminished by it or found it to be distasteful, even ugly.

All orgasms are beautiful. Because *beautiful* is defined as that which gives one the highest degree of pleasure. The primary constituent of an orgasm's beauty seems obvious: an orgasm's physiological components ensure that it feels good. Yet all orgasms are not equal. Speaking as a female body, the duration, intensity, and location of orgasm vary, and they contribute to the particular beauty of an orgasm and to the fact that some orgasms *are* more beautiful than others to the person who is experiencing them. But even a weak orgasm provides a high degree of pleasure in relation to other pleasures in life, such as eating delicious food, participating in a lively conversation, being part of the sunny sky and the desert ground. Beauty can be graceful, striking, roaring, refined, and orgasms can have the same qualities.

Beauty can also be playful. Play plumps us, enriches and amplifies us. When we're full of pleasure, we're beautifully plump, like round hips and bellies and like muscles too. In orgasm, our being itself swells. Play plumps all of a person, soul-and-mind-inseparable-from-body, like sexual arousal plumps the genitals, in readiness for orgasm.

> My lust, which couples with my love for you, has swollen every bit of me, has enlarged all of my materiality and immateriality so that I am full of you, decentered from a more ordinary state of ego.

The Harvard University English professor Elaine Scarry claims, in her philosophical defense of beauty, *On Beauty and Being Just*, "At the moment we see something beautiful, we undergo a radical decentering." Playing with this idea, I say that when we feel the beauty of orgasm, we undergo a radical decentering, which may last beyond the orgasm's length.

> Such decentering can linger, and it perhaps accounts, day after day, month after month, many months after you and I first came together in my bed, for feeling still as if I am aloft.

Scarry suggests that when we happen upon a beautiful object, taste, or concept, it lifts us off the rotating earth to land us changed on shifted ground. Similarly, the aftereffects of orgasm, a beautiful occurrence, cause a lifting, floating, or spinning from which we return to terra firma in a less self-centered state from that in which we left: beauty has transformed terra firma into terra nova.

> You said on Friday that you feel like you're floating. Let me tell you . . . I felt like I was floating all day Friday and it's been happening other times since then. Like my head is high above my body. I had terrific energy after our breakfast and all the weights in the gym felt light, even what I was doing heavier than ever before. Maybe our floating has to do with feeling some of the same things.
>
> It would be fun to put makeup on you. Especially after what you said about liking women's clothes. Made me smile when you asked me, "What if I like it too much?" And I said you were macho enough, so not to worry. "Too macho?" you asked.
>
> Fairy man, fairy woman, floating . . .

Orgasm spirits and moves us into fairyland, a generally unfamiliar world, one of extreme connection with another human being; and that connection exists whether or not we love the person with whom we experience our orgasm. Fairyland is magical, a place or state of extraordinary power.

Fairies travel between human beings' everyday world and regions that the psyche experiences as both lighter and darker than the norm. Our orgasms with one another turn us into fairies or draw out the fairy in us, for during orgasm we are lighter than usual—unburdened, wanton, buoyant, giddy, perhaps foolish; inspired, animated, brightened up, and even radiant—and we are darker too, delving into supplies of energy that we generally hold secret, involuntarily daring to leap toward the twilight of cries and crying, moans and drooling, letting loose the animals that we are, permitting ourselves to be ignorant of sin. The lightness and the darkness of our fairy selves, experiencing orgasm in either masturbation with no one near or in a copulative embrace, is a letting go.

Fairies are so good at letting go. That's because they are large in courage, it's because courage enlarges them. Huge-hearted fairies. Their grasp of life and death is large, yet everything slips through their fingers. The reason is that they do not care about the kind of closure that human beings wish to be conclusive: conclusions that we believe we need after a loved one dies (closure to our grief) or when we end a marriage (closure to our shared history, closure to our love) or at the end of a day's discussion in a university classroom (closure to a concept both obligated to and swirling with a complex of facts). Closure as conclusiveness is a cowardly or lazy way out of the process of living. Living takes time, takes many turns, creates opening after opening. Belief in closure limits our understanding: of the mind's intricate play with ideas and of the gradual muting of grief for a parent or of love for a former spouse, a muting from which flares from the unconscious unexpectedly shoot forth. Belief in closure reduces our capacity for growth, for learning, and for pleasure.

Orgasm, defined as the climax of sexual excitement, is a closure. Yet a climax is not necessarily a finish. An orgasm may have the beauty of finishing touches, which are sexual pleasure's final flourishes, such as the particularity of slow or savage thrusts of cock in cunt or anus, of teeth cutting into the skin that covers a trapezius, of a guttural "I love you" or "I'm coming," of sweaty groin to buttocks. Orgasm does end, but, like emotions, it remains, by embedding itself in the psyche, and although orgasm gradually fades from immediate regard, we can consciously carry it with us, if we wish; we can feel it as a constant pleasure, as a continuity of pleasure in our lives. The continuity of pleasure both comes from and creates sparkling creatures, fairies, who spark pleasure in other people.

In my performance *The Aesthetics of Orgasm*, I wished to give me and my audience pleasure by wearing pink. My hot pink, voile evening gown with a low-cut back and bodice and a flirtatious hemline revealed a lot of my legs from knees to feet, and a matching capelet that sparkles with sequins augmented the costume's fairy glamour.

I've read that when someone wears pink, she attracts love, or at the least, generates happiness in those who are looking at her. Pink unblocks the heart and increases good feelings.

Pink, the color of genitals, ranges, like orgasm, from fierce to tender, and just as orgasm is not a trifling sensation, neither is pink a trifling color.

We perceive pink as a paler version of red and therefore easier to take. Pink doesn't carry the threat of red. It is red's cognate, but we think that red is bold and pink is demure. This formulation of difference between red and pink reveals the trivializing association of pink with femininity, especially with the culturally sweetened notions of little girls' femininity.

Our trifling treatment of pink defends against its potency.

How well the fashion designer Betsey Johnson understands pink's potency. (Betsey designed my pink costume.) The walls of her boutiques are painted fuchsia, and it's easy to find pink clothes in them. Pink sells clothes because pink lifts spirits.

Pink is bubbly, ardent, piquant, sweet, and wild, and we are delinquent hearts when we remain unconscious of pink's complexity and dynamism.

Pink carries the essence of erotic play. Pink can be light and dense, froth and crystal, liquid like a sharp or a sugary juice, pliant like tongues and genitalia, ladylike and generous. Pink refreshes us, as does play, because of its aphrodisiacal lightness.

I don't adhere to the notion that chocolate can be used as an aphrodisiac, although I know that chocolate heightens my own sensual awareness. However, the belief in seventeenth- and eighteenth-century Europe that chocolate acts as a sexual stimulant persists into the present. I'm surprised that I haven't come across a recipe in the chocolate cookbooks that I own for a dish named Chocolate Libido. In *Death by Chocolate*, Desaulniers calls a mousse cake that he invented Chocolate Temptation, and he writes in the book's introduction about his chocolate lust, which he equates with sexual lust. "In my more creative moments," he reveals, "I would blend the two fantasies, conjuring up visions of firm mounds of chocolate mousse topped with Hershey's kisses. Or I would envision Rabelaisian romps in pools of warm chocolate sauce." When foods and people activate us erotically, we find them irresistible. Across from his introduction is a full-page detail: a mass of chocolate chips and walnuts bids us to dig in. The nuts look visceral—golden and meaty—and the chocolates catch the light as would deep-colored stones. The tastes and textures are in my mind's mouth, acting seductively, like the touch and flavor of a person's skin before we've become lovers.

You know, you could decide never to get involved with anyone again, I told myself. You could close your heart after the damage of divorce and parental deaths. You could bring your heart inside, so far inside that even you would hardly know it's beating. The hiddenness of your heart would be like shallow breathing, or like holding your breath.

I give my heart again. My lover's mouth and tongue are soft and dynamic, like mine. So quickly he feels like part of me, my cunt becomes his lips, his saliva is my wetness. Our bodies, clothed alongside each other, moan together, in a union, a communion whose particularities of merging I haven't felt before. Even with our clothes on, I feel a joining that I think I've been afraid of feeling before. I love sex with men. They become feminine. I become masculine. We are both and neither gender. I look at my lover, whose eyes are closed, as I lie on him, as I snake over his body and into his being, and I smile because his pleasure and desire both relax and activate his beauty, which, though distinctly male, is more than willing to be taken—by my strength. He embraces me with power, embraces my torso, then my hips when he's eating me. His passion moves into me, he is much stronger than I am; his hands, running up and down my back, could force me to comply with anything he wants, but they push me, with perfect pressure, into the merging that thrills and stuns me. Even with our jeans on, I feel our hips, groins, thighs, bellies as one. I've read about the loss of identity that people feel with sex. The most captivating discourse comes from philosophers. I've disagreed with them. I've said that during tremendous sexual pleasure, one can feel one's own identity clearly. Now, with my lover, I'm experiencing a change of mind and body through a change of heart, through a vulnerability for which I can't account. My vulnerability surprises me. My lover and I are a surprise to each other; we are a surprise to us. I am letting myself "lose my identity" with him. Let go, as the fairies say and do. O, pin me down with your clear, wild heart, which is all of your body on top of mine, your palms to my palms, our fingers intertwining. O, pick me up and place me where you want me, which is where our identities dissolve into our surprising sexual solution. We are aggressive and tender with each other, creating fairyland with soul-and-mind-inseparable-from-body. We create fairyland together because I am between twenty-two and twenty-five, as well as being in my fifties, and I am eight and two thousand, too; and he is eighteen and twenty-two, as well as being twenty-eight, and he is thousands of years old, like me.

Fearless lovers for a while, we played across the cultural closures of age, with the wonders of each other's sex, and with the pleasure that our hottest pink attraction to each other stimulated in our spirits' seeking happiness and home in each other's body.

I play with the language of my body, the designations given to my pinkness. Words can increase orgasmic capacity. To shun the words, for me, would be a shutting off of imagination, and words can plump the imagination—our creative power—which fashions the beauty of orgasm in soul-and-mind-inseparable-from-body.

Pussy and cunt. They do not connote the same thing. Pussy has a light, amusing, even merry tone, whereas cunt delivers a more aggressive, blunter message, like the passionate imperative, "Fuck me." Many people reduce cunt and pussy to naughty words, but naughty is a facile description; for pussy describes a lovely seductiveness, pink like apple blossoms or a tangy taste, and cunt describes a more demanding enticement, pungent like a curry that sharpens one's sensitivity to flavors, bold as the roses in my garden whose pink an acquaintance of mine called garish and which captivated a little girl I know so much that we cut her a bouquet. Cunt and pussy both connote exuberance, and the words enrich the vulval and vaginal aesthetics originated and developed by the women artists for whom an erotics of women's bodies necessitated a visual representation and understanding of female genital beauty. That understanding disputes Freud's assertion that genitals—male or female—are ugly and, more important, it increases women's orgasmic capacity.

> *What sets me on the verge of the verge of orgasm as I e-mail you is the way you know my cunt, my pussy, the way your fingers play with my moist folds of flesh so that I feel the angelic movement of each of your fingers on a contour or a surface, the way one or more of your fingers so easily finds the entrance to my vagina and then, with equal ease, slips inside, making me so aware of my own body, my own cunt, yet at the same time making me so aware that your body and my own, your fingers and my cunt, are one, making me wetter and ever more giving to your taking, to your giving.*
>
> *I am both baffled by the fact and in love with it—that even though you are everywhere around me in great corporeal force and grace, the materiality of our bodies is entryway, opening, far beyond threshold, and anything but barrier.*

Defenses down. Approach invited. Passage attained.

I'm a pornographer, like the Marquis de Sade. We play with sensually primal language. Perhaps we bring people to the verge of the verge of orgasm. Sade's dark heart, some say, made him a devil, in both his life and writings. Diabolo, a torte recipe given by Medrich in *Cocolat*, thick with heavy cream—three cups—and sweet butter—six ounces. Deep dark chocolate, the cookbooks imply, will undermine if not conquer one's conscience through sensual seduction. Diabolo! The devil made me do it—break my diet with some chocolate temptress, unnerve myself with the nature and extent of my appetites.

Chocolate is a pornographer's delight. Sade loved it—I love it—and in women's magazines and in books and essays about women and sex, women and eating problems, women and beauty ideology, chocolate appears more than occasionally as the food that's sinfully delicious, that provides orgasmic pleasure, that is better than sex. Which reminds me that at our end-of-the-term party for a feminist criticism class several years ago, one of the students, a woman in her thirties, baked a fabulous chocolate cake whose name was Better than Sex.

Deep dark chocolate, deep dark secret: I'd been looking for a fairy lover in the everyday barrage of shitfire. Deep dark chocolate, deep dark forest: I've heard that I look like a dominatrix, but only one dominatrix have I identified with,

Mme Duclos, inside the Château Silling of Sade's 120 *Days of Sodom*. We both tell stories about our lives, our sex, our good looks, our manly behaviors with men's bodies. My midlife authority is precisely a vehicle for identifying with the midlife Duclos, with being, like her, a man in the guise of femininity.

I asked a student in a performance-art class during a critique of his piece, "Do you know where you're standing?" He recognized that I was asking if he knew, as he performed, where his body was. He answered that he didn't know. As men in the guise of femininity, Duclos and I know where we stand, how our bodies attract attention when we tell our stories, how the way we dress, walk, and gesture determines perceptions of us as objects of desire — and fear.

Women who lust, who feel and express their orgasmic capacity, whom people perceive as narcissistic and desirable, who, while they appear to be powerful as hell, also suggest, in their fairy spirit, that their defenses *can* be down, that they *are* inviting approach, that they *do* wish to attain orgasmic passage with *you*, attract shitfire like crazy. Legend, gossip, the media, and even scholars accuse such women of trickery and treachery or, at the least, suspicious behavior. Diabolo! We are not the devil. We have not led anyone astray, though maybe we've seduced some souls who've become richer for our interest in them. We have not forced men to unzip their pants, to pull out their beautiful cocks, to dread our pleasure at being cocksuckers. We are not satans, puckering our crimson lips, black-rimmed eyes gloating over men's imperfect naked bodies, ready to stick a pitchfork into their delicate egos. My conscience is so clean of wile.

Nevertheless, it's no wonder that I've said, only half-jokingly, that at the age of fifty-two I realized I was a man. Men can be devilish and beat the rap of evildoing. They don't have to hear how intimidating they are, or how tempting. And when they do tempt us women, they don't become temptresses. We don't suspect them of wanting to do us in, like Delilah, to sell us down the river because we're coldhearted or greedy or just a bitch. The root of *tempt* is the Latin *temptare*, to try the strength of, to urge. Men must not feel as strong as I do if they've lacked the self-assurance to make love to a woman and not feel that she is using his desire to urge him beyond what *he* desires. Desire is limitless: deal with it.

"Yes, ma'am," says pilot Tom Paris to Kate Mulgrew's Captain Kathryn Janeway on the *Star Trek* series *Voyager*. Like other starship captains in the series, she orders, "Do it!" and the crew obeys. That terse imperative excites me, especially spoken by Janeway, another woman who is a man. "Yes, ma'am," say

Captain Karen Walden's men when her bravery tops theirs as Iraqis attack the Americans' downed helicopter in *Courage under Fire*. Over and over, in one way and another, Meg Ryan's Walden, like any captain, like any man, directs her subordinates to "Do it!" How clear and unsentimental a phrase is "Do it!" How unromantic a sexual command: don't fool around, just fuck me plain and simple. Spoken in sexual circumstances by a woman, "Do it" must make tempted men feel like subordinates, caught in the machinations of the devil, the skills of a dominatrix.

At the risk of further disarming men, let me assert that all of us women don't need or want plying with foreplay, although I've read since I was a girl that we do. Some of us need and love, a lot of the time, decisiveness and force akin to the action hero's when he is at the pinnacle of knowing what he has to do, when he can't afford to make mistakes, when his focus is absolute.

Gibson's Benjamin Martin, a Revolutionary War militia hero in *The Patriot*, wants to kill a lot of King George's soldiers, with the help of his two young sons, who are new to killing and who will be witnessing the mayhem designed by their father. Martin's prayer for success is concise: "Lord, make me fast and accurate."

My fondness for "Do it!" isn't necessarily asking for a fast fuck, which is just right when its passion increases passion.

Like you, my fairy man, I love the sudden synergy of cock and cunt. How quick is orgasm when we are in our fairy passage? As quick as penis meets introitus.

My fairy lover told me that he learned years ago, in martial arts training and in climbing rocks with the mental focus of a monk, the value of no wasted movement. And that is how he made love to me, how we made love together. No wasted movement didn't mean that every movement of ours required a reason for being or that each of them was a deliberate progress toward coming. Rather, no wasted movement meant utmost pleasure. "You're so wet," he'd say to me, delighted. A wet cunt creates ease, the ability to "Do it!" fluidly. Ease is almost an opposite of waste.

"Do it!" asks that we dispense with flesh mulling over flesh, tongue debating finger, finger debating clit, clit debating glans. In a number of *Voyager* episodes, Janeway and her first officer, Chakotay, debate each other about some strategy or offensive on which the captain must imminently embark. Soon enough she's saying to him something like, "That's that, I'm right, we're doing it my way, the debate is over." She knows where she stands in the deep dark forest of the Delta Quadrant, where she has inadvertently lost her ship, and she's as cool as any femme fatale or dominatrix, experts at calculating risks to the flesh and will.

—Here I stand. Here I am with another person. Here I am with another penis, another navel, another set of the same circumstances in a different body led by a different ego, defense mechanisms, and compensatory behaviors.

Here I am in an inescapable way. Here I am, in all my blushes and whatever little pimples exist today on my high round ass.

Orgasm puts you in your place. Here I *am*. Here I am. Or, with one or more partners, here we *are*, here *we* are.

Here I am in the Sonoran Desert with the saguaros, chollas, and prickly pears, or here I am in my rich cream-colored bedroom with the bluejays screeching this early morning along with my coloratura moans, or here we are making our specific heat in the dead of a Chicago winter.

I am here in vaginal orgasm more than in clitoral orgasm. A clitoral orgasm feels as though it spreads across surface flesh and stays in my genital area, whereas a vaginal orgasm aroused because of intercourse often begins with penetration and opens, in a profuse petaling, as penis meets G-spot, then suction and friction occur—of varying speed, rhythm, duration, vaginal/penile depth, and power exchange between my lover and me. In vaginal orgasm I flower to and through my soles and palms and from my brain into my scalp. Nothing gets left out, no organ, no muscle. And my orgasm moves beyond me.

It has, of course, been in my lovers as they and I were sculpting each other with that power exchange of breaths and bodies, saliva, sweat, and cum, and it has radiated into the room or the ground which my lovers and I have inhabited and altered; because I clutched a pillow or ran my nails through sand or made the sounds that sometimes only my lovers heard but sometimes a neighbor could hear as well; and certainly the birds, like other animals, discerned my orgasms with parts of their bodies other than ears.

The zydeco musician Rosie Ledet sings about her "joy box." The lyrics focus on female directions for male control and on the high pleasure of vaginal orgasm. Yet, for me and, I imagine, Rosie, "vaginal orgasm" seems like a misnomer; because the term implies that the pleasure exists or stays in only one place, and, thus defined, orgasm is about closure. However, now that I've enlarged the definition of "vaginal orgasm," I'll use the term more comfortably, knowing that you and I can continue to enlarge our understanding of it, not only through what I say but because the supple parts of our massively unknown selves will play with the term.

Vaginal orgasm helps me know where I stand, where I am. (I speak only for myself, not for all women, because women's genital sensations are not exactly shared.) I know where I stand because cocks that I loved have reached a centrality inside me that is not simply physical. Being in that center of me—which some of the feminists who reclaimed cunt called the *central core*—my fairy lover saw into me, saw through me. Most purely, *he saw me.*

> *Is your cock your center, like my cunt is mine; and if so, do you feel that when we make love I am embracing the center of you?*
> *Yes. We know each other's center in the paradoxical dissolution or exchange of self into the lover, into the decentering, into the loss of identity that is the clearest clarity.*

My fairy lover said, "You're like a little girl." Which meant that he saw me, he knew me as a little girl. He was on-target to my psyche. No wonder his cock found its way so securely inside me without a condom. I knew my trust in him without having to think about knowing it, and considering that all my life I'd religiously used a condom, a diaphragm, or birth control pills so that I wouldn't become pregnant—but also, I now see in retrospect, often enough because I hadn't trusted a man deeply, hadn't felt replete with faith in either his love for me or in our relationship—my trust amazed me to such a degree that I recognized it as part of the reason why I was crying sometimes when my fairy lover and I were talking, making love, or simply smiling as we looked at each other. Even in the past several years, as my periods gradually stopped, I used a condom—maybe out of habit, maybe because of the risk of an STD, maybe because of my ancient lack of *abundant* faith in my own lovingness.

When my lover said, "You're like a little girl," he complimented me without knowing it. He said I'm a sophisticate in public and a little girl at times with him. "It's not that I'm sexually attracted to little girls . . . ," he began without finishing the sentence. Completing it now, I say that he was attracted to my childhood inclinations, living buoyantly in my fairy self, and that his own fairy self felt freed in the presence of mine.

I do love eight-year-old girls. It must be because I am one, still. My fairy lover loved in me whatever the pianist saw.

I was such a little, sexy lady, thinking about posture, makeup, voice, and the seductions of each, paying attention to ways of pleasing a man, letting advice about gender inform my being. Robot femininity could have been the outcome of that early education, from skin-care etiquette to clinical discussions by patriarchal authorities, like Dr. Frank S. Caprio, who wrote *The Sexually Adequate Male* and *The Sexually Adequate Female*, two books that Mom either bought or checked out from the library. But my looking for pleasure rather than for pat answers, and my love of pleasure over passiveness, coupled with my inability to unquestioningly accept sexual "authorities," even as a child, ensured that my sensuality overwhelmed Dr. Caprio's "orders" for gender-deterministic sexual health. My love of pleasure both overdetermined and undermined the ways I learned to fetishize gender, so that my sense of aesthetic drama—which Mom regularly pointed out to me from my teens on—undermined guidance for looking and acting pretty in a nicey-nice way. Many times in my childhood and teens I wanted my body and mind to blend in, but being regular was more of a masquerade than femininity. Velvet, lace, satin, crinoline, nylon; Mom's red lipstick, her pointy-toed high heels, her Persian lamb and mink coats: fabrics for little girls' fancy dresses and underwear along with Mom's material femininity, whose artifacts and effects I tried on, constituted not only a terrain but also a frontier of aesthetic and erotic amplitudes. Having masturbated as a girl in mink, high heels, and lipstick, I've long appreciated the roominess of dressing up for autoeroticism and orgasm.

My friend Jeff teased me only a few years ago, "Joanna, you always dress up in a costume." He was right. I dress up in pleasure for daily life. I dress up in daily life to arrange myself for orgasm. I dress up in order to clear away the everyday crap, the barrage of shitfire; and my dress-up is self-love that clears the way to orgasm.

—I question my interpretation of my primal scene. Because I *could* interpret my reaction differently. I could see it as trauma, I could say that I'm sexually obsessed and that the genesis of my obsession resides in an event that I could not have possibly deciphered and that I never can. I could say that my psyche is full of compensations and that I've been forever mortified by sex. I could say that my sexual revelations, in print and in conversations with my friends, have been defense mechanisms, developed in order to protect myself from feeling that I can never fuck like the big guys, fuck in large scale, heroically, like adults do.

But that interpretation feels wrong, feels itself like a mystification of my reality, of my soul-and-mind-inseparable-from-body. That interpretation feels like a mystification built on theoretical absolutism — trauma results from seeing one's parents in bed — and built, too, on an ideology of anti-pleasure — one's parents' pleasure cannot be digested into a nurturance of one's *own* pleasure.

One learns the significance of pleasure negatively, or rather, through the negation of pleasure. Self-help material about sex and beauty emerges from the negative, from shame and self-repulsion symphonically orchestrated to the theme, "I don't know up from down about my own pleasure or beauty."

Accentuating my appearance increases my orgasmic capacity, situates me on the verge of the verge of orgasm. To be as pretty as I can be was perhaps a compensation for an inadequacy at once lodged in and called up by my primal scene. Being as pretty as I can be enlarged me, so maybe it reduced the large place that my parents' fucking took up in my psyche.

While femininity can paradoxically promote women's abandonment of their bodies in the assertion of a blandly frilly corporeality, femininity can also provide valuably heady pleasures.

Pleasure is available to me even when I hide it from others.

I sit in a movie theater, legs crossed, rotating my hips so slightly that no one would know I'm doing it. I have to keep myself from moaning. I'm rotating my hips because I'm missing my lover. I'm missing the substance of love. My hips first moved like that when I was a little girl, desiring Ricky Nelson or masturbating in bed in the afternoon or before going to sleep at night. I want my lover's hands in my hair and his words in my ears. I want to be making out with him in the back row of a movie theater, because he's as good as chocolate.

My friend Pam, who was acquainted with my fairy lover, surprised me by saying, "He's an angel." "Hmmm," I responded, and then I assented. Lightness of being displayed in his body that was dancing every day down corridors and sidewalks—how energetically gentle and how beautiful. But my agreement with Pam didn't mean that my fairy lover was innocent or perfectly kind or flawlessly good-looking or always sweet to his roots. Rather, my agreement showed that I perceived him to be as gloriously smiling as the angel in Bernini's *Ecstasy of St. Theresa*, as sure in sex and spirit as the arrow that causes her to swoon, and as fluent in passion as her thrown-back head, her parted lips, and the river of her robe.

In orgasm, Bernini's St. Theresa is a figure of insurrection against our too-often-lost love of ourselves. She is ornamented in her robe the way that I ornament myself in femininity. She and I are objects symbolic of anything but scarcity. We operate against the rationing of pleasure, and our adornment ordains our faith in orgy, which is simply unrestrained indulgence, such as the most beautiful orgasm.

Theresa's angel is a sensitively sensual lover, whose smiling gaze at her is infinitely amorous. His fingers part her robe for perfect penetration of the golden arrow that he holds as lightheartedly as a slightly intoxicated celebrant holds a glass of champagne between sips. In the heaven, or the fairyland, that Theresa and her angel create together, he is fucking the shit out of her, which simply means that he is making her real. His attentions ensure that she knows, *I am here*, which is a mystical experience. And there, in that orgy in which a woman's clitoris, labia, cervix, uterus, and vagina are singly or all at once pointedly in focus, they also become sheer gradients and radiations of energy, making the body a unified resonance of pleasure. That orgiastic unit is like a minimalist sculpture, one shape—orgasm as sphere or cone—and it is one sensuousness: all radiance, vibration, fluttering, and sparkling. Paradoxically, Bernini's sculpture, baroque as it is—ornately fervent—is also concisely simple.

Of course, the orgiastic unit's sensuousness dis-integrates the shape, which is osmotic, so the shape passes from orgasmic body into the literal and figurative atmosphere in which that body exists. Theresa's robe is certainly solid, yet its marble ripples and surges into the surrounding space, saturating it with pleasure. Her body is the charged and pretty uninhibited unconscious, which the state of orgasm reveals.

Theresa's body and robe undulate. They are female orgasm described as a wave.

You know I am your deep blue sea, your ship come home, and we are rolling in each other's souls, making waves that swell and break in the same paradise that I perceive to be the place inhabited by Bernini's St. Theresa.

Held in the embrace of art, she is coming for eternity.

I've talked with lovers and some friends about waves of orgasms. "How many?" asked my fairy lover after the first time we made love. "I don't count," I replied. I've never counted.

My candor has perhaps indicted me in a culture that even now, over thirty years after many young women in the late 1960s, such as myself, claimed our bodily pleasure in the Sexual Revolution, mistrusts the woman who is in public clearly intensely involved in her sexuality. That involvement may be perceived as obsession and labeled such because of its very difference from the norm and the normative, which demand women's compliance with the dangerously obsessive mythicizing of their replete if not redundant sexual wiles coupled — in bondage — with the constraint that women should keep their sexuality under wraps.

I think of all the criticism that Madonna received for her frank and frankly sensuous sexual displays in her performances and videos and in her book called *Sex.* When we notice the dangerous obsession and mythicization that I noted above operating on a large public scale, we must understand how insidiously it permeates the lives of we who are less celebrated and therefore more minimally renounced. Contemporary cultural institutions, which range from academia to entertainment, frequently enjoy and enforce women's self-revulsion and self-contempt. Negative criticism, such as that of Madonna, proves this perverse pleasure. So do the numerous stylish academic publications that focus on the body — lesbian, gay, and transgendered, black, white, and brown, male and female, obese and anorexic, menopausal and adolescent — and that advertise an uncovering of profound sexual knowledge only to renege in language, information, personal narrative, or emotional and psychic passion.

Maybe misogynists and our own shame herd us women into pews of ambiguity about our pleasure, for and in ourselves. Maybe we're supposed to be confessing, in an understanding of sin as the plain statement, "I love my body, I love myself."

I've neither lived nor written in confessional mode. When I was a little girl I reveled in my clitoris, labia, and vagina when I pressed my thighs together, experiencing orgasms that continued until I stopped pressing. Sometimes they continued *after* I stopped pressing, for the mind and the cunt continued to connect; and sometimes the orgasms emerged before I pressed my thighs together, as they're emerging at this moment, when I'm writing; and now, in this orgasmic moment, I realize that the moment continues, that one orgasm continues with more and less intensity into many moments, and that my mental concentration can increase or lessen the intensity. The prolonged orgasm is a state of mind and being, like an asana, in which the practitioner both yields and focuses for maximum energy and elongation.

—I read Freud in my early pubescence. His intellect and empirical acumen resonated with my own way of experiencing and perceiving life and people, and it suggested, many years later and through my unconscious, a way of writing as a professional critic: include personal narratives, sex, observation of people, and analysis. I read Guy de Maupassant's short stories concurrently with Freud. Like the Modern Library edition of Freud, a volume of Maupassant lived in the 90 Riparian Road library, and, like Freud, Maupassant felt familiar to me, friendly. His sexually ambivalent characters touched me, tenderly, and his ease with the sexual undercurrents of everyday relations gave me some ease with my own sexual sensations and behaviors. My unconscious absorbed his sophistication and its ability to charm the reader. That charm is profound; it is not the trivialized feminine quality usually connoted by the word. Charm is a kind of literary heroism. It exhibits the fearless enticement of your reader with beauty.

How I wish that the feminist scholar Elizabeth Grosz would have charmed her readers by revealing her swooning beauty in her essay "Animal Sex." Her fourth paragraph disappoints me by offering the possibility of Grosz's almost having discussed female orgasm through telling us about her own. She critiques the description and analysis of her own orgasm: they wouldn't do the sensation justice, they might be perceived simply as confessional or autobiographical, and they might not have relevance for other women. How a brilliant feminist scholar's self-described and self-analyzed experience of orgasm might not be relevant to other women mystifies me. I wish that feminist scholars, especially superb ones such as Grosz, would enter this sexual and scholarly no-man's-land that she herself considers risky.

Feminist scholars describe their eating disorders, their fat bodies, their hairy faces, their rape and sexual abuse, but they do not describe their orgasms. They discuss problems and desires; but carnal pleasure, virtually never.

Grosz thought that evoking the pleasures of her own orgasms would involve "great disloyalty . . . spilling the beans on a vast historical 'secret.'" This reasoning doesn't convince me that Grosz should have kept silent. Why would female orgasm need women's guarding? Isn't feminist scholarship *about* spilling the beans on all kinds of historical secrets? Later in the same paragraph she seems to apologize because "if what is left [after spilling the beans] is not a raw truth of women's desire," it may be "another layer in the complex overwriting of the inscriptions or representations that constitute the body or subjectivity." Layers may constitute *or* constrain pleasure.

The sociologist Wendy Chapkis writes in *Beauty Secrets: Women and the Politics of Appearance*, her groundbreaking 1983 study of women's problematic negotiation of beauty ideals, that freedom from shame and anger about our own perceived lack of beauty, about our never measuring up to an impossible standard, will only occur if we share our beauty secrets with one another. Part of that sharing is friend to friend, and part of it is also public, telling one's own tale, as Chapkis does about her moustache, exposing her animal self. Orgasm, like beauty, is an area of mystery, embarrassment, and taboo. Appropriating Chapkis's desire and admonishment about self-revelation for the sake of ease, community, and freedom, I assert that women benefit from sharing our orgasm secrets.

Through the years, young feminist women students have occasionally asked me how I can bear to devour feminist scholarship, which, to them, concentrates on women's torments, belittlement, and self-berating—even when presenting women's achievements and victories. Those passionate and curious students have told me that such analyses and histories are torture to read, depressing. I've heard them thinking to themselves that feminist scholarship is a misanthropic literature, and I've always affirmed to those students the value of feminist scholarship and the joy it can give its reader; because knowing the truth is inspiring, and it spurs some of us to change what supposed truths have wrought.

From one perspective, a chocolate cake can't have too many layers. More layers mean more feast, more sumptuousness for the eyes and the tongue, and that sumptuousness itself constitutes a raw truth of chocolate. From another perspective, that sumptuousness has nothing to do with the essential pleasure of chocolate, which can be tasted in one bite. Grosz's evocation of the pleasure of orgasm would have given the reader an essential bite of women's carnality, of our animal sex.

Consciously exposing one's animal self isn't easy, even though we may admire others' animality — their sensual aliveness, their instinctual attunement with other living entities and with forces of nature.

My fairy lover was like the animal that I'd been looking for since I was a child — a being with whom I would not have to cling to words or push for love or acceptance, a being who would know my basic self as readily as Theresa trusts her angel because she has faith. My fairy lover was primitive. He said that sex is primitive. I feel peculiar using the word *primitive*. It reeks of unsophisticated politics: they're a primitive people — not Anglo and therefore uncivilized. But primitive means primary and basic. He knew primitive things about me, through our lovemaking, and even before we became lovers. He was primary colors blended to splendor; and he was fairy pink. I wanted to ask, How do you understand me? But I was afraid to ask, afraid I'd ruin a spell that we'd been weaving, a spell created by animals' magic in the presence of one another. He knew me through his breathing me and through his fingertips, both before we ever touched. He told me that on our second date, which we wouldn't have called a date at the time, he felt a "pulsating" in my presence. The pulsating continued. After the second time we made love, I asked him, "Are you my warrior lover?" He didn't answer right away, which scared me, because I thought I'd asked a serious question too soon. But serious questions didn't scare away the animal (for a while), and my fairy lover answered, "I think *so*."

Witnessing her parents fucking shoves a child into the intimately animal. If she does not scare easy, if she can be the animal that humans are, then she stands a chance of not becoming *simply* human, strictly human, which is remotely human — Homo sapiens as the species that is always weighing and judging its life and love away. Orgasm is an avenue out of fear, a fact of warrior heart, angelic lucidity, and fairy vision.

Often when I see you I can't contain myself. Not only do I smile. I start to laugh. Laughter is akin to orgasm, for the contents of the unconscious overwhelm us. Laughter is animal — primitive — and it is angelic — lightness manifested in a delicious burst of emotion. When we laugh in joy we're in the pink — of fairyland — and our hearts are lawless, beyond the cultural negation of pleasure; both the current fears and ancient traumas that burden us, that make our bodies feel heavy to ourselves and others, that make us more full of thoughts than we need to be—they retreat: we are warriors, laughing, though we may not be aware of it, at whatever our enemy or tormentor might be. When I see you I am giddy. I whirl in a radical decentering.

No one else has made me laugh like you make me laugh, and my mirth initiates me into new, though primal, scenes. We are enjoying orgasms—our coming at the same time and separately in each other's arms and nearness—and our beauty grounds my obsession as an act of faith: we are lovers and we are free, in private and in public, in a truth as undeniable as bright pink roses.

—A smiling little girl holding a wand topped with flowers, a wreath of the same bouquet crowning her long, wavy hair, caught my eye from the cover of the October 2003 *Family Fun*. "What a great image!" I thought. It reminded me of Rossetti's paintings, and it reminded me of me. As I continued to wait in the supermarket checkout line, I noticed the copy over her skirt, "Make our magical Flower Fairy Costume." I put the magazine in my cart, eager to find out more about the Flower Fairy. I learned that little girls want to be her: "What's the most popular costume among girl tricksters under the age of seven? When we asked, we heard many a vision filled with fairy dust and brightly colored flowers . . . 'a crown of pink flowers,' added Amelia, five."

When I debuted *The Aesthetics of Orgasm*, I could have worn that crown. Indeed, a vase of pink roses sat on the floor at my feet, as it did in each performance of the piece. By the debut, *fairy* no longer described the man designated "fairy lover" in my raptures and my philosophizing about orgasm. That fairy had disappeared, as had Erne, Florence, and Russell. Yet my parents and my husband are vitally alive, in distance, love, and memory, as are my many passionate attachments to people.

I am living in my history of chocolate, my passionate attachment to an inheritance of pleasure. Chocolate, of course, is my favorite flavor, and I've fashioned myself delicious. I've enriched my body that is my brain from the tastes and textures of that staple—a scent that lingers steady in me from ladies lunches, holidays, vacations, birthdays, and parties of any scale, including those for the dying and the dead, whose actual and perceived infidelities to life and love call for retreats in which chocolate satisfies inchoate longings from the massively unknown self of the living.

The perfume and the experience of chocolate are mine during every loving leap that any action fairy hero takes. I enrich my body that is my brain in the creation of a concoction that I love. Like Florence and Erne, I know how to make things beautiful.

Bring the milk chocolate truffles and the pink roses and carnations and the Merlot. Bring your action hero heart and fairy lightness, because we are creating beauty.

TIMELINE

Many events in *Swooning Beauty* occurred between 1996 and 2003. I do my best to situate them in the reader's mind with chronological clarity. I also think that a timeline, for quick reference, serves ease of reading.

1996
Winter: Dad had triple bypass surgery

1997
September: Mom and Dad sold their house and moved into a condominium

1998
June: Mom moved into Red Oaks

1999
May: Dad moved into Red Oaks
July 9: Dad died
July 11: We scattered Dad's ashes
August 23: Mom moved to Reno

2000
March 3: Mom died
May–June: I created Mel
Early June: Russell moved out of our house
July 2: We scattered Mom's ashes
August: I sojourned at Canyon Ranch
November: I began therapy

2001
July 20: A judge signed Russell's and my divorce papers
August: I sojourned at Canyon Ranch
Mid-October: I made love with a man I call my fairy lover

2002
May 15: I broke my wrist the day that I debuted my performance *The Aesthetics of Orgasm*
Summer–Fall: Fairy lover disappeared

2003
January–October: Mel disappeared, except for an occasional dream

SELECTED BIBLIOGRAPHY

Ammer, Christine. 1995. *The New A to Z of Women's Health: A Concise Encyclopedia.* 3rd ed. New York: Facts on File.

Batchelor, David. 2000. *Chromophobia.* London: Reaktion Books.

Battersby, Christine. 1990. *Gender and Genius: Towards a Feminist Aesthetics.* Bloomington: Indiana University Press.

Bellmer, Hans. 1957. *Petite Anatomie de l'inconscient physique ou l'anatomie de l'image.* Paris: Terrain Vague.

Bly, Robert. 1990. *Iron John: A Book about Men.* Reading, MA: Addison-Wesley.

Bordo, Susan. 1999. *The Male Body: A New Look at Men in Public and in Private.* New York: Farrar, Straus and Giroux.

Boston Women's Health Collective. 1998. *Our Bodies, Ourselves for the New Century: A Book by and for Women.* New York: Touchstone.

———. 2005. *Our Bodies, Ourselves: A New Edition for a New Era.* New York: Touchstone.

Brownmiller, Susan. 1984. *Femininity.* New York: Linden Press/Simon & Schuster.

Chapkis, Wendy. 1986. *Beauty Secrets: Women and the Politics of Appearance.* Boston: South End Press.

Chia, Mantak, and Maneewan Chia. 1986. *Healing Love through the Tao: Cultivating Female Sexual Energy.* Huntington, NY: Healing Tao Books.

Christgau, Robert. 1996. "Children of the Porn." *Village Voice,* July 30, 1996: 67–68.

Classen, Constance. *Worlds of Sense: Exploring the Senses in History and across Cultures.* 1993. London: Routledge.

Classen, Constance, David Howes, and Anthony Synnott. 1994. *Aroma: The Cultural History of Smell.* London: Routledge.

Coe, Sophie D., and Michael D. Coe. 1996. *The True History of Chocolate.* New York: Thames and Hudson.

Cohen Ragas, Meg, and Karen Kozlowski. 1998. *Read My Lips: A Cultural History of Lipstick.* San Francisco: Chronicle.

Columbus, Renaldus. 1559. *De re anatomica.* Venice.

Dahl, Arlene. 1965. *Always Ask a Man: Arlene Dahl's Key to Femininity.* Englewood Cliffs, NJ: Prentice Hall.

DeAngelis, Michael. 2001. *Gay Fandom and Crossover Stardom: James Dean, Mel Gibson, and Keanu Reaves.* Durham, NC: Duke University Press.

Deng, Ming-Dao. 1993. *Chronicles of Tao: The Secret Life of a Taoist Master.* New York: HarperCollins.

De Rougemont, Denis. 1983. *Love in the Western World.* Trans. Montgomery Belgion. Princeton, NJ: Princeton University Press.

Desaulniers, Marcel. 1992. *Death by Chocolate: The Last Word on a Consuming Passion.* New York: Rizzoli.

Desikachar, T. K. V. 1995. *The Heart of Yoga: Developing a Personal Practice.* Rochester, VT: Inner Traditions International.

Ehrenreich, Barbara. 1997. *Blood Rites: Origins and History of the Passions of War.* New York: Metropolitan.

Ensler, Eve. 1998. *The Vagina Monologues.* New York: Villard.

Fanon, Frantz. 1967. *Black Skin White Masks.* Trans. Charles Lam Markmann. New York: Grove Press.

Fein, Ellen, and Sherrie Schneider. 1995. *The Rules: Time-Tested Secrets for Capturing the Heart of Mr. Right.* New York: Warner Books.

Feuerstein, Georg. 1998. *Tantra: The Path to Ecstasy.* Boston: Shambhala.

Foucault, Michel. 1973. *The Birth of the Clinic: An Archaeology of Medical Perception.* Trans. A. M. Sheridan Smith. New York: Pantheon.

Freud, Sigmund. 1953. *The Standard Edition of the Complete Psychological Works of Sigmund Freud.* Trans. James Strachey. Vol. 7 (1901–1905). *A Case of Hysteria, Three Essays on Sexuality, and Other Works.* London: Hogarth Press.

Friedan, Betty. 1963. *The Feminine Mystique.* New York: W. W. Norton.

Frueh, Erne R., and Florence Frueh. 1983. *Chicago Stained Glass*. Chicago: Loyola University Press.

Gordon, Marsha, and Alice E. Fugate. 1998. *The Complete Idiot's Guide to Beautiful Skin*. New York: Alpha Books.

Grahn, Judy. 1993. *Blood, Bread, and Roses: How Menstruation Created the World*. Boston: Beacon Press.

Greer, Germaine. 1971. *The Female Eunuch*. New York: McGraw-Hill.

Grosz, Elizabeth. 1995. "Animal Sex: Libido as Desire and Death." In *Sexy Bodies: The Strange Carnalities of Feminism*, ed. Elizabeth Grosz and Elspeth Probyn. London: Routledge.

Grosz, Elizabeth, and Elspeth Probyn, eds. 1995. *Sexy Bodies: The Strange Carnalities of Feminism*. London: Routledge.

Harries, Karsten. 1997. *The Ethical Function of Architecture*. Cambridge, MA: MIT Press.

Henslin, James M., and Mae A. Biggs. 1971. "Dramaturgical Desexualization: The Sociology of Vaginal Examination." In *Studies in the Sociology of Sex*, ed. James M. Henslin. New York: Appleton-Century-Crofts.

Irigaray, Luce. 1981. "This Sex Which Is Not One." Trans. Claudia Reeder. In *New French Feminisms: An Anthology*, ed. Elaine Marks and Isabelle de Courtivron. New York: Schocken.

———. 1985. *Speculum of the Other Woman*. Trans. Gillian C. Gill. Ithaca, NY: Cornell University Press.

Iyengar, B. K. S. 1979. *Light on Yoga*. New York: Schocken.

Kapsalis, Terri. 1994. "Vaginal Architecture." *Lusitania* 6: 105–12.

———. 1997. *Public Privates: Performing Gynecology from Both Ends of the Speculum*. Durham, NC: Duke University Press.

Keen, Sam. 1991. *Fire in the Belly: On Being a Man*. New York: Bantam.

Keuls, Eva. 1985. *The Reign of the Phallus: Sexual Politics in Ancient Athens*. New York: Harper & Row.

Kipnis, Laura. 2003. *Against Love: A Polemic*. New York: Pantheon.

Laqueur, Thomas. 1990. *Making Sex: Body and Gender from the Greeks to Freud*. Cambridge, MA: Harvard University Press.

Lin, Newman K. N.d. *The Lin Institute*. http://www.actionlove.com/cases/case9819.htm.

Lingis, Alphonso. 2000. *Dangerous Emotions*. Berkeley: University of California Press.

Marcuse, Herbert. 1966. *Eros and Civilization: A Philosophical Inquiry into Freud*. Boston: Beacon.

Matlock, David L. N.d. *Laser Vaginal Rejuvenation Institute of Los Angeles*. http://www.drmatlock.com/briefoverview.htm.

Medrich, Alice. 1990. *Cocolat: Extraordinary Chocolate Desserts*. New York: Warner.

Montez, Lola. 1969. *The Arts and Secrets of Beauty with Hints to Gentlemen on the Art of Fascinating*. New York: Chelsea House.

Morris, Edwin. 1984. *Fragrance: The Story of Perfume from Cleopatra to Chanel*. New York: Charles Scribner's Sons.

Northrup, Christiane. 1995. *Women's Bodies, Women's Wisdom: Creating Physical and Emotional Health and Healing*. New York: Bantam Books.

Pallingston, Jessica. 1999. *Lipstick*. New York: St. Martin's Press.

Pignatelli, Luciana. 1971. *The Beautiful People's Beauty Book: How to Achieve the Look and Manner of the World's Most Attractive Women*. New York: McCall.

Pollock, Griselda. 1999. *Differencing the Canon: Feminist Desire and the Writing of Art's Histories*. London: Routledge.

Post, Peggy. 1997. *Emily Post's Etiquette*. 16th ed. New York: HarperCollins.

Powers, John, and Mary Sue Miller. 1954. *Secrets of Charm*. New York: Holt, Rinehart and Winston.

Raichur, Pratima, and Marian Cohn. 1997. *Absolute Beauty: Radiant Skin and Inner Harmony through the Ancient Secrets of Ayurveda*. New York: HarperPerennial, 1997.

Rinpoche, Sogyal. 1992. *The Tibetan Book of Living and Dying*. Ed. Patrick Gaffney and Andrew Havey. New York: HarperCollins.

Rombauer, Irma S., and Marion Rombauer Becker. 1975. *Joy of Cooking*. Indianapolis: Bobbs-Merrill.

Sade, Donatien-Alphonse-François. 1966 (1931–35). *The 120 Days of Sodom*. Trans. Austryn Wainhouse and Richard Seaver. In *The Marquis de Sade: The 120 Days of Sodom and Other Writings*. New York: Grove Press.

Sams, Jamie, and David Carson. 1999. *Medicine Cards*. New York: St. Martin's.

Scarry, Elaine. 1999. *On Beauty and Being Just*. Princeton, NJ: Princeton University Press.

Sims, J. Marion. 1886. *The Story of My Life*. Ed. H. Marion Sims. New York: D. Appleton.

Smart, Elizabeth. 1992. *By Grand Central Station I Sat Down and Wept*. New York: Vintage.

Steinem, Gloria. 1998. Foreword, in Eve Ensler, *The Vagina Monologues*. New York: Villard.

Sun Tzu. 2001. *The Art of War: A New Translation*. Trans. Denma Translation Group. Boston: Shambhala.

Tolman, Ruth. 1969. *Guide to Beauty, Charm, Poise*. New York: Milady.

Vandenberg, Philipp [Klaus Dieter Hartel]. 1978. *Nefertiti: An Archaeological Biography*. Trans. Ruth Hein. Philadelphia: J. B. Lippincott.

Whitcomb, Helen, and Rosalind Lang. 1974. *Charm: The Career Girl's Guide to Business and Personal Success*. New York: McGraw-Hill.

Wilding, Faith. 2003. "Vulvas with a Difference." In *Domain Errors! Cyberfeminist Practice*, ed. Maria Fernandez, Faith Wilding, and Michelle Wright. New York: Autonomedia.

Wolf, Naomi. 1992. *The Beauty Myth: How Images of Beauty Are Used Against Women*. New York: Anchor.